A CONCISE DICTIONARY ENGLISH-PERSIAN

TOGETHER WITH A SIMPLIFIED GRAMMAR OF THE PERSIAN LANGUAGE

A

CONCISE DICTIONARY

ENGLISH-PERSIAN

TOGETHER WITH A

SIMPLIFIED GRAMMAR

OF THE

PERSIAN LANGUAGE

E.H. PALMER

EDITED BY

G. LE STRANGE

MANOHAR

2022

First published 1883
Reprinted 2022

ISBN 978-93-91928-21-6

Published by
Ajay Kumar Jain *for*
Manohar Publishers & Distributors
4753/23 Ansari Road, Daryaganj
New Delhi 110 002

Printed at
Replika Press Pvt. Ltd.

A

CONCISE DICTIONARY,

ENGLISH-PERSIAN;

TOGETHER WITH A

SIMPLIFIED GRAMMAR

OF THE

PERSIAN LANGUAGE.

BY THE LATE

E. H. PALMER, M.A.

Of the Middle Temple, Barrister-at-Law, Lord Almoner's Reader and Professor of Arabic and Fellow of St. John's College in the University of Cambridge.

COMPLETED AND EDITED
FROM THE MS. LEFT IMPERFECT AT HIS DEATH,
BY

G. LE STRANGE.

LONDON:
TRÜBNER & CO., LUDGATE HILL.
1883.

LONDON:
GILBERT AND RIVINGTON, LIMITED,
ST. JOHN'S SQUARE, CLERKENWELL ROAD.

CONTENTS.

PAGE

Preface v

The Simplified Grammar 1

Table of Irregular Verbs 36

Table for A.H., and A.D. 41

The Dictionary.

PREFACE.

The full and sympathetic "Life of Edward Henry Palmer" which Mr. Besant has lately brought out exonerates me from adding any biographical notice of my friend to his posthumous work. It will, therefore, only be needful to explain what my task has been in preparing this Dictionary for the press.

On my return to London from the East in November, 1882, I learned that all hope had been abandoned, and that there was no doubt that the three brave men, Gill, Charrington and Palmer, had met their fate in the Wady Sudr. A few weeks later I was requested by Mr. N. Trübner to see through the press this Second Part of the Persian Dictionary, some pages of which had already been set up in type. On consulting Mrs. Palmer as to her wishes, I was happy in being able to obtain her full consent to the proposal of Mr. Trübner, and was immediately placed in possession of the slips which Professor Palmer had prepared, the greater portion of which I found had remained at his house, though some were already in the hands of the Publisher.

As long ago as the spring of 1880, Professor Palmer had shown me many bundles of these slips, and fortunately then explained to me the method he intended to pursue in the compilation of the second, or English-Persian part of the Dictionary.

The basis of the work was the First Part, the Persian-English, a copy of which had been cut up, and each paragraph pasted on a separate slip in order that the *English* renderings might be arranged alphabetically.

In this manner a good stock of words was acquired, but much still remained to be done in the way of elimination and addition, while some considerable alterations also were needed to render the English word-list complete; this last especially, inasmuch as in Persian the number of simple verbs is extremely limited, and further, the majority of the Persian compound verbs would only occur in the reversed Dictionary, under the English noun or participle, *not* under the more appropriate infinitive: *e.g.* 'To advise' would be represented by 'Advice,' because the Persians, to express the verb, make use of the phrase 'To give advice.' In 1880 I discussed this with my friend, and remember his then telling me that he intended merely to indicate in its proper place the auxiliary verb to be used with the noun or participle, avoiding thus the repetition involved by adding separate paragraphs for each compound verb; but I found that up to the time of Professor Palmer's last ill-fated journey no steps had been taken to indicate these auxiliary verbs, though the word-list proper had been considerably augmented by him.

No one can be better aware than myself of the disadvantages under which the book labours in never having been revised by the hand of its learned author. I have endeavoured to carry out what I believe to have been the intention of my friend. I have made additions to nearly every paragraph for the purpose above indicated, such as he would assuredly have made had he lived; and I have also completed the list of words from my own reading and colloquial knowledge, and from the works of my predecessors, Messrs A. N. Wollaston, A. Bergé, J. B. Nicolas, and others.

The Persian Grammar which stands at the head of this work originally appeared as the second section in the "Simplified Grammars of Hindustani, Persian and Arabic," published in 1882. For this such slight alterations as were needed in the references have been made, and on one or two occasions I have added an explanation of my own in square brackets [ ]. In all other respects this portion is merely a reprint, for the benefit of those who may be learning Persian but not Hindustani and Arabic.

Furthermore, I have written out a Table of the Persian (so-called) Irregular Verbs, and also a short note with reference to the years of the Hejrah.

As regards the transliteration employed in the work—bearing in mind that the object was merely to give the pronunciation, and that the Persian original invariably preceded,—it has been deemed sufficient to use but one dotted letter (*ḳ*), consequently the Persian homophones of the Arab Alphabet have not been indicated. Furthermore, as in Part I., no difference is shown in the Persian character between the *G* and *K*, since the diacritical bar is never written in Modern Persian, while the letter to be pronounced is clearly indicated in the transliteration following.

G. LE STRANGE.

46, Charles Street, Mayfair,
London.

September, 1883.

POSTSCRIPT.

MR. N. TRÜBNER has lately called my attention to a work professing to be the composition of Sorabshaw Byramji Doctor, but which is in fact no more than an incorrect reprint of Professor Palmer's Persian-English Dictionary. Mr. S. B. Doctor is "Persian Teacher" in the "Surat High School," and his book is printed at the "Irish Presbyterian Mission Press," at Surat, in the year 1880.

Professor Palmer in 1881 had seen this Dictionary, and had some intention of seeking legal redress, but other matters had occupied him up to the time of his last disastrous journey; and it therefore remains to me, in vindication of the literary honour of my friend, to warn the public of this attempt to take away from Professor Palmer the fruit of his labours. Mr. S. B. Doctor, it is true, does notice Johnson's Persian and Arabic Dictionary, together with some others as having "been consulted in the preparation of this Manual;" and here and there in his work we find some pages so altered as to imply that they were borrowed elsewhere; but there is no mention of the work of Professor Palmer, from which has been copied at least nine-tenths word for word. It seems to me needless to print long parallel columns of extracts from the two books in proof of the above assertion: but I will quote a passage which had caught the eye of Professor Palmer, where Mr. Doctor had ignorantly copied an orthographical error, for I find in the handwriting of my friend, "MY MISTAKE REPEATED," written on a slip of paper and stuck into the pirated edition of Surat.

Professor Palmer's Dictionary.

ز

ز *zain*. Z. The eleventh letter of the Arabic and thirteenth of the Persian alphabets.

ژ *zhá*. Zh. The fourteenth letter of the Persian alphabet.

P. ز *zi*. See زا.

A. زابل *zábil*. Short, dwarfish.

P. زاج *záj*. Vitriol.

P.A. زاج ابيز *záj i abyaz*. Alum.

P. زاج سبز *záj i sabz*. Green vitriol.

P. زاج كبود *záj i kabúd*. Blue vitriol.

A. زاحف *záhif*. Fatigued.

&c., &c., &c.

Mr. Doctor's Edition.

ز

ز *ze* is the thirteenth letter of the Persian and eleventh of the Arabic alphabets. In the denotation of numbers by the Arabic letters it stands for 7.

P. ز *ze* (contract. for زا). See زا.

P. زابل *zábil*, *adj*. Short, dwarfish.

P. زاج *záj*, *s*. Vitriol. زاج ابيز Alum. زاج سبز Green Vitriol. زاج كبود Blue Vitriol.

A. زاحف *záhif*, *adj*. Fatigued,

&c., &c., &c.

It is almost needless to point out that the mistake of Professor Palmer, زاج ابيز (for زاج ابيض) has been copied by Mr. S. B. Doctor, *verbatim et literatim*, as is the manner displayed in the remainder of his work.

G. LE S.

PERSIAN GRAMMAR

SIMPLIFIED.

THE ALPHABET.

THE Persian Alphabet is a modification of the Arabic. It is written from right to left.

NAME.	EQUIVALENT.	PRONUNCIATION.
ا *Alif,*	*a, e, i, o,* or *u*	This is the *spiritus lenis* of the Greek, a mere prop to rest an initial vowel on.
ب *Be,*	*b*	As in English.
پ *Pe,*	*p*	As in English.
ت *Te,*	*t*	A soft dental *t* like the Italian.
ث *Se,*	*s*	As in English.
ج *Jím,*	*j*	As in English.
چ *Che,*	*ch*	As in English.
ح *He,*	*h*	An aspirate strongly breathed out from the chest.

NAME.		EQUIVALENT.	PRONUNCIATION.
خ	*Khe*	*kh*	Like *ch* in Welsh or Gaelic, or the German *ch* as pronounced in Switzerland.
د	*Dál,*	*d*	A soft dental *d* as in Italian.
ذ	*Zál,*	*z*	As in English.
ر	*Re,*	*r*	A distinctly pronounced *r*.
ز	*Ze,*	*z*	As *z* in English.
ژ	*Zhe,*	*zh*	Like the French *j* in *jour,* or our *s* in *pleasure.*
س	*Sín,*	*s*	As in English.
ش	*Shín,*	*sh*	As in English.
ص	*Sád,*	*s*	As in English.
ض	*Zád,*	*z*	As in English.
ط	*Tá,*	*t*	Properly pronounced with the tongue full against the front part of the palate, but ordinarily pronounced like ت and ز.
ظ	*Zá,*	*z*	Properly pronounced with the tongue full against the front part of the palate, but ordinarily pronounced like ت and ز.
ع	*'Ain,*	*'a,* etc.	A guttural sound only heard in Arabic: in Persia it is not often pronounced.
غ	*Ghain,*	*gh*	A guttural sound something like the French *r grasseyé.*
ف	*Fe,*	*f*	As in English.

NAME.	EQUIVALENT.	PRONUNCIATION.
ق *Ḳaf,*	*ḳ*	A very guttural *k*, like *ck* in *thick*, only much stronger.
ک *Káf,*	*k*	As in English, but *g* is always hard before all vowels, as گی *gí*, pronounced *ghee*, not *jee*. It is sometimes also pronounced with a slight *y* sound, like the Cockney mode of pronouncing the *g* in *garden*, "gyarden." When it occurs between two vowels it is often sounded like *y*, as اگر *eyer*.
گ *Gáf,**	*g*	
ل *Lám,*	*l*	
م *Mím,*	*m*	
ن *Nún,*	*n*	As in English: before *b* or *f* it is sounded as *m*.
و *Váv,*	*v*	Nearly as in English, but a little inclined to *w*.
ه *He,*	*h*	As in English.
ی *Ye,*	*y*	

These are joined to the preceding letter by prefixing a small curve or stroke, and to the following letter by removing the curve with which they all but *alif* end: thus

DETACHED.	INITIAL.	MEDIAL.	FINAL.
ٮ	ٮـ	ـٮـ	ـٮ
ی ن	ـ	ـ	ـن ـی

* [In modern Persian, print or MS., the diacritical bar distinguishing گ *g* from ک *k* is rarely employed.]

DETACHED.	INITIAL.	MEDIAL.	FINAL.
ح	حـ	ـحـ	ـح
ص	صـ	ـصـ	ـص
ع	عـ	ـعـ	ـع
ف ق	فـ	ـفـ	ـف ـق
ك	كـ	ـكـ	ـك
ل	لـ	ـلـ	ـل
م	مـ	ـمـ	ـم
ه	هـ	ـهـ	ـه

ر و د if deprived of the curve would become unrecognizable; hence they do not join to the left.

The above letters are all consonants.

The vowels are ـُ *u* (as in *bull*), and ـَ *a* (pronounced like *u* in *but*), both written above the letter; and ـِ *i* written below the letter.

Combined with ا *a*, و *w*, and ی *y*, these become آ *aa* (*á*), وُ *uw* (*ú*), یِ *iy* (*í*), وَ *aw* (pronounced as *ow* in *cow*), یَ *ai* (like *i* in *fine*).*

No word can commence with a vowel in the Arabic character: if it does the vowel is introduced by *alif* ا.

When a syllable begins with a vowel, the mark ـٔ *hamzeh* is used to introduce it.

But this *hamzeh* being written above the line requires a

* [Sometimes pronounced like *ey* in *they*.]

prop: this in the case of *a* is ا, in the case of *u* it is و,* and in the case of *i* it is ى,* only that in the initial form this last is [often] distinguished from the ordinary *y* by losing its dots: *e.g.* سؤال *su-ál,* "a question;" مسؤل *mas-ul,* "inquired of;" فائده *fá-idah,* "advantage."

ّ *Tashdíd* doubles the letter it is placed over.

ْ *Sukún* shows that the letter it is placed over has no vowel.

ٱ *Waslah* is only used over an initial *alif* in an Arabic word, or over the Arabic article ال *al,* and shows that it is elided.

ٓ *Maddah* is placed over an initial *alif,* and shows that it should be pronounced long, as آمدن *ámadan,* "to come."

If the first letter of an Arabic word be a sibilant or liquid the article ال is elided before it, and the consonant itself doubled, as عوّامُ ٱلنّاس *'avámmu-nnás,* "common people," عبدُ ٱللّه *'abdu-lláh,* "Abdullah" (the servant of Allah).

[In Persian words و after خ followed by a long vowel is not pronounced, *e.g.* خويش *khísh,* خواستن *khástan.*]

In old Persian, and in the language as spoken in India at the present day, the long و and ى have two sounds, *ú* and *í,* called معروف *ma'rúf,* "known," and *o* and *é,* called مجهول *majhúl,* "unknown." The modern native of Iran does not [often] employ the latter sounds.

* [With or without ء.]

THE ACCIDENCE.

The Parts of Speech.

Like other languages, Persian contains three parts of speech, namely, Nouns, Verbs, and Particles.

It is useful to bear in mind the meaning of these words.

The Noun is the *name* of a thing (*nomen*); the Verb is the *action word;* and the Particle is a useful word not requiring to be defined by inflection or conjugation, but itself used to define, qualify, or restrict other words.

Old Persian—or rather Zend—had a very elaborate grammatical system. This has disappeared, and we have the relations of words to each other expressed in modern Persian with a simplicity equalled only by our own English.

NOUNS.

Cases of Nouns.

The only case-ending for Nouns which has survived is را *rá* for the *objective.*

The other relations which the case-ending of other languages imply are expressed by the *izáfat,* and by the use of such prepositions as بِ *ba,* "to," با *bá,* "with," از *az,* "from," بر *bar,* "upon," در *dar,* "in," etc.

Izáfat implies the relation of one person or thing to another, as genitive and dependent, or substantive and adjective.

Of the application of *izáfat* and the use of the objective case I shall speak when I come to treat of the Syntax.

The Vocative is formed by prefixing ای *ai*, as *ai mard*, "O man!" or (poetical) by affixing ا *á*, as *dústá*, "O friend!"

The language has no article, but a common noun is re-tricted to unity, expressing *one* (specified or not) of the species and no more, by adding ی. When this is the یای مجهول *yá e majhúl* (see p. 5) it makes the word indefinite, whether it be a *noun* or a *verb*.

Nouns Substantive and Adjective.

All nouns are *concrete*, that is, substantive.

A noun only exercises the functions of an adjective by being used in a subservient manner as qualifying another word; *e.g.* مرد خوب *mard i khúb*, "a good man," not as in English (where *good* is abstract and meaningless without the substantive being expressed), but "a man (I mean) a good one:" hence we can use a so-called "adjective" as a substantive, as خوبی *khúbí*, "a good (man)," مُرده *murdah*, "a dead (man)," whereas in English to say "a good," "a dead," is nonsense. There is, in fact, no such thing as an adjective, though one substantive may be used to qualify another.

Number.

The Plural is formed by affixing

ان *án* for rational } creatures;
and ها *há* for irrational }

as مردان *mardán*, "men," سنگها *sanghá*, "stones."

When the word ends in silent ه *h* an euphonic گ is inserted; as بنده *bandah*, "a slave," بندگان *bandagán*, "slaves." If it end in ا *á*, an euphonic ی *y* is introduced; as دانا *dáná*, "wise," *pl.* دانایان *dánáyán*.

Persian, borrowing so much from Arabic, has adopted many plurals from that language. ه at the end of a word, representing the Arabic ة, often becomes ات *át* in the plural, according to the Arabic usage.

In "irrational" words derived from the Arabic, Persians very frequently use the Arabic plural, but they insert a *j* for euphony in the case of the feminine plural in ات *át*; as قلعه *ḳal'ah*, "a fortress, *pl.* قلاع *ḳilá'*,* or قلعجات *ḳal'aját*, "fortresses." They even erroneously transfer this construction to purely Persian words; as نوشته *navishtah*, "a writing," نوشتجات *navishtaját*, "writings;" but this is only done in words implying an irrational being or thing.

* The irregular or "broken" Arabic plurals are treated of in the Arabic Grammar, [and those in common use will be found in the Dictionary].

When the Arabic feminine in ة = ة is affixed to a noun implying a rational object, as معشوق *ma'shúḳ*, "beloved," معشوقه *ma'shúḳah*, "a mistress," it becomes *át*, and not *ját*.

In colloquial Persian ها *há* is used as the plural for nearly all words, rational and irrational alike.

DUAL.

In some words the Arabic dual form is borrowed; as طرف *tarf*, "a side," طرفَين *tarfain*, "the two sides" or "parties": this always ends in يْن *ain*.

GENDER.

From a grammatical point of view the Persian language has no gender. Of such words as پدر *pader*, "father," مادر *máder*, "mother," the gender is self-evident; and in cases where it is necessary to make the distinction other additional words are used, such as ماده *mádah*, "female," نر *nar*, "male"; thus, گاو نر *gáv i nar*, "a bull," گاو ماده *gáv i mádah*, "a cow." For human beings, مرد *mard*, "man," زن *zan*, "woman," are added; as پیرِ مرد *pír i mard*, "an old man," پیرِ زن *pír i zan*, "an old woman."

Sometimes different words are employed, as in English, to distinguish the sexes; as غوچ *ghúch*, "a ram," میش *mísh*, "a ewe" (but in literary Persian میش signifies "a ram"); اسپ

asp, "a horse," مادیان *mádiyán*, "a mare," خروس *khurús*, "a cock," ماکیان *mákiyán*, "a hen."

PRONOUNS.

The Personal Pronouns are:

من *man*, I, *pl.* ما *má*, we.
تو *tú*, thou, „ شما *shumá*, you.
او *ú*, he, „ اوشان *úshán*, they (those).*
این *ín*, this, „ ایشان *íshán*, they (those).

The only thing to notice in من *man* and تو *tu* is that in the objective case they become مرا *mĕrá* (for *man+rá*), ترا *turá* (for *tú+rá*), the *nasal* ن and the *long vowel* both becoming absorbed.

In این *ín* and او *ú*, and their plurals, we notice that *i* or *y* expresses *near* relation, and *u* or *w* expresses *remote* relation.

این *ín*, "this," آن *án*, "that," make ایشان *íshán* and اوشان *úshán* in the plural for rational beings: but they sometimes form the plural quite regularly, as اینان *ínán** and آنان *ánán** for rational, and اینها *ínhá* and آنها *ánhá* for irrational beings.

* [Obsolete.]

Note.—ب "to" or "by" takes an euphonic *d* before these pronouns; as بدین *badín*=بـ این *ba+ín*, "to this," بدان *badán*= بـ آن *ba+án*, "to that."

The plural forms *are not required* for nouns which merely qualify a plural noun, since the plural termination of the noun itself sufficiently explains it; as مردانِ خوب *mardán i khúb*, "good men."

Affixed Pronouns.

The pronouns sometimes take an affixed form, as follows:

م *am*, abbreviated from من *man*, "me *or* mine."
ت *at*, " " تو *tú*, "thou *or* thine."
ش *ash*, "him *or* his."

A ش seems to have once belonged to the pronouns, as we may see from the plurals اوشان *úshán*, شما *shŭmá*, etc.

These affixes are only used of rational beings, and have the usual plural termination in ان *án*, though the final nasal *n* is dispensed in the first person; thus,

ما *má*, "us *or* our."
تان *itán*, "you *or* yours."
شان *shán*, "them *or* theirs."

Interrogative Pronouns.

The sound ك *k* asks a question relative to rational beings; as كه *kih*, "who?" and the corresponding soft sound asks a question relative to irrational things; as چه *chih,* "what?" These, with other words which have become absorbed or amalgamated in the form, make up the remaining interrogatives; *e.g.* کدام *kudám,* "which?" (of two), the *d* being a survival of دو *dú,* "two;" چگونه *chigúnah,* "how?" (for چه *chi,* "what?" and گون *gún,* "phase, colour, sort,") and چون *chún,* "how? like what?" (the گ having a tendency to disappear between two vowels); چند *chand,* "how many" (=چه *chi,* "what?"+اند *and,* "some") (*cf.* اندك *andak,* "a little"); كي *kai,* "when?" etc.

Reflexive Pronouns.

These are formed by adding the personal pronouns خود *khud,* "self," etc.; as,

من خود *man khud,* I myself.
تو خود *tú khud,* Thou thyself, etc.

The affixed forms may also be used with خود *khud*; as,

در خانه خودم *dar khánah-i-khudam,* In my own house.

From خودش *khudash,* "his-self," we get خويش *khísh* ("his own self, his-self") and خويشتن *khíshtan,* "himself." In the last the word تن signifies "body" or "person."

Examples of the Personal Pronouns.

The following examples are useful as showing the various uses and combinations of the pronouns:

من که فلان پسر فلانم *man kih fulán pisar i fulánam*, I, so-and-so, the son of so-and-so.

من که پسرم رفت *man kih pisaram raft,* I whose son went.

تو که پسرت رفت *tu kih pisarat raft*, Thou whose son went.

او که پسرش رفت *ú kih pisarash raft*, He whose son went.

With كه *ki* may be compared the *qui* of European languages. It serves for all relatives, but may be defined by other words, as in the above examples.

Comparison.

The comparative is formed by adding تر *tar*, and the superlative by adding ترین *tarín*. A single example will impress this on the reader's mind:

به *bih*, good, بهتر *bih-tar*, better, بهترین *bih-tarín*, best.

Sometimes the Arabic comparative form افعل *af'al* is used in Persian. [But of this form examples are cited in the Dictionary.]

NUMERALS.

The numerical figures are ۱ ۲ ۳ ۴ ۵ ۶ ۷ ۸ ۹ ۰ (1 2 3 4 5 6 7 8 9 0) They are written from left to right as with us, and are combined in the same way as our own; *e.g.* ۱۸۸۱=1881.

The numerals in Persian are:

1	يك	*yak*	11	يازده	*yázdah*	30	سى	*sí*
2	دو	*do*	12	دوازده	*davázdah*	40	چهل	*chihil*
3	سه	*sih*	13	سيزده	*sízdah*	50	پنجاه	*panjáh*
4	چهار	*chahár*	14	چهارده	*chahárdah*	60	شصت	*shast*
5	پنج	*panj*	15	پانزده	*pánzdah*	70	هفتاد	*haftád*
6	شش	*shash*	16	شانزده	*shánzdah*	80	هشتاد	*hashtád*
7	هفت	*haft*	17	هفتده	*haftdah*	90	نود	*navad*
8	هشت	*hasht*	18	هشتده	*hashtdah*	100	صد	*sad*
9	نُه	*nuh*	19	نوازده	*navázdah*	1000	هزار	*hazár.*
10	ده	*dah*	20	بيست	*bíst*			

They are quite regularly compounded, as follows:

بيست و يك *bíst o yak* (20 and 1) 21.

يك هزار و هشت صد و هشتاد و يك *yak hazár o hasht sad o hashtád o yak*, One thousand eight hundred and eighty and one, 1881.

The ordinals are made by affixing م *um*; as,

يكم	*yakum*,	1st	چهارم *chahárum*,	4th
دوم	*duvum*,	2nd	پنجم *panjum*,	5th,
سِوم	*sivum*,	3rd	and so on.	
[or سيم	*seyum.*]			

For "first" the word نخستين *nukhustín,** or the Arabic اوّل *avval*, may be used.

* [Obsolete.]

The numerals take the noun in the singular; as دو مرد *do mard*, "two men."

We say in English "two head of cattle," and so on. The Persians have several such qualifying words for various objects when used with numerals. The principal are the following:—

Persons,	نفر *nafar*, individuals,	پنج نفر دوست *punj nafar dúst*, 5 friends.
Horse, cattle, etc.	راس *rás*, head,	دو راس اسپ *do rás asp*, 2 horses.
Camels,	قطار *ḳatár*, مهار *mahár*, } string,	سه قطار شتر *sih ḳatár shutur*, 3 camels.
Elephant,	زنجير *zanjír*, chain,	چهار زنجير فيل *chahár zanjír fíl*, 4 elephants.
Jewels & fruit,	دانه *dánah*, grain,	هفت دانه دُر *haft dánah durr*, 7 pearls.
		هشت دانه سيب *hasht dánah síb*, 8 apples.

In colloquial Persian the word تا *tá* is used as a determinative for most objects; as چهار تا كتاب *chahár tá kitáb*, 4 books. (The word "piecee," as "one piecee man," in Chinese Pigeon English, is a relic of the same use of qualificative or determining words.)

THE VERB.

The Persian Verb consists of a root in combination with various participial affixes and the auxiliary verb "To be," of which the simplest form is the affixed substantive verb.

مَ *am*, (I) am,	یِم *ím*, (we) are.
یِ *í*, (thou) art,	یِد *íd*, (ye) are.
دَ *ad*, (he) is,*	اند *and*, (they) are.

Tenses of the Verb.

The root expresses mere action, as رس *ras*, "arriving," hence رس+م *ras+am*, "I arriving," رس+ی *ras+í*, "thou arriving," رس+د *ras+ad*, "he arriving," etc., is the simplest tense, or *aorist*, which must be further defined by context or by particles. The prefix می *mí* (or the older form همی *hamí*) does so define it, and gives it a present meaning; as می رسم *mí rasam*, "I am arriving," etc.

The Root, as the shortest form of the verb, is also used as an imperative, as رس *ras*, "arrive." The prohibitive is made by prefixing مه *ma*, as مرس *ma-ras*, "do not arrive."

---

* When this is used separately it takes the more regular form اَسْت *ast*, "is," as in Greek or Latin.

Then comes an affix expressing *past* action, which is, as in English, generally a *d* or *t* sound, as "ma*d*e," "pas*t*."

In Persian this is, *in most cases*, preceded by a vowel, as

رسید *ras* + *í* + *d*, "arrived."

شنود *shin* + *ú* + *d*, "heard."

استاد *ist* + *á* + *d*, "stood."

The first, or *í* sound, being the most common. Sometimes the د *d* becomes ت *t*; as خواستن *khástan*, "to wish." If to the "stem" thus formed we add ن we obtain the infinitive; as رسیدن *rasídan*, "to arrive." This, further combined with the simple tense in م, ی, د, etc., makes the preterite رسیدم *rasídam*, "I arrived," رسیدی *rasídí*, "thou didst arrive," etc. But the affix ی, as we have seen above (p. 7), makes *any word* indefinite. We therefore get again

رسیدمی *rasídamí*, "did I arrive," or "were I to arrive,"

رسیدی = ی + رسیدی *rasídí*, "didst thou arrive,"

رسیدی *rasídí*, "did he arrive,"

رسیدیمی *rasídímí*, "did we arrive."

رسیدیدی *rasídídí*, "did ye arrive."

رسیدندی *rasídandí*, "did they arrive."

By adding a short *a* ه to the past form the same idea is expressed with a sense of incompleteness. Thus, in English one says, "I am going—eh—to," etc., the hesitating "*eh*" suggesting something to come. This form, *e.g.* رسیده *rasídah*, signifies "having arrived," and is used with those tenses which are formed from auxiliary verbs, without which the sense would be incomplete; as

رسیده ام *rasídah*+*am*, I have arrived.

رسیده٫ *rasídah*+*í*, Thou hast arrived.

رسیده است *rasídah*+*ast*, He has arrived,

and so on.

THE AUXILIARY VERB "TO BE."

We must now speak more fully of the Auxiliary Verb "to be," بو (دن) *bú* (*dan*), "BE(ing)," both being derived from the Sanscrit *Bhuv*. Declining this as far as we can with the affixes given above, etc., we get

Present, بُوم *bŭvam*, I may be.

بوی *bŭví*, thou mayest be, etc.

بُوَد *bŭvad*, he may be.

Past, بُود *búd*, he was, etc.

بوده *búdah*, having been.

Again, by combination with the tenses of another verb,

رسیده بودم *rasídah búdam*, one come I was, etc.

رسیده بودمی *rasídah búdamí*, were I one come,

and so on.

بودن *búdan* makes its imperative باش *básh*. This I shall explain when speaking further on of the "irregular" forms of the verb: for the present we must assume all the forms to be regular.

Then, by the rules given above, we get باشم *básham*, "I may be," and رسیده باشم *rasídah básham*, "I may have been."

With the verb خواستن *khástan*, "to shall," as an auxiliary, the same combination may be made as in English to express the future; *e.g.* خواهم رسید *kháham rasíd*, "I shall arrive."

There is another auxiliary, شُدن *shudan*, root شو *shav*, "to become." This often has the sense of "to go," and is employed to form the passive of an active verb, being analogous in this respect to the English "get," "to get beaten," "get" being connected with "go:" *c.f.* American, "you get," and our own, "get out."

شدن *shudan* may be inflected throughout like رسیدن *rasídan* or any other verb, and the tenses thus obtained may be combined with those of another verb to make the various tenses of the passive.

If, then, we know the *root* and the *past* form or *stem* of any verb we can, with the assistance of the auxiliary verbs, form any tense we may desire: in other words, conjugate it throughout; *e.g.*

رس *ras*, "arriving," "arrival."

رسم *rasam*, I arriving.

رسی *rasí*, thou arriving.

رسد *rasad*, he arriving, etc.

می رسم *mí rasam*, I am arriving.

رسید *rasíd*, "arrived."

رسیدم *rasídam*, I arrived.

می رسیدم *mí rasídam*, I was arriving.

رسیده *rasídah*, having arrived.

رسیده ام *rasídah am*, I have arrived.

رسیده بودم *rasídah búdam*, I had arrived.

رسیدن *rasídan*, "to arrive."

رسیده باشم *rasídah básham*, I may have arrived, etc.

خواهم رسید *kháham rasíd*, I shall arrive.

And in the case of an active verb, as کردن *kardan*, "to do," we may further combine it with شدن *shudan*; as

کرده شدن *kardah shudan*, to be done.

کرده شوم *kardah shavam*, I am done.

کرده می شوم *kardah mí shavam*, I am being done.

کرده شدم *kardah shudam*, I was done.

کرده شده بودم *kardah shudah búdam*, I had been done.

کرده خواهم شد *kardah kháham shud*, I shall be done.

and so on.

Other parts of the verb are ان *án* affixed to root="doing," as رسان *rasán*, "arriving;" انده *andah* affixed to root expressing the agent, as رسنده *rasandah*, "an arriver." With the latter compare the Italian affix *-ante*, having the same meaning.

By prefixing ب *ba*, "to" (see p. 6), we get برسد *ba rasad*, "he is to arrive," *i.e.* "let him arrive," and so on for the other persons of the imperative. This prefix is also used for the "aorist" or indefinite tenses.

Causal verbs are made by inserting ان *án* between the root and the infinitive termination, as رسیدن *rasídan*, "to arrive," رسانیدن *rasánídan*, "to cause to arrive."

PHONETIC LAWS IN PERSIAN.

As in all other languages, certain words in Persian do not appear to follow the ordinary rules of accidence, and are therefore called irregular. It will be always found in such cases that the apparent anomaly is due to some euphonic change, arising either from a desire to avoid an awkward combination of consonants, or to facilitate pronunciation; or else from the survival in some forms of older radical letters which have for similar reasons disappeared in others.

In Persian both these causes act together, and many consonants are found in the root verbs which differ from those of the stem. To account for these we need only notice a few philological facts relative to euphonic changes which exist in Persian.* An acquaintance with these will not only enable the

* Professor Charles Rieu, of the British Museum, has given an admirable

student to inflect so-called "irregular verbs," but to recognise many common European words in their Persian form. They may be briefly stated as follows:—The Old Persian ذ (pronounced like *th* in "there") frequently becomes in Modern Persian ف *f*; *cf.* the Russian *Feodore* for *Theodore.* ك *k* and پ *p* before *t* become خ *kh* and ف *f*.

The two sounds of *k*, namely, *k* and *ch* (as in "kirk" and "church"), account for many irregularities, thus:—*k* passes to *ch*, thence to *z*. *k* and *g*, *d* and *t*, *p* and *b*, are common and more obvious changes.

p is especially liable to be changed into *f* when followed by *r*, as Sanscrit *pra*, Latin *pro*, Persian فر *far*; as Sanscrit *prashita*, "sent," Persian فرشته *firishtah*, "an angel."

Sanscrit *bh*, which becomes *f* in Latin and φ in Greek, becomes simple *b* in Persian; as Sanscrit *bhru*, "a brow," Greek ὀφρύς, Persian ابرو *abrú*. Sanscrit *bhú*, "to be," Latin *fuit*, Persian بودن *bú-dan*.

Sometimes the old Aryan root had an aspirated *d* (*dh*); this becomes either *d* without the *aspirate*, or *h* without the *d*; *cf.* دادن *dádan*, "to give," داد *dád*, "he gave," ده *dih*, "give."

---

exposition of these laws in a pamphlet published by the Philological Society, entitled "Remarks on some Phonetic Laws in Persian," to which I am much indebted for this part of my subject.

The old *d* also changes to *s* before *t* or *d* of the past; as بند *band*, "bind," past بست *bast* for *bandt* (the nasal being lost). *Cf.* Latin *comedo*, *comestum*.

The old Aryan *d* or *dh* is sometimes softened away to *y*, as پای *páy* (Sanscrit *pada*), "a foot," but the *s* into which it changes remains, as شوی *shúy* (Sanscrit *çudh*), "wash," past شست *shust*=*shudht*.

r and *l* interchange indiscriminately. Another change which is exactly paralleled in European languages exists in Persian, namely, *w* or *v* into *gu*, or simply *g*, as Arabic *Wády el kebír*, Spanish *Guadalquiver*, Latin *vulpilla*, French *goupil*. So in Persian we have from the Sanscrit *vṛka*, "a wolf," Zend *vereka*, the Modern Persian *gurg*. *Vistaspa* (Darius Hystaspes), Modern Persian *Gushtasp*. Sanscrit *vṛt*, "to turn" or "become," Latin *vert*, German *werden*, Persian *gard*.

v also occasionally hardens into *p* when preceded in Sanscrit by *ç*, as Latin *equus*, Sanscrit *açva*, Persian اسپ *asp*, "a horse."

The changes of the sibilant are somewhat extraordinary at first sight: thus *ç*, in the instance above given, is equal to *q*. Sometimes this becomes *k*, sometimes *c*, and sometimes simply *h*; *e.g.*

Sanscrit.	Hindustani.	Greek.	Persian.
daça (10)	*das*	δέκα	*deh*.
sapta (7)	*sát*	ἕπτα	*haft*.

As the Sanscrit *s* becomes *h* in Persian, so, *vice versâ*, *h* often becomes *z*: Sanscrit *sahasra* (1000), Persian هزار *hazár* for *hazahr*. *Cf.* Sanscrit *hima*, "snow," Persian *zemistán*, "winter," Latin *hiems*, Slavonic *zima*. *j* also becomes *z*; as

Sanscrit,	Persian.	Greek.
játa, "born,"	*zádah*	
janá, "a woman,"	*zan*	γυνή.

Irregular Verbs.

In studying the so-called Irregular Verbs, we have only to keep the above principles in view, remembering chiefly that

1. ب *b*, پ *p* } become ف *f*.
2. س *s* becomes ه *h*.
3. ه *h*, خ *kh* } become ز *z* or س *s*.

كردن "to do" has كن for its root; the Zend or Vedic form was *keren*, and the form كر *kar* became used for the past and كن *kun* for the present forms.

In ودن *údan* the و *ú* becomes ا *á* in the stem; as

بخشودن *bakhshúdan* (بخشيدن), to bestow,	بخشا *bakhshá*.
آزمودن *ázmúdan*, to try,	آزما *ázmá*.
كشودن *kushúdan*, to open,	كشا *kushá*.
نمودن *namúdan*, to show,	نما *namá*.
ربودن *rubúdan*, to rob,	رُبا *rubá*.

Where the و is a root letter it is retained, but as a consonant *v*; *e.g.*

شنودن *shinúdan*, to hear, شنَوْ *shinav.*

شدن *shudan*=شودن *shúdan*, to become, شَوْ *shav.*

When the infinitive ends in یدن *ídan* and the *í* is part of the root the stem is strengthened by adding a nasal ن; as

آفریدن *áfrídan*, to create, آفرین *áfrín.*

چیدن *chídan*, to collect, چین *chín.*

ختن *khtan* becomes ز *z* (see 3, p. 24), especially after a long vowel:

افراختن *afrákhtan*, to exalt, افراز *afráz.*

آموختن *ámúkhtan*, to learn, آموز *ámúz.*

and sometimes it changes into س *s* or ش *sh* (see 3, p. 24):

شناختن *shanákhtan*, to know, شناس *shanás.*

فروختن *firúkhtan*, to sell, فروش *firúsh.*

فتن *ftan* in some instances becomes ب *b* or و *v* (see 1, p. 24):

تافتن *táftan*, to burn, تاب *táb*

آشفتن *áshuftan*, to disturb, آشوب *áshúb.*

رفتن *raftan*, to go, رَوْ *rav.*

استن *ástan*, ستن *ŭstan* (*ústan*), and یستن *ístan* become آ *a*, ی *í*, and و *ú* respectively:

آراستن *arástan*, to adorn, آرا *árá.*

زیستن *zístan*, to live, زی *zí.*

جستن *justan* (*jústan*), to seek, جو *jú.*

Sometimes ستن *stan* become ن *n* or ين *ín*; as

شکستن *shikastan*, to break, شکن *shikan*.

نشستن *nishastan*, to sit, نشين *nishín*.

Other anomalous changes are شتن *ishtan* into يس *ís*; as

نوشتن *navishtan*, to write, نويس *navís*.

اشتن *áshtan* into ار *ár*; as

داشتن *dáshtan*, to have, دار *dár*.

انكاشتن *ankáshtan*, to think, انكار *ankár*.

There are a few others which practice and the vocabularies will teach, but the phonetic rules given on p. 24 will be found to cover most of the cases met with.*

In some instances the infinitive and the stem belong to different verbs, just as in English "go" and "went" come from different radical forms:

بودن *búdan*, to be, باش *bāsh*.

پيختن *pikhtan*, to twist, پيچ *pích*.

سختن *sakhtan*, to weigh, سنج *sanj*.

گسيختن *gusíkhtan*, to break, گسل *gusil*.

بستن *bastan*, to bind, بند *band*.

---

* [A list of all such verbs is given at p. 37, *et seq.*]

FORMS OF NOUNS.

These are very numerous and various, but although most may be left to practice and the vocabulary, some may be reduced to rule.

Nouns are either primitive, such as "man," or derivative, such as "manly." The last are formed by adding certain terminations to the first, and as these terminations are generally in their turn derived from verbs, and have a signification of their own, a knowledge of them will greatly assist the learner. The principal are:

1. انه *ánah* = "like;" as

    مردانه *mardánah*, manly.

    بزرگانه *buzurgánah*, grandly (like a grandee).

2. آور *ávar*, وَر *avar*, ار *ár*, all from root آوردن *ávardan*, and signifying "bringing," "producing," "displaying" (*cf.* English *-er*, *-or*), etc.

    دِلاور *dil-ávar*, brave (hearty).

    زور اور *zor-ávar*, strong.

    سخن ور *sukhan-var*, eloquent.

3. بار *bár*, "bearing," "abounding in."

    شکربار *shakar-bár*, sugar-laden.

    زنکبار *zangi-bár*, Zanzibár (full of negroes).

4. بان *bán*, وان *ván*, "keeping," "managing;" as

شتربان *shutur-bán*, a camel-man.

باغبان *bágh-bán*, a gardener.

پاسبان *pás-bán*, a watchman.

فام *fám* "colour;" as

سیاه فام *siyáh-fám*, blackish.

5. دار *dár*, تار *tár*, "having," from داشتن *dáshtan*:

فریفتار *faríf-tár*, a deceiver.

خریدار *kharídár*=خرید دار *kharíd-dár*, a purchaser.

خواستار *khástár*=خواست تار *khást-tár*=خواست دار *khást-dár*, a petitioner.

دیدار *dídár*=دید دار *díd-dár*, the visual faculty.

6. دان *dán*, "place" or "vessel for;" as

نمکدان *namak-dán*, a salt-cellar.

قلمدان *ḳalam-dán*, a pen-case.

7. زار *zár*, "place abounding in:"

گلزار *gulzár*, a rose-garden.

8. Similarly سار *sár*; as

کوهسار *koh-sár*, a mountainous country.

شاخسار *shákh-sár*, a place abounding in branches, German *laube*.

سار also signifies "like;" *cf.*

خاکسار *khák-sár*, like dust (vile).

9. ستان *stán*, "place;" as

گلستان *gulistán*, a rose-garden.

هندوستان *Hindústán*, the land of Hindús (Hindústán).

10. ش ِ, هش express the abstract idea of the root; as

نكوهش *nikúhish*, goodness.

دانش *dánish*, wisdom.

آرایش *áráïsh*, adornment.

11. ك *ak* expresses the diminutive of rational objects; as

مردك *mardak*, a little man.

A contemptuous form of diminutive is كه *kah*; as

مردكه *mardakah*, a wretched little man.

For irrational objects the ك is changed into چ, just as in كه *kih* and چه *chĭh* (see p. 12), *e.g.*

بازیچه *bázícheh*, a little game.

كفچه *kaf-cheh*, a ladle (*lit.* a little palm of the hand).

12. كار *kár*, گار *gár*, گر *gar*, all expresses *action* or the *actor*, and are connected with the verb كردن; as

جفاكار *jafá-kár*, cruelty.

دستگار *dast-gár*, skill (دست *dast*, a hand).

جادوگر *jádú-gar*, a conjurer, juggler.

آفریدگار *áfrídagár*, a creator.

آموزگار *ámúz-gár*, a teacher.

كامگار *kám-gár*, successful.

گناهگار *gunáh-gár*, a sinner, guilty.

توانگر *taván-gar*, rich (powerful).

13. گین *gín*, "affected with;" as

غمگین *gham-gín*, grieved.

خشمگین *khashm-gín*, angry.

14. لاخ *lákh*, "place."

سنگ لاخ *sang-lákh*, a strong place.

15. مند *mand*, "possessor of;" as

سودمند *súd-mand*, profitable.

دانشمند *dánish-mand*, wise.

16. ناك *nák* expresses "quality;" as

هولناك *haul-nák*, frightful.

پرهيزناك *parhíz-nák*, abstinent.

17. A final ی *í* signifies "relation," such as that implied in the English adjective; as

هندی *hindí*, Indian.

انگلیزی *inglízí*, English.

After ه this becomes گی; as

بنده *bandah*, a slave.

بندگی *bandagí*, slavery.

خانگی *khánagí*, domestic (for خانه گی).

The final ی *í*, when it represents the *yáe majhúl* (*e*), see p. 7, signifies "unity;" as

مردی *mardí*, one *a* man.

18. نی *ní* signifies "duty," "fitness;" *e.g.*

كردنی *kardaní*, what is to be done (duty).

خوردنی *khurdaní*, good to eat (food).

خریدنی *kharídaní*, purchaseable.

COMPOUND WORDS.

Persian is very rich in compound words, the types most in use for Nouns being exactly analogous to such English compounds as "block-head," "tinder-box," "rosy-cheeks," and the like; *e.g.*

لاله رخ *lálah-rukh*, tulip-cheeked.

گل اندام *gul-andám*, rose-bodied.

سمن بر *saman-bar*, jasmine-bosomed.

Others are made from two verbal roots; as آمد و رفت *ámad o raft*, "coming and going;" or two nouns joined by a preposition, as سربسر *sar ba sar*, "individually," "altogether," *lit.* "head to head."

The Compound Verbs are very numerous, but are for the most part quite simple, the principal ones being the following:

1. A noun followed by either کردن *kardan* "to do," ساختن *sákhtan*, "to make," نمودن *namúdan*, "to display," فرمودن *farmúdan*, "to order," and the like; as

انتظار کردن (ساختن) *intizár kardan* (*sákhtan*), to expect.

کرم نمودن *karam namúdan*, to be generous.

نهضت فرمودن *nahzat farmúdan*, to start (on a march), said of a king, etc.

2. A noun followed by آمدن *ámadan*, "to come" (*cf.* Anglicè "become"):

سیر آمدن *sír ámadan*, to become satisfied.

پُر آمدن *pur ámadan*, to become full.

پدید آمدن *padíd ámadan*, to become apparent.

3. A noun followed by آوردن *ávardan*, the converse of the last; as

پدید آوردن *padíd ávardan*, to make apparent.

4. A noun followed by خوردن *khurdan*, "to eat," used with words expressing passions or grief; as

غم خوردن *gham khurdan*, to be grieved.

تاسّف خوردن *ta-assuf khurdan*, to sorrow.

There are many other compound verbs of this kind, but they will be easily understood when met with, and will be found in the dictionary.

THE SYNTAX.

In Accidence we found how each word was capable of certain modifications to express the accidents of person, number, gender, or time.

We now come to Syntax, which, as its name implies, is the putting together of these individual words, or groups of words, to express one complete idea.

The *Accidence* being known, all that we require further is to learn the *usage* of the language in this syntactical arrangement.

This depends first upon the natural order in which ideas occur. Secondly, upon the history, traditions, habits, and disposition of the people using the ideas; *i.e.* on the natural order modified by habits: in other words, *idiom* or *peculiarity*.

THE SENTENCE.

Now, the complete expression of an idea is called a sentence, which in its simplest form is the mention of a person or thing and the telling something about him or it; *e.g.*

Man is mortal. John went;

but if the verb is *transitive*; *i.e.* if, *as its name implies*, its action goes on to something else, we must have something else for it to go on to ; *e.g.*

John struck James.

All that can possibly be added to this is : (1) something telling us about the state of John or James,—these are adjectives *added to the person ;* (2) the manner of the striking,—these are *adverbs* added to the verb ; (3) the manner in which, or the thing with which, it was done,—these are instruments; or (4) the time or place where and when it was done,—these are the locatives.

The Syntax of Persian is as simple as that of English, which it much resembles in construction.

The Cases of Nouns.

As has been noticed above, the only real case-ending which survives in Persian is را *rá* for the objective; as مرد را کتاب دادم *mard-rá kitáb dádam*, "I gave the man the book," where *mard* is the object (its position in the sentence calling attention to this fact) ; کتاب را بمرد دادم *kitáb-rá ba mard dádam*, "I gave the book to the man," attention being chiefly called in the last sentence to "book," both by the objective affix and by its position in the sentence: the fact that "the man" is in "dative" is then expressed, as in English, by ب *ba*, "to."

CONCORDANCE.

The Concordance of Verbs and Nouns is exactly the same as in English, a singular noun requiring a singular verb, and a plural noun taking a plural verb.

Nouns substantive do not agree with their adjectives or qualifying nouns in number, it being sufficient to mark the plural by the termination in the first named; as

مردان خوب *mardán i khúb*, good men (see p. 11).

The relation of "substantive and adjective," as well as that of the "genitive case," is expressed by the *izáfat* (see p. 6).

اضافت *izáfat* signifies "adding on," and is expressed by placing a short *i* (*kasrah* or *zír*) between the two nouns; as

اسپ مرد *asp i mard*, the man's horse.

اسپ خوب *asp i khub*, a good horse.

The order of words in Persian is Subject—Object—Verb, all qualifying expressions falling into their natural places; *e.g.* a word expressing the condition of the subject follows it; so does a word expressing the condition of the object; while words or expressions signifying time, place, or other circumstances, find their proper place immediately before the verb.

The only marked peculiarity in the arrangement is that the verb comes generally last.

The description of the "tenses" on pp. 16—21 sufficiently indicates their use.

TABLE OF IRREGULAR VERBS.

The following rules and exceptions tabulate all the irregularities of the Persian Verb, and for comment the student is referred to pp. 24—26.

I. Infinitives in ودن *údan* make their Imperative in ا *á*; and in the Present take a euphonic يـ *y*; thus:

نمودن *nemúdan*, "to show;" Imperative, به نما *be-nemá*;
Present, مينمايم *mí-nemáyam.*

II. Infinitives in يدن *ídan*, ادن *ádan*, and ستن *stan*, form the Imperative by dropping these terminations; thus:

فرستادن *firistádan*, "to send;" Imper. بفرست *be-firist.*
پرسيدن *pursídan*, "to ask;" Imper. به پرس *be purs.*
دانستن *dánistan*, "to know;" Imper. بدان *be-dán.*

III. Infinitives in دن *dan*, after ر *r* and ن *n*, and some few in تن *tan*, after ف *f*, form their Imperative by dropping the termination *dan*, or *tan*; thus:

پروردن *parvardan*, "to cherish;" Imperative بپرور *be-parvar.*
كندن *kandan*, "to dig;" Imper. بكن *be-kan.*
بافتن *báftan*, "to weave;" Imper. به باف *be-báf.*

IV. Infinitives in تن *tan*, after خ *kh*, and ش *sh*, form their Imperatives in ز *z*; and ر *r* respectively; thus:

آويختن *ávíkhtan*, "to hang;" Imper. بياويز *biyávíz.*
داشتن *dáshtan*, "to have;" Imper. بدار *be-dár.*

To these rules the following are exceptions:

	Infinitive.	Imperative.
Offend,	آزردن *ázurdan,*	آزار *ázár.*
Disturb,	آشفتن *áshuftan,*	آشوب *áshúb.*
Create,	آفریدن *áferídan,*	آفرین *áferín.*
Come,	آمدن *ámadan,*	آ *á.*
		P. میآیم *mi-áyam.*
Squeeze,	افشردن *afshurdan,*	افشار *afshár.*
Cook,	پختن *pukhtan,*	پز *paz.*
Carry,	بردن *burdan,*	بر *bar.*
Bind,	بستن *bastán,*	بند *band.*
Be,	بودن *búdan,*	باش *básh.*
		P. میباشد *mí-báshad* and میبود *mí-buvad.*
Accept,	پذیرفتن *pazíruftan,*	پذیر *pazír.*
Twist,	پیختن *pikhtan,*	پیچ *pích.*
Join,	پیوستن *paivastan,*	پیوند *paivand.*
Shine,	تافتن *táftán,*	تاب *táb.*
Jump,	جستن *jastan,*	جه *jih.*
Search,	جستن *justan,*	جو *jú.*
		P. میجویم *mí-júyam.*
Pluck,	چیدن *chídan,*	چین *chín.*

	INFINITIVE.	IMPERATIVE.
Get up,	برخاستن *bar khástan*,	برخیز *bar khíz*.
Wish,	خواستن *khástan*,	خواه *kháh*.
Give,	دادن *dádan*,	ده *deh*.
Reap,	درودن *derúdan*,	درو *derú*
		P. میدروم *mí-derevam*.
Run,	دویدن *davídan*,	دو *do*.
		P. میدوم *mí-davam*.
See,	دیدن *dídan*,	بین *bín*.
Deliver,	رستن *rastan*,	ره *reh*.
Grow,	رستن *rustan*,	رو *rú*.
		P. میرویم *mí-rúyam*.
Spin,	رشتن *rishtan*,	ریس *rís*.
Go,	رفتن *raftan*,	رو *ro*.
		P. میروم *mí-ravam*.
Sweep,	رفتن *ruftan*,	روب *rúb*.
Strike,	زدن *zadan*,	زن *zan*.
Consign,	سپردن *sipurdan*,	سپار *sipár*.
Perforate,	سفتن *suftan*,	سنب *sumb*.
Hasten,	شتافتن *shitáftan*,	شتاب *shitáb*.
Become,	شدن *shudan*,	شو *sho*.
		P. میشوم *mí-shavam*.

	INFINITIVE.	IMPERATIVE.
Wash,	شستن *shustan,*	شو *shú.*
		P. میشویم *mí shúyam.*
Break,	شکستن *shikastan,*	شکن *shikan.*
Bloom,	شکفتن *shikuftan,*	شکفت *shikuft.*
Count,	شمردن *shumurdan,*	شمار *shumár.*
Know,	شناختن *shinákhtan,*	شناس *shinás.*
Hear,	شنیدن *shanídan,*	شنو *shino.*
		میشنوم *mí-shanavam.*
Sell,	فروختن *farúkhtan,*	فروش *farúsh.*
Deceive,	فریفتن *firíftan,*	فریب *firíb.*
Squeeze,	فشردن *fishurdan,*	فشار *fishár.*
Hollow,	کافتن *káftan,*	کاو *káv.*
Do,	کردن *kardan,*	کن *kun.*
Burst,	کسستن *kusistan,*	کسل *kusil.*
Sow,	کشتن *kishtan,*	کار *kár.*
Kill,	کشتن *kushtan,*	کش *kush.*
Beat,	کوفتن *kúftan,*	کوب *kúb.*
Sieze,	گرفتن *giriftan,*	گیر *gír.*
Choose,	گزیدن *guzídan,*	گزین *guzín.*
Burst,	گسیختن *gusíkhtán,*	گسل *gusil.*
Become,	گشتن *gashtan,*	گرد *gard.*

	INFINITIVE.	IMPERATIVE.
Say,	گفتن *guftan*,	گو *gú*.
		P. میگویم *mí-gúyam*.
Die,	مردن *murdan*,	میر *mír*.
Sit,	نشستن *nishastan*,	نشین *nishín*.
Write,	نوشتن *navishtan*,	نویس *navís*.
Conceal,	نهفتن *nihuftan*,	نهفت *nihuft*.
Let go,	هشتن *hishtan*,	هل *hil*.
Find,	یافتن *yáftan*,	یاب *yáb*.

RULES FOR FINDING THE YEAR OF THE HEJRAH.

The best complete tables are those edited by F. Wüstenfeld, for the German Oriental Society. The following dates however will be found useful for rough calculation.

A.H.	A.D.	A.H.	A.D.
1	16*th July* 622 =621·54.	700	1300
		803	1400
100	718	900	1494
184	800	1009	1600
300	912	1100	1688
391	1000	1215	1800
500	1106	1300	*Nov.* 12*th*, 1882
597	1200		

The Moslem year consists of 12 lunar months (see Dictionary, s.v. Month) of 30 and 29 days alternately. Now 100 lunar years nearly equal 97 solar years: and hence, to turn Moslem years into Christian years, we must subtract 3 per cent. from the former.

I. To find the equivalent date A.D. of a year A.H.:—From the year A.H. deduct 3 per cent. (or, more exactly, multiply by

·970225), and to the remainder add 621·54. The sum gives the date A.D. of the *end* of the year A.H.

II. To find the equivalent date A.H. of a year A.D.:—From the year A.D. deduct 621·54, and to the remainder add 3 per cent.

ENGLISH AND PERSIAN DICTIONARY.

ABBREVIATIONS AND EXPLANATIONS.

v.	verb.	*n.*	noun.
t.	transitive.	*a.*	adjective.
i.	intransitive.	*pl.*	plural.
n.	neuter.	*pr. p.*	present participle.
a.	active.	*pa. p.*	past participle.
p.	passive.		

For the pronunciation of the Persian letters, see Grammar, pp. 1—3.

In order to save repetition, when the Persian equivalent of an English Verb is made up of noun (or other part of speech) and auxiliary verb, the auxiliary verb to be used is indicated by an initial (*k. sh.* etc.), and no separate paragraph is given. Thus the verb 'to Advise' is to be sought for *s. v.* 'Advice,' where *nasíhat* (*dádan*) will be found. After *bídár*, the Persian for 'Awake,' (*k. sh.*) show that 'to Awaken' is *bídár kardan*, and 'to become Awake,' *bídár shudan.* (See Grammar, pp. 31, 32.).

The following letters stand for these auxiliary verbs, and in the transliteration also they are used to save space.

a.	*ávardan.*	*gr.*	*giriftan.*	*nh.*	*nihádan.*
an.	*andákhtan.*	*gz.*	*guzárdan.*	*r.*	*raftan.*
b.	*búdan.*	*h.*	*hastan.*	*rs.*	*rasídan.*
bs.	*bastan.*	*k.*	*kardan.*	*rsa.*	*rasánídan.*
d.	*dádan.*	*kh.*	*khurdan.*	*s.*	*sákhtan.*
dsh.	*dáshtan.*	*ksh.*	*keshídan.*	*sh.*	*shudan.*
f.	*farmúdan.*	*m.*	*mándan.*	*y.*	*yáftan.*
g.	*gardánidan.*	*n.*	*namúdan.*	*z.*	*zadan.*
gf.	*goftan.*				

It should furthermore be observed, that in cases of repetition a bar (—) stands for the English word commencing the paragraph; and in the transliteration, under like circumstances, the initial letter of the Persian word is alone given.

pr. p. and *pa. p.* are to be understood as indicating the Present or Past Participle of the *English word*, of which the Persian following is the rendering.

Thus we have

Move, *v.i.*, جنبيدن *jumbídan*, etc.; *pa. p.* (*i.e.* Moved). متحرك *mutaharrik*; *pr. p.* (*i.e.* Moving), رج *rajj.*

A

CONCISE DICTIONARY

ENGLISH AND PERSIAN.

A

A, an, یك *yek*

Abandon, ترك كردن *tark k.*; *pr. p.* هاجر *hájir*; *pa. p.* متروك *matrúk*; (shameless) بيحيا *bí-hayá*.

Abashed, شرمنده *sharmandeh* (*s.*) سر افكند *sar afgand*.

Abasing, اهانت *ihánat* (*k.*).

Abatement, تخفيف *takhfíf* (*k.*)

Abbreviation, اختصار *ikhtisár* (*k.*); ايجاز *íjáz*.

Abdication, خلع *khal'* (*k.*); استعفا *isti'fá* (*d.*); اعتزال *i'ti-zál* (*n.*).

Abdomen, شكم *shikam*; ته ناف *tah i náf*.

Abet, مدد دادن *madad d.*

Abhorrence, اكراه *ikráh* (*n.*).

Abhorring, متنفر *mutanaffir* (*b.*); مجتوى *mujtaví* (*h.*).

Ability, لياقت *liyáḳat*; قدرت *ḳudrat*; قوه *ḳuvveh*.

Abject, خوار و زار *khár o zár*. —ness, دونى *dúní*; ذل *zull*; خوارى *khárí*.

Able, زرنك *ziring*. To be —, توانستن *tavánistan*.

Ablution, وضوء *wuzú* (*k.*); غسل *ghusl* (*k.*).

Abode, منزل *manzil*; مكان *makán*.

Abolished, منسوخ *mansúkh* (*k.*); مبطل *mubtal* (*g.*).

Abolition, ابطال *ibtál*.

Abominable, مستكره *mustakrih*; شنع *shani'*.

Abominate, منفور داشتن *manfúr dsh.*

Abortion, اسقاط *iskát.*

Abounding in, مثمور *masmúr.*

About, (concerning), در خصوص *dar khusús*; در حق *dar hakk.* — (around). دور *daur.*

Above, بالا *bálá*; فوق *fauk*; زبر *zabar*

Above-named, مذکور *mazkúr*; موصوف *mausúf*

Abridged, مقتصر *muktasar* (*k.*); مختصر *mukhtasar* (*k.*).

Abridgement, اقتصار *iktisár* (*n.*); اجمال *ijmál* (*k.*).

Abroad, بیرون *bírún.*

Abruptly, ناگاه *ná-gáh*

Abscess, دمبل *dumbal*

Abscond, دررفتن *dar r.*; *pr. p.* متواری *mutawárí.* — (slave), ابیق *abík.*

Absence, غیبت *ghaibat.*

Absent, غیر حاضر *ghair házir*; غایب *gháyib* (*sh.*). — in mind, متفکر *mutafakkir* (*b.*); پریشان *paríshán.*

Absolute, مستقل *mustakill*; مطلق *matlak.*

Absolution, بهل *bihil* (*k.*).

Absorption, جذب *jazb* (*k.*).

Abstain, پرهیز کردن *parhíz k.*; *pr. p.* مجتنب *mujtanib* (*sh.*).

Abstinence ریاضت *riyázat*; پرهیز *parhíz.*

Abstinent عفیف *'afíf*; وریع *vari'.*

Abstract, *n.* مجمل *mujmal* (*s.*); *v.* (to take away) بر داشتن *bar dsh.*

Abstruse, مغلق *mughlak*; دقیق *dakík.* — ness, دقت *dikkat.*

Absurd, پوچ *púch*; بیمعنی *bí-ma'ní*; هرزه *harzeh.*

Absurdity, بطالت *batálat.*

Abundance, فراخی *ferákhi*; وفور *vufúr.*

Abundant, عامر *'ámir*; فایض *fáiz.*

Abuse, *n.*, فحش *fuhsh* (*d.*); شتم *shatm.*

Abusive, زبان دراز *zabán-diráz*, مشاتمه *mushátameh.*

Abyssinian, حبشی *habashí.*

Acacia, مغیلان *mughailán*; سیال *siyál.*

Acceleration, تعجیل *ta'jíl* (*k.*)

Accept, قبول کردن *kabúl k.* *pa. p.* مقبول *makbúl*; *pr. p.* مجیب *mujíb.*

Acceptable, پـذيـره *pazírah*, مستجاب *mustajáb*.

Acceptance (bill), قبوليت *kabúliyat* (*k*.).

Access, آمد و شد *ámád o shud* (*k*.) ; تقريب *takríb*.

Accession, جلوس *julús*.

Accident, اتفاق *ittifák* ; وقـوع *vukú'*.

Accidental, عارضی *'árizí* ; اتفاقی *ittifáki*. — ly, اتـفـاقاً *ittifákan*.

Acclamation, آفرين *áfarín* (*k*.)

Accommodate, مصالحه كردن *musálahah k*.

Accompany, همراه رفتن *hamráh r*. ; *pr. p*. باتـفاق *be-ittifák* ; تشـيـيع *tashyi'* (*n*.)

Accomplice, شريك *sharík*.

Accomplish, سر آمدن *sar ámadan* ; *pa. p*. فاضل *fázil*.

Accomplishment, اتمام *itmám* (*rs*.) ; سر براهی *sar berárhí*.

Accordance with, in —, بحكم *be-hukm*.

According to, مطابق *mutábik* ; حسب *hasb*.

Account (news), خبر *khabar* (*k*.) ; (money), جساب *hisáb* (*d*.). — book, دفتر *daftar*. on — of, برای *baráyí*.

Accoutrements, سلاح *siláh*.

Accumulation, جمع *jam'* (*k*.) ; متراكمه *mutarákemeh*.

Accurate, صحيح *sahíh*. —ly, بدرستی *be-durustí*.

Accursed, ملعون *mal'ún*.

Accusation, تهمت *tuhmat* (*bs*.).

Accuse, شكايت كـردن *shikáyat k*.

Accuser, مدعی *mudda'i*.

Accustomed, to be —, عادت داشـتن *'ádat dsh*. ; *pa. p*. معتاد *mu'tád*.

Ache, درد *dard* (*k*. *kh*.).

Acid, ترش *tursh* (*k*.). —ity حموضت *numúzat*.

Acknowledging, اقرار *ikrár* (*k*.); معترف *mu'tarif* (*sh*.).

Acorn, بلوط *ballút*.

Acquaint, اطلا دادن *ittilá d*.

Acquaintance, آشـنـا *áshná* ; روشناسی *rú-shinásí*.

Acquiescence, رضا *rizá* (*sh*.).

Acquire, حاصل كـردن *hásil k*. يافتن *yáftan*.

Acquisition, تحـصيل *tahsíl* (*k*.) ; اكتساب *iktisáb*.

Acquittal, ابرا *ibrá* (*k.*) ; خلاص *khalás* (*k.*).

Acquittance, فارغ خطی *fáregh khattí.*

Across, عبور *'ubúr* ; از سر بسر *az sar be-sar.*

Act, *v.*, کردن *kerdan* ; *n.* کار *kár* ; فعل *fe'el* ; (play), مجلس *majlis.*

Active, چالاك *chálák*, چست *chust.*

Activity, چستی *chustí* ; چابکی *chábukí.*

Actor, مقلد *mukallid.*

Actual, واقعی *wáki.* —ly, بالفعل *bilfe'l.*

Acute, سخت *sakht.*

Adapt, ترتیب کردن *tartíb k.*

Add, جمع کردن *jam' k.* ; اضافه کردن *izáfeh k.*

Adder, مار جعفری *már-i-ja'afarí.*

Address, سر نامه *sar námeh.*

Adducing, ایراد *írád* (*n.*).

Adhere, چسپیدن *chaspídan* ; *pr. p.* لاصق *lásik.*

Adhesion, لصوق *lusúk.*

Adhesive چسبناك *chaspnák* ; چسپنده *chaspendeh.*

Adieu, خدا حافظ *khudá háfiz* ; الوداع *alvidá'.*

Adjective, صفت *sifat.*

Adjoining, متصل *muttasil* (*sh.*).

Adjournment, بر خاست *bar khást* (*k.*).

Adjudicate, دیوان کردن *díván k.*

Adjuster, ناظم *názim.*

Administration, اداره *idárah* (*k.*).

Admiral, امیر البحر *amír ul bahr.*

Admire, پسند کردن *pasand k.* ; *pr. p.* متعجب *muta'ajjib* (*sh.*).

Admit, راه دادن *ráh d.* ; (agree to), قبول کردن *kabúl k.*

Admonition, نصیحت *nasíhat* (*d.*) ; تنبه *tambih.*

Adopted (son), متبنی *mutabanná* (*k.*).

Adoptive, ملسق *mulassak.*

Adoration, عبادت *'ibádat* (*k.*) ; سجود *sajúd* (*n.*).

Adored, معبود *ma'búd.*

Adorn, زیبیدن *zíbídan* ; *pa. p.* زیبنده *zíbandah.*

Adornment, پیرایش *píráyish* ; زیبندکی *zíbandagí.*

Adult, *a.*, بالغ *bálígh.*

Adulterated, مخلوط *makhlút* (*k.*).

Adulterer, زنا کار *ziná kár* ; فاجر *fájir.*

Adulteress, زانیه *zániyeh*; فاجره *fájireh.*

Adultery, زنا *ziná* (*k.*); فجور *fujúr.*

Advance, *v.*, پیش رفتن *písh raftan*; *n.* (pay), پیشخور *písh khúr*; *v.* پیش دادن *písh d.*

Advance guard, پیش قراول *písh keráúl.*

Advancement, ترقی *tarakki* (*d.*).

Advantage, منفعت *manfa'at*; فایده *fá-ídeh.*

Advantageous, نافع *náfi'.*

Adverb, ظرف *zarf.*

Adversary, دشمن *dushman*; (law), مدعی *mudda'í.*

Adversity, شقاوت *shikávat*; بلا *belá*; نکبت *nikbat.*

Advertisement اعلان *i'lán* (*n.*); انتشار *intishár* (*d.*).

Advice, نصیحت *nasíhat* (*d.*) پند *pand* (*d.*).

Advocate, *n.*, وکیل *vakíl.*

Afar, دور دست *dúr dast.*

Affable, مشفق *mushfik.*

Affability, لطف *lutf*; مهربانی *mihribání.*

Affair, باب *báb*; کار *kár*; امر *amr*; *pl.* امور *umúr*; کاروبار *kár o bár.*

Affection, محبت *muhabbat* (*dsh.*); دوستی *dústí* (*dsh.*). —ate, مهربان *mihribán*; شفیق *shafík.*

Affianced, نامزد *námzad* (*f.*).

Affidavit, قسم *kasm* (*kh.*).

Affinity, نسبت *nisbat*; جهت *jihat.*

Affirmation, تصدیق *tasdík* (*n.*); اثبات *isbát* (*gf.*).

Afflicted, پریشان *paríshán* (*s.*); غمناك *ghamnák*; (with a malady), مبتلا *mubtalá* (*h.*). To be — in mind, غم خوردن *gham kh.*

Affliction, رنجش *ranjish.*

Affluence, نعمت *ni'mat.*

Affluent, دولتمند *daulatmand.*

Affront, *n.*, شتم *shatm*; *v.* بیحرمت کردن *bíhurmat k.*

Afraid, to be, ترسیدن *tarsídan*; *n.* خائف *kháif* (*h.*).

Afresh, مجدداً *mujaddadan.*

After, پس *pas*; بعد از *ba'ad az*; پی *pey*; عقب *'akab.*

Afternoon, عصر *asr*; بعد از ظهر *ba'ad az zuhr.*

Afterwards, بعد از آن *ba'ad az án.*

Again, باز *báz* ; بار دیگر *bár-i-dígar* ; دو باره *do báreh.*

Against, خلاف *khiláf.*

Age, عمر *umr*; سن و سال *sinn o sál*; (time), زمان *zamán.*

Aged, پیر *pír* (*sh.*).

Agent, گماشته *gumáshtah* ; وکیل *vakíl.*

Ages, دهور *duhúr.*

Aggravate, بدتر کردن *badtar k.*

Aggregate, in the, فی الجمله *fíl-jumlah.*

Agression, ظلم *zulm* ; پیشدستی *píshdastí.*

Aggressive, دست دراز *dast diráz* (*k.*).

Agile, چابك *chábuk* ; چست *chust.*

Agitated (mind), مضطرب *muztarib* (*sh.*) ; پریشان *paríshán*; (body), متزلزل *mutazalzal.*

Agitation, اضطراب *iztiráb*; تشویش *tashvísh.*

Agony, سکرات *sakarát.*

Agree to, راضی شدن *rází sh.*

Agreeable دلپسند *dil-pasand.*

Agreement, قرار *ḳerár* (*k.*).

Agriculture, زراعت *zirá'at*; حرث *hirs.*

Agriculturist, دهقان *dehḳán* ; حراث *hurrás.*

Ague, تب و لرزه *tab o larzeh.*

Ah ! ای وای *ai wai !* واه *váh.*

Ahead, جلو *jelo.*

Aid, مدد *madad* (*d.*) ; کمك *kumek* (*k.*).

Aigrette (royal), جیکه *jíkah.*

Aim, قراول *keráúl* (*gr.*) ; (mental), مقصود *maḳsúd.*

Air, هوا *havá* ; باد *bád.*

Airy, هوادار *havá-dár.*

Alabaster, مرمر *marmar.*

Alarm, *n.*, خوف *khauf* ; *v.* ترسانیدن *tarsánídan.*

Alas! های های *hái ! hái !* دردا *dardá !*

Alchemist, کیمیا گر *kímiyágar.*

Alchemy, کیمیا *kímiyá.*

Alcohol, عرق *'araḳ.*

Alcove, طاقچه *táḳcheh.*

Alembic, انبیق *ambíḳ.*

Alert, چابق *chábuḳ.*

Algebra, الجبر والمقابله *aljabr walmaḳábileh.*

Alien, بیگانه *bígáneh.*

Alighting, نزول *nuzúl* (*n.*) ; *pa. p.* پیاده *piyádeh* (*sh.*).

Alike, شبیه *shabíh* ; مثل *misl* ; مانند *mánand.*

Aliment, غذا *ghazá* ; قوت *ḳút.*
Alive, زنده *zindah.*
Alkali, قلی *ḳalí.*
All, همه *hamah* ; جمیع *jamí'.*
Allegation, تقریر *taḳrír* (*n.*).
Allegiance, اطاعت *itá'at.*
Allegory, تمثیل *tamsíl.*
Alleviated, مخفف *mukhaffif* (*ḳ.*).
Alliance, عهد *'ahd* ; حلف *hilf.*
Alligator, نهنك *nihang.*
Alliteration, تجنیس *tajnís.*
Allot, تقسیم کردن *taḳsím k.* ; *pa. p.* مقسوم *maḳsúm.*
Allow, روا داشتن *ravá dsh.* ; اذن دادن *izn d.*
Allowable, روا *ravá* ; حلال *halál.*
Allowance, وظیفه *vazífeh.*
Alloy, عیار *'iyyár* (*k.*).
Allure, فریب دادن *faríb d.*
Allusion, اشاره *isháreh* (*k.*) ; تعریض *ta'ríz.*
Ally, متفق *muttafiḳ.*
Almanac, تقویم *taḳvím.*
Almond, بادام *bádám* ; لوز *lauz.*
Almost, نزدیك *nazdík.*
Alms, صدقه *sadaḳeh* ; زکات *zakát.*
Aloe, صبر *sabir.*
Alone, تنها *tanhá* ; مفرد *mufrad.*

Aloud, با آواز بلند *bá ávázi buland.*
Alphabet, حروف *hurúf.*
Already, هنوز *hanúz.*
Also, هم *ham* ; نیز *níz* ; ایضاً *aizan.*
Altar, مذبح *mazbah.*
Alter, گردانیدن *gardánídan.*
Alteration, تغییر *taghayyur* (*k.*) ; تبدیل *tabdíl* (*k.*).
Altercation, مجادله *mujádileh* ; قیل و قال *ḳíl o ḳál.*
Alternately, بنوبه *be-nobah.*
Although, اگرچه *agar cheh.*
Altitude, ارتفاع *irtifá'.*
Altogether, جمیعاً *jamí'an.*
Alum, زاج ابیض *záji-abyaz* ; زاق *záḳ.*
Always, همیشه *hamíshah* ; دایماً *dáiman.*
Amalgam, مخلوط *makhlút.*
Amanuensis, کاتب *kátib.*
Amass, جمع کردن *jam' k.*
Amateur, مفت *muft.*
Amazed, متعجب *muta'ajjib* (*n.*) ; حیران *hairan* (*sh.*) ; متحیر *mutahayyir* (*m.*).
Amazement, تعجب *ta'ajjub* (*n.*).
Ambassador, ایلچی *ílchí.*

Amber, کاه ربا *káh-rubá.*
Ambergris, عنبرین *'ambarín*; عبیر *'abír.*
Ambiguity, اشتباه *ishtibáh.*
Ambiguous, مشتبه *mushtabih.*
Ambitious, صاحب همة *sáhib himmat*; هوسناك *havvasnák.*
Ambling, یرقه *yurḳeh* (*r.*).
Ambush, کمین *kamín.*
Amend, درست کردن *durust k.*; *pr. p.* تهذیب *tahzíb.*
Amethyst, یاقوت کبود *yáḳúti kabúd.*
Amity, دوستی *dústí*, مهربانی *mihribání.*
Ammunition, اسباب *asbáb.*
Amnesty, عفو نامه *afv námeh.*
Among, در میان *dar miyán.*
Amorous, دلبسته *dilbastah.*
—ly, عاشقانه *'áshekánah.*
Amount, مبلغ *mablagh.*
Ample, واسع *vásih*; فسیح *fasíh.*
Amplitude, توسع *tavassu'*; کشادکی *kushádagí.*
Amputate, بریدن *burídan.*
Amputation, قطع *kat'* (*k.*).
Amulet, تعویذ *ta'víz*; حرز *hirz.*
Amusement, تفرج *tafarruj* (*k.*).
Anagram, تحریف *tahríf.*

Analogy, تجنیس *tajnís*; تطابق *tatábuk.*
Analysis, تجزیه *tajziyah* (*k.*).
Anarchy, هرج مرج *harj-marj.*
Anathema, لعنت *la'nat.*
Anatomy, تشریح *tashríh* (*k.*).
Ancestor, جد *jadd*; *pl.* ابا و اجداد *abá o ajdád.*
Ancestral, جدی *jaddí.*
Anchor, لنکر *langar* (*an.*).
—age, لنکر کاه *l. gáh.*
Ancient, قدیم *ḳadím*; کهنه *kuhnah.*
Ancients, *n.*, متقدمین *mutaḳaddimín.*
And, و *va, o.*
Anecdote, قصه *ḳissah*; حکایت *hikáyat.*
Anemone, شقایق *shaḳáiḳ.*
Angel, فرشته *firishtah*; ملك *malak*; (of death), ملك الموت *malak ul maut*, عزرائل *'azráil.*
Anger, خشم *khashm*; غیظ *ghaiz*; غضب *ghazab.*
Angered, مغضوب *maghzúb.*
Angle, زاویه *záwiyah.* Acute —, زاویهٔ حاده *z-i háddeh.* Obtuse —, زاویهٔ منفرجه *z-i munfarijeh.* Right —, زاویهٔ قایمه *z-i ḳáimeh.*

Angry, خشمناك *khishmnák* (*h.*); كج خلق *kaj khulk* (*b*). To be — with, رنجيدن از *ranjidan az.*

Anguish, تشوير *tashvír.*

Animal, جانـور *jánivar*; حيوان *haiván.*

Animate, زنده كردن *zindeh k.*; *pr. p.* احياء *ihyá.*

Animosity, مخاصمت *mukhásamat.*

Aniseed, رازيانه *ráziyáneh.*

Ankle, كوزك *gúzak.*

Anklet, پـابرنجان *pábaranján*; خلخال *khalkhál.*

Annals, تواريخ *tavárikh.*

Annexation, الحاق *ilháḳ* (*k.*).

Annexed, مضاف *muzáf* (*sh.*).

Annihilate, دمـار بـر آوردن از *damár bar ávardan az*; *pa. p.* منعدم *mun'adim* (*sh.*); نابود *nábúd* (*k.*).

Annotate, حاشيه نوشتن *háshiyeh navishtan*

Announce, خبر دادن *khabar d.*; *pr. p.* مخبر *mukhbir.*

Annoyance, ايـذا *ízá*; اجحاف *ijháf.*

Annual, سنوى *sanavi.*

Annuitant, وظيفـه خوار *vazífeh khár.*

Annul, باطل كردن *bátil k.*; *pa. p.* منسوخ *mansúkh.*

Anointing, تمريخ *tamríkh k.*; تدهين *tadhín* (*k.*).

Another, ديكر *dígar*; غير *ghair.* One —, يك ديكر *yek dígar.*

Answer, جـواب *javváb* (*d.*); *pr. p.* مجاوبت *mujávabat.*

Ant, مورچه *múrcheh.* White —, ديمك *dímek.*

Antagonist, خصيم *khasím.*

Antecedent, متقدم *mutaḳaddim*; ما قبل *má ḳabal.*

Antechamber, دالان *dálán.*

Antelope, آهو *áhú.*

Anterior, پـيشين *píshín*; سابق *sábeḳ.*

Antichrist, دجال *Dajjál.*

Anticipate, سبقت كرفـتن *sabḳat gr.*

Antidote, ترياق *teriyáḳ.*

Antimony, سرما *surmá.*

Antiquities, عتائق *'atáiḳ.*

Antiquity, زمان قـديم *zamáni ḳadím.*

Antithesis, ضد *zidd.*

Antler, شاخ *shákh.*

Anus, کون *kún.*

Anvil, سندان *sandán.*

Anxiety, اضطراب *iztiráb.* To feel deep —, خون جگر خوردن *khúni jigar kh.*

Anxious, دلتنك *diltang* ; فکرمند *fikr mand.*

Any, هیچ *hích.* — one, کسی *kasí.* — thing, چیزی *chízí.* — how, بهرکیف *behar keif.*

Aorist, مضارع *muzári'.*

Apart, جدا *jedá.*

Apartments, منزل *manzil.*

Apathy, سردی *sardí.*

Ape, کبی *kabí.*

Aperient, مسهل *mus-hil.*

Aperture, سوراخ *súrákh.*

Apex, اوج *auj.*

Apocopated, محذوف *mahzúf.*

Apocopation, حذف *hazf*

Apologist, معذر *mu'zir*

Apologising, اعتذار *i'tizár* (*k.*).

Apologue, مثل *masal.*

Apology, عذر *'uzr* (*k.*). To demand an —, عذر خواستن *'uzr khástan.*

Apoplexy, سکته *sakteh* (*z.*).

Apostasy, ارتداد *irtidád* (*n.*).

Apostate, مرتد *murtadd.*

Apostle, پیغمبر *paíghambar* ; رسول *rasúl.* — of Christ, حواری *havári.*

Apothecary, دوا فروش *dawá ferúsh.* — shop, دوا خانه *d. kháneh.*

Apparatus, اسباب *asbáb*; ساز *sáz.*

Apparent, ظاهر *záhir* (*sh.*) —ly, ظاهراً *záhiran.*

Appeal, رجوع کردن *rujú' kerdan.*

Appear, نمودن *namúdan* ; *pr. p.* پیدا *paidá* (*sh.*).

Appearance, نمایش *namáyish.*

Appease, آرامیدن *árámídan.*

Append, آویز کردن *áviz k.*

Appendix, تتما *tatimmá.*

Appetite, اشتها *ishtihá* ; شره *shareh.*

Applause, آفرین *áferín* (*k. gf.*).

Apple, سیب *síb.*

Application, توجه *tavajjah.*

Appoint, مامور کردن *maamúr k.* ; *pa. p.* مقرر *mukarrar* (*k.*) ; *pr. p.* تعیین *ta'yín* (*n.*).

Appointment, منصب *mansab* ; تعین *ta'ayun.*

Apportion, قسمت کردن *ḳismat k.*

Apposite, مناسب *munásib.*

Appraise, قیمت کردن *ḳaimat k.*

Apprehend (seize), گرفتن *girif-tan*; (fear), ترسیدن *tarsídan*.
Apprehension, درایت *dirávet*.
Apprentice, شاگرد *shágird* (s.).
—ship, شاگردی *shágirdí*.
Approach, نزدیك آمدن *nazdík ámadan*; *pr. p.* تقارب *taḳá-rub* (n.).
Approbation, پسند *pasand*; تحسین *tahsín* (k.).
Appropriate, مناسب *munásib*.
Appropriation, تخصیص *taḳhsís* (k).
Approve, پسند آمدن *pasand ámadan*; *pr. p.* استحسان *is-tihsán*; *pa. p.* موجه *muvajjah*.
Approximation, تقرب *takarrub*.
Apricot, زرد آلو *zard álú*; مشمش *mishmish*.
Apron, فوطه *fútah*.
Apt, زرنك *zaring*.
Aptitude, شایستگی *sháyistagí*.
Aquafortis, تیز آب *tíz áb*.
Aquatic, آبی *ábí*.
Aqueduct (under ground), قنات *ḳanát*; کاریز *káríz*.
Arab, عرب *'arab*; عرابی *'arábí*.
Arabia, عربستان *'arabistán*.
Arabic, عربی *'arabí*; تازی *tází*.
Arbiter, ثالث *sális*.
Arbitrary, مطلق *mutlaḳ*.
Arbitration, ثالثی *sálisí*.
Arc, قوس *kaus*.
Arch, *n.*, طاق *ták*; *a.* (cunning), شاطر *shátir*.
Archer, تیر انداز *tír andáz*.
Archery, کمان کشی *kamán keshí*.
Architect, مهندس *muhindas*.
Archive, دفتر *daftar*.
Ardour, غیرت *ghaírat*; همیت *hamíyet*.
Area, ساحت *sáhat*.
Arena, میدان *maidán*.
Argue, منازره کردن *munázarah k*.
Argument, بحث *bahs* (k.); دلیل *dalíl* (s.).
Arid, خشك *khushk*; بایر *báyir*.
Arise, برخاستن *bar khástan*.
Aristocracy, اعیان و نجبا *a'yán o nujabá*.
Aristotle, ارسطو *Aristú*.
Arithmetic, علم حساب *'ilmi hisáb*.
Ark (Noah's), سفینهٔ نوح *safi-nahi Núh*.
Arm, دست *dast*; (upper), بازو *bázú*; (lower), عضد *'azud*.
Armed, مسلح *musallah* (k.); سلحدار *silahdár*.
Armenia, ارمن *Arman*.

Armenian, ارمنی *Armaní.*

Armlet, بازو بند *bázú band.*

Armour, زره *zireh.*

Armpit, بغل *baghal.*

Arms, اسلحه *aslahah (bs.)*; سلاح *siláh.*

Army, لشکر *lashkár;* عسکر *'askar.*

Aroma, بو *bú.* —tic, مطیب *mutayyib.*

Around, دور *daur*, or *dor.*

Arouse, بیدار کردن *bídár k.*

Arrange, تدارك کردن *tadáruk k.*; درست کردن *durust k.*

Arrangement, ترتیب *tartíb (n.)*; تمهید *tamhíd (k.)*; نظم *nazm.*

Array (battle), صف کشیدن *saff ksh.*; (attire), آراستن *árástan.*

Arrears, تتمه *tetummah.*

Arrest, حبس کردن *habs k.*

Arrival, داخل *dákhil*; وصول *vusúl.*

Arrive, رسیدن *rasídan.*

Arrogance, کبر *kibr*, تکبر *takabbur.*

Arrogant, گستاخ *gustákh.* —ly, مغروراً *maghrúran.*

Arrow, تیر *tír.*

Arsenal, توپخانه *túpkháneh*; سلاح خانه *siláh kháneh.*

Arsenic, مرك موش *margi músh.*

Art, فن *fenn*; صنعت *san'at.*

Artery, رك *rig*; شریان *sharyan.*

Artful, حیله ساز *híleh sáz*; کرپز *gurpaz.*

Artichoke, اردشاهی *ardasháhí.*

Article, معرفت *ma'refat.*

Articulation, تلفظ *talaffuz (k.).*

Artifice, حیله *híleh.*

Artificer, کاریکر *káriger.*

Artificial, ساخته *sákhteh.*

Artillery, توپ خانه *túp kháneh.* —man, توپچی *túpchí.*

Artizan, صنعت کر *san'at gar.*

Artlessness, سادکی *sádagí.*

As, چون *chún*; چنانکه *chunánkeh.*

Ascend, بر آمدن *bar ámadan.*

Ascension, معراج *mi'ráj.*

Ascent, صعود *sa'úd (n.)*; عروج *'urúj.*

Ascertain, تحقیق کردن *tahkík k.*; *pr. p.* تشخیص *tashkhís (n.).*

Ascetic, درویش *darvísh*; زاهد *záhid.* —ism, زهد *zuhd.*

Ascribe, نسبت کردن *nisbat k.*; *pa. p.* منسوب *mansúb (h.).*

Ash (tree), اهر *ahar.*

Ashamed, شرمنده *sharmandah.* To be —, سر فرو بردن *sar farú burdan.*

Ash-coloured, شهب *shahab.*

Ashes, خاکستر *khákistar.*
Aside, در کنار *dar kinár.*
Ask, پرسیدن *pursídan*; *pr. p.* مطالبه *mutálabeh* (*k*).
Asker, طالب *tálib.*
Askew (aslant), کج *kaj.*
Asleep, خوابیده *khábídah.*
Asparagus, مارچوبه *már chúbuh.*
Aspect, صورت *súrat*; سیما *símá.*
Asperity, خشونت *khushúnat.*
Aspiring, بلندبین *buland-bín.*
Ass, خر *khar*; اولاغ *úlágh.* Wild —, گور *gúr.* —load, خروار *kharvár.*
Assafœtida, انقوزه *ankúzah*; حلتیت *hiltít.*
Assassin, قاتل *kátil.*
Assassinate, کشتن *kushtan.*
Assassination, قتل *katl* (*k.*).
Assault (military), حمله بردن *hámleh burdan.* A night —, شبگیر *shabgír.* — and battery, لکد و کوب *lakd o kúb*; (robbery), راهزنی *ráhzaní.*
Assay, عیار کردن *'iyár k.*
Assayer, عیار گیر *'iyár gír.*
Assemble, فراهم آوردن *feráham a.*; *pr. p.* مجتمع *mujtama'* (*k.*).
Assembly, مجلس *majlis.*
Assent, اجابت کردن *ijábat k.*

Assertion, اقرار *ikrár* (*k.*).
Assessment, خراج *khiráj* (*k.*).
Assets, جایداد *jáidád.*
Assiduous, ساعی *sá'í*; مقید *mukayyid.*
Assignee, وکیل *vakíl.*
Assignment, تنخواه *tankháh* (*k.*); برات *barát.*
Assistance, مساعدت *musá'adat* (*n.*); کومك *kúmak* (*k.d.*); نصر *nasr.*
Assistant, نایب *náib*; ناصر *násir.*
Associate, شریك *sharík*; رفیق *rafík.* To—with, همراهی کردن *hamráhí k.*
Association, اختلاط *ikhtilát* (*k.*); تشارك *tasháruk* (*n.*).
Assuage, آرام دادن *árám d.*
Assume, تصور کردن *tasavvur k.*
Assure, یقین کردن *yakín k.*; خاطر جمع کردن *khátir jam' k.*
Assuredly, یقینست *yakínast.*
Asthma, ضیق الصدر *zaikus-sadr*; دما *damá.*
Astonish, حیران کردن *hairán k.*; *pa. p.* مات *mát*; متحیر *mutahayyir* (*m.*); *pr. p.* عجیب *'ajíb* (*h.*)

Astonishment, حیرت *hairat*; تحیر *tahayyur*.

Astounded, ماتش میبرد *mát-ash mibarad.*

Astringent, زمخك *zumukhk.*

Astrolabe, اسطرلاب *asturláb.*

Astrologer, astronomer, منجم *munajjim.*

Astronomical, نجومی *nujúmi*; فلکی *falakí.*

Astronomy, علم هیئت *'ilmi hai-at.*

Asunder, جدا *jedá.*

Asylum, بست *bast* (*gr.*); ملجا *maljá.*

At, نزد *nazd*; در *dar*; بـ *bi*; پیش *písh.*

Atheism, الحاد *ilhád.*

Atheist, زندیق *zindík*; ملحد *mulhid.*

Athlete, پهلوان *pahlaván.*

Atmosphere, هوا *havá.*

Atom, ذره *zarrah*; شمه *sham-mah.*

Atonement, کفاره *kaffárah* (*k.*).

Atrocity, ظلم *zulm.*

Attach, آویختن *ávikhtan.*

Attachment, دل بستکی *dil bas-tagí.*

Attack (illness), نزول *nuzúl*; (army, etc.), هجوم *hejúm* (*a.*); حمله *hamleh* (*k.*); تاختن *tákh-tan.*

Attainable, ممکن *mumkin.*

Attempt, سعی *sa'i* (*k.*); (evil), قصد *kasd* (*k.*).

Attend on, حاضر بودن *házir b.*

Attendance, خدمت *khidmat* (*k.*); حاضری *háziri.*

Attention, التفات *iltifát* (*k.*); توجه *tavajjuh.*

Attentive, متوجه *mutavajjeh* (*b.*); آکاه *ágáh* (*b.*).

Attesting, تصدیق *tasdík* (*n.*).

Attire, پوشیدن *púshídan.*

Attorney, وکیل *vakíl.*

Attraction, جذب *jazb* (*n.*); کشش *keshish.*

Attractive, جالب *jálib*; جاذب *jázib.*

Attribute, *n.*, صفت *sifat*; *v.* نسبت کردن *nisbat k.*

Auction, هراج *harráj.*

Auctioneer, هراجی *harrájí.*

Audience (people), حاضرین *házirín*; (interview), حضور *huzúr.*

Audit, محاسبه کردن *muhásabeh k.*

Auger, مته *matah.*

Augmentation, فزونی *fuzúni* (*k.*); زیاد *ziyád* (*k.*); تکثیر *taksír* (*n.*).

Augur, فالگیر *fál-gír.*

Augury, فال *fál* (*gr.*).

August, *a.*, اعظم *a'zam.*

Aunt (paternal), عمه *'ammah*; (maternal), خاله *khálah.*

Auspicious, مبارك *mubárak.*

Austere, عبوس *'abús*; ترشرو *tursh-rú.*

Authentic, صحیح *sahíh.* —ation, تصدیق *tasdíḳ* (*k*).

Author, مؤلف *muallif*; مصنف *musannif.*

Authority, اختیار *ikhtiyár*; حکومت *hukúmat.*

Autocracy, استقلال *istiḳlál.*

Autocrat, مستقل *mustakell.*

Autograph, دستخط *dast khatt.*

Autumn, خزان *khizán*; فایز *fáiz.*

Auxiliary, معاون *mu'ávin*; کمك *kumek.*

Avarice, طمعکاری *tama'kári.*

Avaricious, خسیس *khasís.*

Avenge, انتقام کشیدن *intiḳám ksh.*; *pr. p.* منتقم *muntaḳim.*

Avenue, خیابان

Averse, معرض *mu'riz.*

Aversion, کراهت *kerâhat*; نفرت *nafrat.*

Avert, دفع کردن *daf' k.*

Avidity, حرص *hirs*; طمع *tama'.*

Avoiding, تجنب *tajannub* (*k.*); مجانبت *mujánabat* (*k.*).

Avow, اقرار کردن *iḳrár k.* —edly, عمداً *'amdan.*

Awaiting, منتظر *muntazer* (*h.*).

Awake, بیدار (*k. sh.*).

Aware, آگاه *ágáh.*

Awful, مهیب *muhíb*; مهاب *muháb.*

Awkward, کودن *kaudan.*

Awl, درفش *darafsh.*

Awning, سایبان *sáyebán.*

Axe, طبر *tabar*; تیشه *tíshah.*

Axiom, بدیهی *bedíhí.*

Axis, محور *mihvar.*

Azure, آسمانی *ásmání*; آبی *ábí.*

B

Babbler, فضول *fuzúl.*

Baby, بچه *bacheh.* —hood, بچگی *bachegi.*

Baboon, میمون *maimún.*

Babylon, بابل *Bábil.*

Bachelor, عذب *'azab*; نا کتخدا *ná katkhudá.*

Back, *n.*, پشت *pusht*; (again), باز *baz*; پس *pas*. To bring back, باز آوردن *baz a.* To buy back, باز خریدن *báz kharídan.* To come back, باز آمدن *báz ámadan.* To draw back, باز کشیدن *báz ksh.* To give back, باز دادن *báz d.* To hold back, باز داشتن *báz dsh.* To take back, پس گرفتن *pas gr.* To turn back, باز گردیدن *báz gardídan.*

Backbiting, چغلی *chughulí* (*k.*).

Backbone, زوره *zaurah.*

Backgammon, نرد *nard.*

Backing out of (a promise), متخلف *mutakhallif.*

Backwardness, تقاعد *taḳá'ud.*

Backwards, پس *pas*; رو بعقب *ru be'aḳab.*

Backwater, مرداب *murd-áb.*

Bacon, گشت گراز *gusht-i-guráz.*

Bad, بد *bad*; زبون *zabún.* Bad-living, بدزندگانی *bad zindagáni.* Bad-looking, بد نما *bad namá.* Of bad quality, بد گوهر *bad gauhar.* Badness, بدی *badí.*

Badge, نشان *nishán.*

Baffled, محروم *mahrúm* (*g.*).

Bag, کیسه *kísah*; خریطه *kharítah*; (large), جوال *jowál.* Horse's nose —, توبره *túbrah.* Saddle —, خورجین *khúrjín,* Carpet —, چنته *chantah.*

Baggage, اسباب *asbáb*; بنه *bonah.*

Bail, *n.*, ضمانت *zamánat*; *v.* ضامن شدن *zámin sh.*

Bait, دانه *dánah* (*nihádan*).

Bake, پختن *pukhtan.*

Baker, نان پز *nán-paz.*

Balance, *n.*, میزان *mízán*; (small), ترازو *tarázú*; (of account), باقی *báḳí.*

Balcony, بالا خانه *bálá khánah.*

Bald, کل *kal.*

Bale, *n.*, بسته *bastah.*

Ball, گوی *gúi*; (for gun), غلوله *ghalúlah.*

Bamboo, نی هندی *nai-hindi.*

Band (rope), بند *band*; (men), گروه *garúh.*

Band-box, صندوقچه *sandúkcheh.*

Bandit, راه زن *ráh zan.*

Bandy-legged, کج پا *kaj pá.*

Bang, تراق *tarák* (*kh.*).

Banish, بیرون کردن *bírún k.*

Banister, دست انداز *dast andáz.*

Bank (river), كنار *kinár*; (money), خزانه *khezánah*.

Banker, صراف *sarráf.*

Bankrupt, مفلس *muflis* (*sh.*). —cy, افلاس *iflás.*

Banner, علم *'alam*; بيداق *baidák.*

Banquet, مهمانی *mihmání*; ضيافت *ziyáfat.*

Baptism, تعميد *ta'míd* (*k.*).

Bar (river), بند *band.*

Barb, خار *khár.*

Barbarian, اعجم *á'jam.*

Barber, دلاك *dallák.*

Barberries, زرشك *zirishk.*

Bare, برهنه *barahnah* (*k.*).

Bare-headed (unveiled), سر برهنه *sar barahnah.*

Bargain, شرط *shart* (*k.*).

Barge, زورق *zaurak.*

Bark (tree), پشت *pusht*; (dog), عوعو *'au'au* (*k.*); *v.* عفيدن *'afídan.*

Barked (tree), مقشر *mukashshar.*

Barley, جو *jau.*

Barn, خرمن *khirman.*

Barracks, سرباز خانه *sarbáz kháneh.*

Barrel, برميل *barmíl.* Gun —, لوله *lúlah.*

Barren, عقيم *'akím*; عقير *'akír.*

Barrier, سد راه *saddi ráh.*

Barter, معاوضت كردن *mu'ávizat k.*; تجارت كردن *tejárat k.*

Base, *a.*, شنيع *shaní'*; قبيح *kabí'.*

Based, متمسك *mutamassak* (*b.*).

Baseness, قباحت *kabáhat.*

Bashful, خجل *khijil.* —ness, خجالت *khijálat.*

Basil, ريحان *raihán.*

Basin, لكن *lagan.*

Basis, پايه *páyeh*; بنياد *bunyád.*

Basket, سبد *sabad*; زنبيل *zanbíl.*

Bass (in music), بم *bam.*

Bastard, حرامزاده *harámzádeh.*

Bastinado, *n.*, فلكه *falakeh.* To receive the —, چوب خوردن *chúb kh.* To give the —, چوب زدن *chúb z.*

Bastion, برج *burj.*

Bat, شبپره *shabparah*; (club), چوكان *chaugan* (*z.*).

Bath, حمام *hammám* (*r.*). —keeper, حمامچی *hammámchí.*

Battering, قمع *kam'* (*k.*).

Battery, دمدمه *damdameh.*

Battle, جنك *jang*; وقيعت *vaḳí'at*. Field of —, رزمگاه *razmgáh*.

Battlement, كنگره, *kangurah*.

Bawl, فرياد زدن *faryád z.*

Bay (sea), خليج *khalíj*; (colour), كهر *kahar*; (tree), غار *ghár*.

Bayonet, سر نيزه *sar nízeh*.

Bazaar, بازار *bázár*.

Be, بودن *búdan*; هستن *hastan*.

Beach (sea), كناره *kinárah*.

Bead, شبه *shabeh*; مهره *muhreh*.

Beak, منقار *minḳár*.

Beam (wood), شاه تير *sháh tír*. Sun —, پرتو *partav*.

Bean, باقله *báḳileh*.

Bear, *n.*, خرس *khirs*; (star), Great —, دب اكبر *dabbi akbar*. Little —, دب اصغر *dabbi asghar*. *v.* بردن *burdan*; (fruit), بر آوردن *bar a.*; (children), زادن *zádan*.

Beard, ريش *rísh*; *pa. p.* ريشدار *ríshdár*. —less, ساده رو *sádeh rú*.

Bearer, حمال *hammál*; بر بردار *bar burdár*. Cup —, ساقى *sáḳí*; Tale —, چغل خور *chughul khúr*.

Beast, بهيمه *bahímah*; وحش *vahsh*. — of burden, مال *mál*.

Beat, زدن *zadan*; كوبيدن *kúbídan*.

Beating, زد و كوب *zad o kúb*.

Beau, *n.*, قشنك *ḳashang*.

Beautiful, خوبرو *khúbrú*; خوب صورت *khúb súrat*; خوشكل *khúshgil*; قشنك *ḳashang*.

Beauty, حسن *husn*.

Because, زيراكه *zírákeh*. — that, بنا بر اينكه *bená bar ínkeh*.

Beckon, اشاره كردن *isharah kerdan*.

Become, شدن *shudan*; گشتن *gashtan*; گرديدن *gardídan*. To cause to —, گردانيدن *gardánídan*; (to suit), زيبيدن *zíbídan*.

Bed, خوابگاه *khábgáh*; (of river), رود خانه *rúd kháneh*.

Bedchamber, اطاق خوابگاه *otáḳi khábgáh*.

Bedding, رخت خواب *rakht i kháb*.

Bedfellow, همخواب *hamkháb*.

Bedstead, چارپا *chárpá*.

Bee, زنبور عسل *zambúri 'asal*.

Beef, گشت گاو *gushti gáu.*
Beer, اب جو *ábi-jau.*
Beetle, هماجی *hamáji*; سوسك *súsak.*
Beet-root, چقندر *chuḳandar.*
Befitting, شایسته *sháyesteh*; لایق *láyiḳ.*
Before, پیش از *písh az*; قبل از *ḳabl az*; (in front), جلو *jelo.* To come before, پیش آمدن *písh ámadan.*
Befriend, دوستی کردن *dústi k.*
Beg, التماس کردن *iltimás k.*; (alms), گدای کردن *gedái k.*
Beggar, گدا *gedá*; فقیر *faḳír*; درویش *darvísh.*
Beginner, مبتدی *mubtadí.*
Beginning, ابتدا *ibtidá* (*k.*); شروع *shurú'* (*k.*); آغاز *ágház* (*k.*).
Beginnings, اوایل *avá-il.*
Behalf, in, بواسطه *be-váseteh.*
Behave (well), ادب بجا اوردن *adab bejá a.*; (badly) ترك ادب کردن *tarki adab k.*
Behead, گردن زدن *gardan z.*
Behind, عقب *'aḳab*; پشت *pusht.*
Behold, نگاه کردن *nigáh k.*
Beholden, ممنون *mamnún* (*h.*).

Being (created), مخلوق *makhlúḳ*; (existence), وجود *vujúd.*
Belch, آروغ *árúgh* (*k.*).
Belief, باور *bávar* (*k.*); اعتقاد *i'tiḳád* (*dsh.*).
Believer (true), مومن *múmin.*
Bell, زنك *zang* (*z.*).
Bellowing, بانك *báng* (*z.*).
Bellows, منفخ *manfakh.*
Belly, شکم *shikam*; بطن *batn.*
Belonging to, متعلق *muta'allaḳ* (*sh.*); نسبت *nisbat.*
Beloved, *n.*, معشوقه *ma'shúḳeh.*
Below, پاین *páyín*; فرو *farú.*
Belt, کمر بند *kamar band.*
Bemoan, افسوس خوردن *afsús kh.*
Bend, *v.* پیچیدن *píchídan.* — down, خم شدن *kham shudan.*
Beneath, زیر *zír.*
Benediction, تبرك *tabarruk.*
Benefactor, نیکو کار *níkú kár.*
Beneficence, احسان *ihsán.*
Beneficent, کریم *karím.*
Benefit, منفعت *manfa'at* (*h.*); *pa. p.* مستفاد *mustafád*; *pr. p.* محسن *muhsin.*
Benevolence, رفق *rifḳ.*
Benign, رءوف *raúf.*

Benignity, رءوفت *raúfat.*

Bent, خم *kham,* کج *kaj.*

Benumbed, افسرده *afsurdeh* (*k.*).

Benzoin, سليخه *salíkheh.*

Bequeath, وصيت کردن *vasiyyat k.*

Bequest, وصايت *visáyat*; (for religious purposes), وقف *vakf* (*k.*).

Berry, دانه *dánah*; حبه *habbeh.*

Beseech, التماس کردن *iltimás k.*

Beside, پهلو *pahlú.*

Besides, مگر *magar*; سوا *sivá*; جز *juz.*

Besiege, محاصره کردن *maháserah k.*; *pa. p.* محصور *mahsúr.*

Best, بهترين *behtarín.*

Bestow, بخشيدن *bakhshídan*; *pa. p.* مبذول *mabzúl*; *pr. p.* اعطا *i'tá* (*n.*).

Bet, شرط *shart* (*bs.*).

Betel-leaf, تمبول *tambúl.*

Betray, خيانت کردن *khiyánat k.*

Betrayer, خاين *kháín.*

Betroth, عقد بستن *'akd bs.*

Betrothal, خطب *khatb* (*k.*).

Betrothed, *n.*, نامزد *námzad* (*k.*).

Better, بهتر *behtar* (*k.*). (—than, *b.* از *az*).

Between, ميان (در *dar*) *miyán.*

Beverage, شراب *sharáb.*

Beware! خبردار *khabar dár!* (*b.*).

Bewitched, مفتن *mufattan* (*sh. k.*).

Beyond, آن طرف *án-taraf*; (more), زياده *ziyádah.*

Bible, کتاب مقدس *kitábi mukaddas.* O. T., تورات *torát.* N. T., انجيل *anjíl.*

Bidding (at a sale), سوام *sowám* (*k.*).

Bier, تابوت *tábút*; نعش *na'sh.*

Big, بزرك *buzurg*; (pregnant), حامله *hámileh.*

Bigot, متعصب *muta'assib* (*h.*).

Bigotry, تعصب *ta'assub* (*dsh.*).

Bile, صفره *safrah.*

Bilious, صفراوی *safráví.*

Bill (of exchange), برات *barát*; (bird's), نوك *núk.*

Bind, *v.*, بستن *bastan.*

Binder, جلدگر *jildgar.*

Binding (book), جلد *jild* (*k.*).

Binocular glass, دوربين *dúr bín.*

Bird, مرغ *murgh*; طاير *táir.*

Bird-lime, دبق *dibk.*

Birth, تولد *tavallud.*

Birthday, عيد مولود *'idi maulúd.*

Biscuit, کاك *kák*; بقسومات *baksúmát.*

Bit (piece), تیکه *tíkeh ;* پاره *páreh ;* (of a bridle), دهانه *daháneh ;* لگام *lagám.*

Bite, گزیدن *gazídan.*

Bitter, تلخ *talkh.* —ness, تلخی *talkhí.*

Bitumen, نفط *naft.*

Black, سیاه *siyáh.*

Blackberry, شهتوت *shahtút.*

Blackguard, جو ولاغی *jovalághi;* حرامزاده *harámzádeh ;* لوطی *lúti.*

Blacksmith, آهنگر *áhangar.*

Blacking, سیاهی *síyáhí.*

Bladder, شاشدان *sháshdán ;* مثانه *masáneh.*

Blade, تیغه *tíghah.* Shoulder—, شانه *sháneh.*

Blame, *n.,* لوم *laum ;* ذم *zamm* (*k.*) ; *v.* عیب گفتن *'aib gf.*

Blameable, مقصر *mukassar* (*h.*).

Blameless, بیگناه *bígunáh.*

Bland, ملایم *muláyim.*

Blandishment, ناز *náz* (*k.*).

Blanket, پتو *patú.*

Blasphemy, کفر *kufr* (*gf.*).

Blasts, هبوب *hubúb.*

Blaze, نایره *náireh ;* شعله *sho'leh ;* (on a horse), غره *ghurreh.*

Bleach, گازری کردن *gázurí k.*

Bleed, *v. t*, خون گرفتن *khún gr.;* فصد کردن *fasd k.; v. i.* خون آمدن *khún ámadan.*

Blemish, عیب *'aib ;* لکه *lakkeh.*

Blessing, برکت *barakat* (*d.*) ; درود *durúd* (*gf.*). God bless you ! بارك الله *bárak Allah !*

Blight, زنگ *zang* (*z.*).

Blind, *a*, نابینا *nábíná ;* کور *kúr* (*k.*) ; *n.,* پرده *pardah.*

Blindfold, *v.,* چشم پوشیدن *cheshm púshídan.*

Blindness, کوری *kúrí.*

Blister, آبله *ábilah.*

Blockade, محاصره *muhásareh* (*k.*).

Blockhead, کودن *kodan.*

Blood, خون *khun.*

Bloodshed, خونخواری *khúnkhárí ;* قتل *katl.*

Bloody, خونین *khúnín.*

Blooming, شکفته *shiguftah.*

Blossom, *n.,* شکوفه *shigúfeh ;* غنچه *ghuncheh* (*z.*) ; *v.,* شکفتن *shiguftan.*

Blot, لکه *lakkeh.*

Blow, *n.,* ضرب *zarb* (*kh.*) ; *v.,* وزیدن *vazídan ;* (the nose) دماغ گرفتن *dimágh gr.*

Blue, نیله *nílah;* کبود *kabúd;* آبی *ábí.*

Blunder, غلط *ghallat* (*k.*); خطا *khatá.*

Blunt, کند *kund.*

Blushing, خجالت *khijálat* (*ksh*).

Boar, خوك *khúk;* گراز *guráz.*

Board, تخته *takhtah.*

Boaster, خود ثنا *khud saná.*

Boasting, خود فروش *khud farúsh* (*k.*); گذاف *guzáf* (*k.*); شیخی *sheikhí.*

Boat, کشتی *keshtí;* لوتکه *lútkeh.* —man, کشتیبان *keshtíbán.*

Bodice, سینه بند *sínah band.*

Bodkin, درفش *darafsh.*

Body, تن *tan;* بدن *badan.* Dead —, لاش *lásh.*

Bog, مشیله *mashílah;* مرد آب *murd-áb.*

Boil, *n.*, دنبل *dumbal; v. t.*, جوش کردن *júsh k.; v.i.* جوشیدن *júshídan.*

Bold, دلیر *dalír.*

Boldness, جرئت *jur-at.*

Bolt, پسکله *paskullah;* چفت *chift* (*k.*).

Bond, تمسك *tamassuk.*

Bondage, اسیری *asírí.*

Bone, استخان *ustukhán.*

Bonnet, کلاه *kulláh.*

Book, کتاب *kitáb.* —binder, جلد گر *jild-gar.* —seller, کتاب فروش *kitáb farúsh.*

Boon-companion, همشراب *hamsharáb.*

Boot, کفش *kafsh.* Top —, چکمه *chekmah.*

Booty, غارت *ghárat.*

Borax, بورق *búrak.*

Border, کناره *kináreh;* حاشیه *háshiyeh.*

Bore, سفتن *suftan.*

Born, to be, زادن *zádan; pa. p.* متولد *mutavallad* (*sh.*).

Borrow, قرض گرفتن *karz gr.; pr. p.* (a thing), استعاره *isti'árah* (*k.*); (money), استقراض *istikráz* (*k.*).

Bosom, سینه *sinah;* آغوش *ághúsh.*

Botany, علف چینی *'alaf chíní.*

Both, هر دو *har do.*

Bottle, شیشه *shishah;* (european) بطری *butrí.* Water—, تنك *tung.*

Bottom, ته *tah;* پاین *páin;* (sea, etc.) قعر *ka'ar.*

Bough, شاخ *shákh.*

Bound, *v.*, برجستن *bar jastan*; *n.* (perforce) لابد *lá-budd*; (book), مجلد *mujallad.*

Boundary, حد *hadd* (pl. حدود *hudúd*); سرحد *sar hadd.*

Boundless, نامحدود *ná mahdúd.*

Bountiful, بخشاینده *bakhsháyandeh*; کریم *karím.*

Bounty, فیض *faiz.*

Bouquet, گلدسته *guldastah.*

Bow, *n.*, کمان *kamán.* —shot, پرتاب *partáb.* —string, چله *chilleh.* *v.*, تعظیم کردن *ta'zím k.*; سر فرو کردن *sar farú k.*

Bowels, روده *rúdah.*

Bowl, جام *jám*; بادیه *bádiyeh.*

Box (fight), *v.*, مشت زدن *musht z.*; (chest, large), صندوق *sandúḳ*; (small), قوتی *ḳútí*; جعبه *ja'beh.* Cartridge—, توشدان *túshdán.* Snuff—, انفیه دان *anfiyeh dán.* —on the ears, سیله *sílah* (*d.*). —tree, شمشاد *shemshád.*

Boxer, مشت زن *musht zan.*

Boy, پسر *pisar*; کودك *kúdak.*

Bracelet, دست برنجن *dast baranjan.*

Braces, شلوار بند *shalvár band.*

Brackish, شور *shúr.*

Brag, لاف زدن *láf z.*

Brain, مغز *maghz*; دماغ *dimágh.*

Brambles, خزیز *khazíz*; خار *khár.*

Bran, سبوس *sabús.*

Branch, *n.*, شاخ *shákh.*

Branched out, متفرع *mutafarrah*; —ing off, منشعب *munsha'ab.*

Brand, داغ *dágh* (*k.*).

Brandy, عرق *'araḳ.*

Brasier, مسگر *misgar.*

Brass, برنج *birinj.*

Brave, دلاور *diláver*; دلیر *dalír.*

Bravery, مردانگی *mardánagí.*

Bravo! شاباش *shábásh*; ما شاء الله *máshállah*; به به *bah! bah!*

Braying, ناهق *náhiḳ* (*k.*); عرعر *'ar'ar* (*k.*).

Breach, مغاره *maghára* (*s.*).

Bread, نان *nán* (pronounced *nún*). Leavened —, نان خمیری *náni khamírí.*

Breadth, پهن *pahn*; عرض *'arz.*

Break, *v.*, شکستن *shikastan.*

Breakfast, نهار *nahár.*

Breast, سینه *sínah*; (woman's), پستان *pistán.*

Breath, دم *dam* (*z.*); نفس *nafas* (*ksh. z.*).

Breeches, شلوار *shalvár.*

Breed, اصل *asl.*
Breeze, نسیم *nasím.*
Bribe, رشوت *rishvat* (*kh.*).
Bribery, رشوه خواری *rushveh khárí.*
Brick (unburnt), خشت *khisht.* (burnt), آجر *ájur.* —kiln, کوره *kúreh.* —maker, خشت پز *khisht paz.* —layer, بنا *banná.*
Bride, عروس *'arús.*
Bridegroom, داماد *dámád.*
Bridge, پل *pul;* (of the nose), خیشوم *khaishúm.*
Bridle, دهنا *dahná* (*k.*); لجام *lijám;* (watering), افسار *afsár;* (rein), جلو *jelo.*
Brief, کوتاه *kútáh.* —ly, القصه *alkissah.*
Brigand, راهزن *ráhzan.*
Bright, تابناك *tábnák;* روشن *roshan* (*k. s.*).
Brightness, نورانی *núrání.*
Brilliancy, انارت *inárat.*
Brilliant, مجلی *mujallá.*
Brim, لب *lab.* —full, لبالب *labálab.*
Brimstone, کبریت *kebrít.*
Bring, آوردن *ávardan.* — in, در رسانیدن *dar rasánídan.* — up, پروریدن *parvarídan.* — forth, زایدن *záidan.*

Brink, کنار *kinár.*
Brisk, نشیط *nashít;* جلد *jald.*
Bristle, مو *mú.*
Brittle, تنك *tunuk;* نازك *názuk.*
Broad, عریض *'aríz;* پهنا *pahná.*
Broadcloth, ماهوت *máhút.*
Brocade, کمخاب *kamkháb;* زری *zarí.*
Broiled, بریان *biriyán* (*k.*).
Broker, دلال *dallál.* —age, دلالی *dallálí.*
Bronze, چدن *chudan.*
Brook, جوی *júi.*
Broom, جارو *járú* (*k.*).
Broth, شوربا *shurbá.*
Brother, برادر *barádar.* Adopted —, برادرخوانده *b. khándeh.* Foster —, برادر رضاعی *b-i-rezá'í.* — -in-law, برادر زن *b. zan,* etc.
Brotherhood, اخوت *ukhúvat;* برادری *barádarí.*
Brown, اسمر *asmar;* سرخ *surkh.*
Brow, حواجب *havájib.*
Browse, چریدن *charídan.*
Bruise, آشردن *áshurdan;* کوفتن *kúftan.*

Brush, *n.*, بروش *brúsh*; *v.* پاك كردن *pák k.*
Brushwood, هيمه *hímeh.*
Brutish, بهيمی *bahímí.*
Bubble, حباب *hubáb.*
Bucket, دلو *dalv*; دولچه *dúlcheh.*
Buckle, سكك *sagak.*
Bud, غنچه *ghuncheh*; شكوفه *shekúfeh.*
Buffalo, گاو ميش *gáu mísh.*
Buff-coloured, بادامی *bádámí.*
Buffeting, متلاطم *mutalátim* (*k.*).
Buffoon, مسخره *maskharah*; لوطی *lútí.* —ery, تمسخر *tamaskhur.*
Bug, ساس *sás*; شبگز *shabgez.*
Bugle, شيفور *shaifúr.*
Bugloss, شنگار *shingar*; گاو زبان *gáu zabán.*
Build, بنا كردن *baná k.*
Builder, بانی *bání*; بنا *banná.*
Building, عمارت *'imárat* (*k.*); بنائی *banái.*
Bulb, پياز *piyáz.*
Bulky, سترك *suturg*; پيلتن *píltan.*
Bull, نر گاو *nar gáu.*
Bullet, گلوله *galúleh.*
Bulwark, سنگر *sangur.*

Bunch, خوشه *khúsheh*; دسته *dasteh.*
Bundle, بسته *basteh*; بغچه *bughcheh.*
Burden, بار *bár*; حمل *haml.*
Burn, *v. i.*, سوختن *súkhtan*; *v. t.* سوزيدن *súzídan.*
Burnished, مجلی *mujallá.*
Burst, تركيدن *tarkídan*; *pr. p.* فتق *fatḳ* (*k.*).
Bury, خاك كردن *khák k.*
Burying, تدفين *tadfín* (*s.*); دفن *dafn* (*k.*). — place, گورستان *gúristán.*
Bush, بوته *bútah.*
Busied, مشغول *mashghúl* (*sh.b.*).
Business, كار (و بار) *kár* (*o bár*); مشغله *mashghaleh.* Important —, مهم *muhimm.*
Busybody, فضول *fuzúl.*
Bustard, هوبره *húbareh.*
But, اما *amma*; بلكه *balkeh*; وليكن *valíken*; مگر *magar.*
Butcher, قصاب *ḳassáb.*
Butler, ناظر *názer.*
Butt, *n.*, هدف *hadaf*; *v.*, شاخ زدن *shákh z.*
Butter, كره *karah*; (clarified), روغن *roghan.* — milk, دوغ *dúgh.*

Butterfly, پروانه *parváneh.*

Buttocks, سرين *surín*; كفل *kafl.*

Button, دوكمه or دكمه *dúkmeh.*

— hole, مادگى *mádagí.*

Buy, خريدن *kharídan.*

Buyer, خريدار *kharídár.*

Buying, ابتياع *ibtiya'* (*k.*); اشتراء *ishtirá* (*n.*).

Buying or selling on credit, نسئت *nasiat.*

Buzzing, طنين *tanín* (*k.*).

By, ب *be*; با *bá*; از *az.*

By all means, البته *albattah.*

By chance, اتفاق افتاد *ittifák uftád*; اتفاقاً *ittifákan.*

C

Cabbage, كلم *kalam*; كرنب *kurnub.*

Cabinet, نهانخانه *nihán-khánah.*

Cable, رسن لنكر *rasani langar.*

Cæsar, قيصر *kaisar.*

Cage, قفس *kafas.*

Cajolery, چاپلوسى *cháplúsí* (*k.*).

Cake, نان شرين *náni shirín.*

Calamity, بلا *belá*; مصيبت *musíbat.*

Calculate, حساب كردن *hisáb k.*

Calculation, شمار *shumár.*

Caldron, ديك *díg*; مرجل *mirjal.*

Calendar, تقويم *takvím.*

Calf, گوساله *gausáleh.*

Calico, پيراهن شاهى *píráhani sháhi*; قلمكار *kalamkár.*

Caliph, خليفه *khalífeh*; (*pl.* خلفاء *khulafá*).

Call (awaken), بيدار كردن *bídár k.* — out, صدا كردن *sedá k.*; داد و فرياد كردن *dád o feryád k.*

Calligraphist, خوشنويس *khush-navís.*

Calligraphy, خوشخط *khush-khatt.*

Called, to be, اسم داشتن *ism dsh.*

Calm, ملايم *maláyim*; آرام *árám* (*gr.*). —ness, آسودگى *ásúdagí.*

Calomel, جيوه *jíveh.*

Calumniator, بد زبان *bad zabán.*

Calumny, بهتان *buhtán* (*bs.*); تهمت *tuhmat* (*bs.*)

Camel, شتر *shutur.* Two humped, riding —, بختى *bukhtí.* — driver, شتربان

shuturbán. —litter, تختروان *takhtiraván;* کجاوه *kajáveh.* Female —, ناقه *náḳeh.*
Cameleopard, زراف *zaráf.*
Camomile, بابونه *bábúneh.*
Camp, *n.*, لشکرگاه *lashkar gáh;* خیمه گاه *khaimeh gáh;* *v.* چادر زدن *cháder z.*
Camphor, کافور *káfúr.*
Canal, نشج *nashaj;* کاریز *káríz.*
Cancelled, منسوخ *mansúkh* (*k.*).
Cancer, سرطان *saretán;* هزار چشمه *hezár cheshmeh.*
Candid, صادق *sádiḳ.*
Candidate, امیدوار *ummídvár.*
Candle, شمع *sham'.* —stick, شمعدان *sham'dán.*
Candour, اخلاص *ikhlás.*
Cane, خیزران *khaizurán.* Sugar —, نیشکر *ney-shekar.*
Cannibal, آدمخور *ádamkhúr.*
Cannon, توپ *túp.* Small cannon carried on camel-back, زنبورك *zambúrak.* —ball, گوله *gúleh.* —ade, *v.*, توپ زدن *túp z.* —eer, توپچی *túpchí.*
Canon, قایده *ḳáideh;* قانون *ḳánún.*
Canopus, سهیل *suheil.*
Canopy, سایه بان *sáyeh bán.*
Canter, یورطمه *yúrtmeh* (*r.*).
Canvas پلاس *palás.*
Cap, (*n.*), کلاه *kuláh;* *v.*, (verses), مشاعره کردن *mushá'ereh k.*
Capability, اهلیت *ahliyat.*
Capable, قابل *kábil;* کافی *káfi.*
Capacity (skill), قابلیت *kábiliyat;* (holding), گنجایش *gunjáyish.*
Cape, راس *rás.*
Capital (stock), راس المال *rásulmál,* or راسمال *rásmál;* (town), پایتخت *páitakht;* دار الملك *dár ul mulk.*
Capitulate, تسلیم دادن *taslím d.*
Capricorn, جدی *jidí.*
Caprice, خود سری *khud sarí.*
Captain, سلطان *sultán.*
Captive, اسیر *asír* (*gr.*).
Captivity, گرفتاری *giriftári;* حبس *habs.*
Carat, قیراط *kírát.*
Caravan, کاروان *káraván;* قافله *ḳáfileh.* — serai, کاروانسری *káravánserai;* رباط *ribát.*
Carcase, لاش *lásh;* جیفه *jífah.*
Card, *v.*, پنبه زدن *pambah z.*
Cardamums, قاقله *ḳáḳullah.*

Carder, پنبه دوز *pambah dúz.*

Cards, گنجیفه *ganjífeh.*

Care (fear), پروا *parvá* (*dsh.*); (attention), اهتمام *ihtimám*; رعایت *ri'áyat*; (effort), اجتهاد *ijtihád*; (caution), زینهار *zínhár*; (circumspection), احتیاط *ihtiyát* (*k.*). Take care! دور باش *dúr básh*; خبر دار *khabar dár.*

Careful خبر دار *khabar dár* (*sh.*); متوجه *mutavajjeh* (*b.*).

Careless, ذاهل *záhil*; غافل *gháfil*; بیخبر *bikhabar.*

Caress, نوازش *navázish* (*k.*).

Carnage, قتل *katl.*

Carnal, جسمانی *jismání.*

Carnelion, عقیق *'akík.*

Carp, ازاد ماهی *azád máhí.*

Carpenter, نجار *najjár.*

Carpet (of pile), قالی *kálí*; قالیچه *kálícheh*; (woven), گلیم *gilím*; (felt), نمد *namad*; (at top and bottom of room), یا انداز and سر *sar* and *pá andáz.* Prayer —, سجاده *sajjádeh.* — spreader, فراش *farrásh.* To spread a —, فرش انداختن *farsh andákhtan* (or *kerdan*).

Carraway-seed کرویا *karviyá.*

Carriage, کالسکه *káliskah.*

Carrier, حمال *hammál*; بردار *burdár.*

Carrion, مردار *murdár.*

Carrion-bird, لاشخور *láshkhúr.*

Carrot, زردك *zardak*; گزر *gazar.*

Carry, بردن *burdan.* — away, بر داشتن *bar dsh.* — down, فرو بردن *farú burdan.*

Cart, عرابه *'arábeh.*

Cartilage (of the nose), پردهٔ بینی *pardahi bíní*; خیاشیم *khayáshím.*

Cartridge, فشنك *fishang.*

Carve, (food), بریدن *burídan.*

Carving, *n.*, (stone, etc.), نقش *naksh* (*k.*).

Cascade, آبشار *ábshár.*

Case (legal), دعوا *da'vá*; (box), صندوق *sandúk.* Pen —, قلمدان *kalamdán*; (affair), حال *hál*; امر *amr.* In any case, در هر صورت *dar har súrat*; بهر حال *behar hál.*

Cash, پول نقد *púli nakd.*

Cashmere, ترمه *tirmah.*

Casket, حقه *hukkeh.*

Cassia fistularis, خیار چنبر *khiyár chambar.*

Cast, *v.*, انداختن *andákhtan.* — in a mould, ریختن *ríkhtan.*

Castle, قلعه *kal'ah* ; ارك *arg.*

Castor oil, روغن کرچك *raughani gerchek.*

Castrated, خصی *khasí* (*k.*) ; اخته *akhteh* (*k.*).

Casual, اتفاقی *ittifáki.*

Casualty, سانحه *sániheh.*

Cat, گربه *gurbah.*

Catalogue, فهرست *fihrist.*

Cataract, آبشار *ábshár.* — in the eye, ظفرة *zafarat.*

Catch, گرفتن *giriftan.* — cold, سرما خوردن *sermá kh.*

Catchword, خارجه *khárijeh.*

Caterpillar, کرم دراخت *kirmi dirákht.*

Cattle, مواشی *mavåshí.*

Cauliflower, کلم گل *kalam gul.*

Cause, موجب *mojib*; جهت *jihat* ; سبب *sabab* (*sh.*) ; (author), صاحب *sáhib.* For this cause, از این جهت *az ín jihat.* Final cause, علت غائی *'illati ghái.* Material cause, علت مادیی *'illati máddíy.*

Causeless, بیواسطه *bívásiteh.*

Causeway, خیابان *khiyábán.*

Cautery, کی *kai* (*k.*) ; داغ *dágh* (*k.*).

Caution, احتیاط *ihtiyát.*

Cautious, خبردار *khabar dár* (*h*).

Cavalcade, موکب *maukab.*

Cavalier, سوار *sowwár.*

Cavalry, سواران *sowwárán.*

Cave, غار *ghár* ; کهف *kahf.*

Caviller, نکته چین *nukteh chín.*

Cavilling, عیب جوی *'aib júí* (*k.*).

Cavity, جوف *jauf.*

Cease, وا ایستادن *vá ístádan* ; موقوف بودن *maukúf b.*

Cedar, کاج *káj.*

Cede, تسلیم کردن *taslím k.*

Ceiling, سقف *sakf.*

Celebrated, مشهور *mashhúr* ; *pr. p.* (a mistress in verse), نسیب *nasíb* (*k.*).

Celery, کرفس *karafs.*

Celestial, چرخی *charkhí.*

Cell, تکیه *takiyeh.*

Cellar, زیر زمین *zíri zamín.*

Cement, *n.*, سریش *sarísh* (*k.*). *v.*, دوسیدن *dúsídan.*

Cemetery, قبرستان *kabristan.*

Censer, مجمر *mijmar* ; منقل *mankal.*

Centfoil, صدبرك *sadbarg.*

Centipede, هزار پا *hezár pá.*

Centre, مرکز *markaz* ; مدار *madár.*

Century, صد سال *sad sál.*

Ceremonial, رسمی *rasmí.* — pollution, جنابت *jenábat.*

Ceremony, تکلف *takalluf.* Master of the ceremonies, اشیك اقاسی *íshík aḳási.*

Certain, یقین *yaḳín* (h). —ly, البته *albattah.* —ty, تحقیق *tahḳíḳ.*

Certificate, دست آویز *dast áviz.*

Cesspool, مزبله *mazbalah.*

Chafing-dish, منقل *manḳal.*

Chain, زنجیر *zanjír* (*k. bs.*).

Chair, صندلی *sandali* ; کرسی *kursí.*

Chalk, طباشیر *tabáshír;* گل سفید *gili safíd.*

Chamber, اتاق *otaḳ.*

Chamberlain, حاجب *hájib.*

Chameleon, قلمون *ḳalamún.*

Champion, کاری *kárí.*

Chance, اتفاق *ittifáḳ.* By —, اتفاقاً *ittifáḳan.*

Chandelier, چهل چراغ *chehl chirágh.*

Change, تبدیل *tabdíl* (*k.*); عوض *'ivaz* (*k.*) ; (money), پول خرده *púli khurdah* ; *pa. p.*, متغیر *mutaghayyir* (*sh.*).

Channel, مجری *mujrá.*

Chant, ترانه *tiráneh.*

Chapter, باب *báb.* — of the Ḳorán, سوره *súrah.*

Character(good), نیکنام *níknám;* (bad), بد نام *bad nám* ; (reputation), آبرو *ábrú* ; (quality), کیفیت *keyfiyat.*

Characters, رقوم *ruḳúm.*

Charcoal, زغال *zughál.*

Charge (custody), امانت *amánat* ; (accusation), شکایت *shikáyat.*

Charity, خیرت *khairat* ; صدقت *sadaḳat.*

Charm (written), *n.*, دعا *du'á.*

Chaste, پاکیزه *pákízah.*

Chastisement, عقاب *'iḳáb.*

Chastity, عفت *'iffat* ; عصمت *'ismat.*

Chat, گفتگو کردن *guft gú k.*

Cheap, ارزان *arzán* (*k.*).

Cheapness, ارزانی *arzání.*

Cheat, *n.*, حیله کار *híleh kár* ; *v.*, حیله کردن *híleh k.* ; فریفتن *firíftan.*

Checkmate, شاه مات *sháh mát* (*k.*).

Cheek, رخ *rukh* ; رخساره *rukh-sárah.*

Cheerful, خرم *khurram.*

Cheerfulness, طرب *tarab* ; شادی *shádí.*

Cheerless, نا شاد *ná shád.*

Cheese, پنیر *panír.*

Cheeta, فهد *fahd.*

Chemist, کیمیا گر *kímíyá gar.*

Chemistry, کیمیا *kímíyá.*

Cheque, *n.*, برات *barát.*

Cherish, پـروردن *parvardan* ; *pr. p.*, نواز *naváz* (*k.*).

Cherry, گیلاس *gílás* ; الو بالو *álú bálú.*

Cherub, کروبی *karúbí.*

Chess, شطرنج *shatranj.* —man, مهر *mohr.* —board, بساط *bi-sát.* —square, خانه *kháneh.* The pieces are, king, شاه *sháh* ; queen, فرزین *farzín* ; bishop, فیل *fíl*; knight, اسپ *asp*, or سوار *sowwár* ; castle, رخ *rukh* ; and pawn, پیاده *piyádeh.*

Chest, صندوق *sandúḳ.*

Chestnut, شاه بلوط *sháh balút.*

Chew, خائیدن *kháídan* ; *pr. p.*, مضغ *mazgh* (*k.*). —the cud, خویدن *khavídan.*

Chicken, جوجه *júj eh.*

Chicken-pox, زبرك *zabrek.*

Chiding, معاتبت *mu'átabat* (*k.*).

Chief, خان *khán* ; سرور *sarvar.* —of village, کدخدا *kedkhudá.* — of tribe, رئیس *raís* ; مقدم *muḳaddam.* — of army, (سپه) سالار (*sipeh*) *sálár.* — of 10,000 men, امیر تومان *amír túmán.* — of nomads, ایلخانی *ílkhání.* Chief, or head-servant, پیشخدمت باشی *písh-khidmat báshí* (this last word can be affixed to most names of offices).

Chiefly, غالباً *ghálíban.*

Chiefship, سروری *sarvarí*; خانی *khání.*

Child, طفل *tifl* ; بچه *bacheh.*

Childbirth, وضعت *vaz'at* ; زائیدگی *záídagí.*

Childhood, طفولیت *tufúliyat.*

Childish, طفلانه *tifláneh.*

Children, اولاد *aulád.*

Chill, خنك *khunuk.*

Chimney, دود کش *dúd kesh* —piece, بخاری *bukhárí.*

Chin زنخ *zanakh.*

China (country), چین *Chín*; ختن *Khutan.* —ware, چینی *chíní.*

Chintz, جامه وار *jámah vár*; چیت *chít.*

Chip, تراشه *tarásheh.*

Chisel, اسکنه *askanah.*

Choice, اختیار *ikhtiyár* (*k.*); انتخاب *intikháb* (*k.*).

Choke, خفه کردن *khufeh k.* (*sh.*).

Cholera, وبا *vabá.*

Choose, (بر *bar*) گزیدن *guzídan.*

Chorasmia, خوارزم *khárezm.*

Chosen, منتخب *muntakhib.*

Christ, حضرت عیسی *Hazrat-i-'Ísá.*

Christian, عیسوی *'ísaví*; نصرانی *nasrání.*

Chronicle, تاریخ *táríkh.*

Chronicler, مورخ *muvarrikh.*

Church, کلیسه *kalísah*; کنیسه *kanísah.*

Churn, *n.*, مشك *mashk*; *v.*, دوغ زدن *dúgh z.*

Cinder, خاکستر *khákister*; نیم سوز *ním súz.*

Cinnabar, شنکرف *shangarf.*

Cinnamon, دار چینی *dár chíní.*

Circle, دایره *dáïreh*; چنبر *chambar.*

Circumambulating (of the Ḳaabah, etc.), طواف *tawwáf.*

Circulation, رواج *raváj* (*d.*).

Circumcised, مختون *makhtún* (*sh.*).

Circumcision, ختنه *khatnah* (*k.*).

Circumference, گرد *gird.*

Circumspect, محتاط *muhtát.*

Circumspection, احتیاط *ihtiyát.*

Circumstance, حال *hál* (pl. احوال *ahvál*); کیفیت *keyfiyat.*

Cistern, حوض *hauz*; آب انبار *áb ambár.*

Citadel, ارك *arg.*

Citation (before a court), احضار *ihzár* (*n.*).

Citizen, شهری *shahrí.*

Citron, ترنج *turanj.*

City, شهر *shahr.*

Civil, مؤدب *muaddab*; لطیف *latíf.* — ity, ادب *adab.*

Civilian, اهل قلم *ahli ḳalam.*

Civet, زباد *zabád.*

Claim, دعوی *da'vá.*

Claimant, مدعی *mudda'í.*

Clamour, داد فریاد *dád o feryád.*

Clandestine, خفی *khafí.*
Clarified, مصفی *musaffá.*
Clarify, صاف کردن *sáf k.*
Clarion, سرنا *sarná.*
Class (of people), طایفه *táífeh* ; (school), صنف *sinf.*
Clause, فقره *fikrah.*
Claw, چنك *chang* ; مخلب *mikhlab.*
Clay, گل *gil* ; شل *shul.*
Clean, پاك *pák* (*k.*) ; صاف *sáf* (*k.*) ; پاکیزه *pákízah* (*h.*).
Cleanness, نظافت *nizáfat.*
Clear (evident), بین *bayin* ; صریح *saríh* ; (bright), روشن *roshan.* — profits, پس انداز *pas andáz.* — away, *v.*, بر داشتن *bar dáshtan.*
Clearly, اشکارا *ashkárá.*
Clearness, صراحت *saráhat.*
Cleave, بریدن *burídan.*
Clemency, شفقت *shafakat.*
Clerk, دفتر نویس *daftar navís.*
Clever, چابك *chábuk* ; زرنك *ziring.* —ness, ذهن *zihn.*
Climate, اب و هوا *áb o havá.*
Climb, بر رفتن *bar raftan.*
Clime (country), اقلیم *iklim.*
Cling, چسپیدن *chaspídan.*
Clip, چیدن *chídan.*

Cloak, جبه *jubbeh* ; چوخا *chúkhá.*
Clock, ساعت *sá'at* (*i yek, do,* etc., one, two o'clock). — maker, ساعت ساز *sá'at sáz.*
Clod, کلوخ *kulúkh.*
Close, *a.*, نزدیك *nazdík* ; *v.*, بستن *bastan.*
Closet, خلوتخانه *khalvat khaneh* ; توشه خانه *túsheh khaneh* ; (a privy), مبرز *mabraz* ; خلا *khalá.*
Cloth, پاچه *pácheh* ; (woollen), ماهوت *máhút.* Table —, سفره *sufreh.*
Clothe, پوشانیدن *púshánídan* ; *pa. p.*, ملبس *mulabbas.*
Clothes, رخت *rakht* ; لباس *libás.* Bed —, رخت خواب *rakht-i-kháb.*
Clotted cream, قایمق *káimak.*
Cloud, ابر *abr* ; —y, گرفته *giriftah.*
Clover, ینچه *yuncheh.*
Cloves, میخك *míkhek* ; قرنفل *karanful.*
Club, چوب *chúb.*
Cluster, خوشه *khúsheh.*
Clyster, حقنه *hukneh.*

Coachman, كالسكه چى káliskeh-chí.

Coal, زغال zoghál.

Coarse, درشت durusht; كلفت kuluft; كنده gundah.

Coast, كناره kináreh; ساحل sáhel.

Coat, قبا ḳabá; نيمتنه nímtaneh. Over —, بالا پوش bálá púsh. — of mail. يلمق yalmak.

Coax, نواختن navákhtan.

Cobbler, پينه دوز pínah dúz.

Cobweb, پرده عنكبوت pardahi 'ankabút.

Cochineal, قرمز فرنكى ḳirmezi firengí.

Cock, خروس khurús. Gun —, چقماق cheḳmáḳ. Cistern —, شير shír.

Cockroach, سوسك súsk.

Cocoa-nut, جوز هندي jauzi hindí; نارجيل nárjíl.

Cocoon, پيله pílah.

Code, تنظيم tanzím.

Coeval, همعهد ham'ahd.

Coffee, قهوه ḳahveh.

Coffin, تابوت tábút

Cog, دندانه dandáneh.

Coherent, مربوط marbut.

Cohesion, پيوستكى paivastagí.

Coin, سكه sikkeh; پول púl. Base —, قلب ḳalb. — of copper, ½d., شاهى sháhí. — of silver, worth 10d., قران ḳrán, or هزار دينار hezár dínár. — of gold, 10 ḳráns, تومان túmán. v., ضرب كردن zarab k.

Coincidence, توارد tavárud.

Coiner, ضراب zarráb.

Colchicum, سورنجان súrinján.

Cold, a., سرد sard; n., سرما sarmá; (illness), زكام zukám (kh.).

Coldness, برودت burúdat.

Colic, قولنج kúlinj; پيچ pích (kh.).

Collar, يخه yakheh; (ring), طوق tauḳ.

Collating, مقابل muḳábil (n.).

Colleage, هم پايه ham páyeh.

Collected, in mind, خاطر جمع kháter jam'.

Collection, جمع jam' (k.); فراهم feráham (a.).

Collector of revenue, محصل muhassil; باجكير bájgír.

College, مدرسه madraseh.

Collyrium, سرمه surmah.

Colocynth, خر زهره *khar zahrah.* — gourd, حنظل *hanzal.*

Colonel, سرتیب *sartíb.* Lieut. —, سرهنك *sarhang.*

Colour, رنك *rang* (*k. z.*) ; *pa. p.* رنکین *rangín.* ملون *mulavvan* (*sh.*). To change — (face), رنك رو پریدن *rangi rú parídan.*

Colt, کره *kurrah.*

Column (stone), ستون ; (book), جدول *jadval.*

Comb, شانه *shánah* (*z.*). Curry —, خرخره *kharkhareh.* Cock's —, تاج خروس *táji khurús.*

Combat, مقاتله *muḳátileh* (*n.*).

Combination, سازش *sázish.*

Combustion, تحریق *tahríḳ.*

Come, آمدن *ámadan.* — out, بدر آمدن *bedar a.* — up, بر آمدن *bar a.* — to pass, واقع شدن *váḳiʿ sh.*

Comet, ستاره دمدار *sitárehi dumdár.*

Comfort, دلاسا *dilásá* ; تسلی *tasallá* (*k.*) ; *pa. p.* متسلی *mutasallí* (*sh.*).

Command, *n.*, حکم *hukm* (*k.*) ; فرمان *farmán* (*k.*) ; حکمرانی *hukmrání* ; *v.*, فرمودن *farmúdan.*

Commander-in-chief, سپه سالار *sipeh sálár.*

Commencement, ابتدا *ibtidá* (*k.*) ; شروع *shurúʿ* (*k.*).

Commendable, پسندیده *pasandídah.*

Commendation, مدح *madh* (*k.*) ; تحسین *tahsín* (*n.*).

Commentary, شرح *sharh* (*k.*) ; تفسیر *tafsír* (*n.*).

Commentator, شارح *shárih.*

Commerce, تجارت *tejárat.*

Commiseration, غمخوار *ghamkhár* (*n.*).

Commission (of sins), ارتکاب *irtikáb* (*n.*) ; *v.* کماشتن *gumáshtan.*

Commit, to, سپردن *sipurdan.*

Common, عام *ʿámm* ; مشهور *mashhúr.* — people, عوام *ʿavvám.*

Commotion, تزلزل *tazalzal.*

Communicate, اظهار کردن *izhár* (*k.*).

Compact, تعاهد *taʿáhud.*

Companion, رفیق *rafíḳ* ; شریق *sharíḳ.* Boon —, ندیم *nadím.*

Companionship, مرافقت *murâfikat.*

Company, مجلس *majlis*; صحبت *suhbat*; (of soldiers), دسته *dasteh.*

Comparison, مقابله *mukábileh* (*k.*).

Comparing, قیس *kais.*

Compass, *n.*, قبله نما *kiblah numá.*

Compasses, پرکار *pargár.*

Compassion, مروت *muruvvat* (*n.*); شفقت *shafakat* (*k.*).

Compassionate, دلسوز *dilsúz.*

Compel, بزور کردن *bizúr k.*

Compendium, موجز *mújiz.*

Compensation, تاوان *távân* (*k.*); تلافی *taláfí* (*k.*).

Competence, کفایت *kefáyat.*

Competent, لایق *láik*; کافی *káfí.*

Competition, مجاهده *mujáhedeh* (*k.*); مسابقت *musábekat* (*k.*).

Compilation, تالیف *taalíf* (*k.*).

Compiler, موءلف *muallif.*

Complain, شکایت کردن *shikáyat k.*; *pr. p.* مشتکی *mushtakí* (*sh.*).

Complaint, گله *gelleh*; (illness), ناخوشی *nákhushí*; علت *'illat.*

Complaisance, مسامحت *masámahat.*

Complete, *a.*, تمام *tammám* (*k.*). —ly, بکلی *bekullí.*

Completed, to be, بانجام رسیدن *be-anjám rs.*

Completion, اتمام *itmám* (*rs.*).

Complexion, رنك رو *rangi rú.*

Compliance, رضایت *rezáyat.*

Complicated, پیچیده *píchídeh* (*k.*).

Compliments, سلام *salám* (*d.*); تهنیه *tahniyeh* (*k.*); چم وخم *cham o kham.*

Comply, راضی شدن *rázi sh.*

Composer, مصنف *musannif.*

Composing (verses), تنظیم *tanzím* (*k.*).

Composed of, مترکب *mutarakkib.*

Composition, (lit.) انشا *inshá.*

Composure, جمیعت خاطر *jamí'ati khátir.* To get —, آرام گرفتن *árám gr.*

Compound, *n.*, مرکب *murakkab*; *pr. p.* ترکیب *tarkíb* (*k.*).

Comprehending, مشتمل بر *mushtamel bar*; مدرك *madrik.*

Comprehension, فهم *fahm.*

Comprehensive, جوامع *javámi'.*

Compromise, مصالحه *musálehah* (*k.*).

Compulsion, زور *zúr*; ظلم *zulm.*

Computation, محاسبت *muhásabat.*

Compute, حساب کردن *hisáb k.*; *pa. p.* محسوب *mahsúb* (*h.*).

Concave, اجوف *ajvaf.*

Concealed, مستور *mastúr* (*h.*); پنهان *panhán* (*k.*).

Concealment, کتم *katm.*

Conceit, پندار *pindár.*

Conceited, مغرور *maghrúr.*

Conceive (mental), یاد آمدن *yád ámadan*; (pregnancy) حامله شدن *hámileh sh.*

Concentred, مرکوز *markúz.*

Concern, دخل داشتن *dakhl dáshtan.*

Concerning, در خصوص *dar khusús*; در حق *dar hakk*; نسبت به *nisbat be.*

Concession, اجازه *ijázeh* (*d.*).

Conciliate, راضی کردن *rází k.*

Conciliatory, مصلحت آمیز *maslahat ámíz.*

Concise, مختصر *mukhtasir.*

Conclude, بانجام رسانیدن *be-anjám rasánídan.*

Conclusion, عاقبت *'ákibat*; سرانجام *sar anjám.*

Concoct (a fancy), هوا پختن *havá pukhtan.*

Concord, موافقت *muváfakat.*

Concordance, ساز کاری *sáz kárí*; مطابقت *mutábakat.*

Concubine متعه *mut'ih*; صیغه *sígheh*; مدخوله *madkhúleh.*

Concurrence, مرضی *marzí.*

Condemn, تحکم نمودن *tahakkum n.*; مجرم نمودن *mujram n.*

Condescension, توجه *tavajjuh.*

Condiments, جوارش *javárish.*

Condition, حال *hál*; حالت *hálat.* One of high —, صاحب عالی شان *sáhib 'álí shán*; (stipulation), شرط *shart.* —al, شرطی *shartí.*

Condolence, تعزیت پرسی *ta'ziyat pursí.*

Condoling, غمگسار *ghamgusár.*

Conduct, *n.* (manner), رفتار *raftár*; (leading), هدایت *hedáyat* (*k.*).

Conductor, جلو دار *jelo dár*; راه نما *ráh nemá.*

Conduit, آبراه *ábráh.*

Confectionary, مربی *murabba.*

Confectioner, شیرین ساز *shírín sáz.*

Confederacy, معاهده *mu'áhedeh.*

Confederated, معاقد *mu'áḳid.*

Confer (discuss), مکالمه کردن *mukálemeh k.* — a favour, منت نهادن *minnat nihádan.*

Conference, مجالست *mujálisat.*

Confessing, مقر *muḳirr* (*sh.*)

Confession, اقرار *iḳrár* (*k.*); اعتراف *i'tiráf* (*n.*).

Confidant, همراز *ham ráz*; محرم *mahram.*

Confidence, اعتماد *i'timád* (*d.*); اعتقاد *i'tiḳád* (*b.*).

Confidential, معتمد *mu'tamad.*

Confiding in, متامن *mutaammin.*

Confined, محبوس *mahbús.*

Confines, سرحد *sar hadd*; حدود *hudúd.*

Confirm, ثابت کردن *ábit k.*

Confirmation, استقرار *istiḳrár.*

Confirmed, موکد *múakkad.*

Confirming, تصدیق *tasdíḳ* (*k.*).

Confiscate, ضبط کردن *zabt k.*

Conflagration, احتراق *ihtiráḳ.*

Conflict, جنك *jang.*

Confluence, مجمع *majma'.*

Conformable, موافق *muváfiḳ.*

Conformity, موافقت *muvafaḳat* (*n.*); امتثال *imtisál* (*k.*). In — with, بحسب *behasbi.*

Confound, بر هم زدن *bar ham zadan*; *pa. p.* سر کردان *sar gardán.*

Confront, رو برو کردن *rú berú k.*

Confused, پریشان *paríshán* (*sh.*); برهم *bar ham* (*h.*).

Confusion, تشویش *tashvísh* (*k.*); آشوب *áshúb.*

Confuted, ملزم *mulzam* (*k.*).

Congealed, منجمد *munjamid* (*sh.*); *pr. p.* جمد *jamd.*

Congelation, فسردکی *fusurdagí.*

Congratulations, مبارك بادی *mubárak bádi* (*gf.*); تهنیت *tahniyat* (*k.*).

Congregation, جماعت *jemá'at.*

Congruous, منطبق *muntabiḳ.*

Conjectural, وهمی *vahmí*; قیاسی *ḳiyásí.*

Conjecture, کمان *gumán* (*k.*); تخمین *takhmín* (*k.*).

Conjoined, ملتصق *multasiḳ.*

Conjugation, تصریف *tasríf* (*k.*).

Conjunction, مقرونیت makrúniyat; (in grammar), عطف 'atf.

Conjurer, حقه باز hukkeh báz; جادو گر jádú gar.

Connect, پیوستن paivastan; وصل کردن vasl k.

Connected with, متوصل mutavassil.

Connections, علائق 'aláik.

Connivance, چشم پوشی cheshm púshí (k.).

Connoisseur of wine, میگسار mai-gusár.

Conquer, فتح کردن fath k.; pa. p. مغلوب maghlúb (sh.).

Conqueror, غالب ghálib; ظافر záfir.

Conquest, جهان گیری jehán girí; ملك گیری mulk girí.

Consecration, تقدیس takdís (n.); تخصیص takhsís (k.).

Consecutive, مسلسل musalsal.

Consent, n., رضا rizá (k.); قبول kabúl (k.); v. راضی شدن rází shudan.

Consequence, مآل maal.

Consider, فکر کردن fikr k.; pr. p. متأمل mutaamil (h.).

Consideration, اندیشه andíshah (k.); تأمل taamul (k.); (importance), اعتبار i'tibár.

Consign, سپردن sipurdan.

Consignment, تفویض tafvíz (k.); حواله کردن havâleh k.

Consolation, تسلی tasallá (k.).

Console, دلداری کردن dildárí k.; pa. p. متسلی mutasalli (sh.).

Consort, هنیار hanyár; هنیان hanyán.

Conspicuous, منجالی munjálí.

Conspiracy, سازش sázish; تعهد ta'ahud.

Conspirator, هم عهد ham 'ahd.

Constant, نصوح nasúh.

Constantinople, اسلامبول Islambúl, or استنبول Istambúl.

Constellation, اختر akhtar.

Constipated, منقبض munkabiz (sh.). —ness قبض kabz.

Constituted, متعین muta'ayyin.

Constrained, ملتزم multuzim (b.)

Construct, بنا کردن bená k.

Construction, بنیان bunyán.

Consubstantial, همذات hamzát.

Consul, بالیوز báliyúz.

Consultation, مشورت *mash-varat* (*k.*).

Consume, صرف کردن *sarf k.*

Consummation, زفاف *zifáf* (*d.*).

Consumption, هلاس *hulás.*

Contact, اتصال *ittisál.*

Contagion, سرایت *sirâyat.*

Contagious, منعدی *mun'adí.*

Contained, متضمن *mutazammin* (*b.*). — in, تلو *talv.* Self —, خود داری *khud dárí* (*k.*).

Contaminating, نجس *nejis* (*k.*).

Contemplated, ملحوظ *malhúz.*

Contemplating, مراقب *murákib.*

Contemplation, ملاحظه *mulá-hezeh* (*k.*); مشاهده *mushá-hadeh* (*n.*).

Contemplative, مترسم *mutaras-sim.*

Contemporary, معاصر *ma'ásir.*

Contempt, تحقیر *tahkír.*

Contemptible, حقیر *hakír*; مخذول *makhzúl.*

Contend, نواستن *navástan*; ستیزیدن *sitízídan.*

Contending, منازع *manázi'* (*h.*).

Content, *a.*, راضی *rází*; خرسند *khursand*; *pa. p.* خوشنود *khushnúd*; فارغبال *fáregh-bál.*

Contention, مجادله *mujádeleh* (*k.*); کوشش *kúshish* (*k.*).

Contentious, مجادل *mujádil.*

Contentment, قناعت *kiná'at.*

Contents, مضمون *mazmún.*

Contest, منازعت *munáza'at*; (poetical), مشاعره *mushá'ereh.*

Contiguity, اتصال *ittisál.*

Contiguous, ملاصق *mulásik.*

Continence, احصان *ihsán*; پرهیز *parhíz.*

Continent, پرهیز کار *parhíz gár.*

Contingency, وقوع *vukú'.*

Continually, پیوسته *paivastah.*

Continuance, استمرار *istimrar.*

Continuation, توالی *tavâlí.*

Contortion, پیچش *píchish.*

Contract, قباله *kabáleh*; مقاطعه *mukáta'ah* (*k.*); شرط *shart* (*bs.*).

Contraction, تقلص *takallus*; اختصار *ikhtisár.*

Contradict, بر ضد گفتن *bar zidd gf.*

Contradiction, اختلاف *ikhtiláf.*

Contradictory, مناقض *munákiz.*

Contrariety, مخالفت *mukhá-lefat.*

Contrary, برخلاف *bar khiláf*; مخالف *mukhálif.*

Contrivance, تدبیر tadbír (k.).
Control, ضبط zabt (k.).
Controversy, مناضره munázereh.
Contumacious, مرید maríd.
Contumacy, عناد 'inád.
Contusion, پرت part (kh.).
Convalescence, افاقت ifáḳat.
Convalescent, مفیق mufíḳ.
Convenient, مناسب munásib.
Convent, خانقاه khánekáh.
Convene, هواسیدن havásídan.
Conversation, گفت و گو guft o gú (k.); مکالمه mukálemeh (k.); گفت و شنید guft o shaníd (k.).
Convert, n., جدید jadíd; بدل در یافته badal dar yáfteh; v., بدل کردن badal k.
Convey, ابلاغ کردن iblágh k.
Convex, محدب muhaddab.
Conviction, الزام ilzám (k.).
Convinced, ملزم mulzam (s.).
Conviviality, مباهجت mubáhejat.
Convulse, بهم بر زدن beham bar z.; pa. p. متشنج mutashannej.
Cook, n., آشپز áshpaz; v., پختن pukhtan.
Cookery, طباخت tibákhat.
Cool, خنك khunuk (k.).

Cooling, مبرد mubarrid.
Coolness, خنکی khunukí.
Copious, موفور maufúr; فراون ferávan.
Copper, مس mis.
Copperas, زاج záj.
Coppersmith, مسگر misgar.
Copulate, گایدن gáidan.
Copulation, مجامعت mujáma'at (k.); مباشرت mubásharat (k.)
Copulative, وصلی vaslí.
Copy (writing), سر مشق sari mashḳ; (book), نسخه nuskheh. Rough —, سواد savvád; v., نقل کردن naḳl k.
Coquetry, عشوت 'ishvat (k.).
Coral, مرجان marján; بسد bissad.
Cord, ریسمان rísmán.
Coriander-seed, کشنیز kishníz.
Cork, سر شیشه sari shíshah.
— screw, پیچ pích.
Corn, گندم gandum; غله ghalleh.
Corner, گوشه gúsheh; پیغوله paighúleh.
Corporal, ده باشی deh báshí.
Corporeal, جسمانی jismání.
Corpse, میت maiyit; لاش lásh.

Corpulence, جسامت *jasámat.*

Corpulent, تن آور *tan ávar ;* فربه *farbih.*

Correct, صحیح *sahíh* (*h.*); درست *durust* (*k.*).

Correction, تصحیح *tas-híh.* Under —, زیرچوب *zíri chúb.*

Correspondence (of species), جنسیت *jinsiyat;* (by letter), مکاتبت *mukátabat* (*k.*).

Correspondent, مترسل *mutarassil.*

Corresponding to, مطابق به *mutábiḳ be.*

Corroborated, مشدد *mushaddad.*

Corroboration, تشدید *tashdíd.*

Corroded, زنگ خورده *zang khurdeh.*

Corrupt, فاسد *fásid.*

Corruption, عفونت *'ufúnat.*

Cost, قیمت *ḳaimat* (*d.*).

Costs (law), خرچه *kharcheh.*

Cosy, کیف *kíf.*

Cotton, پنبه *pambah ;* قطن *ḳutn.* — pod, جوزق *jauzaḳ.* — carder, نداف *naddáf.* — carding, ندف *nadf* (*k.*).

Cough, سعال *su'ál* (*k.*) ; سرفه *surfah* (*k.*).

Council, مشورت *mashvarat* (*k.*).

Counsel, رای *rái ;* نصیحة *nasíhat* (*d.*).

Counsellor, مشیر *mushír.*

Count, *v.*, شمردن *shumurdan.*

Countenance, منظر *manzar ;* رو *rú.*

Counterfeit (figure), تقلید *taḳlíd* (*k.*) ; (coin), قلب *ḳalb* (*k.*) ; ساختکی *sákhtagí.*

Counterpane, لحاف *laháf.*

Country, ولایت *viláyat.* Native —, وطن *vatan.* Hilly —, کوهستان *kúhistán.*

Countryman, هم وطن *ham vatan.*

Couplet, بیت *bait.*

Courage, مردانکی *mardánagí ;* دلیری *dalíri.*

Courageous, شجاع *shujá'.*

Courier (on foot), قاصد *ḳásid ;* (mounted), چاپار *chápár ;* غلام *gholám.*

Court (king's), درگاه *dargáh.* Law —, محکمه *mahkamah ;* (of house) حیاط *hayát.*

Courteous, مؤدب *muaddeb.*

Courtesy, ملاطفه *mulátifeh ;* مدارا *mudárá.*

Courtezan, لولی *lúlí;* قحبه *ḳahbeh,*

Courtier, مقرب *muḳarrib.*

Cousin, عمو زاده *'ammú zádeh* (child of pat. uncle); عمه زاده *'ammeh z.* (child of pat. aunt); خالو زاده *khálú z.* (child of mat. uncle); خاله زاده *khálɛh z.* (child of mat. aunt). Male —, پسر عمو *pesari 'ammú*, etc. Fem. —, دختر عمو *dukhtari 'ammú*, etc.

Covenant, عهده *'uhdeh* (*gr.*).

Cover, *n.*, سر پوش *sar púsh*; *v.*, پوشیدن *púshídan.*

Coverlet, لحاف *laháf.*

Covet, طمع کردن *tama' k.*

Covetous, طماع *tammá'.*

Covetousness, طمع کاری *tama' kárí.*

Cow, گاو *gáv.*

Coward, نامرد *námard.*

Cowardice, جبن *jubn.*

Co-wife, همشوی *hamshúi.*

Crab, خرچنك *kharchang.*

Crack, *n.*, شکاف *shikáf*; چاك *chák* (*sh.*); *v.*, شکافتن *shikáftan.*

Cradle, گهواره *gahváreh.*

Craftiness, روباه بازی *rúbáh bází.*

Crane, کلنك *kulang.*

Craze, شوری *shúrí.*

Crazy, خشك مغز *khusk maghz*; دیوانه *díváneh.*

Cream, سر شیر *sari shír.*

Crease, تا *tá* (*n.*).

Create, آفریدن *áfrídan.*

Created beings, مخلوقات *makh-lúḳát.*

Creation, خلقة *khilḳat.*

Creator, آفریدگار *Afrídgár.*
— of the World, جهان آفرین *Jehán áfrín.*

Creatures, خلایق *khaláiḳ.*

Credit, *n.*, (money), نسیة *nasi-yat*; (honour), اعتبار *i'tibár* (*dsh.*); *v.*, باور کردن *bávar k.*

Creditor, قرض خواه *ḳarz kháh.*

Creep, خزیدن *khazídan.*

Crepitatio ventris, گوز *gúz.*

Crescent, هلال *helál.*

Cresses, تیزك *tízak.*

Crest, جقه *jiḳḳeh.*

Crew, حزب *hizb.*

Cricket (insect), چرغد *chirghad.*

Crier, منادی *manádí*; جارچی *járchi*; (of mosque), موذن *muazzin.*

Crime, گناه *gunáh*; تقصیر *taḳsír*; جریمه *jarímah.*

Criminal, گناه کار *gunáh kár*; مذنب *muznib*.

Crimson, قرمز *ḳermez*.

Cripple, چولاق *chúláḳ*.

Crisis (of disease), بحران *bahrán*.

Crisp (hair), جعد *ja'ad*.

Critic, نکته دان *nukteh dán*.

Criticism, نکته چینی *nukteh chíní* (*k.*).

Croaking, نعاب *nu'áb*; نغیق *naghíḳ*.

Crocodile, تمساح *timsáh*.

Crocus, زعفران *za'farán*.

Crooked, کج *kaj*; خم *kham*; عوج *'avaj*. — ness, کجی *kají*.

Crop (of bird), حوصله *hauseleh*; (of field), حاصل *hásel*; حصاد *hesád*.

Cross, چلیپا *chalípá*; صلیب *salíb*.

Cross-beam, نعامت *na'ámat*.

Croup, خروسك *khurúsak*.

Crow, *n.*, کلاغ *kelágh*; زاغ *zágh*; *v.*, بانك زدن *bang z.*

Crowd, ازدحام *izdihám*; خرانبار *khar ambár*.

Crown, تاج *táj*. — of the head, افسر سر *afsari sar*; *pr. p.* تکلیل *taklíl* (*k.*). — property, خالصه *khá-liseh*.

Crowned, تاج دار *táj dár*;

Crucible, بوته *bútah*.

Crucified, مصلوب *maslúb* (*s.*)

Crucifixion, تصلیب *taslíb* (*k.*).

Crude, خام *khám*.

Cruel, بیمروت *bí-muruvvat*.

Cruelty, جان آزاری *ján ázárí*.

Crumb, ریزه *rízah*; خورده *khurdeh*.

Crushed, له *lih* (*k.*); خورد *khurd* (*s.*).

Crust, پوست *púst*.

Crupper, پار دم *pár dam*.

Cry, *n.*, فریاد *feryád*; — *v.*, (weep), گریه کردن *geriyeh k.* — out, صدا کردن *sedá k.*

Crystal, بلور *bullúr*.

Cube, کعب *ka'ab*; ششدر *shashdar*.

Cubit, ذرع *zar'*.

Cuckold, قرمساق *ḳurmsáḳ*.

Cuckoo, کوکو *kúkú*.

Cucumber, خیار *khiyár*.

Cue, اشاره *isháreh*.

Cuff (slap), مشت *musht* (*z.*).

Cuirass, زره *zerah*; جوشن *júshan*.

Cull, چیدن *chídan.*
Culpable, تقصیر وار *taḳsír vár.*
Culprit, مقصر *muḳassar.*
Cultivated, معمور *ma'múr ;* اباد *ábád.*
Cultivation, زراعت *zirá'at* (*k.*); کشته کاری *keshteh kárí.*
Cummin-seed, کمون *kammún.*
Cunning, ذو فنون *zú funún.*
Cup, *n.*, (large tea), پیاله *piyáleh ;* (small coffee), فنجان *finján ;* (large), جام *jám ;* کاسه *káseh ;* قدح *ḳadah.*
Cupboard, طاقچه *táḳcheh.*
Cupola, گنبد *gumbad.*
Cupping, حجامت *hajámat* (*k.*).
Cupper, حجام *hajjám.*
Curable, علاج پذیر *'iláj pazír.*
Curb, لجام *lijám.*
Curds, ماست *mást ;* دوغ *dúgh.*
Cure, شفا *shifá* (*d.*) ; علاج *iláj* (*k.*) ; معالجه *mu'álijeh* (*k.*).
Curiosities, نفیسات *nafísát.*
Curiosity, استقصاء *istiḳsá.*
Curious, سر جو *sirr jú ;* (wondrous), عجب *'ajab.*
Curl, حلقه *halḳeh ;* زلف *zulf.*
Currants, کشمش *kishmish.*
Currency, ترویج *tarvíj* (*dsh.*).
Current (coin), رواج *raváj* (*dsh.*) ; رایج *ráij ;* (stream), جاری *járí.*
Currier, چرم ساز *charm sáz.*
Currying (leather), دبغ *dabgh* (*k.*) ; (a horse), تیمار *tímár* (*k.*).
Currycomb, قشو *ḳasho.*
Curse, لعنت *la'nat* (*k.*).
Cursed, ملعون *mal'ún.*
Curtailing, ابتار *ibtár* (*k.*).
Curtain, پرده *pardah.*
Curve, پیچش *píchish.*
Cushion, بالش *bálish ;* متکا *muttaká.*
Custody (of), حفاظت *hafázat ;* حواله *haváleh.* In —, قید *ḳaid.*
Custom, رسم *rasm ;* عادت *'ádat.*
Customary, رسمی *rasmí.*
Customs, گمرك *gumruk.* — house, گمرکخانه *gumruk-kháneh.*
Cut, بریدن *burídan.* — out, تراشیدن *taráshídan.*
Cuticle, بشرت *basharat.*
Cut-purse, کیسه بر *kíseh bur.*
Cutter (of gems), حکاك *hakkák.*
Cylinder, لوله *lúleh ;* استوانه *ustuvánch.*

Cymbals, سنتور *sumtúr*.

Cypher (zero), صفر *sifr*; (writing), خط رمز *khatti ramz*.

Cypress, سرو *sarv*.

D

Dagger (large), قمه *kammah*; (small), خنجر *khanjar*.

Daily, روزی *rúzí*; هر روز *har rúz*. — allowance, روزانه *rúzánah*.

Daisy, بابونه *bábúnah*.

Dale, دره *derreh*.

Dam, بند *band* (*k.*).

Damage, ضرر *zarrar* (*rsa.*); خلل *khallal* (*k.*); عیب *'aib* (*k.*).

Damascus, شام *Shám*.

Damned, ملعون *mal'ún*.

Damp, *n.*, رطوبت *ratúbat*; *a.*, تر *tarr* (*h. k.*).

Damson, الوچه *álúcheh*.

Dance, رقص *raks* (*k.*).

Dancer, رقاص *rakkás*.

Danger, خطر *khattar*; خوف *khauf*.

Dangerous, خطر ناك *khattar nák*; مهلك *muhlik*.

Dapple-grey, ابرش *abrash*.

Daring, جرئت *jur-at* (*dsh.*); جسارت *jesárat* (*n.*).

Dark, تاريك *tárík*; (colour), تيره *tíreh*.

Darkness, تاريكي *táríkí*.

Darling, محبوب *mahbúb*; عزيز *'azíz*.

Darning, رفو *rafú* (*k.*).

Dart, جريد *jeríd*.

Dash, بهم زدن *biham z.*; *pr. p.* متموج *mutamavvij*.

Dastardly, بيحميت *bíhamiyat*.

Date (fruit), خرما *khurmá*; — stone, نوات *navát*; (epoch), تاريخ *táríkh*; *pa. p.* مؤرخ *muarrakh*.

Daughter, دختر *dukhtar*. — -in-law, عروس *'arús*.

Dauntless, بيمحابا *bímuhábá*.

David, داود *Dáúd*.

Dawn, بامداد *bámdád*; صبح زود *subhi zúd*.

Day, روز *rúz*. — light, روز روشن *rúzi roshan*. Day by day, روز بروز *rúz be rúz*. To-day, امروز *imrúz*. Day after to-morrow, پس فردا *pas fardá*.

Day-book, روز نامه *rúz námeh*.

Dazzling, چشم خيره *cheshm khíreh* (*k. sh.*)

Dead, مرده *murdah* (pl. مردکان *murdagán*).

Deadly, مهلك *muhlik*; هلاهل *heláhil*.

Deaf, کر *kar* (*b.*). — ness, صم *summ*.

Deal, a great, بسیار *bisyár*.

Dealer, سوداکر *súdágar*.

Dealing fairly, راست کردار *rást kerdár*.

Dear (price), کران *gíran*; (affection), عزیز *'azíz*.

Death, مرك *marg*; موت *maut*; وفات *vafát*. Angel of —, اسرافیل *Isráfíl*.

Debarred, محروم *mahrúm* (*k.*).

Debate, مشاورت *mushávarat*.

Debauchee, رند *rind*.

Debilitated, ضعیف *za'íf*.

Debt, قرض *ḳarz*; وام *vám*.

Debtor, قرض دار *ḳarz dar*.

Decanter, تنك *tung*.

Decapitate, کردن زدن *gardan z.*

Decayed, پژ مرده *pazh murdeh*.

Deceased, مرحوم *marhúm*.

Deceit, فریب *firíb*; مکر *makr*; کول *gúl* (*kh.*).

Deceive, فریفتن *firíftan*; *pa. p.* مغبون *maghbún* (*k. sh.*).

Deceiver, خادع *khádi'*.

Deception, تغابن *taghábun*.

Decent, متشخص *mutashakhkhis*.

Decency, شایستکی *sháyistagí*.

Decision (law), حکم *hukm* (*d.*); (mental), مقرر *muḳarrar* (*dsh.*).

Decisive, قاطع *ḳáti'*.

Deck, *n.*, عرشه *'arshah*.

Declamation, انشاد *inshád* (*k.*).

Declaration, اعلان *i'lán* (*k. d.*).

Declination, تنزل *tanazzul*.

Decline, *n.*, (decay), زوال *zavál*; *v.*, در کذشتن *dar guzashtan*; (refuse), نفی کردن *nafí k.*

Declivity, نشیب *nashíb*; شیو *sheiv*.

Decoction, طبیخ *tabíkh*.

Decomposition, انحلال *inhelál*.

Decoration, زینت *zínat* (*k.*); (order), نشان *nishán*.

Decrease, *n.*, نقص *naḳs*. *v.*, کم کردن *kam k.*

Decree, فتوی *fatvá* (*d.*); امر *amr* (*k.*); *pa. p.* مقدر *muḳaddar*.

Decrepit, فرتوت *fartút*; هرم *harim*.

Deducing, منتهج *muntahij* (*k.*).

Deduction, منها *minhá* (*k.*).

Deed (of gift), هبه نامه *hibbeh námeh*; (of sale), قباله *ḳabáleh*; (written), حجت *hujjat*.

Deep, گود *god*; عميق *'amíḳ*.

Deer, آهو *áhú*.

Deface, محو كردن *mahv k.*

Defame, بد نام كردن *bad nám k.*

Defeat, شكست *shikast* (*d. kh.*).

Defect, عيب *'aib*.

Defection, معصيت *mu'siyat*.

Defective, مقصر *muḳassar*.

Defence, صيانت *siyánat* (*k.*); حمايت *himáyat* (*d.*).

Defendant, مدعى عليه *mudda'a 'alaih*.

Defender, حامى *hámí*.

Defensive, دفاع *difá'*.

Defer, دفع انداختن *daf' an*; *pa. p.* موقوف *mauḳúf* (*sh.*).

Deference, احترام *ihtirám* (*n.*)

Deficiency, نقص *naḳs*.

Deficient, قاصر *ḳásir*.

Defile, *n.*, تنگه *tangah*; كتل *kotul*.

Defiled, نجس *nejis* (*k.*).

Defilement, ناپاكى *nápákí*.

Definite, محدود *mahdúd*.

Definition, بيان *bayán* (*k.*).

Deformed, معيوب *ma'yúb*.

Deformity, زشتى *zishtí*.

Defraud, گول زدن *gúl z.*

Defray, خرج كردن *kharj* (*k.*).

Degenerate, نا خلف *ná khalaf.*

Degree, درجه *darajeh*; طبقه *tabaḳeh*.

Deity in, or of, الوهيت *ulúhiyat*.

Delay, تاءخير *taakhír* (*k.*); تاءنى *taanní* (*k.*); دير *dír* (*k.*)

Delegate, مباشر *mubáshir*.

Deliberately, عمداً *'amdan*.

Deliberation, تدبير *tadbír* (*k.*); مشورت *mashvarat* (*k.*).

Delicacies, مستلذات *mustalazzát*.

Delicacy, لطافت *litáfat*.

Delicate, نازك *názuk*.

Delicious, خوش مزه *khush mazah*.

Delight, حظ *hezz*; خوشحال *khush hál* (*s.*).

Delighted, I am, خوشم آمد *khush-am* (*-at*, *-ash*, etc.) *ámad*.

Delirious, مدهوش *madhúsh*.

Delirium, هذى *hezí*.

Deliverance, خلاص *khilás* (*k.*); نجات *neját* (*d.*).

Delivery, تسليم *taslím* (*k.*).

Deluded, غره *gharrah*.

Deluge, طوفان *túfán*.

Demand, *n.*, در خواست *dar khást*; خواهش *kháhesh.* *v.*, طلبیدن *talabídan*; خواستن *khástan.*

Demolition, هدم *hadm* (*k.*); خراب *kheráb* (*k.*).

Demon, دیو *div*; جن *jinn.*

Demoniac, مجنون *majnún.*

Demonstration, اظهار *izhár* (*k.*); برهان *burhán* (*k.*).

Demonstrative, مبرهن *mubarhan.*

Demur, پس و پیش *pas o písh.*

Den, لانه *láneh.*

Denial, انکار *inkár* (*k.*).

Dense, کثیف *kasíf.*

Density, کثافت *kisáfat.*

Depart, روان شدن *raván sh.*

Departure, حرکت *harakat* (*k.*); کوچ *kuch* (*k.*); رحلت *rihlat.*

Dependence, تعلق *ta'alluḳ* (*dsh.*).

Dependent, متعلق *muta'allaḳ* (*b.*); موقوف *mauḳúf.*

Depopulate, ویران کردن *vairán k.*

Deposit, *n.*, امانت *amánat* (*gz.*).

Depraved, فاسد *fásid.*

Depravity, تباهی *tabáhí.*

Depredation, غارت *ghárat* (*k.*).

Depressing, مکب *mukibb* (*k.*).

Deprivation, فقدان *fiḳdán.*

Depth, عمق *'umḳ*; ژرفا *zharfá.*

Deputation, مراسله *muráseleh*

Depute, ماٴمور کردن *maamúr k.*

Deputy, نایب *náib.*

Derision, استهزاء *istihzá.*

Derivation, اشتقاق *ishtiḳáḳ.*

Derivative, فرعی *far'í.*

Derived, مصدور *masdúr* (*b.*).

Dervish, درویش *darvísh.* —'s cup, کشکول *kashkúl.*

Descend, پاین آمدن *páín ámadan*; فرود آمدن *farúd á.*

Descendants, اولاد *aulád*; عقبه *'aḳabah.*

Descent, نزول *nuzúl* (*k.*); نشیب *nashíb*; (origin), نسل *nasl*; نسب *nasab.*

Description, تعریف *ta'ríf* (*k.*); تفصیل *tafsíl* (*k.*); بیان *bayán* (*k.*).

Desert, *n.*, بیابان *biyábán*; دشت *dasht*; *v.*, رو کردانیدن *rú g.*

Deserter, فراری *ferári* (*sh.*).

Deserving, مستحق *mustahaḳḳ* (*b.*).

Design, عزم *'azm* (*k.*); غرض *gharaz* (*k.*); (drawing), نقش *naksh* (*k.*).

Designer, رسام *rassám.*

Desirable, مرغوب *marghúb.*

Desire, آرزو *árzú* (*k.*); خواهش *kháhesh* (*dsh.*); مراد *murád*; رغبت *righbat.*

Desirous, آرزومند *arzúmand*; مشتاق *mushták.*

Desist, دست بردار شدن *dast bar dár sh.*

Desolate, خراب *kharáb* (*k.*); ويران *vairán* (*s.*).

Desolation, ويرانى *vairání.*

Despair, قنوط *kunút*; نا اميدى *ná ummídi.*

Despatch, *n.*, نوشته *navishtah*; *v.*, روانه كرد *raváneh k.*

Desperate, مايوس *máyús.*

Despicable, نكوهيده *nikúhídah.*

Despise, خوار كردن *khár k.*; *pa. p.*, محقر *muhakkar*; مهان *muhán.*

Desponding, يووش *yuvúsh.*

Despot, مستقل *mustakill.*

Despotism, استقلال *istiklál.*

Dessert, نقل *nukl.*

Desisting, متقاعد *mutaká'id.*

Destiny, قدر *kadar*; قسمت *kismat*; بخت *bakht.*

Destitute, بيروزى *bírúzí*; بيكس *bíkas.*

Destitution, بيچاركى *bícháregi.*

Destroyed, خراب *kheráb* (*k.*); منهدم *munhadem* (*s.*).

Destroyer, يبابكار *yabábkár.*

Destruction, تهليك *tahlík*; هدم *hadm*; اعدام *i'dam.*

Destructive, هالك *hálik.*

Detach, جدا ساختن *jedá s.*

Detail, تفصيل *tafsíl.*

Detailed, مفصل *mufassal.*

Detain, باز داشتن *báz dáshtan.*

Detection, انكشاف *inkisháf.*

Detector, كاشف *káshif.*

Detergent, منقى *munakkí.*

Deterioration, زوال *zavál.*

Detestable, مكروه *makrúh*; كريه *karíh.*

Dethronement, خلع *khal'.*

Detraction, نميمه *namímah.*

Detriment, تنقص *tanakkus.*

Devastation, تخريب *takhríb*; پايمال *páimál.*

Development, كشف *kashf* (*k.*).

Deviation, انحراف *inheráf* (*k.*); تجاوز *tajávuz* (*n.*).

Device, حكمت *hikmat.*

Devil, ابلیس *iblís*; شیطان *shaitán*.

Devilish, خناسی *khannásí*.

Devise, تدبیر کردن *tadbír k.*

Devoted, مخلص *mukhlis*; فدوی *fedaví*; محب *muhibb*.

Devotee, زاهد *záhid*; عابد *'ábid*.

Devotion, عبادت *'ibádat*; عاکف *'ákif*.

Devouring, ابتلاع *ibtilá'* (*n.*).

Devout, عابدانه *'ábidánah*; متعبد *muta'abbid*; معتکف *mu'takif*.

Dew, شبنم *shabnam*.

Dewlap, غبغب *ghabghab*.

Dexterity, معرفت *ma'refat*; زرنگی *ziringí*.

Dexterous, نپق *napak*; چابق *chábúk*; زرنك *ziring*.

Diabetes, سلس البول *salas ul baul*.

Diagnosis, تشخیص *tushkhís*.

Dialectics, منطق *mantik*.

Dialogue, جواب سؤال *jawwáb sowál*.

Diametre, قطر *katr*.

Diamond, الماس *almás*.

Diarrhœa, اسهال *is-hál*.

Diary, روز نامه *rúz námeh*.

Dice, ششدر *shishdar*; قمار *kumár*.

Dictation, املا *imlá* (*k.*).

Dictionary, لغت *lughat*.

Die, *n.*, سکه *sikkeh*; *v.*, مردن *murdan*; فوت شدن *faut sh.*; وفات یافتن *vafát y.*

Diet, غذا *ghizá*; پرهیز *parhíz* (*k.*); طعم *ta'm*.

Difference, تفاوت *tafávut* (*dsh. k.*); فرق *fark* (*dsh.*).

Different, جدا *jidá*; علی حده *'alá haddeh*.

Difficult, مشکل *mushkil*.

Difficulty, مشکلی *mushkilí*; اشکال *ishkál*.

Diffident, واهمه *váhimeh*.

Diffuse, افشاندن *afshándan*.

Diffusion, نشر *nashr*; بسط *bast*.

Dig, کندن *kandan*; کاویدن *kávídan*.

Digested, مهضوم *mahzúm* (*sh.*).

Digestible, گواره *gaváreh*.

Digestive, هضمی *hazmí*.

Digestion, تحلیل *tahlíl* (*k. r.*); هضم *hazm* (*k. sh.*).

Digger, کننده *kanendah*.

Digging, حفر *hafr* (*k.*).

Dignified, مشرف *musharraf* (*s.*) ; باوقار *bávikár.*

Dignity, شان *shaan*; منصب *mansab*; دولت *daulat.*

Dilatory, تنبل *tumbul.*

Diligence, تندهی *tandehí*; اهتمام *ihtimám* (*n.*).

Diligent, مقید *mukayyid.* —ly, بجد *be-jidd.*

Diluted, مخلوط *makhlút* (*k.*).

Dimension, مقدار *mikdár.*

Diminish, کم کردن *kam k.*; *pr. p.*, تقلیل *taklíl* (*k.*).

Diminution, کاست *kást.*

Diminutive, تصغیر *tasghír.*

Dimity, دمیاطی *dimyátí.*

Dimness of sight, غشاوة *ghash-ávat.*

Dimple, چاه *cháh.*

Dinner, شام *shám* (*kh.*).

Dip, خیسانیدن *khísánídan.*

Direct, *a.*, راست *rást*; *v.*, ارشاد کردن *irshád k.*; راه نمودن *ráh n.*; *pa.p.*, مهتدی *muhtadi.*

Direction (of letter), نام و مقام *nám o makám*; (way), سمت *samt*; سو *sú*; (guidance), رهنمای *rah namái* (*k.*).

Director, کارکن *kárkun.*

Dirt, چرك *chirk* (*k.*).

Deity, چرکین *chirkín*; کسیف *kasíf* (*sh.*).

Disabled, عاجز *'ájiz.*

Disagree, اختلاف کردن *ikh-tiláf k.*

Disagreeable, نا پسند *ná pasand.*

Disagreement, تناقض *tanákuz.*

Disappeared, نا پدید *ná padíd* (*sh.*).

Disappointed, نا کام *ná kám* (*k.*) ; نا مراد *ná murád* (*k.*).

Disappointment, نغص *naghas.*

Disapprobation, نا پسندی *ná pasandí.*

Disaster, آفت *áfat*; بلا *balá.*

Disavowal, انکار *inkár* (*k.*).

Disbelieve, باور نه کردن *bávar nah k.*

Disc, قرص *kurs.*

Discernment, تفرس *tafarrus.*

Discharge, *v.*, مرخص کردن *mu-rakhkhas k.*; (a gun), خالی کردن *khálí k.*

Disciple, مرید *muríd*; (Xtian), حواری *havárí.*

Discipline, نظم *nazm* (*d.*); تادیب *tádíb* (*k.*).

Disclose, کشف کردن *kashf k.*

Disconcerted, مضطرب *muztarib* (*h.*).

Discontented, ملول *malúl;* دلتنك *diltang.*

Discordant, نا موزون *ná mauzún;* نا ساز *ná sáz.*

Discourse, *n.*, خطاب *khetáb* (*k.*); *v.*, سخن راندن *sukhan rándan.*

Discover, پیدا کردن *paidá k.*

Discovery, اضهار *iz-hár* (*k.*); استکشاف *istiksháf* (*n.*).

Discrimination, تمییز *tamyíz* (*k.*); تفریق *tafrík.*

Discussion, مذاکره *muzákereh* (*k.*).

Disdain, کبر *kibr.* —full, مستغنی *mustaghní.*

Disease, مرض *maraz;* بیماری *bímárí.*

Diseased, مریض *maríz.*

Disgrace, فضاحت *fazáhat* (*k.*); ذلت *zillat;* رسوای *rasváí* (*k.*). —ing one's family, خانه سوز *khánek súz.*

Disguise, تبدیل *tabdíl* (*k.*).

Disgust, نفرت *nifrat* (*s.*).

Dish, پشقاب *pushkáb.*

Dishevelled hair, آشفته موی *áshufteh múi.*

Dishonourable, بی آبرو *bí ábrú* (*sh.*).

Dihonoured, بی حرمت *bí hurmat* (*k.*).

Disinterested, بیغرض *bí-gharaz.*

Dislike, تنفر نمودن *tanaffur n.*

Dislocated, منفك *munfakk* (*sh.*); در رفته *dar rafteh.*

Disloyal, نمك حرام *namak harám.*

Disloyalty, نمك بحرامی *namak be-harámi.*

Dismissal, رخصت *rukhsat* (*d.*).

Dismissed, مرخص *murakhas* (*k. sh.*); معزول *ma'zúl* (*k.*).

Dismount, فرود آمدن *farúd ámadan.*

Disobedience, نا فرمانی *ná farmání.*

Disobedient, نا فرمان *ná farmán;* غیرمطیع *gheyr mutí'.*

Disobey, سر در کشیدن *sar dar ksh.;* عاق شدن *'ákk sh.*

Disorder, تشویش *tashvísh;* *pa. p.*, (mentally), مخبط *mukhabbat.*

Despatch, *v.*, فرستادن *firistádan;* *n.*, نوشته *navishteh.*

Disperse, پراکندن *parágandan;* افشاندن *afshándan;* *pa. p.*, متفرق *mutafarrik* (*k.*).

Dispension, تفرق *tafarruk.*

Dispensive, نشری nashrí.

Displayed, منکشف munkashif (sh.).

Displaying, مکاشفه mukáshifah.

Displeased, کج خلق kaj khulk; دل آزرده dil ázardeh; ناخوش nákhúsh.

Displeasing, نا پسند ná pasand.

Displeasure, رنجش ranjesh (d.); دل کرانی dil geráni.

Disposition (of mind), مزاج mizáj; (of things), ترتیب tartíb (k.).

Dispossessed, بیدخل bídakhl.

Disputant, مباحث mubáhis.

Dispute, مباحثه mubaheseh (k.); قیل و قال kíl o kál (k.).

Disquietude, تشوش tashavvush.

Disregard, v., چشم پوشیدن cheshm púshídan.

Disrespect, بیحرمتی bihurmatí.

Dissatisfaction, سر کرانی sar geráni.

Dissatisfied, سر کران sar gerán (h.); غیر راضی ghair rází.

Dissection, تشریح tashríh (k.).

Dissemble, نازیدن názídan.

Dissimulation, بهانه baháneh (k.); مدارات mudárát (n.).

Dissipated, منتفی muntafí.

Dissipation, هتك hatk.

Dissolve, کداختن gadákhtan.

Distaff, دوکچه dúkcheh.

Distance, مسافت musáfat; دوری dúrí; فاصله fásileh.

Distant, بعید ba'íd; دور dúr.

Distich, بیت bait. Last — of ode, شاه بیت sháh bait.

Distil, چکاندن chakándan. — spirits, عرق کشیدن 'arak ksh.; pr. p., تقطیر taktír (k.).

Distiller, آبکار ábkár. —y, آبکاری ábkárí.

Distinct, متباین mutabáyin.

Distinction, امتیاز imtiyáz (k. y.); تفاوت tafávut (k.).

Distinguished, تشخص tashakhkhus; ممتاز mumtáz (sh.).

Distorted, ملوی malví (sh.).

Distracted, پریشان paríshán (h.); آشفته حال áshuftah hál. To be — شولیدن shúlídan.

Distress, n., مضایقه mazá-ikeh; رنجش ranjesh (y.); در مانده dar mándah; v. a., رنجانیدن ranjánídan; v. p., فرو ماندن farú mándan.

Distribution, تقسیم *taksím* (*k.*); مساهمت *musáhemat* (*n.*).
Distributor, قاسم *kásim.*
District, چکله *cheklah*; ولایت *viláyat*; کوره *kúrah.*
Disturbance, فتنه *fitnah*; غوغا *ghaughá.*
Disturbed, مشوش *mushavvash* (*sh.*); متغیر *mutaghayyir* (*sh.*). To be — در آشفتن *dar áshuftan.*
Disunited, فراق *farák.*
Disused, منسوخ *mansúkh.*
Ditch, خندك *khandak*; نهر *nahr*; گود *gaud.*
Ditto, ایضاً *aizan.*
Dive, غوطه کردن *ghautah k.*
Diver, غوطه خور *ghautah khur.*
Diversion, تفنن *tafannun*; تماشا *tamáshá*; (to one side), انحراف *inheráf* (*k.*).
Divided, منقسم *munkasim* (*k*); دو قسمت *dú kismat* (*k.*). — in two, دو نیم *dú ním.*
Dividend, مقسوم *maksúm.*
Divination, فال *fál* (*gr.*).
Divine, الهی *iláhí.*
Divinity, خدای *khudáí.*
Division, اقتسام *iktisám*; مقاسمه *mukásamah* (*k.*).

Divorce, طلاق *talák* (*d.*).
Divorced woman, مطلقه *mutal-lakeh.*
Divulged, مشاع *mushá'* (*k.*).
Divulging, اباحت *ibáhat* (*n.*).
Do, کردن *kerdan*; ساختن *sákhtan*; کار کردن *kár k.*
Dock, *v.*, ابتار کردن *ibtár k.*
Doctor, طبیب *tabíb*; حکیم *hakím.*
Doctrine, طریقه *taríkat*; مذهب *mazhab.*
Document, مستند *mustanad*; کاغذ *kághaz.*
Dog, سك *sag*; (pointer), طوله سك *túleh sag*; (hound), تازی *tází.* — star, شعری *sha'rí.*
Doleful, غمگین *ghamgín.*
Doll, عروسك *'arúsek.*
Dollar, ریال *riyál.*
Dolphin, دلفین *dulfín.*
Dolt, کودن *kaudan*; غبی *ghabí.*
Dome, گنبد *gumbad* (*gumbaz*).
Domestic, *n.*, نوکر *nokar*; *pl.*, خواص *khavvás*; *a.*, خانگی *khanagí.*
Dominance, تغلب *taghallub* (*n.*).

Dominion, تسلط *tasallut* ; استیلا *istílá*.

Donation, انعام *an'ám*.

Donkey, الاغ *ulágh* ; خر *khar*.

Doom, اجل *ajal*.

Door, در *dar* ; (large), دروازه *darvázeh*. To open the —, در وا کردن *dar vá k*. To shut the —, پیش کردن *písh k*.

Doorkeeper, دربان *darbán*.

Dormitory, خوابگاه *khábgáh*.

Dot, نقطه *nuḳteh*.

Double, دو باره *dú báreh* ; دوتا *dútá* (*k.*). — tooth, ضرس *zirs*.

Doubt, اشتباه *ishtibáh* ; شك *shakk* (*dsh.*) ; گمان *gemán* (*dsh.*) ; شبهه *shubheh*.

Doubtful, مشکوك *mashkúk*.

Doubtless, بی شك و شبهه *bí shakh o shubheh*.

Dough, خمیر *khamír*.

Dove, کبوتر *kabútar* ; قمری *ḳumrí*.

Down, از پای *az páí* ; پائین *páyín* ; زیر *zír*.

Dowry, مهره *mahreh*.

Doze, چرت *chart* (*z.*).

Dracunculus, عاقر قرحا *'áḳir ḳarhá*.

Dragon, اژدها *izhdehá*.

Dragon's-blood, دم الاخوین *dam ul akhavain*.

Drain, بدر رو *badar ro* ; آبریز *ábríz* ; آبشی *áb shí*.

Draper, بزاز *bazzáz*.

Draught (drink), جرعه *jur'ah* ; (air), باد *bad* ; (writing), سواد *savád* (*k.*) ; (money), برات *barát*.

Draughts, نرد *nard*.

Draw, *v.*, (pull), کشیدن *keshídan* ; (a picture), تصویر کردن *tasvír k*.

Drawers, زیر شلوار *ziri shalvar*.

Drawing, نقشه *naksheh* (*ksh.*).

Dread, خوف *khauf*.

Dreadful, هولناك *haulnák*.

Dream, خواب *kháb* (دیدن *dídan*) ; رویا *rúyá* (*dídan*).

Dregs, درد *durd*.

Dress, *n.*, لباس *libás* ; پوشاك *púshák*. — of honour, خلعت *khil'at*. A complete —, یك دست جامه *yek dasti jámeh* ; *v.*, پوشیدن *púshídan*.

Dried, خشك *khushk*.

Drill, مشق *mashḳ* (*k. d.*).

Drink, *v.*, خوردن *khurdan* ; نوشیدن *núshídan*.

Drinkable, مشروب *mashrúb*.

Drinking, شرب sharb.
Drinker, نوشنده núshandeh.
Dripping, شرشر sharshar; تقاطر taḳátur (k.).
Drive, v., راندن rándan; (away), رد کردن radd k.
Drollery, مسخرکی maskharagí.
Drop, n., قطره ḳatreh; چکه chakkeh (k.); v., چکیدن chakídan; pr. p., قطران ḳatrán.
Dropsical, مستسقی mustasḳí.
Dropsy, استسقا istisḳá.
Dross, خبث khubs.
Drought, خشکی khushki; خشك سالی khushk sálí.
Drowned, غرق gharḳ (k. sh.).
Drowsy, وسن vasin; خواب آلوده kháb álúdeh.
Drugs, ادویه adviyeh.
Druggist, دارو فروش dárú ferúsh.
Drum, طبل tabl (z.); دهل duhul (z.); نقاره naḳḳáreh.
Drummer, نقارچی naḳḳár chí.
Drunk, مست mast.
Drunkard, رند rind.
Drunkenness, مستی mastí.
Dry, خشك khushk (k.).

Dryness, یبوست yabúsat.
Dual, تثنیه tasniyeh.
Duck, اوردك úrdak; بط batt.
Due, حق haḳḳ.
Dumb, کنك gung; لال lál; بیزبان bízabán.
Dun coloured, اشهب ashhab.
Dunce, بلید balíd.
Dung, چرکین chirkín; که goh; (of cows), سرکین sargín; (of sheep), پشکل pishkil; (dried-fuel), پاچك páchek.
Dunghill, مزبله mazbaleh.
Durable, استوار ustuvár; پایدار páídár; قایم ḳáim.
Duration, دوام davám.
During, مادام mádám.
Dusk, تاریکی táríkí.
Dust, خاك khák; کرد ǵird; غبار ghubár.
Duty, تکلیف taklíf; (religious), فرض farz.
Dwarf, تنبل timbal.
Dwell, ساکن بودن sákin b.; pr. p., مقیم muḳím (b.).
Dye, رنك rang (z.); pa. p., منصبغ munsabagh.
Dyer, رنك زیر rang ríz; صباغ sabbágh.

Dyeing the hair or nails, خضب *khazb* (*k.*).

Dying, فوات *favát* (*h.*).

Dynasty, طبقه *tabakah*; دوله *dauleh.*

Dysentery, جريان شكم *jarayáni shakam*; اسهال *as-hál.*

Dyspepsia, معده سنگی *mi'dah sangî.*

E.

Each one, هريك *har yek.*

Eager, آرزومند *árzúmand*; مشتاق *mushták.*

Eagle, عقاب *'ukáb*; دال *dál.*

Ear, گوش *gúsh.* —ring, گوشواره *gúshvárah*; آويزه *avizeh.* —of wheat, خوشه *khúsheh.* The cavity of the ear, بنا گوش *biná-gúsh.* —wax, چرك گوش *chirk i gúsh.*

Early, زود *zúd.* — in the morning, على الصباح *'ala ssa-báh*; صبح زود *subhi zúd.*

Earn, مداخل كردن *mudákhil k.*

Earnest, جداً *jiddan.* —money, بيعانه *bai'ánah.*

Earth, خاك *khák*; زمين *zamín.*

Earthen, گلی *gilí.* — ware سفالی *sufálí.*

Earthquake, زلزله *zilzilah.*

Earthworms, خراطين *kharátín.*

Earthly, طينی *tíní.*

Ease, آسانی *ásání*; آسودگی *ásúdagí*; ارام *árám* (*gr.*); آرامش *árámish.*

Easily, آسان *ásán.*

East, مشرق *mashrek*; مطلع *matla'*; شرق *shark.*

Eastern, شرقی *sharkí.*

Eat, خوردن *khúrdan.*

Eatables, خوراكی *khúrákí.*

Eaves, شادروان *shádurván.*

Ebb, جزر *jazr.*

Ebony, آبنوس *ábnús.*

Ebullition, جوش *júsh* (*k.*).

Echo, بنت الجبل *bintu 'ljabal.*

Eclipse (sun), كسوف *kusúf*; — (moon), خسوف *khusúf.*

Economical, كمخرج *kam kharj.*

Economy, خانه داری *kháneh dárí.*

Ecstacy, وجد *wajd*; شعف *sha'f.*

Eddy, موج *mauj.*

Edge, دم *dam*; لب *lab.*

Edging, سنجاف *sanjáf* or زنجف; *zinjaf.*

Edict, امر *amr.*

Edifice, عمارت *'imárat.*

Educate, پروردن *parvardan.*

Education, تربیت *tarbíyet* (*k.*); ترتیب *tartíb* (*k.*).
Eel, مار ماهی *már i máhí.*
Effacement, محو *mahv* (*k.*); ابطال *ibtál* (*k.*).
Effect, *v.*, بسر بردن *basar burdan.* To take —, در گرفتن *dar giriftan*; *n.*, تاثیر *taa'sír.*
Effecting, اجراء *ijrá.*
Effectual, کار گر *kárgar.*
Effeminacy, نرمی *narmí.*
Effervescence, جوش *júsh* (*k.*).
Efficacious, جایگیر *jáy-gír*; پیشرفت *pish-raft.*
Effigy, صورت *súrat.*
Effort, جد *jidd*; جهد *jahd*; اجتهاد *ijtihád*; کوشش *kúshish.*
Effrontery, گستاخی *gustákhí.*
Effusion, ریزش *rízish*; انزال *inzál*; (of blood), سفك *safk.*
Egg, تخم مرغ *tukhmi murgh.* Fried — خاگینه *khágína.* — shell, پوست *púst.*
Egg plant, بادنجان *bádinján.*
Egotism, انانیت *ananíyet.*
Egresses, مخارج *makhárij.*
Egypt, مصر *misr.*
Eight, هشت *hasht.*
Eighteen, هژده *hizhdah.*

Eighth, هشتم *hashtum.*
Eightieth, هشتادم *hashtádum.*
Eighty, هشتاد *hashtád.*
Either—or, یا ـ یا *yá—yá.*
Eject, بدر کردن *badar k.*
Ejectment, اخراج *ikhráj* (*k.*).
Elapse, گذشتن *guzashtan.*
Elapsed, ما فات *má fát*; منقضی *munkazí.*
Elbow, آرنج *áranj.*
Elder, *n.*, شیخ *sheikh*; *a.* مهتر *mehtar.* — tree, خمان *khumán.*
Elders, بزرگان *buzurgán.*
Eldest son, پسر امجد *pisar i amjed.*
Elected, مجتبی *mujtabá.*
Election, انتخاب *intikháb* (*n.*).
Electricity, کاه ربای *káh-rubái.*
Elegance, لطافت *latáfat*; جمال *jamál.* — of style, انشاء *inshá'.*
Elegant, لطیف *latíf*; نغز *naghz*; قشنك *kashang.*
Elegy, مرثیه *marsíyah.*
Element, عنصر *'unsur*; *pl.* عناصر *'anásir*; اصول *usúl.* The four — اخشیجان *akhshíján.*
Elementary, عنصری *'unsurí.*

Elephant, فیل *fíl.* — driver, فیلبان *fíl-bán.*

Elephantiasis, جذام *juzám.*

Elevate, برداشتن *bardáshtan*; افراختن *afrákhtan*; *pa. p.* مرتفع *murtafi'*; *pr. p.* نص *nass.*

Elevation, ارتفاع *irtifá'* (*k.*).

Eleven, یازده *yázdah.*

Eleventh, یازدهم *yázdahum.*

Elicit, استدراك کردن *istidrák k.*

Elision, حذف *hazf.*

Elixir, اکسیر *iksír.*

Elk, کوزن *gauzan.*

Ell, گز *gaz.*

Elm, نارون *nárvan.*

Elongate, دراز کشیدن *diráz ksh.*

Elopement, رم *ram.*

Eloquence, سخن آرای *sukhan-árái*; فصاحت *fasáhat*; بلاغت *balághat*; خوش گفتار *khush-guftár.*

Eloquent, فصیح *fasíh*; سخن دان *sukhan-dán*; بلیغ *balígh*; تر زبان *tar-zaban.*

Emaciated, مهزول *mahzúl.*

Emanation, صدور *sudúr* (*k.*).

Emancipate, آزاد کردن *ázád k.*

Embalm, تحنیط کردن *tahnít k.*

Embankment, پلبندی *pul-bandí.*

Embark, شوار شدن *sowwár sh.*

Embarrassed, دست پچه *dast pácheh* (*sh.*). To be — گیر افتادن *gír uftádan.*

Embassy, سفارت *sifárat.*

Embellishment, پیرایش *pairáyish*; آرایش *áráyish.*

Embers, اخگر *akhgar.* Live — زغال *zughál.*

Emblem, علامت *'alámat.*

Embrace, *n.* آغوش *ághúsh* (*ksh.*); *v.* معانقه کردن *mu'ánakah k.*; بغل کردن *baghal k.*

Embrasure, بارو *bárú.*

Embrocation, ضماد *zimád.*

Embroider, ترازیدن *tarázídan.*

Embroiderer, چکن دوز *chakin-dúz*; مطرز *mutarriz.*

Emdroidery, زر دوزی *zar dúzí.*

Embryo, جنین *janín.*

Emendator, مصحح *musahhih.*

Emerald, زمرد *zumurrud.* — coloured, زمردین *zumurrudín.*

Emery, سنباده *sumbádeh.*

Emetic, مقیي *mukaiyí*; دوائی قی *davá i kay.*

Emigration, جلای وطن *jalá i*

vatan; نقل مکان *naḳl i makán* (*k.*).
Eminence (place), تپه *tappeh*.
— (rank), مشارفت *mushárafat*; سر بلندی *sar-bulandí*; سرفرازی *sar-farází*.
Eminent, سر بلند *sar-buland*; سر افراز *sar-afráz*; والا *válá*.
Emission, نطف *natf* (*k.*).
Emolument, مداخل *mudákhil*.
Emotion, اضطراب *izteráb*.
Emperor, ایمپراطور *ímperátúr*; شاهنشاه *sháhansháh*; قیصر *ḳaisar*; خاقان *kháḳán*.
Emphasis, تاءکید *taakíd*.
Empire, پادشاهی *pádsháhí*; مملکة *mamlakat*; سلطنت *saltanat*.
Employed, مشتغل *mushtaghal* (*sh.*); مشغول *mashghúl* (*k.*).
Employment, شغل *shughl* (*d.*).
Empty, تهی *tihí* (*k.*); خالی *kháli* (*k.*).
Emulating, مواطات *muvátát* (*n.*); مجاهده *mujáhedeh* (*k.*).
Emulation, غیرت *ghairat*.
Enamel, مینا *míná* (*n.*).
Enameller, مینا کار *míná-kár*.
Enamoured, دل آویخته *dil-ávíkhtah*; آشفته *áshufta*.

Encampment, خیمه *haimeh* (*z.*); اردو *urdú* (*z.*).
Enchanter, جادوگر *jádúgar*.
Enchantment, سحر *sihr*.
Enclosure (place), احاطه *iháteh* (*k.*); (letter), ملفوف *malfúf*; مندرج *mundrij*.
Enconium, مداحی *maddáhí*.
Encounter, تقابل *taḳábul*.
Encouragement, خاطر داری *khátir-dárí*.
End, اتمام *itmám*; انجام *anjám*; آخر *ákhar*; انتهاء *intihá*; (extremity), غایت *gháyat*; سر *sar*. — of a day's journey, سر منزل *sar i manzil*. — of the month, سلخ *salkh*.
Endeavour, سعی *sa'i* (*k.*).
Endive, کاسنی *kásní*.
Endless, بیپایان *bípáyán*.
Endorsement, امضا *imzá* (*k.*).
Endowment, وقف *vaḳf*.
Endurance, تحمل *tahammul* (*k.*); مقاسات *muḳását*. May it endure! لا زال *lá zál*.
Enemy, دشمن *dushman*; عدو *'adúv*; خصم *khasam*. A secret —, کاشح *kashih*.
Energy, قوة *kuvvat*.
Enervated, موهون *mauhún*.

Enfeebled, متضعف mutaza'if.
Enfranchise, آزاد کردن ázád k.
Engage, v. t., معین کردن mu'ayyan k. — in, v., تن دادن tan dádan.
Engaged in, to be, در پیوستن dar paivastan.
Engaged, مشغول mashghúl (sh.).
Engagement, کار kár ; وعده va'deh (dsh.).
Engine, منجنیق manjaník.
English, انکلیز or انکلیس Ingilís or Ingilíz.
Engrave, کندن kandan.
Engraver, نقاش nakkásh ; حکاك hakkák.
Engravings, نقوش nukúsh.
Enigma, لغز laghz ; معمی mu'ammá.
Enjoined (by law), مفروض mafrúz.
Enjoy, بر خوردن bar khúrdan.
Enjoying, متمتع mutamatti' (sh.) ; عیش 'aish (k.).
Enjoyment, تمتع tamattu' ; حظ hezz (k.) ; لذت lízzat (ksh.).
Enlarge, بزرك کردن buzurg (k.).
Enlightenment, روشنایی rúshnái (n.).

Enlist, v. t., جمع آوری کردن jam' ávarí k. ; v. n., سرباز شدن sarbáz sh.
Enmity, عداوت 'adáwat ; دشمنی dushmaní.
Ennobled, مشرف musharraf.
Ennobling ; تشریف tashríf.
Enough, بس bas. It is —, کفایت کرد kefáyat kard.
Enquire, سوال کردن suál k.
Enraged, غضبان ghazbán.
Enshrouding (the dead), تکفین takfín (k.).
Ensign (man), نائب دوم náib i duvum.
Ensigns, اعلام a'lám.
Entangled, ژولیده zhúlídah.
Enter, در آمدن dar ámadan ; در شدن dar sh. ; داخل شدن dákhil sh.
Enterprise, بسیج besíj.
Entertainment, ضیافت ziyáfat ; مهمانی mihmání.
Enticing, محرض muharriz (n.).
Entire, یك دست yak-dast ; تمام tammám ; کل kull.
Entirely, بالکل bilkull.
Entrails, روده rúdeh.
Entrance, دخول dukhúl.
Entreat, التماس کردن iltímás k.

Entrenchments, استحکامات *istiḥkámát.*

Entrust, حواله کردن *hawáleh k.*; سپردن *sipurdan*; *pa. p.*, مفوض *mufavvaz.*

Entry and exit, ولوج و خروج *vulúj u khurúj.*

Enumeration, تعدید *ta'díd.*

Envelope, لفافه *lifáfah.*

Envelop, فرا گرفتن *fará girifttan*; *pa. p.*, ملفوف *malfúf.*

Envied, محسود *maḥsúd.*

Envious, حاسد *ḥásid*; حسود *ḥasúd*; رشك خور *rashk-khur.*

Environs, اطراف *aṭráf*; حوالی *ḥawálí*; نواحی *nawáḥí.*

Envoy extraordinary and minister plenipotentiary, وزیر مختار *vazír i mukhtár.*

Envy, *v.*, حسد بردن *ḥasad burdan.*

Ephemeris, زیج *zích.*

Epilepsy, صرع *sar'*. Afflicted with —, مصروع *masrú'.*

Epistle, نامه *náma*; مرسله *mursalah.*

Epitaph, کتابه *kitábeh.*

Epithet, صفت *sifat.*

Epoch, تاریخ *tárikh.*

Equal, *n.*, هم پهلو *ham-pahlú*; همتا *ham-tá*; *a.*, برابر *barábar*; سوی *savíy*; متساوی *mutasáví*; یك انداز *yak-andáz*. — to, معادل *mu'ádil.*

Equalising, تعدیل *ta'díl* (*k.*).

Equality, سویت *savíyet*; تسویة *tasvíyet*; یستوی *yastaví.*

Equation, مساوات *musávát.*

Equator, خط استواء *khatt i istiwá.*

Equilibrium, موازنة *muvázanat.*

Equipment, تجهیز *tajhíz* (*k.*).

Equity, معادلت *mu'ádalat*; انصاف *insáf.*

Equivalent, همقدر *ham-ḳadr.*

Equivocation, طفره *tafrih* (*z.*).

Era, تاریخ *tárikh.*

Eradicate, از بیخ کندن *az bíkh kandan.*

Erasing, محو *maḥv* (*k.*).

Erect, *a.*, منتصب *muntasab*; راست *rást*; *v.*, فرازیدن *farázídan*; *pa. p.*, منصوب *mansúb* (*sh.*); *pr. p.*, نصب *nasb* (*k.*); تعمیر *ta'mír* (*k.*)

Erection, عمارت *'imárat* (*k.*).

Ermine, قاقم *ḳáḳum.*

Errand, پیغام *paighám.*

Error, غلط *ghalat* (*k.*); سهو *sahv* (*k.*); گمراهی *gum-ráhí.*

Eructation, چشاء *jushá'* ; اروغ *árúgh.*

Erudition, دانش *dánish.*

Eruption (skin), آبله *ábileh.*

Erysipelas, بثور *busúr.*

Escape, *v.*, رستن *rastan* ; *n.*, رها *rahá* (*y.*); نجات *naját* (*y.*) ; فرار *ferár* (*k.*).

Escort, بدرقه *badrakeh.*

Especial, مخصوص *makhsus.* —ly, خصوصاً *khusúsan* ; على الخصوص *'ala 'lkhusús.*

Essence, خلاصة *khulásat* ; ذات *zát* ; جوهر *jauhar.*

Established, قرار داد *karár-dád* ; بر قرار *bar karár* (*k.*).

Establishing, مثبت *musab-bit* (*k.*) ; اثبات *isbát* (*n.*).

Establishment, اقامت *ikámat* ; ابقاء *ibká.* — (household), عيال *'ayyál.*

Estate, مال *mál* ; نصاب *nisáb.*

Esteem, اعتبار *i'tibár* (*dsh.*).

Estimate, بر اورد *bar-ávard* (*k.*) ; اندازه *andázah.* ; *pa. p.*, مشخص *mushakhkhas.*

Estrangement, دوری *dúrí* (*k.*).

Et cetera, وغيره *vaghairah.*

Eternal, ابدی *abadí* ; خالد *khálid* ; قيوم *kaiyúm* ; جاويد *jávíd.* —ly, ابداً *abadan.*

Eternity, ابد *abad* ; خلد *khuld* ; سرمد *sarmad* ; ازل *azal* ; بقاء *baká.*

Ethics, اخلاق *akhlák.*

Ethiopian, زنگی *zangí.*

Etiquette, آداب *ádáb.*

Etymology, اشتقاق *ishtikák.*

Euclid, اقليدس *Iklídas.*

Eulogist, مادح *mádih* ; مداح *maddáh.*

Eunuch, خواجه سرا *kh'ája-sará* ; خوجه *khojah* ; خصی *khusí.*

Euphrates, فرات *Furát.*

Europe, فرنگستان *Firangistán.*

European, فرنگی *Firangí.*

Evacuation, تخليه *takhliyeh* (*k.*).

Evade, كناره جستن *kinároh jastan.*

Evaporation, نشف *nashf* (*k.*).

Evasion, حيله *híleh* ; بهانه *bahá-neh* ; تجاهل *tajáhul.*

Even (number), جفت *juft.*

Evening, شام *shám* ; عشی *'ashíy.*

Event, ما وقع *má vaka'* ; ما جری *má jará* ; سر گذشت *sar-guzasht* ; حادثه *hádisa* ; واقعه *váki'ah.*

Ever (any time), هیچوقت *hích vakt.* — (no time), هرگز *hargiz.* — (all times), همیشه *hamísheh.*

Every, every one, هر *har.*

Every kind, هر جنس *har-jins.*

Everywhere, هر جا *har-já.*

Eviction, دفع *daf'* (*k.*).

Evidence, وضوح *wazúh ;* شهادت *shehádat.*

Evident, آشکار *áshkár ;* پدید *padíd.* —ly, ظاهراً *záhiran.*

Evil, بلاء *balá ;* بد کاری *bad-kárí.* The king's —, یرقان *yarakán.* — doer, تبه کار *tabah-kar.* — speaker, بدگو *badgú.* — suggestion, اغواء *ighwá.*

Ewe, میش *mísh.*

Ewer, آفتابه *áftábah.*

Exact, صحیح *sahíh;* درست *durust.* — ly, بعینه *bi'ainihi.*

Exacting an oath, تحلیف *tahlíf* (*k.*).

Exactions, تکالیف *takálíf.*

Exaggeration, اغراق *ighrák* (*k.*).

Exalt, آفراشتن *áfráshtan ;* افراختن *afrákhtan.*

Exaltation, فرازی *farází.*

Exalted, مرفوع *marfú';* سر افراز *sar-afráz.*

Examination, امتحان *imtihán* (*k.*).

Example, مثل *masal ;* تمثیل *tamsíl.* To give an — مثل زدن *masal z.* For — مثلاً *masalan ;* فی المثل *fí'l masal.*

Excavation, حفر *hafr* (*k.*).

Exceed, از حد گذشتن *az hadd guzashtan.*

Exceedingly, بغایت *bigháyat.*

Excellence, فضیلت *fazílat* (*dsh.*) ; فضل *fazl ;* براعت *bará'at.*

Excellency, جناب *janáb.*

Excellent, افضل *afzal ;* ارجمند *arjmand.*

Except, جز *juz ;* بجز *bajuz ;* مگر *magar ;* بغیر *bighaír.*

Exception, استثناء *istisná.*

Exceptional, مستثنی *mustasní.*

Excess, افراط *ifrát ;* بیشی *bíshí ;* تفریط *tafrít* (*k.*).

Excessive, مفرط *mufrit.*

Exchange, *n.* ابدال *ibdál ;* مبادله *mubádalah* (*k.*) ; عوض *ivaz* (*k.*).

Excite, انگیختن *angíkhtan; pa.p.* مولع *múla'.*

Excitement, تغير *taghayyur.*

Exciting thirst, معطش *mu'tish.*

Exclamation, بانك *báng* (*z.*).

Excluded, محروم *mahrúm* (*s.*); بيدخل *bí-dakhl.*

Excommunication, لعنت *la'nat.*

Excoriating, قاشر *ḳáshir.*

Excrement, گوه *gúh*; غائط *gháit.* — of the eye, ششك *shushk.*

Excruciating, دل خراش *dil-kharásh.*

Excusable, معذور *ma'zúr.*

Excuse, *v. t.* عذر نهادن *'uzr nihádan.* — oneself, عذر خواستن *'uzr khástan*; *n.* معذره *ma'zarah*; عذر *'uzr*; پوزش *púzish.*

Execrable, لعين *la'ín*; مكروه *makrúh.*

Execration, ملاعنة *mulá'anat.*

Execute (kill), كشتن *kushtan.*

Executing a business, اجراى كار *ijrá i kár.*

Executioner, جلاد *jallád.*

Executor, وصى *vasíy.*

Exempt from, برى *barí*; معافى *mu'áfá* (*s.*).

Exercise, مشق *mashḳ* (*d.*); — (walk), گردش *gardesh* (*k.*).

Exertion, مجاهده *mujáhedeh* (*k.*); كوشش *kúshesh* (*k.*).

Exhaling, تنسم *tanassum* (*k.*).

Exhausted, خسته *khasteh* (*sh. k.*).

Exhibition, نمايش *namáyish.*

Exhilarated, منفرح *munfarih*; سرخوش *sar-khush.*

Exhilaration, تفريح *tafríh.*

Exhilarating, مفرح *mufarrih.*

Exhortation, موعظت *mau'izat,* (*n.*); وعظ *va'z* (*k.*).

Exigency, اقتضآء *iḳtizá.*

Exiling, تغريب *taghríb* (*k.*).

Exist, بودن *búdan.*

Existence, بودنى *búdaní*; وجود *vujúd*; هستى *hastí.*

Existent, موجود *maujúd.*

Exit, مخرج *makhraj.*

Exorbitant, گذاف *gazáf.*

Expand, گشادن *gushádan.*

Expect, منتظر هستن *muntazer h.*

Expectation, انتظار *intizár* (*ksh.*); ترقب *taraḳḳub*; توقع *tavaḳḳu'* (*dsh.*).

Expecting, متوقع *muta-vaḳḳi'* (*h.*).

Expediency, التزام *iltizám,*

Expedient, مناسب *munásib.*

Expedite, حرکت کردن *hara-kat k.*

Expedition, ایلغار *elghár.*

Expel, بیرون کردن *bírún k.*

Expend, خرج کردن *kharj k.*

Expending, اصراف *isráf* (*n.*).

Expenditure, انفاق *infáḳ*; نفقه *nafaḳah.*

Expense, خرج *kharj*; *pl.* اخراجات *ikhráját.*

Expensive, گران *girán.*

Experience, *v.*, آزمودن *ázmúdan*; *n.* خبرت *khubrat*; آزمایش *ázmáyish*; وقوف *vuḳúf*; تجربة *tajribat.*

Experienced, تجربه کار *tajribah-kár*; جهان دیده *jahán-dídah.*

Expert, سبك دست *sabuk-dast*; چیره دست *chírah-dast*; چالاك *chálák.*

Expertness, چیره دستی *chírah-dastí.*

Expiation, کفاره *kaffáreh.*

Expiration, انقضاء *inḳizá* (*sh.*).

Explained, مشروح *mashrúh* (*sh.*).

Explaining, مبین *mubayyin* (*s*); تبیین *tabyín* (*k.*).

Explanation, شرح *sharh*; بیان *bayán.*

Explicitly and openly, شرح و بسط *sharh u bast.*

Explode, آتش گرفتن *átesh gr.*

Exploration, استکشاف *istik-sháf* (*n.*).

Explore, گرائیدن *garáídan.*

Exposition, اظهار *izhár* (*k.*)

Expressed (juice, &c.), معصور *ma'súr.*

Expression, تلفظ *talaffuz.*

Expulsion, اخراج *ikhráj.*

Exquisite, نفاست *nafásat.*

Extempore, بدیهی *badíhí*; مبده *mubdah.*

Extend, دراز کشیدن *diráz ksh.*; *pa. p.* ممدود *mamdúd*; پهن *pahn.*

Extension, اطالت *itálat*; طول *túl* (*ksh.*); مد *madd*; توسیع *tausí'.*

Exterior, ظاهری *záhirí.*

Extermination, استیصال *istísál* (*k.*).

External, خارج *khárij.* —ly, ظاهراً *záhiran.*

Extinct, منقرض *munḳariz.*

Extinction, انقراض *inḳiráz* (*y.*).

Extinguish, خاموش کردن *khámúsh k.*

Extol, تعریف کردن *ta'aríf k.*

Extort, بزور كرفتن bezúr gr.
Extortion, سختگیری sakhtgírí ; تعسف ta'assuf (k.).
Extract, بر هیختن bar híkhtan ; pr. p., استخراج istikhráj (k.).
Extraction, قلع kal' (k.).
Extraordinary, عجب 'ajab.
Extravagance, سرف saraf.
Extravagant, مسرف musrif ; فضول fuzúl.
Extreme, اقصی aksá. —ly, بغایت bi-gháyet.
Extremity, پایان páyán ; نهایت niháyet.
Exudation, تراوش tarávish.
Exude, تراویدن tarávídan.
Exultant, شاد کام shád kám.
Eye, چشم chashm. Evil—, چشم بد chashm i bad. Squint-eyed, لوچ lúch. The eye-ball or pupil, مردمك mardumak. Eyebrow, ابرو abrú. Eye-glass, اینك ainek. Eyelashes, مژكان mazhagán. Eyelid, جفن jafn.

F.

Fable, فسانه fasánah ; حکایت hikáyat.
Fabric, بناء biná.
Fabulous, کاذب kázib.
Fabricated, ساخته sákhtah.
Face, رو rú, or روی rúy.
Face to face, روارو rú-á-rú.
Facetious, شوخ shúkh. —ness, شوخی shúkhí.
Facilitated, میسر muyassar (h.).
Facility, آسانی ásání ; سهولت suhúlat.
Facing, روبرو, rú be rú ; مواجهة muwájahat ; حقیقت hakíkat.
Fact, کار kár. In —, الحق al hakk.
Factory, کار خانه kár kháneh.
Faculty, اقتدار iktidár.
Fade, خشکیدن khushkídan ; pa. p., پژمرده pazhmurdeh (sh.).
Failing in duty, مقصر mukassar (sh.).
Faint, بیهوش bí-húsh (sh.).
Faintness, غش ghash (k.).
Fair, خوش رو khush rú.
Fair dealing, پاکباز pák-báz.
Fairy, پری parí.
Faith (religion), مذهب mazhab. Article of —, عقیدة 'akídat ; pl. عقائد 'akáid ; (confidence), باور bávar ; اعتقاد i'tikád. Good —, وفا vafá. — ful, وفادار vafá-dár ; ایماندار

ímán-dár. The —ful, مسلمين *muslimín*. —less, بيوفا *bí-vafá*.

Falcon, قوش *kúsh* ; شاهين *sháhín* ; شهباز *shahbáz*.

Fall, *n.* سقوط *sukút* (*k.*) ; *v.* افتادن *uftádan*. — in love, عاشق شدن *'áshik sh.*

Fallow, موات *mavát*.

False, باطل *bátil* ; دغل *daghal* ; جعلى *ja'lí*. — coin, قلب *kalb*. — politeness, تواضع سمرقندى *tavázu'i Samarkandí*. — reports, اراجيف *arájíf*. —hood, دروغ *durúgh* (*gf.*).

Falsified, مزور *muzavvar*.

Fame, نامورى *námvarí*. Good — نام نيك *nám i ník*.

Familiar, *a.* مالوف *maalúf* ; *n.* مونس *mu'nis*.

Familiarity, الفت *ulfat* ; موانست *muvánisat*.

Familiarized, متألف *mutaallif*.

Family, اهل بيت *ahl i beit* ; خانواده *khánavádah* ; عيال *'iyál*.

Famine, قحط سال *kaht-sál*.

Famous, نامدار *nám-dár* ; مشهور *mashhúr* ; نام آور *nám-ávar*. To become —, نام آوردن *nám-ávardam*.

Fan, مروحه *mirvahah* ; باد بزن *bád-bezan*.

Fanatic, متعصب *muta'assib*.

Fanaticism, تعصب *ta'assub*.

Fancy, *n.* خيال *khayál* (*bs.*).

Fanciful, خيالى *khayálí*.

Far, دور *dúr*. How far? تا كجا *tá kujá*.

Fare, طعام *ta'ám*.

Farewell, وداع *vidá'* (*k.*) ; پدرود *padrúd* (*k.*).

Farm, اجاره *ijárah* (*k.*).

Farmer, مستاجر *mustájar*.

Farrier, نعل بند *na'l band*.

Farrier's twitch, پوز مال *púz-mál*.

Fascinated, مفتون *maftún*.

Fascinating, سحر آميز *sihr-ámíz*.

Fascination, افسون *afsún* (*k.*).

Fashions, اطوار *atvár*.

Fast, *v.* روزه گرفتن *rúzah giriftan* ; *a.* زود *zúd* ; (of watch) ; تند *tund*.

Fastened, مضبوط *mazbút* (*k.*).

Fasting, روزه *rúzah*. To avoid —, روزه خوردن *rúzah kh.* One who fasts, صائم *sáïm*.

Fat, *n.* پيه *píyah* ; چرب *charb* ;

n. فربه *farbih* (*s.*) ; سمین *samín.*

Fatal, مهلك *muhlek.*

Fate, تقدیر *taḳdír.* — and destiny, قضا و قدر *ḳazá o ḳadar* ; قسمت *ḳismat.*

Fated, مقدور *maḳdúr.*

Father, پدر *pidar* ; بابا *bábá* ; والد *wálid.* A father-in-law, خسر *khusur.* —ly, پدرانه *pidaránah.*

Fatigue, ماندگی *mándagí* ; خستگی *khastagí* ; تعب *ta'b.*

Fatigued, مانده *mándah.* To be —, در ماندن *dar-mándan.*

Fatness, فربهی *farbihí.*

Fatted, پرواری *parvárí.*

Fault, تقصیر *taḳsír* ; غلط *ghalat* (*k.*) ; عیب *'aib* ; گناه *gunáh.*

Favour, انعام *in'ám* ; لطف *lutf* (*k.*) ; التفات *iltifát* (*y.*) ; توجه *tavajjuh.*

Favourite, مصاحب *musáhib.*

Fawn, آهو بره *áhú-barah.*

Fayence, کاشی *káshí.*

Fear, *n.* ترس *tars.* خوف *khauf* ; بیم *bím* ; باك *bák* ; *v.* ترسیدن *tarsídan* ; هراسیدن *hirásídan.*

Fearful, ترسو *tarsú.*

Fearing, هراسان *hirásán.*

Fearless, بی باك *bí-bák.*

Feast, ضیافت *ziyáfat.* — at the end of the fast of Ramazán, عید فطر *'íd i fatr.* — of the nativity (of Mohammed), عید مولود *'íd i maulúd.* — of Sacrifices, عید قربان *'íd i ḳurbán.*

Feather, پر *par* ; (longest feather in the wing), شهپر *shah-par.*

Feeble, ضعیف *za'íf.*

Feed, *v.* خورانیدن *khúránídan* ; (cattle) چرا کردن *cherá k.*

Feeling, حس *hiss* (*k.*). The sense of —, لامسه *lámisah.*

Feign, بهانه کردن *baháneh k.*

Felicity, سعادت *sa'ádat.*

Fellow (to), زوج *zauj.* Contemptible —, مردك *mardak.* — servants, خواجه تاش *kh'ájah - tásh.* — villager, همدیهی *ham-díhí.*

Felt, *n.* نمد *namad* ; *a.* (perceived), محسوس *mahsús.*

Female, ماده *mádah.*

Feminine, مونث *mu'annas.*

Fence, احاته *ihátah.*

Fennel, شبت *shebit.*

Fenu-greek, حلبه *hulbah.*

Fermentation, جوش *júsh* (*k.*).
Fermented, مخمر *mukhammar.*
Fern, ثمامه *samámeh.*
Ferocious, وحشی *vahshí.*
Ferret, راسو *rású.*
Ferry, گذار *guzár.* — boat, کشتی گذاره *keshtí i guzárah.*
Fertile, خصیب *khasíb*; بارور *bárvar.*
Festival, عید *'íd.*
Festivity, شادی *shádí.*
Fetch, آوردن *ávardan.*
Fetid, گنده *gandah.*
Fetter, غل *ghull*; پای بند *pái-band.*
Fever, تب *tap* or *tab.* High —, تب محرق *tap i muhriḳ.* Hectic —, تب دق *tap i diḳḳ.* Intermittent —, تب نوبت *tapi naubat.* Tertian —, تب غب *tap i ghibb.* Quartain —, تب ربع *tap i rub'.*
Few, کم *kam*; قلیل *ḳalíl.* A —, چندی *chandí*; بعضی *ba'zí.* A — people, تنی چند *taní chand.*
Fibre, ریشه *ríshah.*
Fickleness, تلون *talavvun.*
Fictitious, نقلی *naḳlí.*
Fidelity, وفاداری *vafá-dárí.*

Fie! اف *uff.*
Fief, سیور غال *suyúr-ghál.*
Field (for sowing), مزرع *mazra'*; (sown), کشت *kisht.* — of battle, معرکه *ma'rikah*; نبرد گاه *naburd-gáh*
Fierce, شرزه *sharzah*; درنده *darrandeh.*
Fiery, آتشی *átishí.*
Fife, نی *ney.*
Fifteen, پانزده *pánzdah.*
Fifth, پنجم *panjum.*
Fiftieth, پنجاهم *panjáhum.*
Fifty, پنجاه *panjáh.*
Fig, انجیر *anjír.*
Fight, جنگ *jang* (*k.*).
Figure, شکل *shakl.*
Filbert-nut, فندق *fanduḳ.*
File, سوهان *súhán.*
Filings, برادہ *burádah.*
Fill, پر کردن *pur k.*
Filling up, املاء *imlá* (*n.*).
Fillet, کلاخ *kalákh.*
Filly, کره *kurreh.*
Film on the eye, ناخنه *ná-khunah.*
Filter, *v.* افشردن *afshardan*; صاف کردن *sáf k.*; n. صافی *sáfí.*
Filth, چرك *chirk.*

Filthy, چرکین *chirgín*.

Fin, بال *bál.*

Finally, آخر الامر *ákhir ul amr.*

Finance, ماليات *máliyát.*

Find, *v.* پیدا کردن *paidá k.*

Fine, *n.* جریمه *jarímah;* تاوان *táwán* (*k.*); *v.* مصادره کردن *musádarah k.* —, *a.* باریك *bárík.*

Finger, انکشت *angusht.* Ring-—, بنصر *binsir.* Little —, خنصر *khinsar.* Middle —, وسطی *vastí.* —tips, بنان *banán.*

Finis, تم *tamma.*

Finished, تمام *tammám* (*sh. k.*); منتهی *muntahá* (*sh.*). To be —, بسر شدن *basar shudan.*

Fir, صنوبر *sanauber;* کاج *káj.*

Fire, آتش *átish.* To set — to, آتش زدن *átish z.* To make a —, آتش کردن *átish k.* To light a —, آتش روشن کردن *átish raushan k.*; *v.* (a gun), خالی کردن *khálí k.* Setting on —, احراق *ihráḳ.* —fly, شبتاب *shabtáb.* —lock, چقماقی *chaḳmáḳí.* —place, بخاری *bukhárí.* —wood, هیزم *heyzum.* —worshipper, آتش پرست *átesh parast.* —works, آتش بازی *átesh bází.*

Firm, پایدار *pái-dár;* راسخ *rásikh.* —ly fixed, مکین *makín.* —ness, استحکام *istihkám.*

First, اول *avval;* اولین *avvalín.* —born, بکر *bikr.*

Fish, ماهی *máhí.* The sign Pisces, حوت *hút.* Fisherman, ماهی گیر *máhí-gír.* —hook, قلابه *ḳullábeh.* Fish-net, دام *dám;* طور *túrr.*

Fissure, شکاف *shikáf.*

Fist, مشت *musht.*

Fit, *n.* غش *ghash;* *a.* (proper) لایق *láyiḳ;* سزاور *sezávar.*

Five, پنج *panj.* —hundred, پانصد *pánsad.*

Fix, to be in a, گیر افتادن *gír uftádan;* *v.* ثبت کردن *sabt k.*; نشاندن *nishándan;* *pa. p.*, معین *muʿaiyan;* ثابت *sábit.*

Flaccid, ارخی *arkhá;* نرم *narm.*

Flag, بیراق *bairáḳ;* علم *ʿalam.*

Flagellation, شلاق *shaláḳ.*

Flagon, قرابه *ḳarábah.*

Flame, شعله *shu'lah* ; زبانه *zabáneh.*

Flaming, اشتعال *ishti'ál* (*k.*).

Flashing, بارقه *báriḳah.*

Flask, بغلی *baghalí* ;

Flat, برابر *barábar* ; مساوی *musáví.*

Flatterer, چاپلوس *cháplús.*

Flattery, تملق *tamallaḳ* (*k.*); چاپلوسی *cháplúsí* (*k.*).

Flatulent, بادی *bádí* ; نفاخ *naf-fákh.*

Flavour, مزه *mazah.*

Flaw, کاست *kást* ; نقص *naḳs.*

Flax, کتان *katán.*

Flay, پوست کندن *púst kandan.*

Flea, کیك *kek.*

Flee, گریختن *gurîkhtan.*

Fleeting, فانی *fání.*

Flesh, گوشت *gúsht.*

Flexible, پیچخور *píchkhúr.*

Flight, گریز *guríz* ; فرار *ferár* (*gr.*); (bird's), پرواز *parváz.* Put to —, منهزم *munhazim* (*g.*); *v.*, گریزانیدن *gurízáni-dan.* Taking —, گریزان *gurízán.*

Fling, انداختن *andákhtan.*

Flint (for striking fire), سنك چاقماق *sang í chákmáḳ.*

Flippantly, با شوخی *bá shúkhí.*

Flock, گله *gelleh.*

Flood, سیلاب *sailáb* ; (Noah's), طوفان *túfán.* Flood and ebb tides, مد و جزر *madd u jazr.*

Floor, زمین *zamín.*

Florid, ناضر *názir.*

Flour, ارد *ard.*

Flourish, شکوفتن *shikúftan* ; *pr. p.*, آبادان *ábádán.*

Flow, جاری شدن *járí sh.* ; *pr. p.*, جریان *jariyán* ; روان *raván* ; سایل *sáil* ; (as a river, with noise), شاریدن *sháridan.*

Flower, گل *gul.* — of youth, ریعان *rai'án* ; عنفوان *'un-fuwán.*

Fluent, زبان آور *zabán-ávar.*

Flute, نای *náy.*

Flutter, طپیدن *tapídan.*

Fluxed, to be, دست آمدن *dast ámadan.*

Fly, *n.*, مگس *magas* ; *v.*, پریدن *parídan* ; *pr. p.*, پران *parán* ; پرنده *parendah.*

Fly-flap, مگس ران *magás-rán.*

Foal, کره *kurreh.*

Foam, کف *kaf* (*z.*).

Focus, مورد *maurid.*

Fodder, علف *'alaf.*

Fœtus, جنین *janín.*

Fog, دود *dúd*; مه *meh.*

Fold, ته *tah* (*k.*); تو *tav.* In folds, توبتو *tú ba tú.* Cattle —, اکل *ágel.* To fold together, در نوردیدن *dar navardídan.*

Follow, در پی رفتن *dar pai r.*; عقب رفتن *'aḳab r.*; *pr. p.*, پیروی *pai-raví* (*k.*).

Follower, پیرو *pai-ro*; متابع *mutábi'.*

Folly, حماقت *himáḳat*; نوك *nauk.*

Fomentation, تکمید *takmíd.*

Fondle, بغل کردن *baghal k.*

Food, خوراکی *khurákí*; طعام *ta'ám*; قوت *ḳút*; خوردنی *khurdaní.*

Fool, ابله *ablah*; احمق *ahmaḳ.*

Foolish, بیمعنی *bí-ma'ní.* — ly, بیهوده *bíhúdeh.*

Foot, پا *pá*, or پی *pai.* — soldier, on —, پیاده *piyádah* (*r.*). — of a mountain, دامن *dáman* or دامنه *dámaneh.*

Footstep, قدم *ḳadam.*

For, برای *baráyi*; از برای *az baráyi.*

Forage, علف *'alaf.*

Forbearance, مصابرت *musábarat.*

Forbearing, بردبار *burd-bár.*

Forbid, منع کردن *man' k.*

Forbidden, منهی *manhí*; محظور *mahzúr.* — things, نواهی *naváhí.*

Force, زور *zúr*; زبردستی *zabardastí.* By —, بزور *bazúr.*

Forceps, کلوب *kallúb.*

Ford, گذرگاه *guzar-gáh*; پایاب *páyáb.*

Fore-arm, ساعد *sá'id.*

Forecast, مال اندیش *ma'ál-andísh.*

Forefather, جد *jidd*; *pl.* اجداد *ajdád*; پیشین *píshín.*

Forefinger, سبابه *sabbábah.*

Forehead, جبهه *jubhah*; پیشانی *píshání*; ناصیه *násiyeh.*

Foreign, اجنبی *ajnabí.*

Foreigner, بیگانه *bígáneh*; غریب *gharíb.*

Foreignness, بیگانگی *bígánagí.*

Fore-leg, دست *dast.*

Foremost, مقدم *muḳaddam.*

Forenoon, ضحی *zuhá*; پیش از ظهر *písh az zuhr.*

Foresighted, پیشیاب *písh-yáb.*

Foreskin, غلفت *ghulfat.*

Forest, جنگل *jangal.*

Foretell, پیش گفتن *písh gf.*

Forge, دمگاه *dam-gáh.*

Forged, ساخته *sákhteh.*

Forgery, جعل *ja'l.*

Forget, فراموش کردن *fará-músh k.*

Forgetfulness, نسیان *nisyán* (*k.*) ; فراموشی *farámúshí.*

Forgive, بخشیدن *bakhshídan* ; آمرزیدن *ámurzídan.* — ness, بخشایش *bakhsháyish* ; معاف *mu'áf* (*k.*).

Forgiving, غفور *ghafúr.*

Fork, چنگال *chhangál.*

Form, شکل *shakl* ; قالب *ḳálib* ; پیکر *paikar.*

Formal, رسمانه *rasmáneh.*

Former, پیشین *píshín* ; سابق *sábiḳ* ; قدیم *ḳadím.*

Formerly, پیشینه *píshínah.*

Formidable, نژند *nizhand.*

Formula, دستور العمل *dastúr ul 'amal.*

Fornication, زنا *ziná* (*k.*).

Fornicator, فاسق *fásiḳ.*

Forsake, ترك كردن *tark k.*

Forsaken, مهجور *mahjúr.*

Fort, قلعه *ḳal'ah* ; حصار *hisár* ; حصن *hisn.*

Fortieth, چهلم *chihlum.*

Fortifications, بارو *bárú.*

Fortified, محصون *mahsún* (*k.*).

Fortitude, نجدت *najdat.*

Fortnight, دو هفته *do hafteh.*

Fortunate, سعادت مند *sa'ádat-mand* ; طالعمند *táli'-mand* ; نيك بخت *ník-bakht* ; دولتمند *daulat-mand* ; برومند *barú-mand* ; بختيار *bakht-yár.* May it be — ! مبارك باد *mu-bárak-bád.*

Fortune, بخت *bakht* ; دولت *daulat* ; نصيب *nasíb.* Good —, بختمندی *bakhtmandí.* — teller, فالگير *fálgír.*

Forty, چهل *chehel.*

Forward, پیش *písh.*

Foss, خندق *khandaḳ.*

Fossil, جماد *jamád.*

Foster-brother, برادر رضاعی *birádar-i-rízá'í.* — mother, دایه *dáyeh.* — son, پسر رضاعی *pesari rezá'í.*

Foul, نا پاك *ná pák* (*k.*).

Foul-mouthed, بد زبان *bad zabán.*

Found, *v.*, وضع كردن *vaz' k.*

Foundation, اساس *asás*; بنياد *bunyád*.
Founded, مبنى *mabní* (*b.*).
Founding, تأسيس *ta'sís* (*k.*).
Founder, موءسس *mu'assis*.
Foundling, لقيط *laḳít*.
Fountain, چشمه *chashmah*, or سر چشمه *sar i chashmah*; عين *'ain*; (jet), فواره *favvárah*.
Four, چهار *chehár*.
Fourteen, چارده *chárdeh*.
Fourteenth, چهاردهم *chehardahum*.
Fourth (the), چهارم *chehárum*; one —, ربع *rub'*.
Fowl, جوجه *júјah*.
Fox, روباه *rúbáh*. — cub, روبهك *rúbahek*.
Fraction, كسره *kasreh*.
Fracture, كسر *kasr*.
Fragment, پارچه *párchah*; ريزه *rízah*; *pl.*, خردها *khurdahá*.
Fragrance, خوش بو *khush-bú*; طيب *tíb*.
Fragrant, بويا *búyá*; معطر *mu'attar*.
Frame, چار چوبه *chár chúbah*; قاب *ḳáb*.
Frank, راست گو *rást gú*.
Frankincense, لبان *lubán*.

Frantic, ديوانه *díváneh*.
Fraternity, مواخات *muwákhát*.
Fraud, خدعه *khud'ah*; خديعت *khadí'at*; مكر *makr*; دغابازى *daghá-bází*; تلبيس *talbís*; نتيل *natíl*.
Free, آزاد *ázád*; مبرا *mubarrá*; خلاص *khalás* (*k.*); برىء *barí'*; (leisure), فارغ *fárigh*.
Freedom, خلاصى *khalásí*; آزادى *ázádí*.
Freewill, اختيار *ikhtiyár*.
Freeze, يخ بستن *yakh-bastan*.
Freight, حمل *haml*.
Frenzy, سرسام *sar-sám*.
Frequent, *a.*, بسيار *bisyár*; — ly, بارها *bárhá*; *v.*, آمد وشد كردن *ámad o shud k.*
Fresh, تازه *tázeh*; (air), خنك *khunuk*; (water), شرين *shirín*.
Freshness, تازكى *tázagí*; ترى *tarí*; نضارت *nazárat*.
Fretful, افسرده *afsurdeh*.
Fricassee, قليه *ḳalíyah*; (of butter, onions, &c.), دو پيازه *dú-píyázah*.
Friction, دلك *dalk*.
Friday, روز جمعه *rúz-i-jum'ah*.
Fried, بريان *biryán*.

Friend, دوست *dúst;* یار *yár;* رفیق *rafiḳ;* آشنا *áshná.* Sincere —, صدیق *sadíḳ;* مانوس *ma'nús.*

Friendless, بیکس *bíkas.*

Friendly, دوستانه *dústánah;* یارانه *yáránah.*

Friendship, یاری *yárí;* دوستی *dústí;* تودد *tavaddud;* وداد *vidád.* Sincere —, مصادقت *musádaḳat.*

Fright, هول *haul;* هولناك *haul-nák;* ترس *tars.*

Frighten, ترسانیدن *tarsánídan.*

Frigidity, سردی *sardí.*

Fringe, ریشه *ríshah.*

Frivolous, پوچ *púch;* بیمعنی *bíma'ani.*

Frog, غوك *ghúk;* وزق *vazaḳ.*

From, از *az.*

Front, پیش *písh;* روی *rúy.* — tooth, ثنیة *saníyet.*

Frontiers, سرحد *sar hadd.*

Frost, اریز *aríz;* سرما *sarmá.*

Froth, رغوت *raghwat;* كف *kaf (k.);* زبد *zabad.*

Frown, *n.* اخرو *akhrú (k.);* *v.,* روی درهم کشیدن *rúy dar-ham ksh.*

Frozen, یخور *yákhvar;* بسته *basteh.*

Frugal, خانه دار *kháneh dár.*

Fruit, میوه *mívah;* (berry), فاکهه *fákihah;* ثمر *samar;* بر *bar.* Early —, نو بارة *nau-bárah.*

Fruitful, باردار *bár dár;* بار ور *bár-var;* میوه دار *mívah-dár;* مثمر *musmir.*

Fruition, کامیابی *kám-yábí.*

Fruitless, بی بر *bí bar.*

Frumenty, شهترة *shahtarah.*

Frustrate, محروم کردن *mah-rúm k.*

Fry, بریان کردن *biriyán k.*

Frying-pan, تابه *tábah.*

Fuel, هیمه *heimeh.*

Fugitive, گریخته *guríkhtah;* (slave), ابق *ábiḳ.*

Fulfilment, تکمیل *takmíl (k.).*

Full, پر *pur;* مملو *mamlú;* مالامال *mál-á-mál;* (of food), سیر *sír.*

Fuller, گاذر *gázur.*

Fulness, پری *purí.*

Fumigation, دخنه *dukhneh (k.);* تبخیر *tabkhír.*

Function, کار *kár.*

Functionary, مامور *maamúr.*

Fundamental, اصلی *aslí.*

Funeral, جنازة *jenázah.*

Funny, شوخ *shúkh.*
Fur, پوست *púst*; کورك *kúrk.*
— coat, پوستین *púst'n.*
Furious, ژیان *zhiyán*; متهور *mutahavvir*; متأسد *muta'as-sad.*
Furlough, رخصت *rukhsat* (*d.gr.*)
Furnace, اتون *atún*; تنور *tan-núr.* Bath —, کلخان *kalkhán.*
Furnishing, تجهیز *tajhíz* (*k.*).
Furniture, رخت *rakht*; اسباب *asbáb.*
Furrier, پوستپیرا *púst-pírá.*
Fury, غیظ *ghaiz.*
Fusilier, تفنکچی *tufangchí.*
Fusion, ذوب *zaub* (*k.*).
Fuss, های های *hái hái.*
Fustian, کماش *kumásh.*
Futile, جفنك *jafnak.*
Future, آینده *áyandah*; منستقبل *mustaḳbil.* — state, اخرت *ákhirat.* In —, بعد از این *ba'ad az ín.*
Futurity, عقبی *'uḳbá.*
Fye! ویح *waih*; وای *wái.*

G

Gabble, قیل وقال *ḳíl o ḳál.*
Gabriel, جبرائیل *Jabrá'íl.*

Gadfly, خر پشه *khar-pashah*; خرمکس *khar magas.*
Gaiety, بهبخت *bih-bakht.*
Gain, غنیمت *ghanímat*; اکتساب *iktisáb*; مکسب *maksab*; کسب *kasb*; نفع *naf'.*
Gaining, تکسیب *taksíb* (*k.*).
Gait, راه *ráh.*
Gaiters, لبچین *labchín*; زنکال *zangál.*
Galaxy, کهکشان *kah-kashán.*
Gale, باد *bád.*
Gall, زرد آب *zard-áb.*
Gall-apple, مازو *mázú.*
Gall-bladder, مراره *marárah.*
Gall-nut, ماجو *májú.*
Galled, فکار *figár.*
Gallery, رواق *rivák.*
Gallingale, خولنجان *khúlinján.*
Gallop, *n.*, دو *dú*; *v.*, دویدن *davídan.*
Gallows, چوب دار *chúb dár.*
Gamble, قمار باختن *ḳamár bákh-tan*; بازی کردن *bází k.*
Gambler, مقامر *muḳámir.*
Gambling, مقامرت *muḳámarat.*
Game (wild), شکار *shikár*; صید *said*; (play), بازیچه *bázícheh.* — cock, خروس جنك *khurús i jang.*

Gander, قاز *ḳáz.*
Gang, طایفه *táifeh.*
Gangrene, ناسور *násúr.*
Gaol, زندان *zindán.*
Gaoler, زندانبان *zindánbán.*
Gaping, خمیازه *khamyázah* (*k. sh.*).
Garbled, تحریف *tahríf* (*k.*).
Garden, باغ *bágh*; بستان *bustán*; چمن زار *chaman-zár.*
Gardener, باغبان *bághbán.*
Gargle, غرغره *ghar-gharah* (*k.*).
Garland, اکلیل *iklíl*; یسال *yasál.*
Garlic, سیر *sír.*
Garment, جامه *jámah*; لباس *libás*; *pl.*, ملبوسات *malbúsát.* Under —, زیر پوش *zír-púsh.*
Garrison, ساخلو *sákhlú.* In —, متحصن *mutahassin.*
Garrulous, زیاده گو *ziyádeh gú.*
Garter, زانو بند *zánú band.*
Gasp, نفس زدن *nafas z.*
Gate, در *dar*; (large), دروازه *darvázeh.* — keeper, دربان *darbán.*
Gather (pluck), چیدن *chídan.* — and, گرد آمدن *gird ámadan.*

Gathering, ملتقط *multáḳit* (*n.*); اجتناء *ijtiná'.*
Gauntlet, دستوانه *dast-vánah.*
Gauze, برنجك *birinjak.*
Gaze at, نگاه کردن *nigáh k.*
Gazelle, آهو *áhú.*
Gazette, روز نامه *rúz námeh.*
Gelding, آخته *ákhteh.*
Gem, جوهر *jauhar*; (red), یاقوت احمر *yáḳút i ahmar*; (blue), یاقوت کبود *yáḳút i kabúd.*
Gemini, جوزاء *jauzá'.*
Gender, جنس *jins.*
Genealogy, حسب ونسب *hasab o nasab*; *pl.*, انساب *ansáb.*
General (of division), سرتیپ اول *sartíp i avval*; (of brigade), سرتیپ دوم *sartíp i dúvum.*
Generally, عموماً *'umúman.*
Generated, مولود *maulúd* (*sh.*).
Generation, توالد *taválud.* A single —, نسل *nasl.* From — to —, ابًا عن جدّ *aban 'an jadd.*
Generosity, جوان مردی *javán-mardí*; فتوت *futúvat.*
Generous, جوان مرد *javán-mard.*

Genitale Sperma, نطفه nutfah; نزالت nuzálat.

Genius, ذهن zihn; ذكاوت zakávat; (demon), جن jinn.

Gentian, جنطيانه jintiyánah.

Gentle, ملايم muláyim; حليم halím.

Gently, آهسته áhisteh.

Genuine, صحيح sahíh; اصيل asíl.

Genuineness, صحت sihhat.

Geography, جغرافيا jughráfiyá.

Geomancy, رمل ramal.

Geometrical, هندسی handasí.

Geometrician, مهندس muhandis.

Geometry, هندسه handasah.

Germany, نمسه namsah.

Gesture, وضع vaz'.

Get, to, پيدا كردن paidá k; گرفتن giriftan. — in one's grasp, فرا چنك آوردن fará chang á.; — up, برخاستن bar khástan.

Ghost, عفريت 'afrít. Holy —, روح القدس rúh ul ḳuds.

Gibbet, دار dár.

Giddiness, دوار duvár.

Giddy, سر گردان sar gardán; گيج gíj.

Gift, عطا 'atá' (d.); عطيه 'atíyeh(k.); بخشش bakhshesh; سوغات saughát; (to inferior), انعام in'ám; (to superior), پيشكش píshkesh.

Gild, زر اندودن zar andúdan.

Gilded, مطلى mutallá; زر كار zar-kár.

Gilding, طلا كارى tilá-kárí.

Gimlet, برماه barmáh.

Ginger, زنجبيل zanjabíl.

Giraffe, شتر گاو پلنك shutur-gau palang.

Gird, بستن bastan.

Girder, تير tír.

Girdle, منطقه mantiḳah; كمربند kamar band.

Girl, دختر dukhtar. Slave —, كنيز kaníz.

Girth, تنك tang.

Give, دادن dádan; هبه كردن hibah k.; بخشيدن bakhshídan. — and take, داد ستد dád-sitad.

Giver, دهنده dihendah; بخشنده bakhshandah.

Glad, مسرور masrúr; شاد shád; حظ hezz (h.). — tidings, بشارت bishárat.

Gladiator, سلاح شور siláh-shúr.

Gladness, شادمانی shád-mání; خرمی khurramí; فرح farah; خوشی khushí.

Glance, نظر názar (k.); نگاه nigáh (k.).

Gland, غدة ghuddat.

Glanders, سکاو sakkáu; مشمشه mishmisheh.

Glass, شیشه shíshah; زجاج zujáj; (for drinking), استکان istakán. Mirror, آینه áineh; — blower, زجاج zajjáj; شیشه گر shíshah-gar. — beads, خرز kharaz. — shade for candle, لاله láleh.

Glazier, شیشه بر shíshah bar.

Glean, خوشه چیدن khúsheh chídan.

Gleaner, ریزه خور rízah-khur.

Glen, دره darreh.

Glib-tongued, چرب زبان charb-zabán.

Glibness (of tongue), طلاقت tulákat.

Glimmer, روشنائی rúshnáí.

Glitter, v., درخشیدن darakhshídan; n., تاب táb.

Glittering, زرق برق zark-bark.

Globe, کره kurrah; گوی gúy.

Gloomy, تیره tírah.

Glorifying God, تمجید tamjíd (k.).

Glorious, مفخر mufakhkhar; جلیل jalíl; مباهی mubáhí.

Glory, فخر fakhr; عزت 'izzat; مجد majd; مباهات mubáhát.

Glorying, افتخار iftikhár (n.).

Glossary, لغت lughat.

Glossed over, مزخرف muzkharif.

Glove, دست کش dast-kesh.

Glowing, سوزان súzán.

Glue, سریش sirísh.

Glutton, بسیار خور bisyár-khur; شکم بنده shikam-bandah.

Gluttony, شکم پرستی shikam parastí.

Gnat, پشه pashshah.

Go, رفتن raftan; (polite form), تشریف بردن tashríf burdan. — down, فرو رفتن farú r. — out, بدر رفتن badar r.

Goal, مقصد maksud; مدار madár.

Goat, بز buz; — herd, بز بان buz bán.

Goblet, جام jám.

God, الله Allah; خدا khudá. — the Creator, خدا آفرین

khudá-áfrín. — Most High, حق تعالی *hakk-taʿálá.* By —, والله *walláh;* بالله *billáh;* بخدا *ba Khudá.* For God's sake, خدایرا *khudáerá.* — forbid, مبادا *mabádá;* عیاذاً بالله *ʿiyázán billah;* استغفر الله *astaghfiru 'llah.* — knows best, والله اعلم *walláhu aʿalam.* — be praised, الحمد لله *lilláhi 'l hamd.* — preserve you; adieu, خدا حافظ *khudá háfiz.* O —! یا الله *yá 'lláh;* خدایا *khudáyá.* Please —, انشاء الله *inshállah.*

Godliness, زهد *zuhd.*

Gog and Magog, یاجوج و ماجوج *yájúj u májúj.*

Gold, طلا *tilá.* Red —, زر سرخ *zar i surkh.* Cloth of —, زر بفت *zar-baft.* —dust, زرك *zarak.* — embroidery, زر دوزی *zar-dúzí.* Inlaid with —, زر نگار *zar-nigár.* — leaf, کاغذ زر *kághaz i zar.* Plated with —, زر کوفت *zar-kúft.* — wire-drawer, زر کش *zar-kash.*

Golden, زرین *zarín;* طلائی *tiláí.*

Goldfinch, سقاچی *sakkáchí.*

Goldsmith, زر گر *zar-gar.*

Goloshes, چکمه پوش *chekmeh púsh.*

Gong, ناقوس *nákús.*

Gonorrhœa, آتشك *átishak;* سوزاك *súzak.*

Good, خوب *khúb;* نیك *ník;* خیر *khair;* نیکو *níkú.* — bye, خدا حافظ *khudá háfiz (gf.).* — nature, حسن خلق *hasn i khulk;* خیرة *khairat.* — works, حسنات *hasanát.* —ness, خوبی *khúbí;* نیکوی *níkúí;* نیکی *níkí.*

Goods, اسباب *asbáb;* مال *mál;* املاك *amlák;* اجناس *ajnás.*

Goose, قاز *káz.*

Gorgeous, مجید *majíd.*

Goshawk, باز *báz.*

Gospel, انجیل *Injíl.*

Gossamer, کنتره *kantareh.*

Gourd, کدو *kaddú.*

Gout, نقرس *nikris.*

Governed (the noun), مضاف الیه *muzáf ilaih.*

Government, حکومت *hukúmat.* (*k.*); ایالت *iyálat;* دولت *daulat;* ریاست *riyásat.*

Governor, والی *wálí* ; قـایم مقام *ḳáim maḳám* ; فرمان فرمای *farmán farmai* ; حاکم *hákim*.

Grace, حسن *husn* ; زیب و زینت *zíb u zínat*. — (of God), توفیق *taufíḳ*.

Graceful, چالش *chálish* ; جمیل *jamíl*.

Gracious God ! سبحان الله *sub-hán Alláh*.

Gradation, تدریج *tadríj*.

Grade, مرتبه *martabeh*.

Gradually, درجه بدرجه *darajeh bedarajeh* ; مو بمو *mú be mú*.

Graft, قلمه *ḳalameh* (*k*.).

Grain (corn), غلة *ghallah*. A single —, دانه *dáneh* ; حب *habb* ; حبه *habbah*.

Grammar, نحو *nahv*.

Grammarian, نحوی *nohaví*.

Granary, مخزن *makhzan* ; انبار *ambár*.

Grand, عظیم *'azím*. — child, پسر زاده *pesar zádeh*.

Grandees, عظما *'uzamá'*.

Grandeur, کبرة *kibrat* ; کبر *kibr*.

Grand-daughter, نواسی *navásí*.

Grand-father, جد *jadd*. Maternal —, نانا *náná* Paternal —, جد صحیح *jadd i sahíh*.

Grandmother, جده *jaddeh* ; Paternal — جده صحیحه *jaddah i sahíhah*. Maternal —, مادر مادر *mádar i mádar*.

Grand-son, نوه *navah*.

Granite, سماق *sammáḳ*.

Grant, سند *sanad* ; عطا *'atá* (*k*.) ; اجازه *ijázeh* (*k*.).

Grape, انکور *angúr*.

Grasp, قبض *ḳabz* (*k*.).

Grass, کیاه *giyáh* ; علف *'alaf*. —hopper, ملخ *malakh*.

Grate, بخاری *bukhári*.

Grateful, نمك حلال *namak-halál* ; شکر کذار *shukr-guzár* ; شکور *shakúr* ; حق شناس *haḳḳ shinás* ; احسانمند *ihsánmand*.

Gratified, مستسعد *mustas'ad*.

Grating, شبکه *shabakeh*.

Gratis, مفت *muft*.

Gratitude, تشکر *tashakkur* ; شکر نعمت *shukr i ni'mat*.

Grave, *a*., (majestic), وقور *vuḳúr* ; (tomb), *n*., تربت *turbat* ; قبر *ḳabr* ; کور *gúr*.

Gravel, حصی *hesá* ; سنك ریزه *sang-rízah*.

Gravitation, ثقالت *saḳálat*.

Gravity, سنجیدکی *sanjídagí*.

Gravy, آب کوشت *ab i gúsht.*

Gray, خاکستری *khákisteri*; قبود *ḳabud*; سنجابی *sinjábí*; (horse), نیله *nílah*; قزل *ḳizil.*

Graze, چریدن *charídan.*

Grease, چربی *charbí.*

Greasy, دسم *dasim*; چرب *charb.*

Great, بزرك *buzurg*; کبیر *kabír*; عظیم *'azím*; جلیل *jalíl.* —ness, بزرکی *buzurgí*; عظمت *'azamat*; مهتری *mihtarí.*

Greece, یونان *yúnán.*

Greedy, آزمند *ázmand*; حارص *háris.*

Greek, یونانی *yúnání.*

Green, سبز *sabz.* —grocer, بقال *baḳḳál.* —ness, سبزی *sabzí.*

Greeting, سلام *salám* (*k.*).

Greyhound, سك تازی *sag i tází.*

Grief, رنج *ranj*; غم *gham*; اندوه *andúh*; تاسف *ta'assuf* (*kh.*); حزن *huzn*; غمزدکی *gham-zadagí.*

Grievance, شکایت *skikáyat.*

Grieve, غم خوردن *gham kh.*

Grieved, محزون *mahzún*; غمزده *gham-zadah.*

Grill, بریان *biriyán* (*k.*).

Grim, ترسناك *tars nák.*

Grimace, رو ترش *rú tursh* (*k.*).

Grind, سائیدن *sáídan*; (corn), آسیاب کردن *ásiyáb k.*; (knives), تیزکردن *tíz k.* —stone (mill), سنك آسیا, *sang i ásiyá*; (for knives), سنك فسان *sang i fisán.*

Gristle, غزروف *ghuzrúf.*

Groan, ناله *náleh* (*k.*); آه *áh* (*k.*).

Grocer, بقال *baḳḳál.*

Groin, کش ران *kash i rán.*

Groom, *n.*, مهتر *mehtar.* Head-—, جلو دار *jalo dár*; میر اخور *mír ákhor.*

Groove, ناب *náb.*

Gross, درشت *durusht*; غلیظ *ghalíz.*

Grotto, سرداب *sardáb*; غار *ghár.*

Ground, زمین *zamín*; خاك *khák*; تراب *turáb.* —less, باطل *bátil.* —rent, کرایه *kiráyah.*

Grove, درختستان *dirakhtistán.*

Grow, رستن *rustan*; روئیدن

rú'ídan. — pale, رنك پريدن *rang-parídán.* — up, باليدن *bálídan ;* دميدن *damídan.* —ing, رويندہ *rúyandah ;* روئيدہ *rú'ídah ;* نشاء *nashá' ;* نمو *namú.* —ing up, نشو نما *nashv-namá.*

Growth, باليدكي *bálídagí ;* ناميه *námiyeh.*

Growling, دريغ *darígh (kh.).*

Gruel, شوبا *shaubá.*

Grumble, لند لند كردن *lund lund k.*

Grunt, مخ مخ كردن *mikh mikh k.*

Guarantee, كفالت *kafálat (k.) ; n.* ضامن *zámin.*

Guard, بدرقه *badrakah ;* قراول *kerául ;* پاس *pás (dsh.).* Imperial —, نسقچى *nasakchí.* نكاهبان *nigáh-bán.* —ed, محفوظ *mahfúz (s.).* — house, قراول خانه *keráúl kháneh.*

Guardian, مربى *murabbí.*

Guardianship, محافظت *muháfazat.*

Guarding, احتراس *ihtirás (n.).*

Guess, قياس *kiyás (n.).*

Guest, مهمان *mihmán.*

Guidance, راه نمونى *ráh namúní ;* هدايت *hidáyat.*

Guide, بلد *belad (h.) ;* راه نما *ráh-numá (k.) ;* رهبر *rahbar ;* (spiritual), مرشد *murshid.*

Guilt, كناه *gunáh.* —less, بيكناه *bégunáh.*

Guilty, ماثوم *ma'súm ;* ملزم *malzam.*

Guinea-worm, ريشته *ríshteh.*

Guitar, عود *'úd ;* سه تار *sih-tár* or *sih-tárah ;* زنبوره *zambúrah.*

Gulf, خليج *khalíj.*

Gull, شالو *shálú.*

Gullet, حلقوم *hulkúm.*

Gulley, تنك *tang.*

Gulp, جرعه *jur'ah (k.).*

Gum, صمغ *samagh.* — ammoniac, وشه *washah.* —lac, لاك *lák ;* (of tooth), كوشتى دندان *gúshtí dandán.*

Gun, تفنك *tufang ;* (double barrelled), تفنك دو لوله *tufang i do lúleh.* Long rifled —, شمخال *shamkhál.* Swivel —, شتر نال *shutur-nál ;* زنبورك *zamburek.*

Gunner, توپچى *túp chí.*

Gunpowder, باروت *bárút.*

Gunsmith, تفنكساز *tufang sáz.*

Gust, نفحه *nafheh.*

Gut, معآ *mi'á* ; روده *rúdah.*

Gutter, آبريز *ábríz* ; ناودان *návdán.*

Guttural, حلقى *halkíy.*

Gymnasium, زور خانه *zúrkhánah.*

Gypsum, آهك *áhek.*

Gypsy, قرهچى *karrehchí* ; زنكنه *zanganeh* ; سسمانى *susmání.*

H.

Habit, خو *khú* (*gr.*) ; عادت *'ádat* (*k.*). Religious —, خرقه *khirkah.*

Habitant, ساكن *sákin.*

Habitation, مسكن *maskan* ; مكان *makán.*

Habitual, مستعمل *musta'mel.*

Hag, پيرزن *pír-i-zan.*

Haggard, لاغر *lághir.*

Hail, *v.*, تگرك باريدن *tagarg báridan* ; *n.*, ژاله *zhálah.* —stone, يخچه *yakhcheh.* Hail! مرحبا *marhabá.*

Hair, مو *mú* ; or موى *múy.* —by —, مو بمو *mú-ba-mú.* —cutter, مو تراش *mú-tarásh.* —dye, خضاب *khizáb.* —pencil, قلم موى *kalam i múí.*

Half, نيم *ním* ; نصف *nisf.* —caste, دورك *do rag.* —way, نيم راه *ním ráh.*

Hall, ايوان *aiván* ; دالان *dálán* ; تالار *tálár.*

Halo, هاله *hálah.*

Halt, (stay), توقع كردن *tavakku' k.* — (limp), لنكيدن *langídan.*

Halter, (horse), پالهنك *palhang* ; آبخورى *ábkhurí* ; افسار *afsár* ; — (gallows), ريسمان *rísmán.*

Halting-place, فرود گاه *farúd gáh* ; منزل *manzil.*

Halving, تنصيف *tansíf* (*k.*).

Hammer, چكش *chukush.* — (smith's), خايسك *kháyisk* ; پتك *putk.*

Hamstring, پى كردن *pay k.*

Hand, دست *dast.* — (of watch), عقرب *'akrab.* From — to —, دست بدست *dast ba dast.* —ful, قبضه *kabzah* ; مشت *musht.*

Handicraft, دستكارى *dast-kárí.*

Handkerchief, دست *dast-mál.*

Handle, دسته *dastah.*

Handmaid, كنيز *kaníz.*

Handsel, دست فال *dast-fál.*

Handsome, قشنك *kashang.*

Handwriting, دستخط *dast khatt.*

Hang, آويختن *ávíkhtan* ; بردار كشيدن *bar dár ksh.* — (down), فرو هشتن *farú hishtan.*

Hangings, پرده *pardeh.*

Hankering, رغبت *righbat* (*n.*).

Happen, واقع شدن *vákí' sh.* ; اتفاق افتادن *ittifák uftádan* ; وارد شدن *várid sh.* ; رو دادن *rú-d.* ; سرزدن *sar-z.*

Happiness, فرخندگی *farkhundagí.*

Happy, مسعود *mas'úd* ; خوشنود *khushnúd* ; كامران *kám-rán* ; خوش حال *khush-hál.*

Harangue, خطاب *khitáb* (*n.*).

Harass, آزار كردن *ázár k.* ; اذيت كردن *azíyat k.*

Harbour, بندر *bandar.*

Hard, صلد *sald* ; سفت *sift* ; سخت *sakht* (*k.*). —hearted, سنكدل *sang-dil.* —ness, قساوت *kasávat.* —ship, سختی *sakhtí* ; مصيبت *musíbat.*

Hare, خرکوش *khar gúsh.*

Harem, اندرون *andarún* ; زنانه *zenáneh.*

Harlequin, بمبلی *bambulí.*

Harlot, جنده *jindeh* ; قحبه *kahbeh.*

Harm, ضرر *zarar* (*k.*) ; عيب *'aib* (*h.*).

Harming, ايذا *ízá* (*d.*).

Harmony, وفاق *vifák.*

Harness, يراق *yarák* ; ساز *sáz.*

Harp, بربط *barbat.*

Harper, بربط سرای *barbat saráy.*

Harrier, تازی *tází.*

Harrow, خاك كش *khák-kesh* ; مازو *mázú.* To — the soul, جان كندن *ján-kandan.*

Harsh, درشت *durusht* ; سخت *sakht.*

Harvest, درو *dirau* ; حاصل *hásil* ; حصاد *hesád.*

Hasp, چفت *chift.*

Haste, تعجيل *ta'jíl* (*k.*) ; زودی *zúdí* ; عجلت *'ajlat.* To make —, شتافتن *shitáftan.*

Hastening, استعجال *isti'jál.*

Hastily, عاجلانه *'ájilánah* ; شتابان *shitábán.*

Hasty, تندخو *tund-khú* ; دستپاچه *dast pá-cheh* (*sh.*).

Hat, كلاه *kuláh.*

Hatchet, تبر *tabar.*

Hate, رغم داشتن *raghm dsh.*

—ful, نطیح *natíh ;* مکروه *makrúh (dsh.).* —ed, بغض *bughz ;* کین *kín (dsh.) ;* سحناء *shahná'.*

Haughtiness, کبر *kibr.*

Haughty, متکبر *mutakabher.*

Haul, کشیدن *keshídan.*

Haunch, گرده *gurdah.*

Have, داشتن *dáshtan.*

Haven, بندر *bandar.*

Hawk, باز *báz ;* قوش *ḳúsh.*

Hay, علف *'alaf.*

Hazard, خطره *khatreh ;* بخت *bakht.*

He, او *ú.*

Head, سر *sar ;* کله *kallah.* From — to foot, سرا پا *sar-á-pá.* —ache, درد سر *dard i sar.* —land, راس *rás.* —ing, عنوان *anván.* —long, خودسر *khud sar ;* سرکش *sar kesh.* —stall, افسار *afsár.*

Healing, علاج *'iláj (k.).*

Health, صحت *sihhat ;* خیر و عافیت *khair u 'áfiyat.* Good —, تندرستی *tan-durustí.*

Healthy, تندرست *tan-durust.*

Heap, توده *túdah (k.).*

Hear, شنیدن *shanídan.*

Heard, مسموع *masmú'.*

Hearer, شنونده *shinavendah.*

Hearing, سماعت *samá'at ;* سمع *sam' (k.).* Sense of — مسمع *misma'.*

Hearken, گوش دادن *gúsh d.*

Heart, دل *dil ;* خاطر *khátir.* To get by —, یاد کردن *yád-kerdan.* To cut to the —, بجان رنجیدن *baján ranjídan.* —broken, دل شکسته *dil-shikestah.* —less, بی دل *bí-dil.*

Hearth, بخاری *bukhárí.*

Heartily, بجان *baján.*

Hearty, قلبی *ḳalbi.*

Heat, گرمی *garmí ;* تاب *táb ;* حرارت *harárat.*

Heathen, کافر *káfir ;* بت پرست *but parast.*

Heaven, بهشت *bihisht.* —ly, آسمانی *ásmání ;* جنتی *jannatí.*

Heavens, سماوات *samáwát ;* افلاك *aflák ;* آسمان *ásmán.*

Heaviness, ثقالت *saḳálat ;* گرانی *giràní.*

Heavy, گران *girán ;* ثقیل *saḳíl.*

Hebrew, عبری *'ibríy ;* یهود *ya-húd.*

Hedge, خار بند *khár band.* —hog, خار پشت *khár pusht.*

Heel, پاشنه *páshneh*. At the —s of, در پی *dar-pai*.

Heifer, گوساله ماده *gosáleh mádeh*; کهره *kahreh*.

Height, بلندی *balandí*; ارتفاع *irtifá'*; علاء *'alá'*.

Heir, وارث *wáris*. —apparent, ولی عهد *vali 'ahd*.

Heliotrope, افتاب پرست *aftáb parast*.

Hell, دوزخ *dúzakh*; جهنم *jehannum*.

Hellebore, خربق *kharbuk*.

Hellish, دوزخی *dúzakhí*.

Helm, (ship), سکان *sukkán*.

Helmet, مغفر *mighfar*. —crest, کلاه خود *kuláh khúd*.

Help, کمك *kumek* (*d.*); مدد *madad* (*k.*); یارای *yáráí*.

Helpless, نا چار *ná-chár*; بینوا *bínawá*; بیچاره *bí-cháreh*. —ness, فرو مانده گی *farú-mándagí*.

Hem, حاشیه *háshiyeh* (*bs.*).

Hemistich, مصراع *misrá'*.

Hemlock, شوکران *shavkerán*.

Hemorrhage, رعاف *ru'áf*.

Hemorrhoids, بواسیر *bavásír*.

Hemp, *n*, قنب *kinab*.

Hen, مرغ *murgh*.

Henbane, بنج *banj*.

Hence, (from), ازینجا *azínjá*; (reason), از این سبب *az ín sabab*. —forth, بعد از این *ba'ad az ín*.

Henna, حنا *hinná*.

Heptagon, مسبع *musabba'*.

Her, او *ú*; (possessive), ش *-esh*; مال او *mál i ú*.

Herald, منادی *munádi*.

Herb, نبات *nabát*. pot —, بقله *baklah*. Dry —, حشیش *hashísh*. —age, گیاه *giyáh*; سبزه *sabzeh*.

Herd, گله *galah*; رمه *ramah*.

Herdsman, گله بان *galah bán*.

Here, اینجا *ínjá*. — and there, جا بجا *já ba já*.

Hereafter, آیند *áyandeh*.

Hereditary, موروثی *maurúsí*.

Heresy, رفض *rafz*.

Heretic, رافضی *ráfizi*; خارجی *khárejí*.

Heritage, میراث *mírás*; ارث *irs*.

Hermaphrodite, خنثی *khunsá*.

Hermit, زاهد *záhid*; گوشه نشین *gúsheh níshín*.

Hermitage, تکیه *takiyeh*.

Hernia, فتق *fatk*.

Hero, گرد *gurd*; غازی *ghází*; پہلوان *pahlaván*.

Heroism, شجاعت *shujá'at*.

Heron, ماهی خوار *máhí-khár*.

Herring, شاه ماهی *sháh máhí*.

Hesitate, پائیدن *pá-ídan*.

Hesitating, مذبذب *muzabzab*.

Hesitation, تردد *taraddud* (*k.*).

Hexagon, شش کوشه *shash-gúshah*; مسدس *musaddas*.

Hexagonal, شش جهتی *shash-jihatí*.

Hiccough, سکسکه *saksakeh* (*k.*).

Hidden, نهان *nihán*; مخفی *makhfí* (*s.*); مختفی *mukhtafí*; خفیة *khafiyah*; مستتر *mustatar*; پوشیده *púshídah* (*k.*); پنهان *panhán* (*k.*).

Hide, پوشیدن *púshídan*; (one self), قایم شدن *ḳáim sh.*

Hide, *n.*, چرم *charm*.

Hiding-place, مکمن *makman*.

Hideous, مکره *mukrih*; زشت *zisht*.

High, بلند *buland*; رفیع *rafí'*; عالی *'álíy*; بالا *bálá*. In — estimation, بعزة *ba'izzat*. — station, عالی مقام *'álí muḳám*. — and low, شریف و وضیع *sharíf u vazí'*. The Most —, تعالی *Ta'ála*.

Highness (your), اعلا حضرت *a'lá hazrat*.

High-road, جاده *jádah*.

High treason, یاغی *yághí*.

Highwayman, راه زن *ráh-zan*.

Hill, کوه *kúh*; تپه *tappeh*.

Hilly, کوهی *kúhí*. — country, کهستان *kuhistán*.

Hilt, قبضه *ḳabzeh*.

Hinderance, منع *man'* (*k.*).

Hindering, مزاحم *muzáhim* (*n.*); مانع *máni'* (*k.*).

Hindoo, هندی *hindí*.

Hinge, لوله *luleh*.

Hint, اشاره *ishárah* (*k. d.*).

Hippodrome, میدان *maidan*.

Hippopotamus, اسپ دریا *aspi-daryá*.

Hips, سرین *surín*; کفل *kafal*.

Hire, کرایه *keráyeh* (*k. d.*); اجاره *ijáreh* (*d.*).

Hired labourer, اجیر *ajír*.

His, ش *-ash*; او *ú*; مال او *mál i ú*.

Hiss, سوتك *sútak* (*z.*).

Historian, مورخ *muvarrikh*; راوی *rávi*.

History, تاریخ táríkh; pl., تواریخ tawárikh; ماثور ma'sur.

Hit, n., ضرب zarb (k.); v., زدن zadan.

Hitherto, تا حال tá hál; تا هنوز tá hanúz.

Hive, مش mash.

Hoard, گنج ganj.

Hoar frost, اریز ariz; پژه puzheh.

Hoariness, شیب shaib.

Hoarse, صدا گرفته sedá girifteh.

Hock, (horse's), پای pai.

Hoe, بیل bíl (k.).

Hog, خوك khúk; گراز guráz.

Hold, (contain), v. گنجیدن ganjídan; (keep), گرفتن giriftan; نگاه داشتن nigáh dsh.

Hole, سوراخ súrákh; روزنه rauzenah.

Holiday, عید 'íd; تعطیل ta'tíl.

Holiness, پارسای pársái; قدس ḳuds.

Hollow, a., اجوف ajvaf; خالی khálí; n., گود gaud; کاواك kávák.

Holsters, قبل ḳobol.

Holy, مقدس maḳaddas; قدوس ḳadús. — Ghost, روح القدس rúh ul ḳuds. — place, قدم گاه ḳadam gah.

Homage, بیعت bai'at (k.).

Home, وطن vatan; خانه kháneh. To make a —, وطن کردن vatan k. Is so and so at —? فلان خانه است or تشریف دارد fulán kháneh ast? or tashrif dárad?

Homicide (man), خونی khúní; (action), قتل ḳatl.

Homogeneous, مجانس mujánis.

Hone, مشحذ mishhaz.

Honest, ایمان‌دار imándár.

Honesty, راستی و درستی rástí u durustí; دیانت diyánat.

Honey, عسل 'asal. — bee, مگس عسل magas i 'asal. — comb, شان shán.

Honour, آبرو ábrú; حرمة hurmat; مکرمت makrumat; عزت 'izzat; ناموس námús. Dress of —, خلعت khil'at; v., تعظیم و تکریم کردن ta'zím o takrím k.

Honourable, مجید majíd; معظم mu'azzam; محترم muhtaram (dsh.).

Honouring, اکرام ikrám (n.); تبجیل tabjíl.

Hood, باشلق *báshliḳ.*
Hoof, سم *sum.*
Hook, قلاب *ḳulláb.*
Hoop, حلقه *halḳeh.*
Hooping-cough, سرفه سالی *surfahi sálí.*
Hoopoe, هدهد *hudhud.*
Hope, امید *ummíd* (*dsh.*); امل *amal*; بویه *búyah*; ترصد *tarassud* (*n.*); توقع *tavaḳḳu'* (*dsh.*).
Hopeful, امیدوار *ummídvár.*
Hopeless, نا امید *ná-ummíd*; نومید *naumíd.*
Horizon, افق *afaḳ.*
Horizontal, مسطح *musattah.*
Horn, شاخ *shákh* (*z.*).
Horned, شاخدار *shákhdár.*
Hornet, زنبور سرخ *zambúr i surkh.*
Horoscope, زایچه *záicheh.*
Horrible, سهمکین *sahm-gín*; هولناك *haulnák.*
Horror, هیبت *haibat*; هول *haul.*
Horse, اسپ *asp*; مرکب *markab*; (thorough bred), اصیل *asíl*; (pony or half bred), یابو *yábú.* Ambling —, یرغه *yurgheh.* Led —, یدك *yedek.* — cloth, جل *jull.* — doctor, بیطار *baitár.* — man, سواره *suvárah.* — manship, سواری *suvárí*; — shoe, نعل *na'l.* — radish, ترب *turb.*
Hospitable, مهمان دوست *mihmán dúst.*
Hospital, دار الشفا *dár us shefá.*
Hospitality, مهمانی *mihmání*; مهمانداری *míhmán dárí.*
Host (landlord), میزبان *mízbán*; (of men), جماعت *jamá'at.*
Hostage, گرو *garú*; کفیل *kafíl.*
Hostile, عداوت گزین *'adávat guzín*; مخالف *muḳhálif.*
Hostility, عداوت *'adávat.*
Hot, گرم *garm.*
Hound, توله سگ *túleh sag.*
Hour, ساعت *sá'at.*
Houris, حور *húr.*
Hourly, ساعت بساعت *sá'at ba sá'at.*
House, خانه *khánah*; دار *dár*; مکان *makán.*
Household, خانواده *khánevádeh.*
Householder, خانه دار *khánah-dár.*

Housekeeping, خانه داری *khánahdárí.*

How? چه طور *chih taur*; چگونه *chigúnah.* — are you? احوال شماچه طور است *ahvál i shumá chih taur ast*; مزاج شریف چه طور است *mizáj i sharíf cheh taur ast.* — far? چه قدر راه *cheh ḳadr ráh.* — ever much, هر چند *har-chand.* — many? چند *chand.* — much, چه قدر *cheh ḳadr.*

Howl, غریو *gharív* (*k.*).

Human, آدمی *ádmí.* — being, آدمی زاده *ádmi-zádah.* — nature, انسانیت *insáníyet*; بشریت *bashariyet.* — race, بنی آدم *beni ádam*; نوع البشر *nau ʿul bashar.*

Humane, کریم *karím*; صاحب مروت *sáhib muruvvat.*

Humanity, آدمیت *ádamíyet*; بشریت *bashariyet*; انسانیت *insáníyet*; مردمی *mardumí*; مروت *muruvvat.*

Humble, فرو تن *farú-tan*; خاکسار *khák-sár*; متواضع *mutavázi*ʿ.

Humid, راطب *rátib.*

Humidity, نمی *namí.*

Humiliation, تحقیر *taḥḳír* (*k.*).

Humility, افتادگی *uftádagí*; تواضع *tavázu*ʿ; انکسار *inkisár*; وضاعت *vazáʿat*; خشوع *khushú*ʿ.

Humour (of body), خلط *khilt.*

Hump, کوهان *kúhán.* — backed, کوز پشت *kúz-pusht.*

Hundred, صد *sad.* Two —, دویست *duvíst.* Three —, سصد *sisad.*

Hunger, گرسنگی *gursnagí*; جوع *jau*ʿ.

Hungry, گرسنه *gursnah.*

Hunt, شکار کردن *shikár k.*

Hunter, شکاری *shikarí.*

Hunting, شکار *shikár.* — ground, صید گاه *said-gah.*

Huntsman, میر شکار *mír shikár.*

Hurl, در انداختن *dar andákhtan.*

Hurricane, طوفان *túfán.*

Hurry, زودی *zúdí.*

Hurt, *v.*, آزاردن *ázárdan*; *n.*, درد *dard.*

Hurtful, مضر *muzirr.*

Husband, شوهر *shauhar.*

Husbandman, حارث *háris;* مزارع *muzárî;* کشت کار *kisht-kár.*

Husbandry, دهقانی *dihḳání.*

Hush! خاموش *khámúsh.*

Husk, پوست *púst.*

Hut, کمه *kumah.*

Hyacinth, سنبل *sumbul.*

Hyæna, کفتار *kaftár.*

Hydrophobia, کلاب *kaláb.*

Hymn, تسبیح *tasbíh.*

Hyocyamus, سیکران *saikerán.*

Hyperbole, مبالغه *mubálaghah.*

Hypochondria, تهی گاه *tihí-gáh.*

Hypocrisy, تزویر *tazvír;* نفاق *nifáḳ;* دو رنگی *dú-rangí.*

Hypocrite, منافق *munáfiḳ;* ریا کار *riyá-kár.*

Hypocritical, سالوس *sálús;* دو رنگ *dú-rang.*

Hypothesis, فرض *farz.*

Hypothetical, مجازی *mujází.* —ly, فرضاً *farzan.*

Hyssop, زوفا *zúfá.*

I.

I, من *man.* I am, منم *manam.* I who am, منکه *man kih.*

Ibex, مرال *marál;* بز *buz.*

Ice, یخ *yakh.* — chest, یخدان *yakhdán.* Iced-water, برف آب *barf-áb.*

Idea, خیال *khiyál;* تصور *tasavvur;* فکر *fikr.*

Ideal, معنویه *ma'navíyeh.*

Identical, همین *hamín;* عینی *'ainí.*

Idiom, اصطلاح *istiláh.*

Idiot, کول *gúl;* ابله *ablah.*

Idiotcy, دیوانکی *divánagí.*

Idiotic, دیوانه *díváneh.*

Idle, هوشا *húshá;* سست *sust;* معطل *mu'attal.* — talk, یافه داری *yáfah-dárí.* —ness, بیکاری *bí-kárí;* تنبلی *tumbulí.*

Idol, بت *but.*

Idolator, بت پرست *but-parast.*

Idolatry, بت پرستی *but-parastí* (*k.*).

Idol-temple, بت کده *but-kedah;* بت خانه *but-khánah.*

If, اگر *agar.* — not, اگرنه *agarnah.*

Ignite, *v. t.*, سوزانیدن *súzánidan;* *v. t.*, شعله کشیدن *sho'leh ksh.*

Ignoble, نا جنس *ná-jins;* بد رگ *bad rag.*

Ignominy, فضیحت *fazıhat.*

Ignorance, نا دانی *ná-dání;* جهل *jahl;* جهالت *jahálat.* Feigning —, متجاهل *mutajáhil.* The times of — (before Mohammed), جاهلیت *jáhilíyet.*

Ignorant, نا شناس *ná-shinás;* جاهل *jáhil;* نکر *nakir.* Very —, جهول *jahúl.* —ly, نا دان *ná-dan.*

Ill, to be, نا خوش هستن *ná khúsh h.* —disposed, بد نهاد *bad-nihád.* —doing, بد کار *bad-kár.* —fated, بد بخت *bad bakht.* —ness, ناخوشی *ná khúshí.* —tempered, بد خوی *bad-khúy;* زشت خوی *zisht-khúy.* —timed, بی هنگام *bí-hangám.* —treatment, بد رفتاری *bad raftárí* (*k.*); ظلم *zulm* (*k.*). —favoured, زشت *zisht.* —starred, بد اختر *bad-akhtar.*

Illegal, ناحق *ná hakk;* حرام *harám.*

Illegitimate-child, حرام زاده *harám zádeh.*

Illiberal, بخیل *bakhíl.*

Illuminate, افروختن *afrúkhtan;* *pa. p.*, منور *munavvar* (*k.*).

Illumination, چراغان *cherághán* (*k.*).

Illusion, خواب و خیال *kh'áb u khayál.*

Illustration, (drawing), تصویر *tasvír;* (in argument, بیان *bayán.*

Illustrious, بزرگ وار *buzurg-vár;* نام آور *nám-ávar.* Most —, اشرف *ashraf.* — race, دودمان *dúdmán.*

Image, صنم *sanam;* صورت *súrat.*

Imagination, توهم *tavahhum;* تصور *tasavvur;* واهمه *váhimah;* خیال *khayál* (*k.*). Vain —, خیال خام *khayál i khám.*

Imaginations, خیالات *khayálát.*

Imagined, متصور *mutasavvar;* موهوم *mauhúm.*

Imagining, مخیل *mukhaiyil;* متخیل *mutakhaiyil.*

Imam, امام *imám; pl.*, ائمه *a-immah.*

Imbecile, ضعیف العقل *za'íf ul 'akl.*

Imitated, مقلد *mukallad.*

Imitation, تقلید (در آوردن) *taklíd* (*dar a.* or *k.*), تتبع *tattabu';* متابعت *mutába'at.*

Imitator, مقتدی *muktadí.*

Immature, نا بالغ *ná-báligh;* خام *khám.*

Immeasurable, نهشمار *nuhshumár;* بیحد *bíhadd.*
Immediately, فی الحال *fi 'l hál;* فوراً *fauran.*
Immemorial, مستدام *mustadám.*
Immense, بیکران *bí-girán.*
Immersed, مغروق *maghrúḳ;* مستغرق *mustaghraḳ (sh.).*
Immersion, تغریق *taghríḳ (k.);* استغراق *istighráḳ.*
Imminent, نزدیك *nazdík.*
Immobile, قایم *ḳáim.*
Immodest, بی شرم *bí sharm;* بی حیا *bí hayá.*
Immolate, قربان کردن *ḳurbán k.*
Immoral, فاسد *fásid.* —ity, فسوق *fusúḳ.*
Immortal, لا یموت *lá yamút.*
Immortality, ابدی *abadí.*
Immovable, بی حرکت *bí harrakat.*
Immunity, آزادی *ázádí,*
Immutable, بی تغیر *bí taghayyur.*
Impale, *v.* خازوق زدن *kházúḳ z.*
Impartial, راست بین *rást-bín.*
Impartiality, عدل *'adl.*
Impatience, نا شکیبائی *ná shakíbáí.*
Impatient, بیصبر *bí-sabr.*
Impediment, مزاحمت *muzáhamat;* سنك راه *sang i ráh;* خار راه *khár i ráh.*
Imperative امر *amr.*
Imperfect, ناقص *náḳis.* —ion, قصور *ḳusúr.*
Imperial, شهنشاهی *shahanshâhí;* خاقانی *kháḳání.*
Impersonation, تشبه *tashabbuh (k.).*
Impertinence, گستاخی *gustákhí;* بیهودگی *bí-húdagí.*
Impetuous, تند رو *tund ro.*
Impetus, هجوم *hujúm.*
Impiety, کفر *kufr.*
Impious, کافر *káfir;* بیدین *bídín.*
Implement, آلت *álat.*
Implicate, تهمت بستن *tuhmat bs.*
Implied, مضمر *muzmar.*
Imploring, مستدعی *mustad'í (n.).*
Import, آمدنی *ámadaní;* مدخل *madkhal.*
Important, مهم *muhimm.* — affairs, مآرب *ma'árib.*
Importune, پله کردن *pillah k.*
Importuning, متقاضی *mutaḳází.*

Importunity, الحاح *ilháh ;* ابرام *ibrám.*

Impose on, گول دادن *gúl d.*

Imposition, حیله *hílah.*

Impossibilities, محالات *mahálát.*

Impossible, محال *mahál ;* غیر ممکن *ghair mumkin ;* نا شدنی *ná shudaní.*

Impostor, شیاد *shaiyád ;* غابن *ghábin.*

Imposture, دغا *daghá.* Accusing of —, تکذیب *takzíb* (*k.*)

Impotence, تعجیز *ta'jíz.*

Impotent, عاجز *'ájiz ;* عنین *'anín.*

Impoverished, مفقر *mufḳar* (*sh.*) ; محتاج *muhtáj* (*s.*).

Impregnable, منیع *maní'.*

Impregnation, ابستن *abistan* (*s.*).

Impressed, متاثر *muta'assar ;* مطبوع *matbú'* (*k.*).

Impression, اثر *asar ;* تأثیر *ta'sír.* Making an — on, موثر *músir.*

Imprison, حبس کردن *habs k.*

Imprisonment, قید *ḳaid* (*k.*).

Improbable, دور *dúr ;* غیر معقول *ghair ma'ḳúl.*

Impromptu, بدیهت *badíhat ;* بداهت *badáhat.*

Improper, بیجا *bí-já ;* نا بایسته *ná-báyistah ;* نا مناسب *ná-munásib ;* نا لایق *ná-láiḳ.*

Improvement, ترقی دادن *taraḳḳí d.*

Improvidence, غافلی *ghájílí.*

Improvisator, مبده *mibdah.*

Imprudence, غفلت *ghiflat.*

Imprudent, بی تدبیر *bí tadbír.*

Imprudently, غفلتاً *ghiflatan.*

Impudence, شوخی *shúkhí ;* شوخ چشمی *shúkh-chashmí ;* وقاحت *vaḳáhat.*

Impudent, نا داری *ná-dárí ;* شوخ دیده *shúkh-dídah ;* وقح *vaḳih ;* فضول *fuzúl.*

Impulse, تحریك *tahrík* (*d.*).

Impunity, with, بیسزا *bísezá.*

Impure, نا پاك *ná-pák ;* پلید *palíd ;* نجس *najis.*

Impurity, نجاست *najásat.*

Imputation, تهمت *tuhmat* (*bs.*).

Impute, نسبت دادن *nisbat d.*

In, ب *ba ;* در *dar ;* اندر *andar ;* میان *miyán ;* توی *tuy.*

Inability, در ماندگی dar mán-dagí.

Inaccessibility, مناعت manáʻat.

Inaccessible, منیع muniʻ.

Inaccurate, نا راست ná rást.

Inactive, سست عنان sust-ʻinán.

Inadmissible, نا روا ná-ravá.

Inadvertence, غفلت ghiflat.

Inadvertent, غافل gháfil.

Inasmuch as, از بسکه az baskih.

Inattention, تغافل tagháful.

Inattentive, غافل gháfil.

Inauspicious, نا مسعود ná-masʻúd; نحس nahs.

Incalculable, بیقیاس bí-ḳiyás.

Incantation, افسون afsún; رقیه ruḳyah.

Incapable, ناقابل ná ḳábil.

Incapacity, نا رسائی ná-rasáí.

Incarnation, تجسم tajassum.

Incautions, بیخبر bí khabar.

Incendiary, شر انگیز sharr-angíz.

Incense, بخور bakhúr.

Incessant, دایم dáim.

Incessantly, دمبدم dam ba dam; پیوسته paivasteh.

Incest, فجور القرابه fujúr al ḳarábah.

Inch, گره garah.

Incident, واقعه váḳiʻah; اتفاق ittifáḳ.

Incidental, اتفاقی ittifáḳi.

Incipient beard, خط سبز khatt i sabz.

Incision, قطع ḳatʻ.

Incitement, ترغیب targhíb (k.); اطماع itmáʻ (n.).

Incivility, بی ادبی bí adabí.

Inclement, سخت sakht.

Inclination, ارادت irádat; (mental), میل meyl; (leaning), تکیه takiyeh; (in prayer) رکعه rukʻah.

Inclined, مایل máil; میلان mílán; چسپیده chaspídah.

Inclining, متمایل mutamáyil.

Including, متضمن mutazammin; شامل حال shámil i hál; مندرج mundarij.

Incoherent, بی موافق bí muváfiḳ.

Income, حاصل hásil; مداخل mudákhil.

Incomparable, بیچون bí-chún; بی نظیر bí-nazír; بی همتا bí-hamtá; بیمانند bí mánand.

Incompetent, غیر کافی ghair káfí.

Incomplete, نا تمام *ná-tamám* ; نا فرجام *ná-farjám.*

Incomprehensible, بی قیاس *bí ḳiyás.*

Inconceiveable, نا متصور *ná-mutasavvar.*

Incongruous, نا ساز *ná sáz.*

Inconsiderate, سر سری *sar-sarí* ; نا سکالیده *ná-sakálídah.*

Inconsistent, مناقض *munáḳiz* ; منافی *munáfí.*

Inconstant, طیاش *taiyásh* ; طایش *táish* ; نا استوار *ná ustuvár* ; نا پایدار *ná páidár.*

Incontinence, بد پرهیزی *bad parhízí.*

Incontinent, بد کار *bad kár.*

Inconvenience, مضرت *mazar-rat* ; Putting to — مکلف *mukallif.*

Inconvenient, دشوار *dushvár* ; زحمت *zahmat.*

Incorporate, مجسم *mujassam.*

Incorporation, ضمیمه *zamímah* (*sh.*).

Incorrect, نا درست *ná durust* ; نا صواب *ná saváb.*

Incorrectness, غلط *ghalat.*

Incorruptible (man), پاك دمانی *pák damáni* ; بیغرض *bí gharaz* ; (matter) غیر فنا *ghair faná.*

Increase, توفیر *taufír* ; فزون *fuzún* ; افزایش *afzáyish* ; افزونی *afzúní* ; اضافه *izáfeh* ; ترقی *taraḳḳi* ; *v.* افزودن *afzúdan.*

Increasing, متزاید *mutazáyid* ; افزون *afzún.*

Incredible, نا واجب اعتبار *ná vájibi i'tibár.*

Incrustate, اندودن *andúdan.*

Incumbent, لازم *lázim* ; واجب *vájib.*

Incurable, لا دوا *lá davá* ; لا علاج *lá 'iláj.*

Incursion, حمله *hamleh* ; چپو *chapau* (*k.*).

Indebted, مدیون *madyún* ; مقروض *maḳrúz.*

Indecency, هرزگی *harzagí.*

Indecent, لا ینبغی *lá yambaghí* ; ناسزا *ná-sazá.* Speaking —ly, هراء *hurá'.*

Indeed, بدرستی *ba-durustí* ; یقیناً *yaḳínan.*

Indefinite, غیر معین *ghair mu'ayyan.*

Indelible, ثابت *sábit.*

Indemnification, تضمین *tazmín*; مجازات *mujázát*.

Independence, استقلال *istiklál*; استغناء *istighná'*.

Independent, مستغنی *mustaghní*; مختار *mukhtár*; (well off), خوش باش *khúsh-básh*.

Index, فهرست *fihrist*.

India, هندوستان *Hindústán*; هند *Hind*.

Indian, هندو *hindú*; هندی *hindí*.

Indicate, اشاره کردن *isharah k.*; *pa. p.* مشار الیه *mushár ilaih*.

Indication, دلالت *dalálat*.

Indictment, حکم نما *hukm namá*.

Indifference, غفلت *ghiflat*.

Indifferent, بیزار *bí-zár*.

Indigence, تنك دستی *tang-dastí*; بیمایکی *bí-máyagí*.

Indigent, محتاج *muhtáj*; تنك دست *tang dast*, or دست تنك *dast-tang*; نیاز مند *niyáz-mand*; حاجت مند *há-jat-mand*.

Indigestible, ناکوار *nágavár*.

Indigestion, وخامت *vakhámat*; تخمه *tukhmah*.

Indignant, خشمناك *khishmnák*.

Indignation, تنفر *tanaffar*.

Indignity, خفت *khiffat*.

Indigo, نیل *níl* · وسمه *vasmeh*.

Indirect, پیچیده *píchídah*.

Indiscernable, ناپیدا *ná paidá*.

Indiscreet, بی امتیاز *bí imtiyáz*.

Indisputable, بی شك و شبهه *bí shakk o shubheh*.

Indistinct, نا صاف *ná sáf*.

Individual, نفر *nafar*; کس *kas*; شخص *shakhs*.

Indolence, تکاسل *takásul* (*n.*); سستی *sustí* (*k.*).

Indolent, سست *sust*.

Inducement, ترغیب *targhíb* (*k.*); تحریك *tahrík* (*k.*).

Indulgence, التفات *iltifát*.

Indulgent, مهربان *mihribán*.

Indulging one's passions, هوس باز *havvas-báz*.

Industrious, جاهد *jáhid*; ساعی *sá'i*.

Industry, کسب *kasb*; اجتهاد *ijtihád*; جد و جهد *jidd o jahd*.

Inebriated, مست *mast*.

Ineffable, ما لا کلام *má lá kalám*, or لا کلام *lá ka-lám*.

Inefficatious, بیثمر *bí samar*.

Inelegance, بد صورت *bad súrat*.

Inept, بی لیاقت *bí liyákat.*
Inequality, فرق *fark.*
Inestimable, بی بها *bí bahá.*
Inevitable, نا گریز *ná-guríz;* چار نا چار *chár ná chár.*
Inexpedient, نا مناسب *ná munásib.*
Inexperienced, خام *khám.*
Inexpert, بی سلیقه *bí-salíkah.*
In extenso, بالتمام *bittamám.*
Infallibility, بی خطای *bí khatá-i.*
Infallible, بلا خطا *bilá khatá.*
Infamous, بد نام *bad-nám;* رسوا *rusvá;* مابون *mábún.*
Infamy, رسوای *rusvá'í.*
Infancy, طفولیت *tufúlíyat.*
Infant, بچه *bachah;* (suckling), رضیع *razí'.*
Infantry, سر باز *sarbáz;* پیاده *piyádeh.*
Infatuate, آشفتن *áshuftan;* pa. p., فریفته *firífteh.*
Infection, سرایت *saráyat (k.).*
Infectious, معدی *mu'dí.*
Inferior, اسفل *asfal;* زیرین *zírín;* فرودست *farú-dast;* کهتر *kihtar.*
Inferiority, پستی *pastí;* دونی *dúní.*

Infernal, دوزخی *dúzakhí.*
Infidel, کافر *káfir; pl.* کفار *kuffár.*
Infidelity, کفر *kufr.*
Infinite, بیکران *bígirán;* نا متناهی *ná-mutanáhí.*
Infinitive (verb), مصدر *masdar.*
Infirm, ضعیف *za'íf;* نا توان *ná-taván.* — ity, نا توانی *ná-taváni;* (*pl.*), اسقام *askám.*
Inflamed (with love), مشغوف *mashghúf;* (wound), ملتهب *multahib.*
Inflaming, جانسوز *ján-súz.*
Inflammation, سوزش *súzish;* (wound), التهاب *iltiháb.*
Inflated, دمی *damí (s.).*
Inflexible, سخت *sakht.*
Inflexion, (grammar), تصریف *tasríf (k.);* صرف *sarf (k.).*
Influencing, تاثیر *taasír (k.).*
Influenza, زکام *zukám.*
Inform, اطلاع کردن *ittilá' k;* فهمانیدن *fahmánídan;* خبر دادن *khabar d.*
Information, تخبیر *takhbír;* وقوف *vukúf.* To obtain —, وا رسیدن *wá-rasídan.*
Informed, واقف *vákif;* مطلع *muttali'.* To be —, اطلاع داشتن *ittilá' dáshtan.*

Informer, نمام *nammám*; جاسوس *jásús*.

Infringement, فسخ *faskh* (*k.*).

Infuse, خيسيدن *khísídan*.

Infusion, خسانده *khasándah*, or خيسانده *khísándah*.

Ingenious, زكي *zakíy*, or ذكي *zakíy*; ذهين *zahín*; ظريف *zaríf*.

Ingenuity, جودت *júdat*; حذاقت *hizáḳat* and حداقت *hadáḳat*; كياست *kiyásat*; شهامت *shahámat*; (purity), زكاوت *zakáwat*.

Ingenuous, ازكياء *azkiyá*; صادق *sádiḳ*.

Ingot, شوشه *shúshah*; خفچه *khafchah*; (of gold), خشت زر *khisht i zar*.

Ingratitude, بيوفاى *bí-vafá-í*; كفران *kufrán*.

Ingredient, جز *juz*.

Ingress and egress, در آمد بر آمد *dar ámad bar ámad*.

Inhabitant, ساكن *sákin* (*b.*); (*pl.*), سكناء *sukaná*, or سكان *sukkán*; باشنده *báshandah*; (*pl.*), اهالى *ahálí*.

Inhabited, آباد *ábád*.

Inhabiting, متوطن *mutavattin*.

Inhale, دم زدن *dam z.*

Inherent, اصلى *aslí*.

Inheritance, ارث *irs* (*gr.*); ميراث *mírás* (*y.*).

Inherited, موروث *maurús*.

Inheriting, وراثت *varásat*.

Inheritor, وارث *váris*.

Inhibition, نهى *nahí* (*k.*).

Inhospitable, لئيم *laím*.

Inhuman, فظ *fazz*; بيمروت *bi-muruvvat*.

Inimical, معاند *mu'ánid*. —ly, خصمانه *khasmánah*.

Iniquitous, حرام خور *harám-khur*. — things, مناكير *manákír*.

Iniquity, فساد *fasád*; فسق *fisḳ*.

Initial, حرف ابتدا *harf i ibtidá*.

Initiation, دخل *dakhl* (*d.*); مداخله *mudákhalah* (*n.*).

Injection, تنقيه *tanḳiyeh*.

Injudicious, پوچ *púch*; بيتدبير *bítadbír*.

Injunction, تاكيد *ta'kíd*.

Injure, آزردن *ázardan*; ضرر رسانيدن *zarar rsa.*

Injured, متأذى *muta'azzí*.

Injurious, مضر *muzirr*.

Injury, اذيت *azíyet*; ايذا *ízá*; گزند *gazand*.

Injustice, ظلم *zulm*; بيداد *bí-dád.*

Ink, مركب *murakkab.* Indian —, مركب چين *m-i chín.*

Inkstand, دوات *davát*; (pen and ink case), قلمدان *kalam-dán.*

Inlaid, مرصع *murassa'*; (with gold), طلا كوب *telá kúb*; (with mosaic work), خاطمی *khátimí*; (with tiles), کاشی کاری *káshí kárí.*

Inn, کاروان سرای *káraván saráí*; مهمان سرا *mihmán sará.*

Innate, مادر زاد *mádar-zád*; غریزی *gharíziy*; طبیعی *tabí'í.*

Innocence, بی گناهی *bí-gunáhí.*

Innocent, بی گناه *bí-gunáh*; معصوم *ma'súm*; عاصم *'ásim*; بری الذمه *barí uz zimmah.*

Innovating, ابداع *ibdá'* (k.).

Innumerable, نا محصور *ná-mahsúr*; نا معدود *ná-ma'dúd*: بیشمار *bí-shumár.*

Inoculation, آبله کوبی *ábilah kúbí.*

Inodorus, بی بو *bí-bú.*

Inorganic, جمادی *jamádiy.*

Inopportune, بی وقت *bí vakt.*

Inquest, تفحص *tafahhus* (k.).

Inquietude, اضطراب *izteráb.*

Inquire, پرسیدن *pursídan*; وا جستن *wá-justan.*

Inquiring, متفتش *mutafattish.*

Inquiry, پرسش *pursish* (k.); استفسار *istifsár*; پژوهش *pizhúhish*; تفقد *tafakkud* (n.); تفتیش *taftísh*; سراغ *surágh* (thus دزدرا سراغ کردند *duzd-rá surágh kerdand*, They found the thief). Strict —, تفحص *tafahhus.* Subject of —, پرسیدنی *pursídaní.*

Inquisitor, مفتش *mufattish.*

Insane, دیوانه *díwánah*; جنونی *junúní*; مجنون *majnún*; (with love), مدله *mudallah.*

Insanity, جنون *junún*; دیوانکی *díwánagí.*

Inscribe, مرقوم کردن *markúm k.*

Inscription, کتابت *kitábat*; *pl.* نوشتجات *navishtaját*; خط *khatt.*

Inscrutable, بی نشان *bí-nishán.*

Insect, حشرت *hashrat*; جانورك *jánvarak.*

Insecurity, خطر *khatar.*

Insensibility, بیهوشی *bí húshí.*

Insensibly, بتدريج *be-tadríj.*

Insert, داخل كردن *dákhil k.*

Insertion, تعبيه *ta'bíyeh.*

Inside, اندرون *andarún*; توى *túy.*

Insignia, التمغا *at-tamghá.*

Insignificance, حقر *hakr.*

Insignificant, نا چيز *ná chíz.*

Insincere, بيوفا *bí-vafá.*

Insincerity, منافقت *munáfikat.*

Insinuation, ايهام *íhám* (*n.*); اشاره *ishárah* (*k.*).

Insipid, بى نمك *bí-numak*; بيمزه *bí-mazah.*

Insistence, اصرار *isrár* (*k.*);

Insolence, شاهدى *sháhidí*; شوخى *shúkhí.*

Insolent, شوخ *shúkh.*

Insoluble, لاحل *lá hall.*

Insolvent, نا دار *ná-dár.*

Insomuch as, چندانكه *chandánkih.*

Inspection, نگاه *nigáh* (*k.*); معاينه *mu'áyanah* (*k.*); نظارت *nazárat* (*n.*); ملاحظه *mulá-hezeh* (*k.*).

Inspector, ناظر *názir.* — general of tents, خيام باشى *khiyám báshí.*

Inspiration, الهام *ilhám* (*n.*).

Inspired, ملهم *mulham.*

Inspiring, تخويف *takhvíf* (*k.*).

Inspissated juice, رب *rubb.*

Instability, بى قرارى *bí-karárí.*

Installation, نصب *nasb* (*k.*).

Instalment, قسط *kast.*

Instance, *n.*, مثال *misál.* For — مثلاً *masalan*; فرضاً *far-zan.*

Instant, نفسى *nafasí*; لمحه *lamheh.* —ly, در ساعت *dar sá'at*; بمجرد *bamujarrad*; در دم *dar dam*; در حال *dar hál.*

Instead of, بجاى *ba jái*; عوض *ivaz.*

Instigating, تحريص *tahrís* (*k.*).

Instigation, اغوا *ighvá.*

Instigator, محرك *muharrik.*

Instinct, عقل *'akl*; فراست *firásat.*

Institutes, one who, مقنن *mu-kannin.*

Institution, اختراع *ikhtirá'* (*k.*). —s, آئين *á'in*; قانون *kánún.*

Instruct, ياد دادن *yád d.* —ion, تعليم *ta'lím* (*k.*); تربيت *tarbiyat* (*n.*); تلقين *talkín* (*n.*).

Instructor, معلم *mu'allim.*

Instrument, آلت *álat* ; ادات *adát*, *pl.* ادوات *adawát*. — for boring, مثقب *musaḳḳib*. Musical —, نا انبان *ná-ambán* ; ساز *sáz*. Wind —, نفیر *nafír*.

Insubordination, تمرد *tamarrud*.

Insufferable, لا تحمل *tahammul*.

Insufficient, کم *kam* ; قاصر *ḳásir*.

Insulation (of a wire), خارج *khárij* (*k.*).

Insulator, کرکری *gargarí*.

Insult, شتم *shatm* (*d.*) ; دشنام *dushnám* (*d.*) ; خفت *khiffat*.

Insurance, بیمه *bímah* (*k.*).

Insurrection, خاستکی *khástagí* ; شورش *shurish* ; فتنه *fitnah*.

Integrity, دیانت *diyánat* ; راستی *rástí* ; صلاح *saláh*.

Intellect, عقل *'aḳl* ; ذهن *zihn* Acuteness of —, ذکاء *zaká*.

Intellectual, معقول *ma'ḳúl*.

Intelligence, (news), خبر *khabar* ; (wit), زکاوت *zakávat*.

Intelligent, فهیم *fahím* ; شناس *shinás* ; رمیز *ramíz* ; عاقل *'áḳil* ; زیرك *zírak* ; هشیار *hushyár* ; دریابنده *daryábandah* ; با خبر *ba-khabr* ; بخرد *ba khird* ; روشن کهر *raushan-guhar*. Very —, فهام *fahhám*.

Intelligible, مدرك *mudrak*.

Intemperance, مستی *mastí*.

Intemperate, نا معتدل *ná-mu'tadil*.

Intend, آهختن *áhikhtan* ; قصد کردن *ḳasd k* ; *pa. p.*, منوی *manvíy* ; *pr. p.*, عازم *'ázim*.

Intensity, شدت *shiddat*.

Intention, قصد *ḳasd* (*k. n.*) ; طویت *taviyet* ; زمم *zamam* ; عرضه *'arzah* ; عمد *'amd* ; پیش نهاد *písh-nihád* ; همت *himmat* ; *pl.*, همم *himam* ; نیت *niyat* ; آهنك *áhang*.

Intentional, بالقصد *bilḳasd*. —ly, عمداً *'amdan*.

Inter, دفن کردن *dafn k*.

Intercalary, کبیسه *kabísah*.

Intercept, کرفتن *giriftan*.

Intercession, شفاعت *shifá'at* (*k.*) ; وساطت *vasátat* (*k*).

Intercessor, شفیع *shafí'* ; شافع *sháfi'*.

Intercourse, معاشرت *mu'ásharat* ; آمد و رفت *ámad o raft* ; اختلاط *ikhtilát* ; (carnal), مضاجعت *muzája'at*.

Interdicting, تحریم *tahrím* (*k.*); منع *man'* (*k.*).

Interest (money), سود *súd*; مرابحه *murábahah*; (concern), اعتنا *i'tiná*; علاقه *'alákah*.

Interested, غرض *gharaz*. Self-—, غرضمند *gharz-mand*.

Interference in, مداخلت *mudákhalat* (*n.*). — with, معارض *mu'áriz* (*b.*); مزاحم *muzáhim* (*sh.*).

Interim, اثنا *asná*.

Interior, درون *darún*; بواطن *bavátin*.

Interjection, صوت *saut*.

Interlaced, مشبك *mushabbak*.

Interlocutor, کلیم *kalím*; متکلم *mutakallim*.

Intermarriage, وصلت *vaslat* (*k.*).

Intermediary, متوسط *mutavassit*.

Interment, دفن *dafn*.

Intermingled, مخلوط *makhlút* (*k.*).

Intermission, تقطع *takattu'*.

Intermittent fever, تب نوبت *tab-i-naubat*.

Internal, باطنی *bátini*; درونی *darúní*.

Interpolation, مخالطه *mukháleteh* (*s.*).

Interpose, درمیان آمدن *dar miyán ámadan*.

Interposition, دخل *dakhl* (*k.*).

Interpretation, تأویل *ta'víl* (*n.*); ترجمه *tarjumah* (*k.*); (of dreams), تعبیر *ta'bír* (*k.*).

Interpreter, ترجمان *tarjumán*; مترجم *mutarjim*; (of dreams and omens), فالگیر *fálgír*.

Interregnum, فترة *fitrat*.

Interrogation, استفهام *istifhám*.

Interrogate, پرسیدن *pursídan*.

Interrogatively, باستفسار *be-istifsár*.

Interrogator, پرسنده *pursendah*.

Interruption, intersection, قطع *kat'* (*n.*).

Interval, بین *bain*; تفریق *tafrík*; اثنا *asná*. At —s, غباً *ghibban*.

Intervening, طاری *tárí*; حایل *háyil*; دخل *dakhl*.

Interview, دیدار *dídár*; مواصلت *muvásalat*; ملاقات *mulakát*.

Intestate, بی وصیت *bí vasíyat*.

Intestine, روده *rúdah* (*n.*); *in pl.*, جگر بند *jigar-band.*

Intimacy, موانست *muvánasat*; سر آشنائی *sar-áshnáí*; دم سازی *dam-sází.*

Intimate friend, همدم *ham-dam*; همنشین *ham-nishín*; محرم *muhrim.*

Intimation, اشاره *isháreh* (*k.*).

Intimidation, تخویف *takhvíf* (*k.*).

Into, در *dar*; اندر *andar*; توی *tuy.*

Intolerable, غیر متحمل *ghair mutahammel.*

Intoning, ترنم *tarannum*; ترتیل *tartíl.*

Intoxicated, مست *mast*; سر مست *sar-mast*; سکران *sukrán*; نشوان *nashván*; سرشار *sar-shár.* Like one —, مستانه *mastánah.*

Intoxicating, مسکر *muskir.*

Intoxication, سکر *sukr*; نشه *nash-h*; نشوت *nashvat*; مستی *mastí.*

Intractable, سرکش *sar kesh.*

Intreaty, التماس *iltimás* (*k.*); الجا *iljá* (*k.*).

Intrenchment, سنگر *sangur*; النك *alang.*

Intrepid, فاتك *fátik*; بیباك *bí bák.*

Intrepidity, شجاعة *shajá'at*; شیری *shírí*; دلاوری *dilávarí*; دلیری *dilírí*; جانبازی *ján-bází.*

Intricate, ژولیده *zhúlídah*; درهم *dar-ham*; معقد *mu'akkad.* An — business, آشفته کار *áshuftah kár.*

Intrigue, سازش *sázish*; عشقبازی *'ishk-bází.*

Intrinsic, حقیقی *hakíkí*; معنوی *ma'naví*; ذاتی *zátí.*

Introducing, ادخال *idkhál*; معرفی *mu'arrafí* (*k.*).

Introduction (of book), دیباچه *díbácheh.*

Intrust, سپردن *sipurdan*; تسلیم کردن *taslím k.*

Intrusted, مسلم *musallam.*

Intwine, *v. i.*, پیچیدن *píchídan*; *v. t.*, پیچانیدن *pichánídan.*

Inundation, سیلاب *sailáb*; سیل *sail.*

Invalid, ناخوش *nákhush.*

Invalidate, باطل کردن *bátil k.*

Invaluable, عزیز *azíz.*

Invariable, دایم *dáim.*

Invasion, تعدی *ta'addí* ; یورش *yúrish* (*k.*) ; هجوم *hujúm* (*k.*).

Invective, زبان درازی *zabán dirází* ; لعنت *la'nat.*

Inveigle, فریفتن *firíftan.*

Invention, ابتداع *ibtidá'* (*k.*) ; اختراع *ikhtirá'* (*k.*) ; ایجاد *íjád* (*k.*) ; احداث *ihdás* ; نو آورد *nau-ávard.*

Inventor, محدث *muhdis* ; واجد *wájid* ; موجد *mújid.*

Inventory, فهرست *fihrist.*

Inversely, بر عکس *bar 'aks.*

Inversion, تقلیب *taḳlíb* (*k.*) ; عکس *'aks* ; (of letters), تحریف *tahríf.*

Invert, بر گشتن *bar gashtan* ; بر گردیدن *bar gardídan* ; *pa. p.*, معکوس *ma'kús* ; منعکس *mun'akis* ; مقلب *muḳallab* ; مقلوب *maḳlúb* ; نگون *nigún* ; *pr. p.*, متبدل *mutabaddal.*

Investigation, تنقیح *tanḳíh* (*k.*) ; تجویز *tajvíz* (*k.*) ; باز خواست *báz-kh'ást* (*k.*) ; تحقیق *tahḳíḳ* (*k.*).

Investigator, a minute —, خورده دان *khurdah-dán.*

Investment (of a town), محاصره *muhasereh* (*k.*) ; (with honours), متقلد *mutaḳallid* (*k.*).

Invidious, حاسد *hásid.*

Invigoration, تقویت *taḳvíyat* (*k.*).

Inviolable, بی فتور *bí futúr* ; بست *bust.*

Invisibility, غیب *ghaib.*

Invisible, نا پدید *ná-padid* ; نا دیدنی *ná dídaní.* — things, غیوب *ghuyúb* ; غائبانا *gháïbáná.*

Invitation, دعوت *da'vat* (*k.*).

Invited, مدعو *mad'ú* (*h.*).

Invocation, دعا *du'á* (*k.*).

Invoice, فهرست *fihrist.*

Involuntary, بی اختیار *bi ikhtiyár.*

Involved, مشتمل *mushtamel* (*b.*).

Invulnerable, معصوم *ma'súm.*

Inward, باطن *bátin* ; درونی *darúní.*

Irascibility, تغیظ *taghayyuz.*

Irascible, سر تیز *sar-tíz.*

Iris (flower), زنبق *zambaḳ.*

Iron, آهن *áhan* ; حدید *hadíd* ; (cast), چدن *chadan* ; (for ironing), اتو *utú* (*ksh.*).

Made of —, آهنی *áhaní;* آهنین *áhanín.* — mace, کوپال *gúpál.*

Ironclad (ship), زره پوش *zireh púsh.*

Irony, هجو *hajv.*

Irrefutable, بی جواب *bí javáb.*

Irregular, بی توزکانه *bí-túzagánah;* بیقاعده *bí ḳá'ideh.*

Irregularity, بی رسمی *bí-rasmí.*

Irreligious, بد کیش *bad-kísh;* بی دین *bí-dín.*

Irremediable, بی چاره *bí cháreh.*

Irresolute, دو دل *do dil.*

Irresolution, تردد *taraddud.*

Irresponsible authority, استقلال *istiḳlál.*

Irreverence, بی احترامی *bí ihtirámí.*

Irreverent, بی احترام *bí ihtirám.*

Irrigate, آب دادن *áb d.*

Irrigation, آبیاری *ábyárí.*

Irritable, کج خلق *ḳaj khulḳ.*

Irritate, رنجیده ساختن *ranjídah s.*

Irritation, آشفتگی *ashuftagí.*

Isinglass, سریش ماهی *sirísh i máhí.*

Islam, اسلام *islám.*

Island, جزیره *jazírah.*

Isolated, تکتک *tektek;* مجرد *mujarrad.*

Isolation, تفرید *tafríd.*

Issue, *n.*, اولاد *aulád.*

Issuing, صادر *sádir* (*sh. k.*); اصدار *isdár.*

Isthmus, تنکه *tangah.*

It, او *ú;* آن *án;* این *ín.*

Itch, خارشت *khárisht;* خارش *khárish;* حکة *hikkat;* جرب *jarab.*

Itching, خراش *kharásh.*

Item, فرد *fard.*

Itinerary, راه *ráh.*

Itself, of —, بنفسه *be-nafsah.*

Ivory, عاج *'áj;* دندان فیل *dandán-i-fíl.*

Ivy, لبلاب *labláb;* ویشه *wíshah.*

J

Jabber, مغلطه کردن *maghlitah k.;* قیل و قال کردن *ḳíl o ḳál k.*

Jackal, شغال *shaghál.*

Jackdaw, زاغ *zágh.*

Jacket, نیمتنه *nímtaneh;* Quilted silk —, کج اکند

kaj-ágand. Sheepskin —, پوستین *pústín.*

Jacob, James, یعقوب *Ya'kúb.*

Jade (stone), یشم *yashm.*

Jail, زندان *zindán.*

Jailor, زندانبان *zindánbán.*

Jam, مربا *murabbá.*

Jar (large), خم *khum;* خمره *khumrah;* (small), سبو *sabú;* کوزه *kúzah.*

Jargon, کج زبان *kej zabán.*

Jasmine, یاسمین *yásmín.*

Jasper, یشب *yashb;* (another kind), یاش *yásh.*

Jaundice, مرض زهره *marzi zahrah.*

Javelin, نیزك *nízak.*

Jaw (bone), چانه *chánah* (z.). Upper —, فك اعلی *fakk i a'lá.* Lower —, فك اسفل *fakk i asfal.*

Jealous, غیور *ghaiyúr;* حسود *hasúd.*

Jealousy, رشك *rashk;* حسد *hasd.*

Jeering, طعنه زنان *ta'nah-zanán* (*k.*); ریش خند *rísh khand* (*k.*).

Jehovah, هو *hú;* یاهواه *Yáhváh.*

Jerboa, یربوع *yarbú'.*

Jerk, تکان *takán* (*d. kh.*).

Jerusalem, بیت المقدس *Bait al Mukaddas.*

Jest, لاغ *lágh;* بزله *bazlah;* وشیه *vashyah;* لطیفه *latífah.* — ing, هزل *hazl* (*k.*).

Jester, مسخره *maskharah.*

Jesus, حضرت عیسی *Hazrat-i-'Isá.*

Jet (stone), شوه *shavah;* (of water), فواره *favvárch.*

Jew, Jewish, یهودی *yahúdí;* عبرانی *'ibrání.*

Jewel, جوهر *johar;* زیور *zívar;* (worn in the turban), سرپیچ *sar-pích.*

Jeweller, جوهری *jauharí.*

Jockey, چابکسوار *chábuk sovvár.*

Jocose, شوخی *shúkhí.*

Join, پیوستن *paivastan;* پیوند کردن *paivand k.*

Joined, منضم *munzamm* (*k.*); واصل *vásil* (*sh.*); مقرون *makrún.*

Joining in a drinking bout, منادمت *munádamat.*

Joint, بند *band;* شلو *shalv;* مفصل *mufsal.* —ly, شراکتاً *sharákatan.*

Jointure (woman's), مهر *mahr.*

Joists, همون *hamún*; شه تیر *shahtír*.

Jokes, هزلیات *hazalíyát*.

Joking, مزاح *mazáh* (*k.*); مزاحت *mazáhat* (*n.*).

Jollity, شوخی *shúkhí*.

Jolt, تکان *takán* (*kh. d.*).

Jonas, یونس *Yúnas*.

Joseph, یوسف *Yúsuf*.

Jot, ذره *zarreh*; نکته *nukteh*.

Journal, روز نامه *rúz námeh*.

Journey, سفر *safar*. A day's —, منزل *manzil*.

Jovial, خوشگذران *khúsh guzarán*. —ity, بشاشت *bashá-shat*.

Joy, سرور *surúr*. فرح *farah*; نشاط *nashát*; مسرة *masarrat*. —ful, فرحناك *farah-nák*; خرم *khurram*.

Judaism, یهودیه *yahúdíyeh*.

Judge, *n.*, قاضی *kází*; *pl.*, قضاة *kuzát*; حاکم *hákim*; *v.*, دیوان کردن *díván k.*

Judgment, فتوی *fetvá*. —hall, محکمه *mahkamah*. The last —, محشر *mahshar*; روز قیامت *rúz-i-kiyámat*.

Judicature, شریعت *sharí'at*.

Judicious, با درایت *bá dirâyet*; عقلی *'aklíy*.

Jug, کوزه *kúzah*.

Juggler, حقه باز *hukkah-báz*; شعبده باز *shu'bdah-báz*; بازیگر *bázigar*.

Juggling, art of, شعبده بازی *shu'bdah-bází* (*k.*).

Jugular vein, ورید *varíd*.

Juice, شیره *shírah*; عرق *'arak*. Expressed —, عصاره *'usárah*; (of dates, &c.), دوشاب *dúsh-áb*.

Juicy, آبدار *ábdár*.

Jujube fruit, عناب *'unnáb*. —tree, کنار *kunár*.

Jump, *n.*, خیز *khíz* (*k.*); جست *jast* (*k.*); *v.*, جستن *jastan*.

Junction, اتصال *ittisál*.

Jungle, جنگل *jangal*.

Junior, اصغر *asghar*.

Juniper, اردج *ardaj*.

Jupiter, مشتری *Mushtarí*.

Jurisdiction, قلمرو *kalam-rav*.

Jurisprudence, فقه *fikh*.

Jurisprudist, فقیه *fakíh*; *pl.*, فقهاء *fukahá*.

Just, عادل *'ádil*; منصف *munsif*; حق *hakk*. — men, ابرار *abrár*. Most—, اعدل *a'dal*.

Justice, عدالت *'adálat* ; عـدل *'adl* ; نصفت *nisfat* ; داد *dád*.

Justification, ابرار *ibrár* (*n.*) ; تزکیت *tazkiyat* (*k.*).

Justly, انصافاً *insáfan*.

Juvenile, جوان *javán*.

Juvenility, جوانی *javání*.

K

Kaliyan (Persian water pipe), قلیان *ḳaliyán*.

Keen, تیز *tíz*.

Keep, داشتن *dáshtan* ; نگاهداشتن *nigáh-dsh*.

Keeper, نـگـهـبان *nigah-bán*. — of the records, سر دفـتر *sar-dafter*. — of the seal, مهر دار *muhr-dár*. — of a vineyard, رز بان *raz-bán*.

Keepsake, یاد کار *yád-gár*.

Kennel, سگخانه *sagkháneh*.

Kernel, مغز *maghz*.

Kestrel, یوه *yúh*.

Kettle, کتری *ketrí* ; قدر *ḳidr* ; دیـك *dig* ; (small), دیگچـه *dígcheh*. — drum, کـوس *kús* ; نـقاره *naḳḳárah*. — — player, نـقـارچی *naḳḳárachí*.

Key, کلید *kilíd* ; اقلید *iḳlíd*.

Khosroes, کسری *kasrá*.

Kick, لکد *lakd* (*z.*).

Kid, بزغاله *buz-ghálah* ; هیرك *hírak* ; بـره *barah*. White kid or cotton shoes, گـیـوه *gívah*.

Kidney, گرده *gurdah* ; کلـیـه *kulyah*.

Kill, کشتن *kushtan*.

Killed, قـتیل *ḳatíl*.

Killing (in comp.), کشان *kushán*.

Kiln, کوره *kúrah*.

Kind (genus), جنس *jins* ; گونه *gúnah* ; نوع *nau'* ; *pl.*, انواع *anvá'* ; قسم *ḳism* ; (friendly), مهربان *mihribán* ; شفیق *shafiḳ* ; لطیف *latíf*.

Kindle, بـر فـروخـتـن *bar farúkhtan* ; سوزانیدن *súzánídan*.

Kindling, سوزنده *súzendah*.

Kindness, مهربـانی *mihribání* ; عاطفت *'atifat* ; نوازش *navázish* ; احسان *ihsán*.

Kindred, اقربا *aḳribá* ; خویش *khísh* ; پـیوند *paivand*.

King, شاه *sháh* ; پادشاه *pád-sháh* ; سـلطان *sultán* ; ملك *malik*. O — ! شها *shahá*.

— of kings, شهنشاه *shahan-sháh.* — of the bees, يعشوب *ya'shúb.*

Kingdom, مملکت *mamlakat;* ولايت *viláyet.* — of heaven, ملکوت *malkút.*

Kingfisher, چلق *chilliḳ.*

Kinsman, ذوالقربی *zu'l ḳurbá;* خویشاوند *khísháv and; pl.,* اقارب *aḳárib.*

Kiss, *n.,* بوس *bús (d.);* بوسه *búsah (d.); v.,* بوسیدن *búsídan.* — ing and hugging, بوس و کنار *bús o kenár.* — ing and licking (as a cat her kittens), ماچ و موچ *mách u múch.*

Kitchen, آشپز خانه *ásh-paz khánah;* مطبخ *matbakh.* — garden, پالیز *páliz.*

Kite (bird), غلیواج *ghalíwáj;* or غلیواز *ghalíwáz;* زغن *zaghan;* موش خور *músh-khúr;* (paper), کاغذك *kághazak.*

Knapsack, جامه دان *jámah-dán;* بقچه *buḳchah.*

Knave, چاره کر *chárah-gar.*

Knead, سرشتن *sirishtan;* خمیر کردن *khamír k.; pa. p.,* معجون *ma'jun.*

Knee, زانو *zánú (z.).* — to —, همزانو *ham-zánú.*

Knife, کارد *kárd.* Butcher's —, ساطور *sátúr.* Pen —, قلمتراش *ḳalamtarásh.* Pocket or clasp —, چاقو *cháḳú.* Shoemaker's —, نشکرده *nishgirdah.*

Knit, بافتن *báftan.*

Knob, قبه *ḳubbah.*

Knock, *n.,* ضرب *zarb;* (at the door), دستك *dastak; v.,* کوبیدن *kúbídan.* — down, فرو کوفتن *farú-kúftan.*

Knot, کره *girah (z.);* عقد *'aḳd;* عقده *'uḳdah.*

Knotted, معقود *ma'ḳud.*

Know, شناختن *shinákhtan;* دانستن *dánistan;* فهمیدن *fahmídan.*

Knowing, داننده *dánendah;* عرفان *'irfán.* — for certain, متیقن *mutayaḳḳin.*

Knowledge, معرفت *ma'rifat;* علم *'ilm;* دانستکی *dánistagí;* جزرسی *juz-rasí;* اکاهی *agáhí.* — of God, تعرف *ta'arruf.*

Known, معلوم *ma'lúm* (*h.*); معروف *ma'rúf.*

Knuckle, بند انگشت *band i angusht.*

Koran, قرآن *ḳur'án*; فرقان *furḳán.*

Krán (one franc), قران *ḳrán.*

L

Label, سر نامه *sar námeh.*

Laborious, محنتی *mihnatí*; کار کن *kár kun.*

Labour, کار *kár* (*k.*); عمل *'amal* (*k.*); محنت *mihnat*; مزدوری *mazdúrí.*

Labourer, عامل *'ámil*; *pl.*, عمله *'amaleh*; (hired), مزدور *mazdúr.* Agricultural —, برزگر *barz-gar.*

Labouring hard, تجاهد *tajáhud.*

Lac (gum), لك *lak.*

Lace, توره *túrah*; (cord), قیطان *ḳaitán*; زنجیره *zanjírah.*

Ladder, نردبان *nardubán*; سلم *sullam*; زینه *zínah.*

Ladies' man, عشق باز *'ishḳ-báz.*

Ladle, کفچه *kafcheh*; چلك *chilk.*

Lady, خانم *khánum*; خاتون *khátún*; بیگم *baigam*; کد بانو *kad-bánú.*

Lag behind, باز ماندن *báz mándan.*

Lake, دریاچه *daryácheh.*

Lamb, بره *barah.* Fattened —, شیر مست *shír-mast.*

Lame, لنك *lang* (*k.*).

Lament, زاریدن *zárídan*; نویدن *navídan*; نالیدن *nálídan*; *pa. p.*, مندوب *mandúb*; *pr. p.*, نالان *nálán.*

Lamentation, زاری *zárí* (*k.*); شیون *shívan* (*k.*); نوحه *nauhah* (*k.*); ندبت *nudbat*; فغان *fighán*; ناله *nálah* (*k.*); فریاد *faryád* (*k.*). Great —, زار زار *zár-zár.*

Lamp, چراغ *chirágh*; سراج *siráj*; مصباح *misbáh*; (Chinese), فانوس *fánús.*

Lampblack, دودهٔ چراغ *dúdah i chirágh*; خوال *khuvál.*

Lampoon, جرشفت *jarshaft*; هجو *hajv.*

Lance, جرید *jaríd*; نیزه *naizeh.*

Lancet, نیشتر *níshtar*; نشتر *nishtar.*

Land, زمین *zamín.* Cultivated —, کشت زار *kisht-zár.*

— and money, ملك و مال *mulk u mál.* — not needing artificial irrigation, ديمی *dímí.*

Landed property, تعلقه *ta'allu-ḳah*

Landholder, زمين دار *zamín-dár.*

Landscape, چشم انداز *cheshm andáz.*

Land-tax, مال ديوان *mál i díván.*

Lane, كوچه *kúchah*; كوی *kúy.*

Language, لغة *lughat*; زبان *zabán.* Belonging to —, لغوی *laghaví.*

Languid, مانده *mándah.*

Languor, فتر *fatar*; سستی *sustí*; فتور *futúr.*

Lantern, فانوس *fánús*; (of a building), مشكوت *mishkút*; منار *minár.*

Lap, *n.*, كنار *kinár*; *v.*, ليسيدن *lísídan.*

Lapidary, حجار *hajjár.*

Lapis lazuli, لاجورد *lájvard.*

Lapse of time, مرور دهور *murúr i duhúr.*

Lapwing, هدهد *hudhud.*

Lard, چربی خوك *charbí-yi-khúk.*

Large, بزرك *buzurg*; كلان *kalán*; متسع *muttasi'*

Largesse, انعام *in'ám.*

Lark, عزلاغ *ghazlágh*; چكاوك *chakávak.*

Lascivious, شهوتی *shahvatí*; بد نفس *bad-nafas.* — ness, مستی *masti.*

Lash, قمچی *ḳamchí.*

Lasso, كمند *kamand.*

Last, *a.*, آخر *ákhar*; پسين *pasín*; *v.*, ماندن *mandan.*

Lasting, دير پا *dír-pá*; دايم *dáim* (*b*); بقا *baḳá* (*dsh.*); دوام *davám* (*k.*).

Lastly, عاقبة الامر *'áḳibat ul amr.*

Latch, چفت *chift.*

Late, دير *dir* (*ámadan*); (deceased), مرحوم *marhum.*

Lateness, ديری *dírí.*

Lath, چوب *chúb.*

Lathe, خراد *kharád.*

Lather, كف *kaf* (*k.*).

Latitude, عرض *'arz.*

Latter, وا پسين *vá-pasín*; آخر *ákhir.*

Lattice window, بالكانه *bálká-nah*; پنجره *panjareh.*

Latticed, مشبك *mushabbak.*

Laudable, رضیه razíyeh; مستحسن mustahsin; حمید hamíd. — actions, حمائد hamáid.

Laugh, v., خندیدن khandídan; pr. p., خندان khandán.

Laughter, خندگی khandagí; خنده khandah (k.). Loud —, قهقهه ḳahḳahah (k.).

Laundress, رخت شو rakht shú.

Laundry, رختشو خانه rakhtshú kháneh.

Laurel, سر خس sar khas.

Lavishing, اسراف isráf k.).

Lavishly, مسروفاً masrúfan.

Law (of the Koran), شریعت sharí'at; شرع shar'. Common —, عرف 'urf. — of retaliation for homicide, قصاص ḳisas.

Lawful, حلال halál; مباح mubáh; جواز jawáz. Making —, تحلیل tahlíl (k.). —ness, حلیت hillíyet.

Lawless, بیداد bí-dád; فاسد fásid.

Lawsuit, دعوا da'vá.

Lawn, چمن chaman.

Laxative, مسهل mus-hil.

Laxity, رخوت rikhwat.

Lay, v., گذاشتن guzáshtan; نهادن nihádan. — eggs, تخم کردن tukhm k.

Laziness, سستی sustí.

Lazy, تنبل tambal; کور دل kúr-dil; نا رای ná-rái; نفه nafih.

Lead (metal), سرب surb; رصاص rasás. Red —, سرنج sirinj. White —, سفیدا safídá; (plummet), بلت bult.

Lead, v., بردن burdan; دلالت کردن dalálat k.

Leader, سر دار sar-dár; قاید ḳáid; پیشوا píshwá. — of an army, سر جنك sar-jang. of the Hajj, میر حج mír i hajj. — at prayer, امام Imám.

Leading into error, مغالطت mughálatat.

Leaf (tree), برك barg; (paper), ورق varaḳ. The fall of the —, برك ریزی barg rízí.

League, معاقدت mu'áḳadat; عهد 'ahd.

Leak, n., رخنه rikhnah; چکه chikkeh; v., تراویدن tarávidan.

Lean, a., لاغر lághar; نزار nizár; نحیف nahíf. —ness,

لاغری *lághirí*; *v.*, تکیه زدن *takyeh z.*

Leap, *n*, خیز *khíz* (*k.*); *v.*, جستن *jastan*; بر جستن *bar jastan*; یوزیدن *yúzídan*; *pr. p.*, جهان *jihán*. — year, سال کبیسه *sál-i kabísah.*

Learn, یاد گرفتن *yád-gr.*; آموختن *ámúkhtan*; درس گرفتن *dars gr.*

Learned, دانا *dáná*; عالم *'álim.* Profoundly —, متبحر *mutabahhir.* — man, ملا *mullá.* — men, علما *'ulamá*; فواضل *fawázil.*

Learner, نو آموز *nau-ámúz.*

Learning, آموزش *ámúzish*; علم *'ilm*; حکمت *hikmat.*

Lease, اجاره *ijárah* (*k. gr.*); کرایه *keráyeh* (*k.*).

Least, ادنی *adná.* At —, اقل قلیل *aḳall i ḳalíl.*

Leather, چرم *charm*; جلد *jild.* Raw white —, یشمه *yashmah.* Soft —, انبان *ambán.* — of horse's or ass's hide, کیمخت *kímukht.*

Leathern, چرمینه *charmínah.*

Leave, *n.*, اجازت *ijázat*; اذن *izn* (*d. gr.*); رخصت *rukhsat* (*gr.*), دستوری *dastúri*; *v.*, (to quit) پرداختن *pardákhtan*; ترك كردن *tark k.* To take — of, مرخص شدن *murakhkhas sh.* — off, وا ایستادن *vá ístádan.*

Leaven, *n.*, مایه *máyeh*; *v.*, ور آوردن *var a.*; *pa. p.*, مخمر *mukhammar.*

Leavings, باقیه *báḳiyeh.* — of a meal, پس خور *pas-khur.*

Lebanon, Mount, لبنان *libnán.*

Lecherous, شهوت *shahvat.*

Lecture, درس *dars* (*d.*).

Lecturer, مدرس *mudarris.*

Led horse, یدك *yadak.*

Ledger, دفتر *daftar.*

Leech, زالو *zálú* (*an.*); زلو *zalú.*

Leek, گندنا *gandaná*; کراث *karrás.*

Left (side), چپ *chap*; یسار *yasár.* — handed, چپدست *chap-dast.*

Leg, پا *pá*; ساق *sák*; اشقالنك *ishḳálang.*

Legacy, میراث *mírás*; ترکه *tarikah*; *pl.*, متروکات *matrúkát.*

Legal, شرعی *shar'íy*; مشروع *mashrú'*.

Legate, ایلچی *ílchí*.

Legatee, موصی الیه *muvassá ilaíh*.

Legation, سفارت *sefárat*.

Legend, افسانه *afsánah*; حکایت *hikáyat*.

Legerdemain, حقه بازی *hukkeh bází*.

Legible, ما یقرا *ma yukrá*.

Legislature, حکمرانی *hukmrání*; حکومت *hukúmat*.

Legitimacy, حلالزادکی *halálzádagí*.

Legitimate, حلال زاده *halál zádeh*.

Leisure, فراغت *farághat*. —ly, آهسته *áhisteh*.

Lemon, لیمو *límú*. —ade, آب لیمو *áb límú*.

Lend (money), قرض دادن *karz d.*

Length, طول *túl*; درازی *dirází*. At —, آخر الامر *ákhar ul amr*.

Lengthen, دراز کردن *diráz k.*

Lenient, ملایم *muláyim*.

Lenity, ملایمت *muláyimat*.

Lentil, بلسن *bulsun*; مجك *machak*; منجو *manjú*; عدس *'adas*.

Leopard, پلنك *palang*; نمر *nimr*.

Leper, مبروص *mabrús*.

Leprosy, برص *baras*.

Leprous, ابرص *abras*.

Less, (fewer) کم *kam (k.)*; کمتر *kamtar*; (smaller), کهتر *kih-tar*; کوچکتر *kuchiktar (k.)*.

Lesson, درس *dars (d.)*; سبق *sabk*. Giving —s, مدارست *mudárasat (n.)*.

Lest, مبادا *mabádá*.

Let (permit), اذن دادن *izn d.*; (on hire), اجاره دادن *ijárah d.* — go, ویل کردن *veil k.* — alone, کذاشتن *guzáshtan*.

Lethargy, پینکی *pínakí*.

Letter (of the alphabet), حرف *harf*; *pl.*, حروف *hurúf*. — by —, حرفًا عن حرف *harfan 'an harf*. — with diacritical point, معجمه *mu'jamah*; (epistle), کاغذ *kághaz*; مکتوب *maktúb*. Short — (between equals, or from superior to inferior—a note), رقعه *ruk'ah*. — from a prince,

رقم *raḳm;* فرمان *farmán;* (a royal order), شقه *shiḳḳah.* — from a servant, عرض *'arz;* عریضه *'arízeh.* — of recommendation سفارش نامه *sefárish námeh.* — of apology, اعتذار نامه *i'tizár námeh,* etc., etc.

Lettuce, کاهو *káhú;* خس *khus.*

Levee, مجلس عام *majlis i 'ám.*

Level, مسطح *musattah* (*s.*); هموار *hamvár* (*s.*); *pa. p.,* موطاء *muvattá.*

Lever, دیلم *dílum.*

Levite, Levitical, لاوی *láviy.*

Levity, سبکی *sabukí;* طیش *taish;* (of speech), خطل *khatal;* (of conduct), خفت *khiffat.*

Levy (of taxes), باج *báj;* خراج *khiráj.*

Lewd, شهوتی *shahvatí.* —ness, شهوت *shahvat.*

Lexicography, علم لغت *'ilm-i-loghat.*

Lexicon, کتاب لغت *kitáb-i-loghat.*

Liar, کاذب *kázib;* دروغ گو *durúgh-gú.* A great —, کذاب *kazzáb.*

Libel, مذمت *muzammat;* هجو *hajv.*

Liberal, سخی *sakhíy;* فیاض *faiyáz;* سامح *sámih;* جواد *jawwád.* —ity, جود *júd;* سخاء *sakhá';* سخاوت *sakhávat;* ندی *nadá;* کرامت *karámat.*

Liberated, خلاص *khilás* (*k.*).; رستکار *rastakár* (*k.*); رها *rahá* (*k.*).

Liberating, منقذ *munḳiz* (*n.*).

Liberation, رهای *rahái;* نجات *najat.*

Libertine, رند *rind;* قلاش *ḳallásh.*

Liberty, عتق *'itḳ;* آزادکی *ázádagí.* Setting —, اطلاق *itláḳ* (*k.*).

Libidinous, هواس *havvás;* نیاك *naiyák.*.

Libra, میزان *mízán.*

Library, کتب خانه *kutub-khánah.*

License, اجازه *ijázah* (*d.*).

Lick, لیسیدن *lísídan.*

Lid, پوش *púsh;* سر *sar.*

Lie, *n.*, کذب *kizb;* دروغ *durúgh* (*gf.*); *v.*, — down دراز شدن *diráz sh.*

Lieutenant, نائب اول *náib i avval.*

Life, زیست *zíst;* زندگی *zindagí;* زندگانی *zindagání;* جان *ján;* حیوات (or حیات) *haiyát.* Eternal —, دار البقا *dár ul baḳá.* The next —, زندگانی دوم *zindagání i duvam.* The present and future —, دو جهان *dú-jehán.* Solitary —, انزوال *inzivál.* —less, بی جان *bí-ján* — time, عمر *'umr.*

Lift, بلا کردن *bálá k.* — up, بر داشتن *bar dsh.*

Ligature, بستگی *bastagí;* وثاق *visáḳ.*

Light (up), بر فروختن *bar farúkhtan.* —, *n.*, روشن *raushan* (*k.*); نور *núr;* روشناءی *rúshnáí;* روشنی *raushaní;* شعاع *shu'á'.* —, *a.*, (not heavy), سبك *sabuk;* خفیف *khafíf;* (digestible), هنیء *haní'.* —headed, سبك سار *sabuk-sár.* — of conduct, خف *khiff;* خفیف *khafíf.* — souled, سبك روح *sabuk-rúh.*

Lightning, برق *barḳ;* صاعقه *sá'iḳah.*

Like, چو *chu;* چون *chún;* همچو *hamchú;* مثل *misl;* مشابه *mushábih;* متشکل *mutashakkil;* بسان *basán;* (in composition), آسا *ásá;* سا *sá;* تای *táy;* *v.*, میل داشتن *meyl dsh;* پسندیدن *pasandídan.*

Likelihood, احتمال *ihtimál.*

Likely, گویا *guyá;* محتمل *mohtamil.*

Likeness, تشبیه *tashbíh* (*k.*); تصویر *tasvír;* شکل *shekl.*

Likewise, ایضاً *aizan.*

Lilac, یاس *yas,*

Lily, سوسن *súsan.* Water —, نیلوفر *nailúfar.*

Limb, عضو *'uzv;* *pl.*, اعضا *á'zá.*

Lime, آهك *áhak;* گچ *gach;* (fruit), لیمو *límú.*

Limit, حد *hadd;* *pl.*, حدود *hudúd;* سنور *sinúr;* سنیر *sinír;* *pa. p.*, محدود *mahdúd.*

Limp, لنگیدن *langídan;* *pr. p.*, افتان خیزان *uftán khízán.*

Limpid, صاف *sáf.*

Line, *n.*, سطر *satr;* *pl.*, سطور *sutúr;* خط *khatt;* *pl.*, خطوط *khutút.* Circular —, خط مستدیر *khatt i mustadír.* Curved —, خط منحنی *kh. i munhaní*. — of demarcation, خط فاصل *kh. i fásil.* Ecliptic —, خط محور *kh. i mihwar.* Meridional —, خط نصف نهار *kh. i nisf i nahár.* Parallel —, خط متوازی *kh. i mutawází.* Perpendicular —, خط عمود *kh. i ʿamúd.* Right —, خط مستقیم *kh. i mustaḳím.*

Lineage, نسل *nasl*; نسب *nasab.*

Linen, بز *bazz*; کتان *kattán.*

Linendraper, بزاز *bazzáz.*

Linguist, زبان دان *zabán-dán.*

Lining (of a garment), آستر *ástar* (*k.*); بطانت *bitánat.*

Link, حلقه *halḳeh.*

Linseed, بزر الکتان *bizr ul kettán*; کتان *kettán.*

Lintel, آستانه *ástánah.*

Lion, شیر *shír*; (obsolete or poetic), لیث *lais*; هزبر *hizabr*; غضنفر *ghazanfar*; ضیغم *zaigham*; ارسلان *arslán*; اسد *asad*; ببر *babr*; حیدر *haidar.*

Lip, لب *lab*; شفة *shifat.* cracked or ulcerated —, سلنج *silunj.*

Liquefaction, گدازش *gudázish.*

Liquid, مایع *máiʿ*; اب *áb*; *a.*, مذاب *muzáb*; ذائب *záib.*

Liquor (spirituous), شراب *sharáb*; عرق *ʿaraḳ.*

Liquorice, ملهطی *malhatí*; سوس *sús.*

Lisp, لکنت *luknat* (*k.*).

List, فهرست *fihrist*; سیاهه *siyáhah.*

Listen, گوش دادن *gúsh d.*; *pr. p.*, استماع *istimáʿ* (*k.*); اصغاء *isghá*ʿ.

Listener, مستمع *mustamiʿ.*

Listless, غافل *gháfil.*

Literal, لفظی *lafazí.* —ly, لفظاً *lafzan.*

Literary composition, تصنیف *tasníf* (*k.*).

Literature, ادب *adab.*

Litigation, تنازع *tanázuʿ* (*k.*); خصومت *khusúmat* (*n.*).

Litter (carried by two mules), تخت روان *takht-raván*; (two on one mule), کجاوه *kajáveh.* Camel or elephant —, هودج *haudaj*; محافه *maháfah.*

Little (few), قلیل *ḳalíl*; اندك *andak*; (small), کوچك *kú-*

chak. A —, قــدری ḳadrí; برخی barkhí.

Live, زستــن zistan, or زیستــن zístan; روز کار بردن rúz-gar burdan; (dwell), ساکن بودن sákin b.; منزل داشتن manzil dsh.

Livelihood, آبخــورد ábkhurd; معیشت ma'íshat; آب و دانـه áb u dánah.

Liver, جکر jigar; کبد kibd.

Living, زنـده zindah. A — creature, جاندار ján-dár.

Lizard, بزمجه buzmajah; سوسمار súsmár; چلپـاسا chalpásá; نـزك nizk; سقنقور saḳunḳúr.

Load, بار bár (k.); حمل haml (k.); (carried on the head), سـر بـار sar-bár. Ass —, خـروار karvár; v., (a gun), پر کردن pur k..

Loadstone, آهنربا áhan-rubá.

Loaf, قرص نان ḳurs-i-nán.

Loan (money), قــرض ḳarz (d. gr.); (article), عاریت 'ári-yet (k.); استعاره isti'arah (k.).

Loathing, نفرت nifrat (k.); کراهیت keráhiyat (n.).

Lobby, دالان dálán; کفش کن kafsh kun.

Lobster, خرچنك khar chang.

Lock (of door), قـفل ḳufl (k.); (of hair), حلقه halḳeh; زلـف zulf; (of gun), چقماق chaḳ-máḳ.

Lockjaw, لقوه laḳvah.

Locksmith, قـفل ساز ḳufl sáz.

Locum-tenens, جا نـشـیـن já-nishín

Locust, ملخ malakh.

Lodging, منزل manzil.

Logic, منطق mantiḳ.

Logwood, بقم baḳm.

Loins, کمر kamar.

Loiter, عقب رفتن 'aḳab r.

Lonely, تـنها tanhá.

Long, دراز diráz; طویل tavíl; مدید madíd. — ago, دیـر باز dír-báz. How —? تـاکـی tá key.

Longing, اشتـیـاق ishtiyáḳ; خواهش kháhish (n.); مـیـل meyl (k.). — of a pregnant woman, وحم wahm.

Longitude, طول túl.

Long-suffering, دیـر رنج dír-ranj.

Look, نـکه nigah, or نـکاه nigáh (k.); نظـر nazar (k.); نـکـر

nigar (*k.*); *pr. p.*, نگران *nigran.*

Loom, منسج *minsaj*; کارگاه *kár gáh.*

Loose, نا بسته *ná basteh*; باز *báz*; (flaccid), هز *hiz*; سست *sust.* To let —, سر دادن *sar dádan*; سرکردن *sar-k.*

Looseness, رخاوت *rakhávat.*

Loquacious, پر گو *pur gú.*

Lord, خداوند *khudávand*; خان *khán*; *pl.* خوانین *khavánín*; بك *beg*, or بيك *beig*; مولی *maulá*; امير *amír*, *pl.*, (noblemen), امرا *umará*; ارباب *arbáb*; مولانا *mauláná.* The —, رب *rabb.* O our —! ربنا *rabbaná.*

Lordship, خداوندی *khudávandí.*

Lose, گم کردن *gum k.*; (at play), باختن *bákhtan.*

Loss, زيان *ziyán* (*burdan*); خسارت *khasárat* (*ksh.*). To be at a —, قافيهٔ تنك شدن *ḳáfiyeh i tang shudan.*

Lost, گم *gum* (*k. sh.*); گمراه *gum-ráh*; ضائع *zá'i* (*k.*); مفقود *mafḳúd.*

Lots, قرعه *ḳar'ah* (*an.*).

Lotus, نيلپر *nilupar.*

Loud, بلند *buland.* — sounding, بلند بانك *buland báng.* — toned, بلند آواز *buland-áváz.*

Louse, قمل *ḳamal*; شپش *shipish.*

Love, عشق *'ishḳ* (*dsh.*); محبت *mahabbat* (*dsh*); صبابت *sabábat*; (for a mistress, &c.), عشق حقيقی *'ishḳ i haḳíḳiy.* Falling in —, تعشق *ta'ashshuḳ* (*k.*).

Love-sick, شوريده *shúrídeh.*

Lover, عاشق *'áshiḳ*; *pl.*, عشاق *'ushsháḳ*; دلداده *dildádah*; دلدار *dil-dár*; محب *muhibb.*

Low, پست *past*; فرو *farú* (*k.*); ادنی *adná.* — person, نذل *nazl.*

Lowest, اسفل *asfal.*

Lowing (of cattle), خوار *khuvár*; بانك *báng* (*z.*).

Lowliness, خشوع *khushú'.*

Lowly, مسكين *miskín.*

Lowspirited, دل تنك *diltang.*

Loyal, مطيع *mutí'.*

Lucerne, يونجه *yúnjeh.*

Lucid, صاف *sáf.*

Lucifer-match, كبريت *kebrít.*

Luck (good), نيك بختى *ník bakhtí;* (bad), بد بختى *bad bakhtí.*

Lucrative, مفيد *mufíd;* نافع *náfi'.*

Ludicrous, مضحك *muz-hik.*

Luggage, اسباب *asbáb;* بنه *bonah.*

Lukewarm, نيم كرم *ním-garm;* ملول *malúl.*

Lumbar, صلبى *sulbíy.*

Luminous, درخشنده *dirakh-shandeh.*

Lump, كنده *kundah.*

Lunacy, ديوانكى *díránagí.*

Lunar, قمرى *ḳamaríy.*

Lunatic, ديوانه *díránah.*

Lungs, سل *sull;* شش *shush.*

Lurk, كمين كردن *kamín k.*

Luscious, لذيذ *lazíz.*

Lust, شبق *shabaḳ;* هوا و هوس *havá u havvas;* هواى نفسانى *havá i nafsání;* شهوت *shahvat.*

Lustful, شهوت پرست *shahvat parast.*

Lustre, روشنائى *raushnáí.*

Lute, بربط *barbat;* يشكرده *yashkardah;* چنك *chang.*

A small Turkish lute with three strings, يونغار *yún-ghár.*

Luxuriance, كثرت *kesrat.*

Luxuriant, فراوان *faráván.*

Luxurious, عياش *'ayyásh.*

Luxury, عشرة *ishrat;* عياشى *'ayyáshí.*

Lying, دروغ كو *durúgh gú.*

Lying-in (woman), زاچه *zá-cheh.*

Lying in ambush, كامن *kámin.*

Lynx, سياه كوش *siyáh-gúsh.*

M.

Mace (spice), بزباز *bazbáz;* بسباسه *basbásah;* (club), كرز *gurz;* چماق *chumáḳ.*

Mace-bearer, چوبدار *chúb-dár.*

Macerate, آغاريدن *ágháridan.*

Machination, مكر *makr.*

Machine, منجنيق *manjaníḳ;* آلات *álát.*

Mad, شيدا *shaidá;* مجنون *maj-nún* (s.); ديوانه *díváneh* (s.); شيفته *sheiftah.*

Madam, خانم *khánum.*

Made (artificial), ساخته *sákhtah;* مصنوع *masnú'.*

Madness, خبط *khabt*; شیدای *shaidái*; شوریدگی *shúrídagí*.

Magazine, مخزن *makhzan*; خزانه *khezánah*; in comp., خانه, as, powder —, باروت خانه *bárút kháneh*.

Magian, مجوس *majús*; مجوسی *majúsí*; گبر *gabr*. — (religion), مجوسیة *majúsíyet*.

Magic, سحر *sihr*; نفاثت *nafásat*; جادو *jádú*; (natural), سیمیا *símiyá*.

Magician, جادو گر *jádú-gar*; سحار *sahhár*.

Magistrate, حاکم *hákim*; (one who gives a فتوی *fatvá*), مفتی *muftí*.

Magnanimous, بزرگ همت *buzurg-himmat*.

Magnet, آهن ربا *áhan-rubá*; آهنکش *áhan-kesh*; مقناطیس *maknátís*.

Magnificence, بزرگواری *buzurg-wárí*; اجلال *ijlál*; زرنك *zarank*.

Magnificent, معظم *mu'azzam*.

Magnified, مفخم *mufakhkham* (*s.*); مشرف *musharraf* (*s.*).

Magnitude, بزرگی *buzurgí*.

Magpie, کلاغ جیکو *kilágh i jíkú*.

Maidservant, کنیز *kaníz*.

Mail (coat of —), جوشن *jaushan*.

Maimed چولاق *chúlák* (*k.*); افلیج *iflíj*.

Maintenance, معیشت *ma'íshat*.

Maize, ذرت *zurrat*.

Majesty, حضرة *hazrat*, *pl.* حضرات *hazarát*; جلال *jalál*; جلالت *jalálat*. Your —! عالی حضرت *'álá hazrat*; قبله عالم *kiblah i 'álam*.

Major, یاور *yáver*.

Make, ساختن *sákhtan*; کردن *kerdan*; سازیدن *sázídan*.

Maker, سازنده *sázendah*.

Malady, مرض *maraz*; علت *'illat*.

Male, نر *nar* (as شیر نر *shír i nar*, — lion); ذکر *zakar*; ذکورت *zukúrat*. — and female, نرماده *nar-mádah*.

Malediction, لعنت *la'anat*.

Malefactor, مجرم *mujrim*.

Malevolence, بد خواهی *bad khwáhí*.

Malice, کینه *kínah*; شر *sharr*.

Malicious, بد اندیش *bad-andísh* ; شتر کینه *shutur-gínah.*

Malignancy, خیرکی *khíragí.*

Malignant, خیره *khírah.*

Malleable, نرم *narm.*

Mallet, میخ کوب *míkh-kúb* ; (for clods), کلوخ کوب *kulúkh-kúb.*

Man, مرد *mard, pl.* مردان *mardán* ; آدم *ádam* ; نفر *nafar* ; مردمان *mardumán* ; *in pl.* (people), مردم *mardum.* Village head —, ده خدا *dih-khudá.* Wealthy —, دنیا دار *dunyá-dár.* Worthless —, دنی *daníy.*

Manacles, دست بند *dast band.*

Management, تدبیر *tadbír* ; نظارت *nazárat.*

Manager, پیش کار *písh-kár* ; کار پرداز *kár-pardáz.*

Mandate, فرمان *farmán.*

Mandragora, یبروج *yabrúj*, or یبروح *yabrúh.*

Mane (horse's), یال *yál.*

Manful, دلیر *dalír.*

Mange, گر *gar.*

Manger, آخر *ákhor* ; معلف *ma'laf.*

Mango, انبه *ambah.*

Manhood مردی *mardí* ; بلوغت *bulúghat.*

Manifest, *a.*, مبین *mubín* ; ظاهر *záhir* ; باهر *báhir* ; *pa. p.*, منصوص *mansús* ; *pr. p.*, مصرح *musarrih* ; اظهار *izhár* (*k.*).

Manifestation, ابراز *ibráz.*

Manikin, مردمك *mardumak.*

Mankind, بشر *bashar* ; انسان *insán* ; انس *ins* ; (men and devils), انس و جان *ins va jánn* ; ناس *nás.* All —, کافهٔ انام *káfah i anám.*

Manly, مردانه *mardánah.*

Manliness, مردی *mardí.*

Manna, شیرخشت *shír-khisht* ; ترنجبین *taranjubín* ; (sweet-meat), گز *gaz.*

Manner, طور *taur* or *túr* ; اسلوب *uslúb* ; چگونکی *chigúnagí* ; طریقة *taríkah* ; نمط *nimt.* In such a —, بنوعی *ba-nau'í* ; بر وجهی *bar vajhí.* Every —, هر صورت *har-súrat.* In this —, همچنین *ham-chunín*, or همچین *ham-chín.* In that —, همچنان *ham-chunán.* In no —, هیچگونه *hích-gúnah.*

In the same —, همیجان *hamíján.*

Manners, آداب *ádáb.*

Mansion, سرای *saráy*; دار *dar.* Thus: the — of peace, (Bagdad,) دار السلام *dár us salám*; the — of perdition, (hell), دار البوار *dár ul bavár*; the — of safety (the towns of Ḳum or Kirman, etc.), دار الامان *dár ul amán.*

Mantle, ردا *ridá.*

Manual, دستی *dustí*; (book), رساله *risáleh.*

Manufactory, کارخانه *kár kháneh.*

Manumission, اعتاق *i'táḳ* (*k.*).

Manure, زبل *zibl.*

Manuscript, دستخط *dast khatt*; نسخه *nuskheh.*

Many, بسیار *bisyár*; خیلی *khailí*; کثیر *kasír*; بسی *basí*; بسا *basá*; متعدد *muta'addid.* How —? چند *chand*; چه قدر *cheh ḳadr?*

Map, نقشه *naḳshah.*

Maple-wood, سارمه *sármah.*

Marble, مرمر *marmar*; رخام *rukhám.*

March (of an army), کوچ *kúch* (*k.*); رحلت *rihlat* (*k.*); رحیل *rahíl*; پسیچ *pasích.*

Marches, سرحد *sar hadd.*

Mare, مادیان *mádiyán*; (one having a yearling colt), مفلی *muflí.*

Margin, حاشیه *háshiyeh*; کران *karán*; کرانه *karánah.*

Marginal lines, جدول *jadval.*

Marine, بحری *bahrí*; دریای *daryáí.*

Mariner, ملاح *malláh.*

Marjoram, سعتر *sa'tar.*

Mark, نسان *nishán* (*k. d.*), or نشانه *nishánah*; (stain), داغ *dágh*; عیار *'iyár*; وسم *vasm*; اثر *asar*; *in pl.*, مآثر *ma'ásir*; آثار *ásár.*

Marked, مرسوم *marsúm*; موسوم *mausúm*; معلم *mu'lam.*

Market, بازار *bázár* (*k.*); سوق *suḳ*; ینپلو *yampalú.* Belonging to a —, بازاری *bázárí.*

Marriage, عروسی *'arúsí* (*k.*); کتخدای *kat-khudáí*; نکاح *nikáh* (*k.*); ازدواج *izdiváj* (*n.*); مناکحة *munákahat.* — feast, عرس *'urs*; ولیمه *válímah.* — portion, مهر *muhr.* —

settlement, كابين *kábín*; صداق *sadáḳ*.

Married (man), منكوح *mankúh*; زوج *zauj*; (woman), منكوحه *mankúhah*; زوجه *zaujah*.

Marrow, لب *lubb*; مغز *maghz*. Spinal —, نخاع *nukhá'*; حرام مغز *harám-maghz*.

Marrowless, بی مغز *bí-maghz*.

Marry, زن كردن *zan k.*; زن خواستن *zan kh.*; زن گرفتن *zan gr.*; *pr. p.* تأهل *ta'ahhul* (*s.*); (betrothing), خطب *khatb* (*n.*).

Mars (planet), مریخ *Mirríkh*; بهرام *Bahrám*.

Marsh, مرد آب *murd áb*; مشیله *mashílah*.

Marshmallows, خطمی *khatmíy*.

Marshal, امیر نظام *amír i nizám*.

Marten, سوسر *súsar*.

Martin پرستك *parastuk*.

Martingale, زیر بند *zír-band*; تعلیمی *ta'límí*.

Martyr, شهید *shahíd*, *pl.*, شهداء *shuhadá*.

Martyrdom, شهادت *shahádat* (*y.*). Place of —, مشهد *mashhad*.

Marvel, عجب *'ajab*.

Marvellous, عجیب *'ajíb*.

Masculine, مذكر *muzakkar*; تذكیر *tazkír*.

Mason, بنا *banná*; معمار *mi'már*.

Masonry, معماری *mi'márí*.

Mass, جملگی *jumlagí*; جماعت *jamá'at*.

Massacre, *n.*, قتل *ḳatl* (*k.*); مقاتله *muḳáteleh* (*k.*); *v.*, كشتن *kushtan*.

Massive, ضخیم *zakhím*. —ness, ضخامت *zakhámat*.

Mast (of a ship), تیر كشتی *tír i kishtí*.

Master, صاحب *sáhib*; اقا *áḳá*; مولی *maulá*; تاش *tásh*; (of a family), كتخدا *kat-khudá*. Generous —, خداوند نعمت *khudávand i ni'mat*.

Masticate, جایدن *jáídan*; خایدن *kháídan*.

Mat, حصیر *hasír*; بوریا *búryá*.

Match (lucifer), كبریت *kebrít*; (for a lamp, a linstock), پتیل *patíl*; (equal), برابر *barábar* (*sh.*).

Matchlock, شمخال *shamkhál*. —man, تفنگچی *tufangchí*.

Material, (essential), مـــادى *máddíy;* هيولانى *haiyuláni;* (stuff, etc.), قماش *ḳumásh.*

Materiality, جسمانيت *jismání-yet.*

Materials, اسباب *asbáb.*

Maternal, مادرى *mádarí.* — aunt, خاله *khálah.* — uncle, خالو *khálú.*

Mathematician, مهندس *mu-handis.*

Mathematics, رياضى *riyází.*

Matrimony, نكاح *nikáh.*

Matrix, يوكان *yúgán;* رحم *rihm.*

Matron, مخدره *mukhaddarah.*

Matter, what is the —, چه چيز است *cheh chíz ast.* No —, عيب نيست *'aib nist;* (pus), قيح *ḳaih;* (adhering to the corners of the eyes), كيغ *kígh.* —, (the first principle of everything), هيولا *haiyúlá* (ἡ ὕλη).

Mattock, كلند *kuland.*

Mattress, دوشك *dúshek;* بستر *bistar.*

Mature, بالغ *báligh;* منش *manish.*

Maturity, رسيدگى *rasídagí.*

Matutinal, سحرى *saharí.*

Maxim, پند *pand.*

May be that, شايد كه *sháyad-keh.* — it not be, مباش *ma-básh.* — it do you good, (said when anyone eats, etc.), عافيت شما باشد *'áfiyat-i-shumá báshad.*

Me, to me, مرا *mará;* (affixed), م *-am.*

Meadow, چمن *chaman;* مرغزار *murgh-zár;* راغ *rágh.*

Meal (flour), آرد *árd;* (repast), طعام *ta'ám:* خوراكى *khúrákí.*

Mean, *a.*, ذليل *zalíl;* كمين *kamín;* كمينه *kamínah;* سفله *siflah;* رذيل *razíl;* نا ستوده *ná-sitúdah;* فرو مايه *farú-máyah;* دون *dún;* خسيس *khasís;* حقير *haḳír.* Most —, احقر *ahḳar.* Of— intelligence, خيره راى *khírah-rái.* — persons, خسان *khasán.*

Meaning, معنى *ma'ní.* —less, ما لا يعنى *má lá ya'ní.*

Meanness, صغر *sughr;* نا كسى *ná-kasí;* سفل *safl:* خست *khissat.*

Means, واسطه *vásitah;* وسايط

vasáit ; وسیله *vasílah* ; توسل *tavassul*. — of living, معاش *ma'ásh*. By all —, بهر حال *ba har hál*. By no —, بهیچ وجه *be hích vajh*.

Meanwhile, در این اثنا *dar ín asná*.

Measles, سرخك *surkhak* ; سرخچه *surkhichah* ; حصبة *hasbat*.

Measure, *n.*, وزن *vazn* (*k.*); *pl.*, اوزان *auzán* ; پیمایش *paimáyish* (*k.*) ; پیمانه *paimánah* ; قفیز *kafíz* ; (of grain), کیل *kail* ; *v.*, پیمودن *paimúdan* ; *pa. p.*, مکیول *makyúl* ; *pr. p.*, مکایل *mukáil*.

Measurement, مساحت *masáhat*.

Measurer, پیما *paimá*. Land —, مساح *masáh*.

Meat, گوشت *gúsht* ; (roasted), کباب *kebáb*.

Mechanics, منجنیق *manjaník*.

Medal, تغمه *tughmeh*.

Meddle, *v.*, پس و پیش کردن *pas o písh k.*

Meddler, فضول *fuzúl*.

Mediation, توسط *tavassut* (*k.*) ; وساطت *vasátat* (*n.*).

Mediator, وسیط *vasít* ; میانچی *miyánchí*.

Medical, طبی *tabbíy*. The — art, طب *tibb*.

Medicine, دوا *davá*, *pl.*, ادویه *adviyah* ; دارو *dárú*. — snuffed up, نفوخ *nufúkh* ; نشوع *nushú'*.

Mediocrity, اوسط *ausat*.

Meditation, فکر *fikr* (*k.*) ; تفکر *tafakkur* (*k.*) ; اندیشه *andísheh* (*k.*) ; تاءمل *taammul* (*k.*).

Medlar, ازگل *azgal* ; زعرور *za'rúr*.

Meek, حلیم *halím* ; ملایم *muláyim*. —ness, حلم *hilm*.

Meeting (with), ملاقات *mulákát* (*k.*) ; وصال *visál* (*n.*) ; (interview), چار چشم *chár-chashm* (*sh.*) ; دو چار *du-chár* (*sh.*) ; تلاقی *talákí* ; ملتقی *multakí* ; جلسه *jalsah* (*séance*) ; مجلس *majlis*.

Melancholic, سوداءی *saudáí*.

Melancholy, شوریده خاطر *shúrídah-khátir* ; سودا *saudá* ; کابت *kábit* ; مالخولیا *málikhúliya*.

Mellifluous, شیرین *shírím*.

Mellow, رسیده *rasídah*.

Melodious, خوش ادا *khush-adá.*

Melody, ترانه *taránah*; نغمة *naghmat*; سرود *surúd*; لحن *lahn.*

Melon, خربوزه *kharbúzah*; خربزه *kharbuzah.* Water —, هندوانه *hinduváneh.*

Melt, گداختن *gudákhtan*; *pr. p.*, تسبيك *tasbík* (*n.*).

Melter, سباك *sabbák.*

Member (partner), شريك *sharík*; رفيق *rafík*; (limb), عضو *'uzv*, *pl.*, آعضاء *a'zá.*

Membrum virile, كير *kír*; آلت مباشرة *álat i mubásharat*; نره *narah.*

Memoir, تذكره *tazkerah.*

Memorandum, ياد داشت *yád-dásht.*

Memory, ياد *yád* (*dsh.*); حفظ *hifz* (*k.*). Retentive — (the word قوت *kúvvat* being understood), حافظه *háfizah.*

Mend, تعمير كردن *ta'mír k.*; (clothes), رفو كردن *rafv k.*

Mendicant, گدا *gedá*; فقير *fakír.*

Menial, نوكر *naukar.*

Menses, حيض *haiz.*

Menstruous woman, حايضه *háizeh.*

Mensuration, مساحت *musá-hat.*

Mention, ذكر *zikr* (*k.*); *pa. p.*, مذكور *mazkúr*; مزبور *mazbúr.* — above, موءمى اليه *mú'má ilaih.*

Mentor, لله *lalah.*

Mercenary, موءتجر *mu'tajar*; (hired-labourer), اجير *ajír.*

Merchandise, سوداگرى *saudá-garí*; تجارت *tijárat.*

Merchant, تاجر *tájir*, *pl.*, تجار *tujjár*; سوداگر *saudágar*; بازرگر *bázargar.*

Merciful, رحيم *rahím*; رحمان *rahmán*; بخشايشگر *bakhshá-yishgar.* Most —, ارحم *arham*; بيرحم *bírahm.*

Merciless, بيدريغ *bí-dirígh.*

Mercury (metal), سيماب *símáb*; زيبق *zíbek*; (planet), عطارد *'utárid.*

Mercy, رحمت *rahmat*; رحم *rahm.*

Merely, محض *mahz.*

Meridian, هجير *hajír*; ظهر *zuhr.*

Merit, لیاقت *liyáḳat* ; سزاواری *sezávárí.*

Meriting, استحقاق *istiḥḳáḳ* (*k.*).

Meritorious, سزاوار *sezávár* (*b.*) ; لایق *láyiḳ* (*sh. h.*).

Merry, دلخوش *dilkhúsh* ; دلشاد *dilshád* ; خرم *khurram.*

Mesh, شبکه *shabakeh.*

Mesopotamia, الجزیره *Aljazíreh* ; دیار بکر *Diyár Bekr.*

Message, پیغام *paighám* ; پیغم *paigham* ; پیام *paiyám* ; پیم *paiyam.*

Messenger, فرستاده *feristádeh.* Foot —, قاصد *ḳásid.* Mounted —, چاپار *chápár.* — from heaven, رسول *rasúl* ; پیامبر *paiyámbar*, etc.

Messiah, مسیح *masíh.*

Messmate, رفیق *rafíḳ.*

Metal, فلز *filizz.*

Metallic, فلزی *filizzíy.*

Metamorphosis, مسخ *maskh.*

Metaphor, مجاز *mujáz* ; استعاره *istiʿáreh.* —ical مجازی *majázi.*

Metaphysics, الهیت *iláhiyat.*

Metempsychosis, تناسخ *tanásukh.*

Meteor, شهاب *shiháb.*

Metheglin, شهد آب *shahd-áb.*

Methinks, گویا *guyá.*

Method, سلیقه *salíḳah, in pl.* اسالیب *asálíb.* Without —, بی سروپا *bí-sar u pá,*

Metre (measure), مقیاس *miḳyás* ; وزن *vazn* ; (verse), بحر *bahr.*

Metropolis, پای تخت *páitakht* ; دارالخلافت *dár ul khiláfat.*

Mew (cat's), مو مو *mau mau* (*k.*),

Midday, ظهر *zuhr* ; نیمروز *nímrúz.*

Middle, میانه *miyánah* ; میان *miyán* ; اوسط *ausat* ; وسط *vast.*

Middling, مقارب *muḳárib.*

Mid-night, نیم شب *ním-shab* ; دل شب *dil i shab.*

Midst, اثناء *asná* ; قلب *ḳalb.*

Midsummer, قیظ *ḳaiz* ; تابستان *tábistán.*

Midway, نیمه راه *nímah-ráh*

Midwife, قابله *ḳábilah.*

Mien, صورت *súrat.*

Might, بأس *bá's.* —y, قادر *ḳádir* ; عظیم *ʿazím.*

Migration, نقل *naḳl* (*k.*) ; انتقال *intiḳál* (*k.*).

Minute, *n.*, دقیقة *daḳíḳah* A few —s, دمی چند *damí chand*; *a.*, (small), خرد *khurd.* —ly, بدقة *bediḳḳat.*

Miracle (performed by a prophet), معجزه *mu'jizah*, *pl.*, معجزات *mu'jizat*; (which happens), کرامت *kerámat*; خارق عادت *khárik i 'ádat*; خرق عادت *khirḳ i 'ádat.* A — of beauty, نگار عالم *nigár i 'álam.*

Mirage, سراب *saráb.*

Mire, خلاب *khaláb.*

Mirror, آئینه *á-inah*; آبگینه *ábgínah*; مرآت *mirát*; — holder, (a court officer), آئینه دار *á-inah-dár.*

Mirth, شادمانی *shádmání*; انبساط *imbisát.* —ful, شاد *shád*; خوش *khúsh.*

Misadventure, بلا *balá.*

Misanthropy, حوشیة *húshíyet.*

Misapprehension, غلط *ghalat.*

Misbehaviour, بدرفتاری *bad raftárí.*

Miscarriage, اسقاط *isḳát* (*k.*).

Mischief, شرارة *sharárat.*

Mischievous, شریر *sharír.*

Misdeeds, ذمیمة *zamímeh*, *pl.*, ذمائم *zamáim.*

Miser, بخیل *bakhíl*; زکور *zakúr*; جوکی *júkí.*

Miserable, نکد *nakid*; منکوب *mankúb*; بیچاره *bícháreh.*

Misery, اضطرار *iztirár*; شقاوت *shaḳávat.*

Misfortune, نکب *nakb*; مصیبت *musíbat*, *pl.*, مصائب *masáib*; بلیة *balíyet*, *pl.*, بلیات *balıyát*; افت *áfat*, *pl.*, آفات *áfát*; وبال *vabál*; شومی *shúmí.*

Miss, *v.*, خطا کردن *khatá k.*; *pr. p.*, گم *gum* (*sh.*).

Mission (embassy), سفارة *sefárat.*

Missionary, کشیش *keshísh.*

Missive, مراسله *murásaleh.*

Mist, دود *dúd*; بخار *bukhár.*

Mistake, غلط *ghalat* (*k.*); خطا *khatá* (*k.*).

Misletoe, کاولی *kávalí.*

Mistress (sweetheart), دل آرام *dil-árám*; شاهد *sháhid*; مه پاره *mah-párah*; (of house), خانم *khánum.*

Mistrustful, بد گمان *bad gumán* (*k.*).

Misty, پرمه *pur mih.*

Misunderstanding, سهو *sahv*

Minute, *n.*, دقیقه *daḳíḳah* A few —s, دمی چند *damí chand*; *a.*, (small), خرد *khurd.* —ly, بدقة *bediḳḳat.*

Miracle (performed by a prophet), معجزه *mu'jizah*, *pl.*, معجزات *mu'jizat*; (which happens), کرامت *kerámat*; خارق عادت *khárik i 'ádat*; خرق عادت *khirḳ i 'ádat.* A — of beauty, نگار عالم *nigár i 'álam.*

Mirage, سراب *saráb.*

Mire, خلاب *khaláb.*

Mirror, آئینه *á-inah*; آبگینه *ábgínah*; مرآت *mirát*; — holder, (a court officer), آئینه دار *á-inah-dár.*

Mirth, شادمانی *shádmání*; انبساط *imbisát.* —ful, شاد *shád*; خوش *khúsh.*

Misadventure, بلا *balá.*

Misanthropy, حوشیة *húshíyet.*

Misapprehension, غلط *ghalat.*

Misbehaviour, بدرفتاری *bad raftárí.*

Miscarriage, اسقاط *isḳát* (*k.*).

Mischief, شرارة *sharárat.*

Mischievous, شریر *sharír.*

Misdeeds, ذمیمة *zamímeh*, *pl.*, ذمائم *zamáim.*

Miser, بخیل *bakhíl*; زکور *zakúr*; جوکی *júkí.*

Miserable, نکد *nakid*; منکوب *mankúb*; بیچاره *bícháreh.*

Misery, اضطرار *iztirár*; شقاوت *shaḳávat.*

Misfortune, نکب *nakb*; مصیبت *musíbat*, *pl.*, مصائب *masáib*; بلیة *balíyet*, *pl.*, بلیات *balíyát*; آفت *áfat*, *pl.*, آفات *áfát*; وبال *vabál*; شومی *shúmí.*

Miss, *v.*, خطا کردن *khatá k.*; *pr. p.*, گم *gum* (*sh.*).

Mission (embassy), سفارة *sefárat.*

Missionary, کشیش *keshísh.*

Missive, مراسله *murásaleh.*

Mist, دود *dúd*; بخار *bukhár.*

Mistake, غلط *ghalat* (*k.*); خطا *khatá* (*k.*).

Misletoe, کاولی *kávalí.*

Mistress (sweetheart), دل آرام *dil-árám*; شاهد *sháhid*; مه پاره *mah-párah*; (of house), خانم *khánum.*

Mistrustful, بد گمان *bad gumán* (*k.*).

Misty, پرمه *pur mih.*

Misunderstanding, سهو *sahv*

(*k.*); (quarrel), مجادله *mujádeleh* (*k.*).

Mix, درگذاشتن *dar-guzáshtan*; سرشتن *sirishtan*; آمیختن *ámíkhtan*; آشوردن *áshúrdan*. — up, بر آمیختن *bar ámíkhtan*; *pa. p.*, ممتزج *mumtazaj*; ممزوج *mamzúj*; (blended), مخلوط *makhlút*; *pr. p.*, مزج *mazaj*; آمیز *ámíz*. — together in society, مخالطة *mukhálatat*.

Mixture, خلط *khalt*; میزك *mízak*; آمیزش *ámízish*.

Moan, ناله *náleh* (*k.*).

Moat, گودال *gaudál*.

Mob, هنگامه *hangámeh*; ازدحام *izdihám*.

Mocker, ساخر *sákhir*.

Mockery, ریشخند *rísh khand*.

Mocking, تضحك *tazahhuk* (*n.*).

Mode, روش *ravish*; نمط *namat*; سیاقت *siyákat*; اسلوب *uslúb*, *pl.* اسالیب *asalíb*; وضع *vaz'*, *in pl.* (fashions), اطوار *atvár*.

Model, نمونه *namúnah* (*k.*).

Moderate, وراع *varrá'*; معتدل *mu'tadíl*.

Moderation, میانه روی *miyánah-raví*; اعتدال *i'tidál*.

Modern, حالی *hálí*; جدید *jadíd*, *pl.* (people), متاخرین *muta'ákhkharín*.

Modest, شرمسار *sharm-sár*; پرده نشین *pardah-nishín*. —ly, آهیز *áhíz*.

Modesty, شرم *sharm*; شرمساری *sharm-sárí*; حیاء *hayá*; حجاب *hijáb*; آزرم *ázarm*; انفعال *infi'ál*.

Modification, تعدیل *ta'díl* (*k.*).

Modulation, نوا *navá*.

Mogul, or Mongolian, مغل *mughal*.

Mohammedan, محمدی *muhammadí*; مسلمان *musalmán*. — religion, مسلمانی *mussalmání*; اسلام *islám*.

Moist, نم *nam* (*k.*); نمناك *namnák*; نمگین *nam-gín*; نملو *namlú*; سیر آب *sír-áb*; رطب *ratb*; تر *tar* (*k.*).

Moisten, آغاریدن *ághárídan*; خیسیدن *khísídan*; آغشتن *ághashtan*.

Moisture, رطوبت *rutúbat*; نداوت *nadávat*; آب *ab*.

Mole (animal), موش کور *músh i kúr*; (on face), خال *khál*.

Molest, آزاردن *ázárdan*.

Molester, سرکوب *sar-kúb.*

Moment, لحظة *lahzat ;* لمحه *lamhah.* At that —, هماندم *hamán-dam.* One —, یکدم *yak-dam.*

Momentary, یکساعت *yak-sá'at.*

Monarch, پادشاه *pádisháh.*

Monarchy, پادشاهی *pádisháhí.*

Monastery, خانقاه *khánḳáh ;* دیر *dair ;* صومعه *súmi'ah.*

Monasticism, رهبانیت *ruhbá-níyet.*

Monday, دو شنبه *dú-shambah.*

Money, پول *púl ;* (cash), پول نقد *púl-i-naḳd.* — paid in advance, سلم *silm ;* رمون *ramún ;* عربون *'arbún.* — and goods, نقد و جنس *naḳd u jins.* Ready — purchase, خوش خرید *khush-kharíd.* Small —, change, خرده *khur-dah.* False —, قلب *ḳalb.* A sum of —, مبلغ *mablagh.* — changer, صراف *sarráf.*

Mongrel, دورگه *du-ragah.*

Monitor, ناصح *násih ;* واعظ *va'iz.* — of a school, خلیفهٔ کتاب *khalífah i kuttáb.*

Monk, راهب *ráhib, pl.* رهبان *ruhbán.*

Monkey, بوزنه *búzinah ;* قرد *ḳird ;* میمون *maimun.*

Monopolist, محتکر *muhtakir.*

Monopoly, انحصار *inhisár.*

Monotheist, موحد *muvahhid.*

Monsoon, موسم *mausum.*

Monster, عفریت *'afrít.*

Monstrous (size), عظیم *'azím.*

Month, ماه *máh ;* شهر *shahr, pl.,* شهور *shuhúr.* The Moslem (lunar) months are 1st, محرم *muharram ;* 2nd, صفر *safar ;* 3rd, ربیع الاول *rabí' ul avval ;* 4th, ربیع الاخر *rabí' ul ákhir ;* 5th, جمادی الاولی *jumádí ul avval ;* 6th, جمادی الثانی *jumádí ussáni ;* 7th, رجب *rejeb ;* 8th, شعبان *sha'-bán ;* 9th, رمضان *ramazán ;* 10th, شوال *shavvál ;* 11th, ذو القعده *zu'l ḳa'dah ;* 12th, ذو الحجة *zu'l hijjah.* The ancient Persian (solar) year is used for the crops. It begins at *No rúz,* the Vernal Equinox (21st March). 1st, فروردین *farvardín* (April) ; 2nd, اردیبهشت *ardí bihisht* (May) ; 3rd, خرداد *khur-dád* (June) ; 4th, تیر *tír*

(July); 5th, مرداد *mardád* (August); 6th, شهریر *shahrír* (Sept.); 7th, مهرماه *mihrmáh* (Oct.); 8th, آبان *ábán* (Nov.); 9th, آذر *ázur* (Dec.); 10th, دی *dai* (Jan.); 11th, بهمان *bahmán* (Feb.); 12th, اسفندارمز *asfandármuz* (ending 21st of March).

Monthly, ماهیانه *máhiyánah*; ماهوار *máhwár*; ماه بماه *máh ba máh*. — allowance, مشاهره *musháharah*. — wages, ماهانه *máhánah*; ماهواری *máhvárí*.

Monument, یاد کار *yád-gár*.

Mood (tense), صیغه *síghah*, *pl.* صیغ *siyagh*.

Moon, ماه *máh*; مه *mah*; قمر *ḳamar*. New —, ماه نو *máh i nau*. Crescent —, هلال *hilál*. Full —, بدر *badr*. Little —, مهچه *mahcheh*. —faced, ماهرو *máh-rú*. Beautiful as the —, مهوش *mahvash*. — light, مهتاب *mahtáb*; ماهتاب *máh-táb*.

Moral, *a.*, صالح *sálih*.

Morality, صلاح *saláh*.

Morals, اخلاق *akhlák*.

More, بیش *bísh*; بیشتر *bishtar*; زیاده *ziyádeh*; اکثر *aksar*.

Moreover, علاوه برین *'aláveh bar-ín*.

Morning, صبح *súbh*; صباح *sabáh*; بامداد *bámdád*; بام گاه *bám-gáh*; (dawn), فجر *fajr*. Next —, بامدادان *bámdádán*.

Morocco leather, ادیم *adím*.

Morose, سخت *sakht*. —ness, درشتی *durushtí*.

Morrow, to-, فردا *fardá*. The day after to-morrow, پس فردا *pas-fardá*; پسین فردا *pasín-fardá*.

Morsel, نواله *niválah*.

Mortal, *n.*, فانی *fání*; *a.*, مهلك *muhlik*. —ity, فناء *faná*.

Mortar (plaster), کچ *gach*; (for pounding), هوان *haván*; هاون *hávan*. Pestle and —, هوان دسته *haván dastah*.

Mortgage, رهن *rahn* (*gz.*).

Mortgaged, رهین *rahín*.

Mortgagee, مرتهن *murtahin*.

Mortgager, راهن *ráhin*.

Mortification (of passions), ریاضت *riyázat*; (of matter),

عفونت *'ufúnat*; (of mind), زحمت *zahmat* (*ksh.*).

Mortify (a wound), گندیده شدن *gandídeh sh.*; (passions), ضبط کردن *zabt k.*; (a person), آزار دادن *ázár d.*

Mortmain, وقف *vakf.*

Mosaic (wood), خاتمی *khátimí.*

Moslem, مسلمان *musalmán*; مسلم *muslim.*

Mosque, مسجد *masjid, pl.*, مساجد *masájid.* The great — of a city, جامع *jámi'.*

Mosquito, پشه *pashah.*

Moss, پوژه *púzhah.*

Most, بیشترین *bíshtarín.* —ly, اغلب *aghlab.*

Mote, ذره *zarreh.*

Moth, پروانه *parvánah*; فراش *farásh.* — eaten, بید خورده *bíd khúrdah.*

Mother, مادر *mádar*; ماما *mámá*; ام *umm*; والده *válidah.* — in law, خوشدامن *khush-dáman*; مارندر *márandar*; خشو *khushú*; خش *khash*, or *khush.* — of pearl, صدف *sadaf.*

Motion, حرکت *harakat*; جنبش *jumbish*; تحرك *taharruk.* —less, ساکن *sákin.*

Motive, دست آویز *dast áviz*; مقصود *maksúd*; تقریب *takríb*; غرض *gharaz.*

Motto, علامت *'alámat.*

Mould (form), قالب *kálib*; (soil), خاك *khák.*

Mouldy, زنك زده *zang zadeh.* — ness, زنك *zang.*

Moulting, نسول *nusúl* (*k.*).

Mound, تپه *tappeh.*

Mount (rise), بر شدن *bar shudan*; (a horse), سوار شدن *sovvár sh.* — on, بر نشستن *bar nishastan.*

Mountain, کوه *kúh*; جبل *jebel.* — ous, کوهسار *kúh-sár*; کهستان *kuhistán.*

Mourn, افسوس خوردن *afsús kh.*; گریه کردن *geriyeh k.*

Mourner (hired,) نوحه گر *nauhah-gar.*

Mournful, دلتنك *dil-tang*; غمناك *ghamnák.*

Mourning, تعزیه *ta'zíyeh* (*k.*). Belonging to —, ماتمی *mátumí.*

Mouse, موش *músh.* Field —, موش دشتی *músh i dashtí.*

Mouth, دهن *dahan*; دهان *dahán*; فم *fam*; فو *fú, pl.*,

افواه *afvah*. — of a firearm, لوله *lúlah*. Inside of the —, نج *naj* or *nuj*. Parts round the —, پوز *púz*. —ful لقمه *luḳmah*.

Movables, اسباب *asbáb*.

Move, *v. i.*, جنبيدن *jumbídan*; *v. t.*, جنبانيدن *jumbánídan*; تكانيدن *takánídan*; *pa. p.*, متحرك *mutaharrik*; *pr. p.*, رج *rajj*.

Movement, حركت *harakat* (*d. kh*); تكان *takán* (*d.*).

Mover, محرك *muharrik*.

Mow, درويدن *diravídan*.

Mower, درونده *diravandeh*.

Much, بسا *basá*; خيلی *khaili*; بسيار *bisyár*; فراوان *farávan*; از بس *az bas*. As —, so —, چندان *chandán*; چندين *chandín*. Too —, زياد *zíyád*.

Mucus (of the nose), مخاط *mukhát*.

Mud, گل *gil*; خلاب *khaláb*.

Muddy, شل و گل *shul o gil*; تار *tár*.

Mulberry, توت *tút*.

Mulct, تاوان *táwán*; غرامت *gharámat*. — for manslaughter, ديت *diyat*.

Mule, قاطر *ḳátir*; استر *astar*; بغل *baghl*.

Muleteer, قاطرچی *ḳatirchí*; چاروا دار *charvá-dár*.

Multiplication (in arithmetic), ضرب *zarb* (*k.*).

Multiply, افزائيدن *afzáídan*.

Multitude (crowd), انبوه *ambúh*; (number), تعدد *ta'addud*.

Mummy, موميای *múmiyái*.

Mundane, دنياوی *dunyávi*.

Munificence, بخشندگی *bakhshandagí*; بذل *bazl*.

Munificent, سخی *sakhí*; جواد *javvád*.

Murder, قتل *ḳatl*. Charged with —, خون گرفته *khún-giriftah*. Fine for —, خون بها *khún-bahá*.

Murderer, خونی *khúní*; قاتل *ḳátil*.

Murmur, زمزمه *zemzemeh*.

Murmuring (complaint), گله *gilah* (*k.*); شكوا *shakvá* (*k.*).

Muscle, عضلة *'azalat*; (fish), صدف *sadaf*.

Mushroom, قارچ *ḳárch*; چترمار *chatar i már*; سماروغ *samárúgh*.

Music, موسیقی *músíḳí.* — gallery, نوبت خانه *naubat-khánah.*

Musical scale or gamut, پردهٔ لحان *pardah i ilhán.* — instrument, ساز *sáz.*

Musician, مطرب *mutrib.*

Musk, مشك *mushk.* A pod of —, نافه *náfah.* — rat, کرموش *ḳar-músh.* — scented, مشك بو *mushk-bú*; مشکین *mishkín.*

Musket, تفنك *tufang*; بندوق *bandúḳ*; توپك *topak.* —eer, بندوقچی *bandúḳchí.*

Muslin, ململ *malmal*; اقابانو *aḳábánú.*

Mustachios, بروت *burút.*

Mustard, خردل *khardil.* — seed, سرشف *sarshaf.*

Mutability, تغیر *taghayyur.*

Mutable, or Mutation, تبدیل *tabdíl* (*k.*); تغییر *taghyír* (*k.*).

Mute, لال *lál.*

Mutilated, ابتر *abtar*; چولاق *chúláḳ.*

Mutineer, یاغی *yághí* (*sh.*); عاصي *'ásí* (*sh.*).

Mutiny, یاغی گری *yághí gerí* (*k.*); فساد *fasád.*

Mutter, رکیدن *rakídan.* — in a rage, زکیدن *zakídan.*

Mutton, گوشت گوسفند *gúsht-i-gúsfand.*

Mutual, جانبین *jánibain.* —ly known, متعارف *muta'árif.*

Muzzle (dog), دهن بند *dahan band*; (of gun), دهن *dahan.*

Myrobalan, هلیله *halílah.*

Myrrh, مر *murr.*

Myrtle, آس *ás*; مورد *múrd.*

Mysterious, مخفی *makhfí.* —ly, سراً *sirran.*

Mystery, راز *ráz.* Divine —, حکمة الهی *hikmat i Iláhí.* Skilled in —, رموز دان *rumúz-dán.*

Mystic, *n.*, صوفی *súfí.* —al, باطن *bátin.* —ism, تصوف *tasavvuf.*

Mythological, موهوم *mauhúm.*

Mythology, موهومات *mauhú-mát.*

N

Nail (finger), ناخن *nákhun*; (peg), مسمار *mismár*; میخ *míkh.*

Naked, برهنه *barahnah;* لوخت *lúkht;* عریان *'uryán;* عاری *'ári.* —ness, برهنگی *barahnagí.*

Name, *n.,* نام *nám (d. gz.);* اسم *ism (nh.), pl.,* اسامی *asámí* and اسماء *asmá'.* The name showing descent is called کنیه *kunyeh;* the title is لقب *lakab;* the "nom de plume" is تخلص *takhallus.* In the — of God, بسم الله *bismillah; v.,* نامیدن *námídan; pa. p.,* مسمی *musammá (n.).* —ly, یعنی *ya'ní.* —sake, سمی *samíy.*

Nap (sleep), چرت *churt (z.);* (of cloth), کلك *kuluk.*

Nape (of the neck), قفا *kifá.*

Naptha, نفط *nift.*

Napkin, دستمال *dast-mál.*

Narcissus, نرگس *nargis;* نسترن *nastaran;* عبهر *'abhar.*

Narcotic, مخدر *mukhaddir;* مسکر *muskir.*

Narration, وصف *vasf (k.).*

Narrative, تقریر *takrír (n.).*

Narrator, راوی *rávi.*

Narrow, تنك *tang.* — place, مضیق *muzík, pl.,* مضایق *muzáik.* — minded, تنك دل *tang-dil.* —ness, تنگی *tangí.*

Nasty, نا پاك *nápák;* کسیف *kasíf.* —ness, کسافت *kisáfat.*

Nation, قوم *kaum;* ملت *millat.* — al, ملتی *millatí.*

Native (of), متوطن *mutavattin.* — place, مولد *maulid;* وطن *vatan.*

Nativity, میلاد *mílád;* ولاد *vilád;* ولادت *viládat.*

Natural, ذاتی *zátí;* طبعی *tab'iy;* طبیعی *tabí'iy;* شمایلی *shamáilí;* خلقی *khalkíy.*

Naturalized, محسوب *mahsub (s.).*

Nature, طبع *tab';* طبیعت *tabí'at;* طینت *tínat;* فطرت *fitrat;* نهاد *nihád;* نجار *nujár;* جبلت *jibilat;* سجیة *sajhat;* سرشت *sirisht.* Dame —, مادر روزکار *mádar i rúzgár.* Good —, نیك خو *ník-khú.*

Naughty, بد *bad.* — ness, سکیت *sagíyet.*

Nausea, تهوع *tahavvu'.*

Nautical, Naval, بحری *bahrí.*

Navel, ناف *náf*; ناخ *nákh*.

Navigator, جاشو *jáshú*.

Navy, بحريه *bahriyah*.

Near, نزديك *nazdík*; نزد *nazd*; قريب *karíb*. —ly, تقريباً *takríban*; عنقريب *'ankaríb*.

Neat, تميز *temíz*. —ness, نظافت *nizáfat*.

Necessaries, لوازم *lavázim*; ضروريات *zarúriyát*; حوائج *haváij*.

Necessarily, لا بد *lá budd*; بالضرورة *bizzurúrat*; لا جرم *lá jaram*.

Necessary, *n.*, ضروری *zarúrí*; لازمي *lázimí*; نفقه *nafakat*; واجبي *vájibí*; در كار *dar kár*. That which is —, ما لازم *má lazam*. It is —, بايد *báyad*; لازم است *lázem ast*; ضرور است *zurúr ast*; واجب است *vájib ast*. To be —, بايستن *báyistan*.

Necessitous, حاجت مند *hájatmand*; محتاج *muhtáj*.

Necessity, ضرورت *zarúrat* (*n.*); لزوم *luzúm*; التزام *iltizám*.

Neck, گردن *gardan*; عنق *'ank*; رقبه *rakbat*. —cloth, or tie, گردن بند *gardan band*.

Necklace, گلو بند *gulú-bánd*.

Nectarine, شليل *shalíl*.

Need, احتياج *ihtiyáj* (*dsh.*).

Needle, سوزن *súzan*. — case, سوزندان *súzandán*. —work, چكن *chakin*; قلابدوزی *kulláb dúzí*.

Needless, بيجهت *bíjihat*.

Needy, محتاج *muhtáj*.

Nefarious, فضيح *fazíh*.

Negation (in logic), سلب *salb*.

Negative, نفی *nafiy*. —ly, نفياً *nafiyan*.

Neglect, اهمال *ihmál* (*n.*); غفلت *ghiflat* (*k.*).

Negligence, غفلت *ghaflat*; خوابيدگی *kh'ábídagí*; تكاهل *takáhul*. Wilful —, تغافل *tagháful*.

Negligent, غافل *ghâfil* (*sh.*); مهمل *muhmil*; متهاون *mutahávin*.

Negotiation, كار و بار *kár o bár*; معامله *mu'ámeleh* (*k.*).

Negro, حبشی *habashí*; زنگي *zangí*.

Neighing, شيهه *shíhah* (*k.*); صهيل *sahíl* (*k.*).

Neighbour, همسایه *hamsáyeh;* مجاور *mujávir;* جار *jár, pl.* جیران *jírán;* همجوار *ham-javár.* —s and dependants, جار و بالجار *jár o bi'ljár.* A next door —, همدیوار *ham-dívár.* —hood, همسایگی *ham-sáyagí;* جوار *jivár;* نواحي *naváhí;* مجاورت *mujávarat.*

Neither, nor, نه نه *nah nah.*

Nephew, برادر زاده *birádar zádeh;* پسر برادر *pesari birá-dar;* (sister's son), خواهر زاده *kháher zádeh,* etc., *pl.* بنی عم *bení 'amm.*

Nerve, عصبه *'asabeh;* عضلت *'azlat.*

Nervous, ترسان *tarsán.*

Nest, آشیان *áshyán;* آشیانه *ásh-yánah;* کاشانه *káshánah.*

Net, شبکه *shabakeh;* دام *dám;* طور *túr.*

Nettle, گزنه *gaznah.*

Neutral, بیطرف *bítaraf.*

Never, هرگز *hargiz;* قطعا *kat'an.* —theless, امّا *amma.*

New, نو *nau,* or *no;* (fresh), تازه *tázah;* (modern), جدید *ja-díd;* نو پیدا *nau-paidá.* — comer, نو آینده *nau-áyendah.*

New year's day, نوروز (عید *'íd i) nau-rúz.*

News, خبر *khabar;* اخبار *akh-bár.* Good —, نوید *navíd;* مژده *muzhdah.* Announcing —, مستبشر *mustabshir.* —paper, روز نامه *rúznámeh.*

Next (to), متصل *muttasil;* پیوسته *paivasteh;* (after), بعد *ba'ad;* پس *pas.* — day, روز دیگر *ruz-i-dígar.* — year, سال آینده *sal i áyandeh.*

Nib of a pen, نوك قلم *nauk i kalam.*

Nice, قشنك *kashang;* نیك *ník.*

Niche, طاقچه *tákcheh.*

Niece, دختر برادر *dukhtar i birá-dar;* برادر زاده *birádar zádeh;* (sister's daughter), دختر خواهر *dukhtar i kháhar,* etc.

Niggard, بخیل *bakhíl;* لئیم *layím,* —liness, بخل *bukhl,* —ly, خسیس *khasís.*

Nigh, قریب *karíb.*

Night, شب *shab;* لیل *lail.* To —, امشب *imshab.* Last —, دیشب *dí-shab.* The — before last, پریشب *parí-shab.* — and day (inces-santly), شبانروز *shabánrúz.*

—ly, هر شب *har shab.* — after —, شباشب *shabá-shab.* — time, or at —, شبانگاه *shubángah;* شب گاه *shab-gáh;* شب هنگام *shab-hangám.* Dark —, شب دیجور *shab i daijúr.* Travelling by —, شب رو *shab-ro.* — attack, شب خون *shab-khún;* شبگیر *shab-gír.* Vigilant during the —, شب زنده دار *shab-zindah-dár.* The — watch, شب گرد *shab-gard.* — gown, پراهن شب *piráhan i shab.*

Nightingale, بلبل *bulbul;* عندلیب *'andalíb;* هزار *hazár.*

Nightmare, کابوس *ḳábús;* نیدل *nídul;* برخفچ *barkhafch.*

Nightshade, کاکنج *kákenj.*

Nimble, چابك *chábuk;* چالاك *chálák.*

Nimrod, نمرود *nimrúd.*

Nine, نه *nuh.* —teen, نوزده *núzdah.* —teenth, نوزدهم *núzdahum.* —ty, نود *navad.*

Ninth, نهم *nuhum.*

Nippers, انبر *ambur.*

Nipple, پستان *pistán;* (gun), خروسك *khurúsak.*

Nitre, نطرون *natrún.*

No, not, نه *na;* خیر *khair,* or *kheyr;* نه خیر *nah kheyr.* — (with the imperative), مه *mah.* It is —, نیست *níst.*

No! no! not at all, نی نی *nai-nai.*

Noah, نوح *Núh.*

Nobility, نجابت *najábat;* شرفیت *sharfíyet;* شرف *sharaf.*

Noble, شریف *sharíf;* نجیب *najíb;* ماجد *májid;* مکرم *mukarram.* Of — race, بزرك زاده *buzurg-zádah.* — and plebian, خاص و عام *kháss u-'ámm.* —ness, نباهت *nabáhat.* —man, امیر *amír;* امیرزاده *amírzádah.*

Nobles, بزرکان *buzurgán;* اشراف *ashráf;* شرفاء *shurafá';* اعیان *a'yán;* امرآء *umará;* نجباء *nujabá';* اکارم *akárim.* Great —, اماجد *amájid.*

Nobly, بزرکانه *buzurgánah.*

Nobody, هیچکس *híchkas.*

Nod, اشاره *ishárah* (*k.*).

Noise, آواز *aváz* (*k.*); صدا *seda* (*k.*); بانك *báng;* (uproar), غوغا *ghaughá;* نژغار *nazh-ghár;* ولوله *valvalah.* To make a —, هنکامه کردن *han-*

gámah k. —less, خاموش *khámúsh.*

Nolens volens, خواهنخواه *kh'áh na kh'áh ;* طوعاً و کرهاً *tau'an o karhan.*

Nomad, ایل *íl, pl.* ایلیات *íliyát.*

Nom-de-plume, تخلص *takhallus.*

Nominal, اسمی *ismí.* —ly, اسماً *isman.*

Nomination, تسمیة *tasmíyet (k.).*

None, هیچ *hích.*

Nonsense, پوچ *púch (gf.)*; حرف مفت *harf i muft.*

Noon, ظهر *zuhr.*

Noose, خم کمند *kham-kamand ;* کمند *kamand (an.).*

Nor, نه *nah.*

North, شمال *shimál.*

Nose, بینی *bíní.* —bag, توبره *túbrah.* —gay, گلدسته *guldastah ;* دستهٔ گل *dastah i gul.*

Nostril, منخر *minkhar ;* پرهٔ بینی *parrah i bíní.*

Not, نه *nah ;* غیر *ghair.* — at all, اصلاً *aslan ;* هیچ *hich.*

Notch, ناب *náb;* (of an arrow),

سوفار *súfár ;* (in a blade), دمریزه *damrízah.*

Note (letter), کاغذ *kághaz ;* رقعه *ruḳ'ah ;* (in book), حاشیه *háshiyeh ;* (of music), مقام *maḳám.* Modulated —, الحان *alhán.* — book, کتابچه *kitábcheh*

Nothing, هیچ *hích.* This generally requires another negative, as هیچ نمی دارم *hích na mí dáram,* I have nothing.

Notice (of), اطلاع *ittilá' (d.)*; خبر *khabar (d.).* To take — of, نگاه کردن *nigáh k.*

Notification, اعلان *i'lán (k.).*

Notion, خیال *khiyál ;* ظن *zann.*

Notoriety, شهرت *shuhrat.*

Notorious, مشهور *mashhúr ;* معروف *ma'rúf.* —ly, مشهوراً *mashhúrán.*

Notwithstanding, باوجود *bá-vujúd ;* باوصف *bá-vasf.*; با آنکه *bá-ánkih.*

Noun, اسم *ism.*

Nourish, پروردن *parvardan.* —er, پرور *parvar.* —ment,

طعام ta'ám ; قوت ḳút ; خوراك khúrák.

Novel, *a.*, نو *nau*, or *no*. —ty, حدوث *hudús* ; حادثه *hádisah* ; نو آئين *nau-á'ín*.

Novice, نو آموز *nau ámúz*.

Now, حالا *hálá* ; الحال *al hál* ; الان *al-án* ; اکنون *aknún* ; کنون *kanún*.

Nowhere, هيچ جا *hich já*.

Noxious, موذی *mu'zí* ; ضار *zárr*.

Nubile, بالغ *báligh*.

Nude, عاری *'árí*, عريان *'uryán*.

Nugatory, باطل *bátil*.

Nuisance, اذيت *azíyat* ; وبال *vabál*.

Null and void, ابطال *ibtál* (*k.*).

Nullity, نيستی *nístí*.

Numb, بيحس *bí hiss* (*s.*) ; سست *sust* (*sh.*).

Number, عدد *'adad* (*k.*), *pl.*, اعداد *a'dád*. —ed, معدود *ma'dúd* ; شمرده *shumurdah* ; معتد *mu'tadd*.

Numeral, هندسه *hindiseh*.

Numeration, عد *'add*.

Numerous, بسيار *bisyár* ; خيلی *khaili* ; متوافر *mutaváfir*.

Nun, راحبه *ráhibeh*.

Nurse, دايه *dáyah*. Wet —, شير ده *shír-dah*.

Nurture, پرورش *parvarish* (*k.*).

Nut, جوز *jauz* ; (filbert), فندق *fanduḳ*. Wall—, گردو *girdú*. —shell, پوست *púst*. —meg, جوز بويا *jauz i búyá*.

Nutricious, مغذی *mughazzí*.

Nux vomica, جوز القی *jauz ul ḳai*.

O

O! ای *ai!* يا *yá!*

Oak, بلوط *ballút*. —apple, مازو *mázú*.

Oakum, نبج *nabj*.

Oar, خاده *khádah* ; پارو *párú*.

Oath, سوگند *saugand* (*kh.*) ; قسم *ḳasm* (*kh.*), *pl.*, اقسام *aḳsám* ; يمين *yamín* (*k.*), *pl.*, ايمان *aimán* ; حلف *half*

Oats, زن *zann*.

Obdurate, سنگدل *sangdil*. —ness, سختی *sakhtí*.

Obedience, طاعت *tá'at* ; اطاعت *itá'at* (*k.*) ; طوع *tau'* ; استطاعت *istitá'at* (*n.*) ; اذعان *iz'an* ; تبعيت *tab'íyet* ; مطاوعة *muta-va'ah* ; انقياد *inḳiyád* (*r.*).

Obedient, مطیع *mutí'* (*sh.*); ممتثل *mumtasil*; حکم انداز *hukm-andáz*; فرمان بردار *farmán-bardár* (*sh.*).

Obeisance, کورنش *kúrnish*; کورنشات *kurnishát*; تعظیم *ta'zím* (*k.*).

Obey, سر نهادن *sar nihádan*. I —, بر آن ام *bar án am*; *pa. p.*, متبوع *matbú* (*sh.*); مطاع *mutá'*; مخدوم *makhdúm*.

Object (seen), مظهر *muzhar*; منظر *manzar*; (mental), مقصد *maksad*; مقصود *maksúd*; مراد *murád*; نیت *niyyat*. — to, *v.*, مخالف کردن *mukhálif k.*

Objection, اعتراض *i'tiráz* (*k.*).

Obligation, منت *minnat* (*dsh.*); وجوب *vujúb*; امتنان *imtinán*. Imposing an —, من *mann* (*k.*). — in writing, مچلکه *muchalkah*.

Obligatory, لازم *lázim*.

Obliged (to do so and so), ملزوم *malzúm*; (to a person), ممنون *mamnún* (*h. s.*).

Obliging, مشفق *mushfik*.

Oblique, کج *kaj*.

Obliterate, قلم در کشیدن *kalam dar kashídan*; *pa. p.*, مندرس *mundaris*; *pr. p.*, ماحی *máhí* (*k.*); نسخ *naskh* (*k.*).

Oblivion, ذهول *zuhúl*; نسیان *nisyán*.

Oblivious, ذاهل *záhil*.

Oblong, مستطیل *mustatíl*.

Obloquy, بهتان *buhtán*.

Obscene, فاحش *fáhish*; خبیث *khabís*; شطاح *shattáh*.

Obscenity, فحش *fuhsh* (*gf.*); خنو *khanv*; هرزگی *harzagí*.

Obscure (dark), تاریك *tárík*; شب رنك *shab-rang*; (in language), غامض *ghámiz*.

Obscurity, تیرگی *tíragí*.

Obsequies, تدفین *tadfín*.

Obsequious, موء تمر *mu'tamar*; دروب *darúb*. — ness, فرو تنی *farú taní*.

Observance, مراقبت *murákabat*. — of justice, حق بین *hakk-bín*.

Observation (of the stars), تنجم *tanajjum* (*k.*).

Observatory, رصد گاه *rasad-gáh*.

Observe (stars), رصد کردن *rasad k.*; (look at), ملاحظه کردن *muláhezeh k.*

Observer, راقب *rákib* ; راصد *rásid* ; رصاد *rassád*. Superficial —, ظاهر پرست *záhir-parast.*

Obsolete, منسوخ *mansúkh.*

Obstacle, مانع *máni'* ; سد *sadd.*

Obstinacy, معاندت *mu'ánadat* ; اصرار *isrár.*

Obstinate, خرمست *khar-mast* ; خود سر *ḳhud-sar* ; عاند *'ánid.*

Obstructed, مسدود *masdúd* (*s.*).

Obstruction, سد *sadd* ; سده *saddah.*

Obtain, یافتن *yáftán* ; پیدا کردن *paidá k.*

Obtuse, کودن *kaudan.* —ness, حماقت *himáḳat.*

Obvious, پیدا *paidá* ; پدید *padíd* ; آشکار *áshkár.* —ly, ظاهراً *záhiran.*

Occasion, باعث *bá'is* ; محل *mahall* ; (leisure), فرصت *fursat* ; (cause), سبب *sabab.*

Occasionally, اتفاق *ittifáḳ.*

Occult, مبهم *mubham.*

Occupant, متصرف *mutesarrif.*

Occupation, کسب *kasb* ; کار *kár* (*k.*) ; حرفة *hurfat* ; شغل *shughl* (*dsh.*), *pl.*, اشغال *ashghál* ; اشتغال *ishtighál.*

Occur, واقع شدن *váḳi' sh.* ; سر زدن *sar z.* ; روی نمودن *rúy n.*

Occurrence, سر گذشت *sar guzasht* ; واقعه *váki'ah* ; in *pl.*, مواقع *maváḳi'.*

Occurring (to the mind), خطور *khutúr.*

Ocean, دریای محیط *darya i muhít.*

Ochre, گل زرد *gil i zard.*

O'clock, ساعت *sá'at.*

Octagonal, مثمن *musamman.*

Ocular, چشمي *chashmí.*

Oculist, کحال *kuhhál.*

Odd (not even), طاق *ták* ; (queer), غریب *gharíb.*

Ode, قصیده *ḳasídah*, *pl.*, قصائد *ḳasáid.*

Odious, مستقبح *mustaḳbih* ; مکروه *makrúh.*

Odium, تنفر *tanaffur.*

Odoriferous, معطر *mu'attar* ; عنبر بار *'amberbár* ; مشموم *mashmúm.* — herbs, ریاحین *riyáhín.*

Odour, بوی *búy* ; رایحه *ráihah*, *pl.* روایح *raváih* ; نشق *nashḳ* ; نشوت *nashvat.*

Of, از *az.*

Off, far, دور *dúr.*

Offal, مردار *murdár.*

Offence, تقصیر *taksír* ; جرم *jurm.* To take — خشم گرفتن *khishm gr.*

Offend, شتم کردن *shatm k.* ; رنجانیدن *ranjánídan* ; *pa. p.*, (at) ; کجخلق *kajkhulk* (*b.*).

Offender, خاطیٔ *kháti'.*

Offensive, کریه *karíh.*

Offer, تقدیم *takdím* (*k.*) ; (a sacrifice), ذبح *zibh* (*n.*).

Offering, *n.*, (sacrifice) قربان *kurbán* ; (present), پیشکش *píshkesh* (*k.*).

Office, عهده *'uhdah* ; منصب *mansab.* — of Imam, امامت *imámat.* — of a Vizier, وزارت *vizárat* ; (room), دفتر خانه *daftar khánah.*

Office-holder, منصب دار *mansabdár.*

Office-keeper, دفتری *daftarí.*

Officer, عهده دار *'uhdah-dár* ; صاحب منصب *sáhib mansab.* — of cavalry, دفعدار *daf'-dár.* Superior —, وکیل اول *vakíl i avval.* First non-commissioned —, وکیل *vakíl* ; بیك زاده *beg-zádah* ; حوالدار *havaldár.* Second non-commissioned, وکیل دوم *vakíl i dúvum.* Police — who examines weights, etc., محتسب *muhtasib.* — of state, دیوان بیگی *díván begí* ; (controller), مستوفی *mustaufí.*

Officially, رسماً *rasman.*

Officious, گستاخ *gustákh.* —ness, چالاکی *chálákí.*

Offspring, موالید *maválíd.* A beloved —, نودره *naudarah.*

Often, بارها *bárhá* ; اکثر *aksar.*

Ogling, غمزه *ghamzah* (*k.*).

Ogre, غول *ghúl.*

Oh, ا *a* ; ای *ai* ! یا *yá.* — God, اللهم *Allahumma* !

Oil, روغن *raughan.*

Oiled paper, چربه *charbah.*

Oilman, روغن فروش *raughan ferúsh.*

Oilpresser, عصار *'assár.*

Oily, روغنی *rauganí* ; چرب *churb.*

Ointment, مرهم *marham.*

Old (ancient), کهنه *kuhnah* ; قدیم *kadím* ; بارینه *párínah* ; دیرینه *dírínah* ; عتیق *'atík* ; (worn), کهن *kuhn* ; ژنده *zhandah* ; (aged), پیر *pír.*

Very —, سال خورده *sál-khúrdah* ; بزرك سال *buzurg-sál.* — age, پیری *píri.* — man, پیر *pír.* Like an — man, پیرانه *piránah.* A decrepit — man, زرفان *zarfán* ; خرف *kharif.*

Oleander, خر زهره *kar zahrah.*

Olive, زیتون *zeitún.*

Olive-oil, زیت *zeit* ; کوکو *kúkú.*

Omelet, نیمرو *nímrú.*

Omen, فال *fa'l* or *fál* (*gr.*). Of happy —, نیك فال *ník-fál.* Taking a good —, تفاول *tafávul* (*k.*) ; تیمن *tayammun* (*n.*).

Omission, سهو *sahv* (*k.*).

Omit, در گذشتن *dar guzashtan.*

Omnipotence, جبروت *jubrút.*

Omnipotent, جبار *jabbár* ; قدیر *kadír.*

Omniscience, همه بینی *hamah biní.*

Omniscient, غیب دان *ghaib-dán.*

On, بر *bar* ; بالا *bálá* ; روی *rúyi.* — foot, پیاده *píyádeh* (*sh.*). — horse back, سواره *sovvâreh* (*sh.*).

Onager, گور *gûr.*

Once, یکبار *yak-bár* ; باری *bári.* At —, یکبارکی *yak-báragí.* All at —, بیکبار *ba yekbar.*

One, یك *yek* ; (somebody), یکی *yakí* ; (sole), یگانه *yagánáh* ; یکه *yakkah* ; (single), یگان *yagán* ; (an unit), احد *ahad* ; واحد *váhid.* — by —, یکایك *yekáyek.*

One another, یکدیکر *yek dígar.*

Oneself, خود *khud.*

Onion, پیاز *piyáz* ; بصل *basal.*

Only, همین *hamín* ; همان *hamán* ; (merely), فقط *fakat.*

Onset, هجوم *hujúm.*

Onwards, پیشتر *píshtar.*

Onyx, عقیق *'akík.*

Ooze, گل *gil.*

Opal, عین الهره *'ain ul hirreh.*

Open, واز *váz* (*k. sh.*) ; باز *báz* (*k. sh.*) ; وا *vá* (*k. sh. n.*) ; *v.*, (بر *bar*) کشادن *kushádan* ; (بر *bar*) کشودن *kashúdan* ; فرا زدن *fará z.* — a vein, رك زدن *rag z.* ; *pa. p.*, مفتوح *maftúh* (*sh. k.*) ; منفرج *mun-farij.*

Opening, *n.*, تفتیح *taftíh* ; کشف *kashf* ; کشایش *kushá-yish.*

Openly, آشکارا *áshkárá.*

Opera, تماشا *tamáshá.*

Operation (surgical), جراحی *jarráhí* (*k.*).

Operative, کاریگر *kárígar.*

Operator, جراح *jarráh.*

Ophthalmia, چشمدرد *chashm-dard*; رمد *ramad.*

Opiate, معجون *ma'jún.*

Opinion, ظن *zann*; مظنه *mazannah*; رای *rái*; فکر *fikr*; زعم *za'm*, or *zu'm.* In my —, نزدمن *nazdiman.* To give an —, رای دادن *rái-d.*

Opinionated, خود رای *khud-rái.*

Opium, افیون *afyún*; تریاك *tariyák.*

Opponent, مخالف *mukhálif*; مضاد *muzádd*; اضداد *azdád.*

Opportune, به جا *be-já.*

Opportunity, فرصت *fursat*; قابو *ḳábú.*

Oppose, مخالفت نمودن و کردن *mukhálifat n., k.*; معارض *mu'áriz k.*; معترض *mu'tariz*; متعرض نمودن *muta'arriz n.*

Opposite, مقابل *muḳábil*; روبرو *rú be rú*; بر خلاف *bar khiláf*; محاذی *muhází.*

Opposition, خلاف *khiláf*; مضادت *mazáddat*; معارضت *mu'árazat*; تعارض *ta'áruz*; تخالف *takháluf*; تعرض *ta'arruz*; اعتراض *i'tiráz.*

Oppress, ظلم کردن *zulm k.*; *pa. p.*, ستم دیده *sitam-dídah*; مظلوم *mazlúm*; *pr. p.*, تظالم *tazálum.*

Oppression, ستم *sitam*; دراز دستی *diráz dasti*; ظلم *zulm*; مظلمت *mazlamat*; تظلم *tazal-lum*; بدعت *bid'at.*

Oppressor, جفاکار *jafá-kár*; جفاگر *jafá-gar*; ظالم *zálim.*

Opprobrious, شوخ *shúkh*; بد زبان *bad zabán.*

Opprobrium, فضیحت *fasíhat.*

Optical, بصری *basari.*

Optics, علم بصر *'ilm i basar.*

Option, اختیار *ikhtiyár.* —al, اختیاری *ikhtiyárí.*

Opulence, مالداری *máldárí*; غنا *ghaná*; توانگری *tavángarí*; ثراء *sará*; تمول *tamavvul.*

Or, یا *yá.*

Oracle, وحی *vahí.*

Oral, شفاهی *shifáhí.*

Orange, نارنج *náranj*; نارنك *nárang*; پرتغال *purtughál.*

Mandarine —, نارنگی *nárangí.*

Oration, خطاب *khitáb;* کلام *kalám.*

Orator, سخن سرا *sukhun-sará;* سخن گو *sukhun-gú.*

Oratory, نماز گاه *namáz gáh.*

Orb, جرم *jirm.*

Orbit, دوران *daurán.*

Orchard, دوحة *dauhat;* باغ *bágh.*

Order (arrangement), انتظام *intizám* (*n.*); ترتیب *tartíb* (*k.*); نسق *nasaḳ;* نظم و نسق *nazm o nasaḳ.* To be put in —, آراستن *árástan; pa. p.,* منتظم *muntazam;* مأمور *ma'múr.* —, (command), فرمایش *farmáyish* (*d.*), *pl.* فرمایشات *farmáyishát;* قدغن *ḳadaghan* (*k.*); حکم *hukm* (*n.*); امر *amr* (*n.*); *v.,* فرمودن *farmúdan.*

Ordinal, فرعی *far'í.*

Ordinance (of God), فریضه *farízah;* شرع *shar'.*

Ordinary (usual), رایج *ráij;* (common), عام *'ámm.* —ly, عادتاً *'ádatan.*

Ordination, نصب *nasb* (*k.*).

Ordnance, توپخانه *túpkháneh.*

Ordure, گوه *gúh,* or گه *guh.*

Ore, فلز *filizz.*

Organ, آلت *álat.*

Organization, نظام *nizám* (*d.*).

Organism, ترکیب *tarkib.*

Oriental, شرقی *sharḳí.*

Orifice, سوراخ *súrákh.* — of the ear, سماخ *simákh.*

Origin, اصل *asl;* بنیاد *bunyád;* بیخ *bíkh;* نژاد *nizhád;* نژاده *nizhádah;* ماروك *ma'rúk.* Of good —, نیك ذات *ník zát.*

Original, *a.,* اصلی *aslí.* The — of anything, *n.,* ماخذ *ma'khaz.* —ly, اولاً *avvalan.*

Orion, جبار *jabbár.*

Ornament, *n.,* زینت *zínat* (*d.*); آرایش *áráyish;* طراز *taráz;* پیرایه *pairáyah;* تزین *tazayyun n.* —al, زیوری *zívarí;* *v.,* آرائیدن *áráídan;* آراستن *árástan.*

Ornamented with a wreath, مکلل *mukallal.* — with jewels, مرصع *murassa'.* — with a scarf, موشح *muvashshaḥ.*

Ornaments, زیور *zívar.*

Orphan, يتيم *yetím*, *pl.* ايتام *aitám*; يتامى *yatámá*.

Orpiment, زرنيخ *zarníkh*.

Orthodox, رشيد *rashíd*; راشد *ráshid*; متدين *mutadaiyin*. — teaching, مسترشد *mustarshid*.

Orthodoxy, صدق *sidḳ*.

Orthography, املاء *imlá*.

Ortolan, پرکیری *pargírí*.

Oscillation, تکان *takán* (*n.*).

Osprey, نسر *nisr*.

Ostensible, ظاهر *záhir*.

Ostentation, کبریا *kibriyá*.

Ostentatious, خود بين *khud-bín*.

Ostrich, شترمرغ *shutur-murgh*; نعام *na'ám*.

Other, دیکر *dígar*; غير *ghair*.

Otherwise, ورنه *varnah*; واکر نه *va agar nah*; و الا *va illá*.

Otter, سك آبى *sag i ábí*; کربه آبى *gurbah i ábí*.

Ottoman, عثمانى *'osmání*.

Ought, بايد *báyad*; شايد *sháyad*, بايست *báyist*. As it — to be, كما ينبغى *kamá yambaghi*; (anything), چيزى *chízí*; (cypher), صفر *sifr*.

Ounce, وقية *vuḳíyat*; أوقيه *úḳíyah*; (animal), يوز *yúz*.

Our, مان *i-mán*.

Ours, مال ما *mál i má*.

Out, بيرون *bírún*. — of doors, بدر *badar*.

Outer side (of a garment), ابره *abrah*.

Outcast, مردود *mardud*.

Outlet, مفر *mafarr*.

Outline, دايره *dáireh*.

Outpost, قراول *ḳarávul*.

Outrage, *v.*, تعدى کردن *ta'addi k*.

Outside, خارج *khárij*. — the door, دم در *dam i dar*.

Outwardly, ظاهراً *záhiran*.

Oval, بيضوى *baizaví*; بادامى *bádámí*.

Oven, تنور *tannúr*; اتون *atún*;

Over, بر *bar*; زبر *zabar*; (across), عبور *'ubúr*; (more) زياده *ziyádeh*; (remaining), باقى *báḳí* (*m.*).

Overcast, کرفته *girifteh*.

Overcoat, بالا پوش *bálá púsh*; بارانى *báráni*.

Overcome, شکست دادن *shikast d.*; غلبه کردن *ghalabah k.*; *pr. p.*, مستولى *mustaulí* (*n.*).

Overflowing, سیلان *sailán* (*sh.*).

Overhead, بر سر *bar sar.*

Overhearing, تسمع *tasammu'* (*n.*).

Overlooking (a fault, &c.), قطع نظر *kaṭ' i nazr* (*n.*); چشم پوشی *cheshm púshí* (*k.*).

Overnight, شبانه *shabáneh.*

Overplus, ما بقی *má baḳá.*

Overreach, گول زدن *gúl z.*.

Overseer, ناظر *názir*; داروغه *dárúghah.* — of the kitchens, بقاول *baḳával.*

Oversight, سهو *sahv.*

Overtaking, فایز *fáiz* (*n.*).

Overthrow, شکست *shikast* (*y.*); هزیمت *hazímat*; افکن *afgan.*

Overturn, وارونه کردن *várúnah k.* (*sh.*).

Overwhelm, غرق کردن *gharḳ k.*

Owe, قرض داشتن *ḳarz dsh*; بده داشتن *bidih dsh.*

Owl, بوم *búm*; چغد *chughd.*

Own, خویش *khish*; خود *khud.*

Owner, مالك *málik* (*b.*); صاحب *sáhib* (*k.*). Rightful —, حق دار *haḳḳ-dár.*

Ox, گاو *gáv.*

Ox-goad, گاو شنك *gáu-shang.*

Oxus (river), جیحون *jaihún.*

Oxymel, سکنجبین *sikenjabín.*

Oyster, صدف *sadaf.*

P.

Pace, گام *gám* (*r.*); قدم *ḳadam* (*r. z.*); (gait), رفتار *raftár.* Quick —, زلط *zalt.* Quick-paced, خوش گام *khush-gám.*

Pacific, سلیم *salím.*

Pacification, مصالحت *masálahat.*

Pacifying, تسکین *taskín* (*k.*); آرام *árám* (*d.*).

Pack (mule), بار *bár*; *v.*, — up, بر بستن *bar bs.*

Packing-needle, جوال دوز *juvál-dúz.*

Pack-saddle, پالان *pálán.*

Packthread, بندور *bundúr.*

Packet, بسته *bastah.*

Pad, خو گیر *khú-gír*; *v.*, حشو کردن *hashv k.*

Paddock, چراگاه *charágáh.*

Padlock, قفل *ḳufl.*

Pæderast, کونی *kúní.*

Pagan, بت پرست *but parast.* —ism, کفر *kufr.*

Page (leaf), صفحه *safhah*, *pl.*, صفحات *safahát*; (boy), پیشخدمت *pish-khidmat*; غلام *gholám*.

Pageant, تماشا *tamáshá*.

Pagoda, بت کده *but-kedeh*; بت خانه *but-khánah*.

Pail, دلو *dalv*; دول *dúl*.

Pain, درد *dard*; ایذا *ízá*; وجع *vaj'*, *pl.*, آلام *álám*; زحمت *zahmat* (*ksh.*). In —, موجع *muja'*.

Painful, درد آلود *dard álúd*; الیم *alím*.

Paint, *n.*, رنك *rang*; *v.*, نکاشتن *nigáshtan*; (a picture), کشیدن تصویر *kashídan*; تصویر کشیدن *t. svír ksh*; (lay on colour), رنك کردن *rang k.*; *pa. p.* منقش *munakkash*; *pr. p.*, رنك آمیزی *rang-ámízí*.

Painting and ornaments, نقش و نکار *naksh o nigár*.

Painter, مصور *musavvir*; قلم کار *kalam-kár*; رنکساز *rang-sáz*; صورت کر *súrat-gar*.

Painting, نقش *naksh* (*k.*); تصویر *tasvír* (*k.*).

Pair, زوج *zauj*, *pl.*, ازواج *azváj*; جفت *juft* (*k. gr.*).

Pairing (of birds), جفتی *juftí*.

Palace, قصر *kasr*; کوشك *kúshk*; ایوان *aiván*; دولت خانه *daulat-khánah*.

Palanquin, تخت روان *takht raván*.

Palatable, کوار *guvár*.

Palate, حنك *hanak*; مذاق *muzák*.

Pale, نیمرنك *ním-rang*; کم رنك *kam-rang*; اصفر *asfar*. —faced, زرد رو *zard-rú*; روی زرد *rúy zard*. To turn —, رنك رو پریدن *rang i rú parídan*.

Palliation, معاف *mu'áf* (*k.*); تخفیف *takhfíf* (*n.*).

Palm (hand), کف *kaff*; کف دست *kaff i dast*; (tree), نخل *nakhl*; خرما *khurmá*.

Palpably, ظاهرًا *záhiran*.

Palpitate, تپیدن *tapídan*.

Palpitation (of the heart), خفقان *khafakán*.

Palsied, افلج *aflaj* (*h.*); رعشه *ra'shah* (*dsh.*).

Palsy, فالج *fálij* (*dsh.*).

Paltry, دون *dún*.

Pampered, پرورده *parvardeh*.

Pamphlet, رساله *risáleh*.

Pan, حسین *hasín* ; دیزی *dízí* ; Frying —, طاجن *tájin*. The knee —, سر زانو *sar i zánú*.

Pane (of glass), جام *jám*.

Panegyric, مدح *madh*.

Panegyrist, مداح *maddáh*.

Panel, تخته *takhtah*.

Pang, درد *dard*.

Panic, هزیمت *hazímat*.

Panniers (for fruit), لوده *laudah* ; (for persons), کجاوه *kajáveh*.

Pant, نفس زدن *nafas z*.

Panther, پلنك *palang* ; یوز *yúz*. Young —, یوزك *yúzak*.

Paper, کاغذ *kághaz* ; قرطاس *ḳirṭás*. A — kite, کاغذ باد *kághaz i bád*.

Papyrus, حفا *hafá*.

Parable, مثال *misál*.

Parade-ground, میدان *maidan*.

Paradise, جنت *jannat* ; بهشت *bihisht*. The sublime —, خلد برین *khuld i barín*.

Paradisiacal, بهشتی *bihishtí*.

Paradox, لغز *laghz*.

Paragraph, فصل *fasl*.

Parallax, اختلاف منظر *ikhtiláf i manzar*.

Parallel استوآء *istivá* ; متوازی *mutavází* ; مساوی *masáví*.

Paralysed, مفلج *mufallaj* (*sh.*)

Paralysis, فلج *falj*.

Paralytic, شل *shal* ; مشلول *mashlúl* ; مفلوج *maflúj*.

Paramour, عاشق *'áshiḳ*.

Parapet, کنکره *kangurah*.

Paraphernalia, اسباب *asbáb* ; جهیز *jahíz*.

Paraphrase, تفصیل *tafsíl* (*n.*).

Parasang (a league), فرسخ *farsakh* ; فرسنك *farsang*.

Parasite (man), طفیلی *tufailí*.

Parasol, چطر *chatr* ; آفتابگیر *áftáb-gír*.

Parboiled, نیم پخته *ním-pukhtah*.

Parcel, بوغچه *búghcheh*.

Parch, برشتن *birishtan*. To be —ed, خوشیدن *khúshídan*.

Parchment, پوست *púst*.

Pardon, مغفرت *maghfirat* (*n.*) ; عفو *'afv* (*k.*) ; غفران *ghufrán* ; *v.*, بخشیدن *bakhshídan*. To beg —, عذر خواستن *'uzr khástan*. I beg your —, معاف بفرمائید *mu'áf bifarmáyíd*. I ask — of God استغفر الله *astaghfiru 'llah* ;

pa. p., معاف *mu'áf* (*k.*) مغفور *maghfúr*.

Pardoner, غفار *ghaffár*.

Pare (nails), ناخن گرفتن *ná-khun gr.*; (hoofs), سم تراشیدن *sum taráshídan* (*gr.*).

Parentage, نسب *nasab*; اصل *asl*.

Parenthetical, معترض *mo'tariz*.

Parents (both), والدین *váli-dain*.

Paring, تراشه *tarásheh*.

Parley, مکالمه *mukálemeh* (*n.*).

Parliament, دار الشورا *dár ush shúrá*.

Parody, تقلید *taḳlíd*.

Parole, قول *ḳaul*.

Paroxysm, طغیان *tughyán*.

Parrot, توتی or طوطی *túti*.

Parry, دفع کردن *daf' k.*

Parse, ترکیب کردن *tarkíb k.*

Parsee, گبر *gabr*.

Parsimonious, مقتر *muḳtir*; لئیم *layím*; خسیس *khasís*.

Parsimony, بخل *bukhl*; امساك *imsák*; بخیلی *bakhílí*.

Parsley, کرفس *karafs*.

Parsnip, گزر *gazar*.

Parson, کشیش *keshísh*.

Part, قسم *ḳism*; پاره *páreh*; تکه *tikkah*; جزء *juz'*; بهره *bahrah*; بخش *bakhsh*; جزوی *juzví*. For the most —, بیشتر *bíshtar*. On his —, عن قبله *'an ḳibalih*; از جانب او *az jánib-i-ú*; *v.*, جدا کردن *jidá k.*

Partake, شراکت داشتن *shirákat dsh.*

Parterre, خیابان *khiyábán*.

Partial, طرفدار *taraf-dár*; متعصب *muta'assib*.

Partiality, جانبداری *jánib-dárí*; پاسداری *pás-dárí*.

Partially, قدری *ḳadrí*.

Participating, بهره مند *bahrah-mand*; مداخله *mudákheleh*.

Participle (active), اسم فاعل *ism-i-fá'il*; (passive), اسم مفعول *ism-i-maf'úl*.

Particle, خرده *khurdah*; شمه *shammah*; (in grammar), حرف *harf*.

Particular, خاص *kháss*; مخصوص *makhsús*. —ly, علی الخصوص *'alá-l-khusús*.

Particularity, خصوص *khusús*, *pl.*, خصوصیات *khusúsíyát*.

Parting (leaving), ودع *vad'* (*n.*); (of hair), فرق *farḳ*.

Partitioning (division), اقتسام *iktisám* (*n.*).

Partly, پاره *páreh*.

Partner, شريك *sharík*, *pl.*, شركاء *shuraká'*; مساهم *musáhim*; مشترك *mushtarik*; انباز *ambáz*.

Partnership, مشاركت *mushárakat*; انبازی *ambází*; اشتراك *ishtirák*.

Partridge, كبك *kabk*. Francolin —, دراج *durráj*. Small — or quail, تيهو *tíhú*.

Parturition, نتاج *nitáj*.

Party, گروه *gurúh*; جمعيت *jamíat*. Dinner —, مهمانی *mihmání*.

Pass (in mountains), *n.*, تنك راه *tang i ráh*; كتل *kotul*; كردن *gardan*; *v.*, گذشتن *guzashtan*.

Passage (of a river, etc.), عبور *'ubúr* (*k.*); گذر *guzar* (*k.*); گذار *guzár* (*k.*); راه گذار *ráh-guzár*; (an escape), منفذ *manfaz*; (of time), مرور *murúr*; (in a book), عبارت *'ibárat*.

Passenger, عابر *'ábir*; مسافر *musáfir*.

Passion (to get in a), باهم آمدن *báham ámadan*.

Passionate, خشمناك *khashmnák*; تند مزاج *tund mizáj*. —ly, غضباً *ghazaban*.

Passive, متحمل *mutahammil*; (verb), مفعول *maf'úl*.

Passport, گذرنامه *guzarnámah*; راه داری *ráh-dárí*; تعليقه *ta'líkah*.

Past, گذشته *guzashtah*; منقضی *munkazí*; سابقه *sábikah*. The —, ما سلف *má salaf*; ما تقدم *má takaddam*. — tense, ماضی *mázi*.

Paste, سريش *sirísh*; خمير *khamír*.

Pasteboard, دفتين *daffatain*; كاغذ وصلی *kághaz i vaslí*.

Pastern, وظيف *vazíf*.

Pastimes, ملاهی *maláhí*.

Pastor, گله بان *galah-bán*.

Pastoral care, گله بانی *galahbání*.

Pasturage, or Pasture, مرعی *mar'á*; چراگاه *chará-gáh*; چمن *chaman*; علف زار *'alafzár*; *v.*, چريدن *charídan*.

Pasty, سنبوسك *sambusak*.

Patch (of cloth, etc.), پینه *pínah*; لدام *ladám*. — upon —, رقع بر رقع *ruḳ'ah bar ruḳ'ah*.

Patcher, پاره‌دوز *párah dúz*.

Patched, مرقع *muraḳḳa'*.

Paternal, پدری *pidrí*. — love, عشق مجازی *'ishḳ i mujáziy*.

Path, معبر *mi'bar*, *pl.*, معابر *ma'ábir*. A mountain —, شعب *sh'ib*.

Pathetic, دلسوس *dilsús*.

Patience, صبر *sabr*; صبوری *sabúrí*; شکیب *shakíb*; شکیبائی *shakibáí*.

Patient, بردبار *burdbár*, صابر *sábir*; صبور *sabúr*. To be —, شکیبیدن *shakíbídan*; (sick man), مریض *maríz*. —ly, صبراً *sabran*.

Patriot (word not used in Persian), حبیب الوطن *habíb al vatan*. —ism, حب الوطن *hibb ul vatan*.

Patrol, راه دار *ráh-dár*; پاسبان *pásbán*.

Patron, پشت پناه *pusht-panáh*; ولی نعمة *valí ni'mat*.

Patronage, دستگیری *dast-girí*.

Patronymic, نسبت *nisbat*.

Pattern, نمونه *nimúnah*.

Paucity, کمی *kamí*.

Paunch, بطن *batn*.

Pauper, مسکین *miskín*.

Pause, وقف *vaḳf* (*k.*).

Pavement, سنکفرش *sangfarsh*.

Pavilion, سرا پرده *sará-pardah*.

Paw, پاچه *páchah*; پنجه *panjah*.

Pawn (at chess), بیدق *baidaḳ*, or بیذق *baizaḳ*; (pledge), رهن *rahn* (*gz.*); کرو *giro* (*gz.*).

Pay (wages), مواجب *mavájib*; مزد *muzd*; موظف *muvazzaf*.

Paymaster, بخشی *bakhshí*. — general, میر بخشی *mír-bakhshí*.

Payment, اداء *adá* (*k.*); کرایه *kiráyah* (*d.*); اجرت *ujrat* (*n.*).

Pea, نخود *nukhúd*; ماش *másh*.

Peace, سلامت *salámat*; سلام *salám*; آشتی *áshtí*; صلح *sulh* (*k. d.*); هدنت *hudnat*.

Peaceable, سهل جو *sahl-jú*.

Peach, شفتالو *shaftálú*; هلو *hullú*.

Peacock, طاءوس *tá'ús*. Like a —, طاءوسی *tá'úsí*.

Peak, سر *sar* ; نوك *nauk.*

Pear, گلابی *gullábí.*

Pearl, مروارید *marvaríd* ; لؤلؤ *lú'lu'*; در *durr* ; درر *durar.* Unique —, در یتیم *durr i yatím.*

Peasant, رعیت *ra'íyat* ; دهقان *dehḳán.*

Pebbles, سنك ریزه *sang-rízah.*

Peculation, تصرف *tasarruf.*

Peculiar, مخصوص *makhsús.*

Peculiarity, اختصاص *ikhtisás* ; خاصگی *khássagí.*

Pedant, فضیلت فروش *fasílat ferúsh.* —ry, فضیلت فروشی *fasílat ferúshí.*

Pedestrian, راجل *rájil.*

Pedigree, تنسل *tanassul* ; حسب و نسب *hasab o nasab.*

Pedlar, پیلور *pílavar.*

Peel, پوست *púst* ; *pa. p.*, مقشور *maḳshúr* ; منقشر *munḳashir.*

Peep, نظر *nazar* (*k.*).

Peevish, کج خلق *kaj khulḳ.*

Peg, میخ *míkk.*

Pelican, سریخه *saríkhah.*

Pelisse, کرك *kurk.*

Pellucid, شفاف *shifáf.*

Pen, قلم *ḳalam* ; کلك *kilk* ; خامه *khámah.* The piece of wood for nibbing pens on, خامه زن *khámah-zan.* —case, قلم دان *ḳalam-dán.* —knife, قلم تراش *ḳalam-tarash.*

Penalty, جریمه *jarímah.*

Pencil, مداد *midád.*

Pendulous, آویزه *ávízah.*

Pendulum, لنگر *langar.*

Penetrate, سرایت کردن *siráyat k.* ; *pr. p.*, نفذ *nafz* (*k.*) ; نافذ *náfiz* (*b*) ; نفوذ *nufúz* (*n.*).

Penetration, بینش *bínish* ; ذهن *zihn.*

Peninsular, جزیره *jazíreh.*

Penis, کیر *kír.* Penem magnum habens, خر نفسه *khar-nafsah.*

Penitence, کفارت *kafárat* ; توبه *taubah.*

Penitent, مستغفر *mustaghfir* ; پشیمان *pashímán* ; نادم *nádim.*

Pension, وظیفه *vazífeh* ; راستاد *rástád* ; (in lands), جاگیر *jágír.* —er, وظیفه خوار *vazífeh khár.*

Pentagon, پنج گوشه panj-gúshah. —al, مخمس mukh-ammas.

Pentateuch, توریت taurít.

Penurious, طمعکار tama' kár; لئیم layím. —ness, حرص hirs; بخل bukhl; خسیست khusísat.

Penury, بینوائی bí-navá-í.

People, مردمان mardumán; امم umam; خلق khalḳ, in pl., طوائف taváif. Common —, عوام 'avvám. Great —, اکابر akábir. Intelligent —, عقلاء 'uḳalá. — of the world, زمانیان zamániyán; جهانیان jaháníyán; عالمیان 'álamiyán. — of former times, شدگان shudagán; v., آباد کردن ábád k.

Pepper, فلفل (z.). Long —, دار فلفل dár-filfil.

Peppermint, نعنع na'na'.

Per cent, فی صد fí sad.

Per pound, فی من fí man.

Perambulation, طواف taváf (n.).

Perceive, دریافتن dar-yáftan; pa. p., محسوس mahsús (k.).

Perception, ادراك idrák (n.); دریافت dar-yáft (n.).

Perch (roost), چکس chakas; چوب chúb.

Perchance, شاید sháyad; گویا gúyá.

Percolation, وقوب vuḳúb (n.).

Percussion (gun, etc.), طرقه taraḳeh.

Perdition, هلاك halák; هلاکت halákat; تهطر tahattúr.

Peremptory, قاطع ḳáti'; موکد muakkad.

Perfect, کامل kámil; تمام ta-mám; مکمل mukammal; (tense), ماضی mází. More or most —, اکمل akmal; اتم atamm. —ly, هیچمدان hích-madán; بالکل bil-kull.

Perfecting, تکمیل takmíl (k.); اکمال ikmál (n.).

Perfection, کمال kamál; اتمام itmám.

Perfidious, غدار ghaddár.

Perfidy, غدر ghadr; خیانت khiyánat; غل ghill.

Perforate, سنبیدن sumbídan; سفتن suftan.

Perforation, ثـقـب sakb (k.). ; سـفـت suft (k.) ; سـوراخ súrákh (k.).

Perforce, جبراً jabran.

Perform, بجـا آوردن bajá a ; كذاردن guzárdan ; كردن kardan. Bound to —, مستمسك mustamsik (h.).

Performance (act), كار kár (k.) ; عـمـل 'amal (k.) ; (finishing) اتـمـام itmám (rsa.); (of a promise), استيفاء istífá' (n.); اجـرا ijrá (k.) ; نجز najz (n.) ; (play), تـمـاشا tamáshá.

Performer, عامل 'ámil ; فـاعل fá'il. Musical —, رامش كر rámish-gar.

Perfume, عطر 'itr, pl., عطريات 'itríyát ; بخور bukhúr ; خوشبو khush bú ; نـكهت nak-hat ; دستنبويه dastambúyah.

Perfuming, تبخير tabkhír (k.). — one's self, تبخـر tabakh-khur (n.).

Perfumed, معطر mu'attar. — pastille, شمـامـه shamámah, pl., شمايم shamáim. — with ambergris. معنبر ma'amber.

Perfumer, عطار 'attár.

Perfunctory, غـافل gháfil; كاهل káhil.

Perhaps, شـايـد sháyad ; مـكر magar ; باشد كه báshad keh.

Peril, خطر khatar ; بـاك bák ; بيم bím.

Perilous, خـطـر نـاك khatar-nák ; مهلك muhlik.

Period, مدت muddat ; نوبه nau-beh ; دوره daurah.

Perish, نيست شـدن níst-sh. ; هلاك شدن halák sh. ; pr. p., تـهلـكه tahlikah (n.) ; نفـق nafak (b.). —able, زايـل zá-il.

Perjury, قسم زور kasam-i-zúr (kh.) ; سوكند دروغ saugand i durúgh (kh.).

Permanence, قيام kayám ; بـقاء baká.

Permanency, اسـتـدامـت isti-dámat.

Permanent, پايدار páidár ; قايم kaim ; باقى bákí.

Permeating, سرايت siráyat (k.).

Permission, اذن izn (d. khástan) ; رخـصـت rukhsat (d. khástan) ; اجازت ijázat (khástan) ; پروانـكى parvánagí.

Permitted (allowed), مـأذون ma'zún ; هلال halál ; جائـز já'iz ; روا ravá. — to go, مرخص murakhkhas.

Permitting, روا دار ravá-dár.

Permutation, تبدل tabaddul.

Pernicious (anything), مفسدت mafsadat.

Perpendicular, مستقيم musta-ḳím.

Perpetration, ارتـكاب irtikáb (n.) ; اجرا ijrá (k.).

Perpetrator, مرتكب murtakib.

Perpetual, دائم dáim ; استمراری istimrárí (k.) ; مستدام mus-tadám (n.) ; واتن wátin. May it be —! دام dáma ; thus : دام اقبالـه dáma iḳbáluhu. May his prosperity continue —ly ! همواره hamvárah.

Perpetuate (may he), ادام adáma ; thus : may God prolong his days, ادام الله ايامه adáma 'lláhu aiyámahu.

Perpetuation, ادامـت idámat (k.) ; ابـقآء ibḳá (n.) ; تـأبيد ta'bíd (k.).

Perpetuity, دوام davám ; دايمی dáimí ; مداومت mudávamat.

Perplexed, حيران hairán (k.) ; متحير mutahayyir (h.) ; متردد mutaraddid (k.) ; پريـشـان paríshán (s.). To be —, شوريدن shúrídan.

Perplexity, اشـكـال ishkál (dsh.) ; اضـطـراب iztiráb ; كشاكش kashákash.

Perquisite, مـداخل mudákhil ; مزد muzd.

Persecution, ستم sitam (k.) ; ظلم zulm (k.) ; تعاقب ta'á-ḳub (n.).

Persecutor, ظالم zálim.

Persepolis, اصطخر Istakhar.

Perseverance, اصرار isrár (n.) ; مـقـاومـت muḳávamat (n.) ; مواظبـت muvázabat.

Persevering, مصر musirr (h.) ; مقاوم muḳávim (b.).

Persia, ايران Írán ; عجم 'Ajam.

Persian, ايرانی Írání ; عجـمـی 'Ajamíy ; (language), فارسی Fársí. Ancient —, پهلوی Pahlaví ; دری Darí.

Persistence, استبداد istibdád.

Person, كس kas ; نـفـر nafar ; شخـص shakhs, pl. اشخاص ashkhás ; تن tan. Every —, هـمـكـنـان ham-kunán. Unmarried —, عزب 'azab.

Noble —, ذات شریف *zat i sheríf.* —s of distinction, خاصان *khássan.* Intelligent —, عرفاء *'urafá.*

Personality, ذات *zát.*

Personally, فی نفسه *fi nafsihí.*

Personification, تشبیه *tashbih* (*k.*).

Perspective, منظره *manzareh.*

Perspicacious, دیده ور *dídah-var.*

Perspicacity, ذهن *zihn.*

Perspicuous, مبین *mubín.*

Perspiration, عرق *'arak* (*k.*).

Perspire, خویدن *kh'aydan.*

Persuasion, اغوا *ighvá* (*k.*); تحریک *tahrík* (*k.*); رای *ráí* (*z.*).

Pert, گستاخ *gustákh.*

Pertinacious, مصر *musirr*; مداوم *mudávim.*

Pertinacity, استقرار *istikrár.*

Pertinent, موافق *muváfik.*

Pertness, شوخی *shúkhí.*

Perturbation, آشفتگی *áshuf-tagi*; اضطراب *iztiráb*; تشویش *tashvísh.*

Perusal, ملاحظه *muláhezeh* (*h.*); مطالعه *mutále'eh* (*k.*).

Pervading, ساری *sárí* (*h.*).

Perverse, کج طبع *kaj-tab'*; لجوج *lajuj.* —ness, خود سری *khud sarí.*

Perversion, انحراف *inhiráf* (*k.*); احباط *ihbát* (*k.*).

Perverted, معوج *mu'avvaj* (*g.*).

Pest, وبال *vabál*; آفت *áfat.*

Pestilence, وبا *vabá*; طاعون *tá'ún.*

Pestle, دسته *dastah.*

Pet, عزیز *'azíz* (*k.*).

Petal, برگ *barg.*

Petition, عرض *'arz* (*k.*); عرضی *'arzí* (*dsh.*); داعیه *dá'iyeh*; التماس *iltimás* (*k. n.*); (in writing), عریضه *'arízah, pl.*, عرائض *'aráiz*; عرضداشت *'arz-dásht.* —er, عارض *'áriz.*

Putrefaction, تحجر *tahajjur* (*k.*).

Petroleum, مومیا *múmiyá*; نفط *naft.*

Petticoat, فستان *fistán.*

Petty charges, بعضی خرچ *ba'zí-kharch.*

Petulance, بطر *batar*; افسردکی *afsurdagí.*

Petulant, کج خلق *kaj khulk.*

Pewter, روح *rúh.*

Phantom, طیف *taif*; خیال *khi-yál.*

Pharaoh, فرعون *Fir'aun.*

Pharmacy, ادویه adviyeh.

Pheasant, قرقاول ḳarḳáúl.

Philosopher, فیلسوف feilasúf, pl., فلاسفه falásifeh; حکیم hakím, pl., حکماء hukamá.

Philosophy, فلسفه falsafah; حکمت hikmat; علم ʻilm.

Phlebotomy, فصد fasd (k.).

Phlebotomist, فصاد fassád; رگ زن rag-zan.

Phlegm, بلغم balgham; (mucus), نخاعت nukháʻat.

Phœnix, سیمرغ simurgh; رخ rukh; هما humá.

Photograph, عکس ʻaks (k.). —er, عکاس ʻakkás. —y, عکسی ʻaksí.

Phrase, اصطلاح istiláh.

Phraseology, محاورة muhávarah.

Physic, دارو dárú; دوا davá. Art of —, پزشکی pizishkí.

Physical, طبیعی tabíʻi.

Physician, حکیم hakím; طبیب tabíb, pl., اطباء atibbá; پزشك pizishk; بزشك bizishk.

Physiognomy, قیافه ḳayáfah.

Physiology, موجودات maujúdát.

Pick out, وا چیدن vá-chídan.

Pickaxe, کلند kulund.

Pickle, ترشی turshi (an.); آچار áchár.

Picquets, قراول ḳarávul; طلایه taláyah.

Picture, تصویر tasvír; نقش naḳsh; نگار nigár. — gallery, نگار خانه nigár-khánah.

Piebald, ابلق ablaḳ; ابرق abraḳ.

Piece, قطعه ḳatʻah; پارچه pár-cheh; پاره párah; تکه tikkeh. — goods, قماش ḳumásh.

Pierce, سبوختن sabúkhtan; سفتن suftan; pr. p., همز hamz (k.); pa. p., مثقوب masḳúb.

Piety, تقوی taḳvá; تقاوت taḳá-vat; نسك nusk. Man of —, زنده دل zindah-dil; صاحبدل sáhib-dil

Pig, خوك khúk; خنزیر khinzír. Wild —, گراز guráz.

Pigeon, کبوتر kabútar; کفتر kaftar.

Pile (of velvet, &c.), خاو kháv; (heap), توده túdah.

Piles (hemorrhoids), بواسیر bavásír.

Pilfering, or Pilferer, دزدی *duzdí* (*k.*).

Pilgrim (to Mecca), حاج *hájj*; حاجی *hajjí*, *pl.*, حجاج *hujjáj*; (to other shrines), زوار *zavvár*. —age (to Mecca), حج *hajj* (*k.*); (to other places), زيارت *ziyárat* (*k.*).

Pill, حب *habb*, *pl.*, حبوب *habúb*. — box, قوتی *kútí*.

Pillage, غارت *ghárat* (*k.*); چپاو *chápáú* (*k.*).

Pillar, ستون *sutún*, *pl.*, اساتين *asátín*; ركن *rukn*, *pl.*, اركان *arkán*; عماد *'imád*; عمدة *'umdat*; قوام *ḳavám*, *pl.*, قوايم *ḳawáím*.

Pillory, دو شاخه *dú-shákhah*.

Pillow, متكا *muttaká*; تكيه *takyeh*; بالش *bálish*; بالين *bálín*; وساده *vasádah*, *visádah*, *vusádah*; وساد *vasád*, *visád*, *vusád*. A soft —, نازبالش *náz-bálish*.

Pilot, ناخدا *nákhudá*; كشتی بان *kishtí-bán*.

Pimp, قلتبان *ḳaltabán*; قرمساق *ḳurmsáḳ*.

Pimple, بشره *basrah*; كورك *kúrk*.

Pin, سنجاق *sanjáḳ*.

Pincers, انبر or انبور *ambúr* (*gr.*); منقاش *minḳásh*.

Pinch, نشكنج *nishkunj*.

Pine (tree), صنوبر *sinaubar*; (cedar), كاج *káj*; (juniper), ناژو *názhú*. *v.*, — away, كاهيدن *káhídan*. — cone, چلغوزه *chilghúzah*.

Pink (flower), ميخك *míkhek*; (colour), گلرنك *gulrang*.

Pinnacle, قله *ḳullah*.

Pioneer, پيش رو *písh rau*.

Pious, پارسا *pársá*; صالح *sálih*; تقی *taḳí*. — men, اتقياء *atḳiyá*.

Pipe (smoking), چبوق *chibúḳ*. — stem, چوب چبوق *chúb i chibúḳ*. Water —, قليون *ḳaliyún*; (tube), نی *nay*; لوله *lúlah*; زيش *zísh*.

Piper, نی زن *nay zan*.

Pisces, حوت *hút*.

Piss, شاشه *sháshah* (*k.*); بول *baul* (*k.*).

Pistachio, پسته *pistah*; فستق *fustuḳ*.

Pit, چال *chál*; گودال *gaudál*; مغاك *magháḳ*. — of the

chin, چاه زنخ cháh i zanukh; زنخدان zanukh-dán.

Pitch, قیر ḳír.

Pitcher, کوزه kúzah.

Piteous, جگر سوز jigar súz.

Pith, لب lubb.

Pitiful, رحمان rahmán.

Pitiless, بیرحم bírahm.

Pitted with small pox, آبله خورده ábileh khurdeh.

Pity, مرحمت marhamat (n.); رافت ráfat; رقت riḳḳat; ترحم tarahhum (n). To have — on, بخشودن bakhshúdan. It is a —, حیف است haif ast. —ing, راحم ráhim.

Pivot, مدار madár.

Place, مقام maḳám; مکان makán, pl., اماکن amákin; جا já; جای jáy; محل mahall; موضع mauzi'; موقع mauḳi'; جا داد já-dád; درگاه dar-gáh. A desolate —, خرابه kharábah. — of worship, سجده گاه sijdah-gáh. — where four roads meet, چهار سواره chehár-suvárah. — for rubbish, خاك دان khák-dán. Market —, چهار سو chehár-sú. In —, بجا

ba já; برجا bar já;—v., نهادن nihádan; نهیدن nahídan; pa. p., موضوع mauzú'.

Placid, حلیم halím; سلیم salím.

Placenta, مشیمه mashímah.

Plagiarism, سرقة sarḳat.

Plague, وبا vabá; طاعون tá'ún.

Plain (ground), میدان maidán; فضاء fazá'; صحراء sahrá; جلغه julghah. — for exercising horses, جولان گاه jaulán-gáh. Extensive uncultivated —, دق و لق daḳ o laḳ; (level), هموار hamvár; (clear), بین baiyin; (artless), ساده sádah. —ly, آشکارا áshkárá.

Plaint, دعوی da'vá; نالش nálish; شکایت shikáyat.

Plaintiff, مدعی mudda'iy; داد خواه dád-kh'áh. — and defendant, متخاصمین mutakhasimain.

Plait, بافتن báftan.

Plaits, چین chín.

Plan (map), نقشه naḳsheh; (mental), تدبیر tadbír.

Plane (superficies), بسیط basít. Joiner's —, رنده rundah (z.). — tree, چنار chenár.

Planed, منجور manjúr.

Planet, سیاره *saiyárah.*

Plank, تخته *takhteh.*

Plant, *n.*, نبات *nabát* ; سبزی *sabzí*.. Young —, نهال *nihál* ; *v.*, (flowers) تولك كردن *túlak k.*

Plantain, موز *mauz.*

Plantation, درختزار *dirakhtzár.*

Plaster (dressing), مرهم *marham*, *pl.*, مراهم *maráhim.* — of Paris, گچ *gach* ; (lime), آهك *áhak* ; *v.*, دوسیدن *dúsídan.*

Plate, پوشقاب *púshkáb.*

Plated, ملمع *mulamma'.*

Platform (mud), سکو *sakú* ; (wooden), تخته *takhtah.*

Plato, افلاطون *Aflátún.*

Platter, طبق *tabak.*

Play, بازی *bází* (*k.*) ; لعب *la'b* (*k.*) ; لهو *lahv* ; (gambling), قمار *kimár.* Stage —, تمثیل *tamsíl* ; *v.*, باختن *bákhtan* ; بازیدن *bázídan.* — on an instrument, نواختن *navákhtan* ; *pr. p.*, ملاعبت *mulá'abat* (*n.*) ; (on an instrument), نوازندگی *navázandagí.*

Player (gamester), لاعب *lá'ib* ; بازنده *bázandah* ; (instrumental), نوازنده *navázendah.*

Playfellow, همدم *hamdam.*

Playful, دلخوش *dilkhúsh.*

Plaything, بازیچه *bázícheh.*

Plead, دعوی کردن *da'vá k.*

Pleasant, فراخروی *ferákh-rúí* ; خوش دماغ *khush-dimágh* ; خوش آینده *khush-áyendah.*

Pleasantry, بذله *bazlah* ; بـزله *bazlah* ; لطیفه *latífah*

Please, خوش آمدن *khush ámadan* ; پسندیدن *pasandídan.* Striving to —, رضا جوی *rizá-júí* ; *pa. p.*, راضی *rází* ; مشعوف *mash'úf* ; سرخرو *surkh-rú.* If you —, زحمت کشیدید *zahmat kashídíd.* If it — God, انشاء الله *inshá 'alláh.*

Pleasure, خوشی *khushí* ; عشرت *'ishrat* ; عیش *'aish* ; لذت *lizzat* ; حظ *hazz.* To take — in, حظ کردن *hazz k.*

Pledge, گرو *girau* (*gz.*) ; رهن *rahn* (*gz.*) ; *pa. p.*, مرهون *marhún* ; رهین *rahín.*

Pleiades, ثریا *Suraiyá* ; پروین *Parvín.*

Plenipotentiary, وزیر مختار *vazír mukhtár.*

Plenteous, Plentiful, وافر *váfir*; فراوان *feráván*.

Plenty, موفور *maufúr*; وافر *váfir*; فرط *fart*.

Plethoric, دموی *damavíy*.

Pleurisy, جرسام *jirsám*; برسام *bar-sám*.

Pliant, پیچ خور *píck-khur*.

Pliers انبر *ambur*.

Plot (against), معاهده *mu'áhe-deh*; سازش *sázish*.

Plough, قلبه *kulbah*; خیش *khísh* (*k.*). —man, قلبه ران *kulbah-rán*. —share, گاو آهن *gáu i áhan* — tail, هش *hish*; *v.*, شیاریدن *shiyárí-dan*; سباریدن *sabárídan*.

Pluck, *v.*, چیدن (بر *bar*) *chí-dan*.

Plug, دسام *dısám*; سر *sar*.

Plum, آلو *álú*; آلوچه *álúcheh*.

Plumbago, سرمه *surmah*.

Plumb-line, شاهول *sháhúl*; بلد *balad*.

Plume, طره *tarrah*.

Plump, چاق *chák*.

Plunder, *n.*, یغما *yaghmá* (*k.*); نهب *nahb* (*k.*); نهیبی *na-híbí*; *v.*, توزیدن *túzídan*; *pr. p.*, توز *toz*; نهیب *nahíb*; *pa. p.*, منسلب *munsalib*,

Plunderer, سالب *sálib*; یغمائی *yaghmáí*.

Plunge, غوطه *ghautah* (*kh.*).

Plural, جمع *jam'*.

Plush, مخمل *makhmal*.

Pneumatic, هوای *havái*.

Poach (game), *v.*, شکار دزدیدن *shikár duzdídan*.

Poached (egg), نیمرو *nímrú* (*k.*).

Pock-marked, آبله دار *ábileh dár*.

Pocket, جیب *jíb*. — hand-kerchief, دستمال *dastmál*.

Pod, پیله *pílah*.

Podex, کون *kún*.

Poem, نظم *nazm*. — consist-ing of rhyming couplets, مثنوی *masnaví*.

Poet, شاعر *shá'ir*, *pl.*, شعراء *shu'ará*.

Poetry, شعر *shi'r*; اشعار *ash'ár*. The art of —, شاعری *shá'irí*.

Point (dot), *n.*, نقطه *nuktah*; (end), سر *sar*. The four car-dinal points, خوافق *khaváfik*. To — out, اشاره کردن *ishá-reh k.*

Poison, زهر *zahr* (*d.*); *pa. p.*, مسموم *masmúm*.

Pole (star, etc.), قطب *ḳutb*. Telegraph —, etc., تیر *tír*.

Pole (Polish), له *lah*.

Police, شحنکی *shahnagí*; کشیك *kashík*. — man, کشیکچی *kashíkchí*.

Polish, *v.*, زودن *zúdan*; *n.*, (lustre), صیقل *saiḳal*; جلا *jilá* (*d.*); *pa. p.*, مصقول *masḳúl*.

Polisher, جلا کر *jalá-gar*; صاقل *sáḳil*.

Polite, ادیب *adíb*; مودب *mu-addab*; فرهیخته *farhíkhtah*. —ness, ادب *adab*.

Politic, مفید *mufíd*.

Politics, Polity, سیاست *siyásat*.

Pollute, آلودن *álúdan*; نجس کردن *najis k.*; آغشتن *ágashtan*; *pa. p.*, منجس *munajjas* (*k.*); ملوث *mulavvas* (*k.*).

Pollution, آلودکی *álúdagí*; آلایش *áláyish*.

Poltroon, بیدل *bídil*.

Polytheism, شرك *shirk*.

Polytheist, مشرك *mushrik*.

Pomade, روغن *roghan*.

Pomegranate, نال *nár*; انار *anár*. — blossoms, کلنار *gulnár*. — tree,ناربن *nár-bun*.

Pommel (saddle), قربوس *ḳarbús*; (sword), قبضه *ḳabzah*.

Pomp, شوکت *shaukat*; شکوه *shikúh*; تجمل *tajammul*; احتشام *ihtishám*; حشمت *hashmat*; جاه *jáh*; طمطراق *tamturáḳ*; طنطنه *tantanah*; دبدبه *dabdabah*.

Pond, اصطخر *istakhr*; دریاچه *daryácheh*.

Ponder, فکر کردن *fikr k.*

Ponderous, ثقیل *saḳíl*, —ness, ثقلت *saḳlat*.

Pony, یابو *yábú*.

Pool, حوض *hauz*; آبکیر *ábgír*.

Poor, مفلس *muflis*; شقی *shaḳíy*; درویش *darvísh*; مقل *muḳill*; غریب *gharíb*, *pl.*, غربآء *ghurabá'*; مسکین *miskín*; *pl.*, مساکن *masákin*; فقیر *faḳír*; فقراء *fuḳará*.

Poorly, فقیرانه *faḳíránah*.

Poplar (white), سفیدار *safídár*; (oriental), چنار *chinár*.

Poppy, خشخاش *khaskhásh*; کوکنار *kúknâr*.

Populace, عوام *'avvám*.

Population, معموری ma'múrí.

Populous, آباد ábád (k.); ابادان ábádán.

Porcelaine, چینی chíní.

Porcupine, خارپشت khár-pusht.

Pores (skin), مسام masám.

Pork, گوشت خوك gúsht-i-khúk, or euphemistically, گوشت بلبل gusht-i-bulbul.

Port, بندر bandar; دریا بند daryá-band.

Portal, باب báb.

Portent, طالع tálí'.

Porter (carrier), حمال ham-mál; بار کش bár kesh; (doorkeeper), در بان dar-bán. — at a caravanserai, دالان دار ćulán-dár.

Portfolio, جزدان juz-dán.

Portico, دهلیز dihlíz; پیشگاه písh-gáh; رواق rivák.

Portion, بهره bahrah; پاره párah; جز juz, pl., اجزاء ajzá'; نبذة nubzat; نبذی nubzí. — of a farm re-let, کتکنه kat-kenah.

Portrait, تصویر tasvír.

Position, وضع vaz'.

Positive, یقین yakín (b). — injunction, توکید taukíd. —ly, یقیناً yakínan.

Possess, v., داشتن dáshtan; یافتن yáftan; pr. p., متصرف mutasarrif. Termination signifying "possessed of," مند -mand; وار vár; ور var; دار dár.

Possession, تصرف tasarruf (k.); ملاکت malákat, in pl., تصرفات tasarrufát: املاك amlák. To gain — of, بدست آوردن badast a.

Possessive case, اضافت izáfat.

Possessor, صاحب sáhib.

Possibility, احتمال ihtimál; امکان imkán.

Possible, ممکن mumkin; شدنی shundaní.

Possibly, شاید sháyad.

Post (on horse), چاپار chápár; (on foot), قاصد kásid. — (office), منصب mansab; (stake), چوب chúb.

Posterior, موخر mu'akhkhar.

Posteriors, دبر dubr.

Posterity, اعقاب a'káb; اولاد aulád.

Postponement, توقف tavak-kuf (k.).

Postscript, ذیل *zail.*

Pot (metal), دیك *dig*; (earthen), کوزه *kúzah.* — companion همکاسه *ham-kásah*; همقدح *ham-ḳadah.*

Potage, آش *ásh.*

Potash, قلیا *ḳilyá.*

Potation, نوشت *núsht.*

Potato, سیب زمین *sib-i-zamín.*

Potent, قادر *ḳádir.*

Potsherd, خزف ریزه *khazf-rízah.*

Potter, سفالگر *sufálgar*; کوزگر *kúzagar*; خزاف *khazzáf*; خزفی *khazafí.*

Pouch, کیسه *kísah*; کیف *kíf.*

Poultice, پخته *pukhtah.*

Pound (sterling), لیره *lírah*; *v.*, آشوردن *áshúrdan*; کوبیدن *kúbídan.*

Pour, ریختن *rikhtan*; *pr. p.*, مفیض *mufíz* (*n.*).

Poverty, مسکینی *miskíní*; مسکنة *maskinah*; فقیری *faḳírí*; مفلسی *muflisí*; درویشی *darvíshí*; نا داشتی *ná-dáshtí.*

Powder, سفوف *sufúf.* Gun —, باروت *bárút.* — flask, باروتدان *bárút dán.* — magazine, باروت خانه *bárút-khánah.*

Power, قدرت *ḳudrat*; قوت *ḳuvvat*; طاقت *táḳat*; زور *zúr*; توان *taván*; توانائی *tavánái*; دست رس *dast-ras*; دستگاه *dast-gáh*; مجال *majál*; مکنت *maknat*; (authority), اقتدار *iḳtidár.*

Powerful, توانا *tavāná*; قدیر *ḳadír*; مقتدر *muḳtadir*; محتشم *muhtashim*; متمکن *mutamakkin*; زور آور *zúr-ávar*; زبر دست *zabar-dast.*

Powerless, ناچار *náchár*; rendering —, اعجاز *i'jáz.*

Pox (the small-), آبله *ábilah*; (syphilis), کوفت *kúft.*

Practicable, شدنی *shudaní*; کردنی *kardaní.*

Practical, عملی *'amalíy.*

Practice, استعمال *isti'mál* (*k.*); مشق *mashḳ* (*k.*); ممارست *mumárisat*; عادت *'ádat.*

Practise, *v.*, طرح افکندن *tarh afgandan*; *pa. p.*, مسلوك *maslúk*; مستعمل *musta'mal.*

Praise (to a man), مدح *madh*; نعت *na't*; نیایش *niyáyish*; آفرین *áfrín*; ثناء *saná'*;

ستايش *sitáyish ;* (to God), حمد *hamd ;* تسبيح *tasbíh ;* تحميد *tahmíd ;* تهليل *tahlíl.* — be to God, الحمد لله *al-hamdu lilláh ; v.,* ستائيدن *sitáídan ;* ستودن *sitúdan.*

Praises (one who), وصاف *vas-saf ;* واصف *vásif.*

Prating, هرزه كوى *harzah gúí.*

Prayer, نماز *namáz (gf.)*; صلات or صلوت *salát (gf.), pl.,* صلوات *salavát.* The call to —, اذان *izán.* The crier to —, موذن *muezzin.* — niche, محراب *mihráb.* A place of —, مصلى *musallá.* — carpet, سجاده *sajjádeh.* One whose — is heard مستجاب الدعوات *mustaját ud da'vát.* One who prays, دعا كوى *du'á-gúí.*

Preacher, واعظ *vá'iz ;* خطيب *khatíb.*

Preaching, وعظ *va'z (k.)*; مواعظة *muvá'izeh (k.)*; موعظت *mau-'izat (n.).*

Preamble, سرآغاز *sar-ágház ;* مقدمه *mukaddameh.*

Precaution, تدارك *tadáruk ;* تدبير *tadbír.*

Precede, پيش رفتن *písh r.*

Precedence, سبقت *sabkat ;* صدارت *sadárat ;* مبادرت *mubádarat.*

Preceding, سابق *sábik ;* سلف *salaf ;* مبادر *mubádir.* That which precedes, ما سبق *má sabak.*

Precept, اندرز *andaraz ;* وصيت *vasíyet, pl.,* وصايا *vasáyá.*

Preceptor, معلم *mu'allim ;* موءدب *mu'addib.*

Precinct, حد *hadd.*

Precious, ارجمند *arjmand ;* عزيز *'azíz ;* ثمين *samín ;* نفيس *nafís.* — stone, جوهر *jauhar.*

Precipice پرتگاه *partgáh.*

Precipitation, تهور *tahavvur ;* شتابزدكى *shitáb-zadagí.*

Precipitous, پرت *part ;* سراشيب *saráshíb.*

Precise, صحيح *sahíh.*

Preclude, مانع كردن *máni' k.*

Preconception, پيش انديشى *písh andíshí (k.).*

Predecessors, سابقين *sábikín.*

Predestination, قضا *kazá ;* تقدير *takdír.*

Prediction, كهانت *kahánat* (*gf.*).

Predilection, ميل *meyl.*

Predominance, استيلا *istílá.*

Predominant, مستولی *mustaulí.*

Pre-eminence, برآمدگی *bar-ámadagí.*

Pre-eminent, ممتاز *mumtáz.*

Preface, دیباچه *díbácheh* ; عنوان *'unván* ; مقدمه *muḳaddamah.*

Preferable, راجح *rájih* (*h.*).

Preference, ترجیح *tarjíh* (*d. dsh.*) ; مراجعت *murájahat n.*

Preferred, مقتفی *muḳtafá.*

Pregnancy, حمل *haml.*

Pregnant, آبستة *ábistah* ; آبست *ábist* ; حامله *hámilah* (*b.*).

Prejudice, *v.*, متعصب ساختن *muta'assib s.*

Prejudical, مضر *muzirr.*

Premature, بیوقت *bí-vaḳt.*

Premeditation, تدبر *tadabbur* (*k.*).

Premises (logical), مقدمات *muḳaddamát.*

Preparation, تدارك *tadáruk* (*k.*) ; ترتیب *tartíb* (*s. d.*).

Prepare, آمادن *ámádan* ; درست کردن *durust k.* ; سچیدن *sichídan*; *pa. p.*, مستعد *mus-ta'idd* (*sh.*) ; مهیا *muhaiyá* (*k.*) ; حاضر *házir* (*h. k.*). One who —s, مهیی *muhyí.*

Preponderance, استیلا *istílá* (*n.*).

Preposition, حرف جر *harf i jarr.*

Prepossession, رغبت *righbat.*

Preposterous, بیهوده *bihúdah.*

Prepuce, غلف *ghalaf.*

Prerogative, حق *haḳḳ.*

Presage, فأل *faal.*

Prescription (doctor's), نسخه *nuskheh* (*d.*).

Presence, حضور *huzúr* (*dsh.*) ; قبل *ḳibal.* In the — of, رو برو *rú-ba-rú* ; بحضور *bahu-zúr.*

Present (not absent), حاضر *házir.* At —, الحال *al hál* ; حالا *hálá* ; الان *al-án.* (gift), بخشش *bakhshish* ; دهش *dihish* ; تحفة *tuhfat* ; سوغات *saughát* ; (to inferior), انعام *in'ám* ; (to superior), پیشکش *pish-kesh.* A wedding — (from the bridegroom), رو نما *rú-numá.* Asking for a —, مستوهب *mustauhib.*

Presenting, اقدام *iḳdám* (*n.*).

Preservation, محافظه *muháfezeh* (*k.*).

Preserved, مأمون *ma'mún.*

Preserves (fruit, &c.), آچـــار *áchár*; مربا *murabbá* (*s.*).

Preserving, وقاء *vaḳá'*. — one's self from sin, اعتصام *i'tisám.*

President, صــدر نـشـين *sadr nishín.* — of the republic, رئيس دولت جـمـهـور *raís i daulat i jamhúr.*

Press (wine or oil), بـرشـك *barshak*; مـصـر *ma'sar*; *v.*, شكنجيدن *shikanjídan*; افشردن *afshurdan.*

Presumed (it is to be), احتمال كـلى مـيـرود *ihtimal-i-kulli míravad.*

Presumption, تجاسر *tajásur*; تصدى *tasaddí.*

Presumptuous, صائل *sáil*; مغرور *maghrúr.*

Pretence, بهانه *bahánah.*

Pretender, داعى *dá'í.*

Pretending, ادعاء *iddi'á* (*k.*).

Pretension, دعـوى *da'vá*, *pl.*, دواعى *davá'i.*

Pretext, بهانه *bahánah.*

Pretty, خــوشــگل *khush-gil*; خوبصورت *khúbsúrat.*

Prevalent, اغلب *aghlab* (*b*); غالب *ghaleb* (*sh.*); رواج *raváj* (*dsh.*).

Prevarication, تناقض *tanáḳuz* (*gf.*).

Prevention, مـنـع *man'* (*k.*); دفع *daf'* (*k.*).

Preventive, مزاحم *muzáhim.*

Previous, مـقـدم *muḳaddam*; اسبق *asbaḳ*; سابق *sábiḳ.*

Prey (plunder), ياغـمـه *yághmah*; (game), صيد *said* (*k.*).

Price, قيمت *ḳaimat*; بها *bahá*; ارز *arz*; ارج *arj*; ثـمـن *saman*; (hire), اجاره *ijárah.* — current, نرخ *nirkh.*

Prick, خـلـيـدن *khalídan*; جلانيدن *khalánídan*; آزدن *ázadan.*

Pride, غـرور *ghurúr*; ابـراح *ibráh*; مـغـرورى *maghrúrí*; استـكـبار *istikbár*; رعونت *ru'únat*; نخوت *nakhvat*; تعظم *ta'azzum.* — and egotism, ماءى و منى *má'í u maní.*

Priest, پيش نماز *písh-namáz.* Chief — of the Magi, پـيـر مغان *pír i mughán.* Christian —, كشيش *kashísh.*

Prime, مهتر *mehtar.*

Priming, چاشنی *chashní* (*n.*).

Primitive, پیشین *píshín.*

Prince, شاهزاده *sháhzádah*; (title *after* the name), میرزا *Mírzá.*

Princess, شاهزاده خانم *sháh-zádeh khánum.*

Principal, اصلی *aslí*; اول *avval*; (money), سرمایه *sar máyeh.* —ly, غالباً *gháliban.*

Principle, اصل *asl*; ماده *mád-dah*; منشاء *manshá'.*

Print, *v.*, چاپ کردن *cháp k.*; طبع کردن *tab' k.*; *pa. p.*, مطبوع *matbú'.*

Printer, طباع *tabbá'.*

Printing, طباعت *tibá'at.*

Prior, مقدم *mukaddam*; اقدم *akdam.*

Priority, تقدیم *takdím*; تقدم *takaddum*; قدامت *kadámat.*

Prison, زندان *zindán*; سجن *sijn*; محبوس خانه *mahbús khánah,*

Prisoner, محبوس *mahbús*; قیدی *kaidí*, *pl.*, زندانیان *zindáni-yán.* — of war, اسیر *asír.*

Privacy, خلوت *khalvat.*

Private (soldier), سر باز *sar-báz.* — apartment, خلوت خانه *khalvat khánah.*

Privately, نهانی *nihání.*

Privation, عطل *'utal.*

Privative, عدمی *'adamíy.*

Privilege, استحقاق *istihkák.*

Privy, مبرز *mabraz*; مزبله *maz-balah*; خلا *khalá.*

Prize, انعام *in'ám.*

Probability, احتمال *ihtimál.*

Probable, محتمل *muhtamil.*

Probably, گویا *guyá.*

Probation, امتحان *imtíhán.*

Probe, میل *míl.*

Probity, صدق *sidk.*

Problem, مسئله *mas-aleh.*

Proboscis, خرطوم *khartum.*

Proceed, روارو کردن *ravá-rav k.*; رفتار کردن *raftár k.*

Proceedings, حرکات و سکنات *harakát o sakanát*; (of a lawsuit), رو بکاری *rú-ba kári.*

Process, وضع *vaz'.*

Procession, طواف *tavváf.*

Proclaimed, مشتهر *mushtahar* (*h.*).

Proclaiming, تشهیر *tash-hír* (*n.*).

Proclamation, ندا *nidá* (*k.*); صلا *salá* (*k.*); اشتهار *ishti-hár* (*d.*).

Procrastination, لیت و لعل *lait o la'al* (*k.*); تعلل *ta'allul* (*n.*).

Procurable, دستیاب *dást-yáb.*

Procure, بهم رسانیدن *baham ra-sáníd an*; *pa. p.*, پیدا *paidá* (*k.*); حاصل *hásil* (*k.*).

Procuress, دلاله *dallálah.*

Prodigal, *a.*, مبذر *mubazzir*; مسرف or مصرف *musrif*; *n.*, تلفکار *talaf-kár.*

Prodigality, اسراف *isráf*; تبذیر *tabzír.*

Prodigious, عظیم *'azím.*

Prodigy, اعجوبه *u'júbah.* — (fem.) of beauty, عجبا *'ajbá.*

Produce, *n.*, ما حصل *má hasal*; حاصل *hasil*; حصول *husúl*; پیدایش *paidáyish*; *v.*, در آوردن *dar a.*; *pr. p.*, ابداع *ibdá'* (*n.*); احضار *ihzár* (*k.*).

Products, حاصلات *hásilát.*

Production, پیدا *paidá* (*k.*).

Profanation, تدنیس *tadnís* (*k.*).

Profane, فاسق *fásik.* —ly, پلیدانه *pilídáneh.*

Profanity, نفاق *nifák.*

Profess, اظهار کردن *izhár k.*

Profession (trade), سنعت *san'at*; پیشه *píshah.* — of faith, تشهد *tashahhud.*

Professor, استاد *ustád*; مدرس *mudarris.*

Proffer, تقدیم *takdím* (*k.*).

Proficiency, قابلیت *kábiliyat.*

Proficient, قابل *kábil.*

Profit, منفعت *manfa'at*; فائیده *fáidah*; بهره *bahrah*; استفاده *istifádah*; ربح *ribh*; سود *súd* (*y.*); حاصل *hásil* (*gr.*).

Profitable, سود مند *súd-mand*; مفید *mufíd*; فائده مند *fáidah-mand.*

Profligacy, فسق *fisk*; فجور *fujúr.*

Profligate, *n.*, رند *rind.*

Profound learning, تبحر *tabah-hur.*

Profuse, موفر *muvaffar*; غایت *gháyat.*

Progenitor, جد *jadd.*

Progeny, نسل *nasl*; ذریة *zar-ríyet*; سلالة *sulálat.*

Progress, فرا روی *fará raví.* To make —, ترقی کردن *ta-rakki k.*

Prohibit, *v.*, وا داشتن *vá dáshtan*; *pa. p.* ممنوع *mamnú'*; محجور *mahjúr*; ممتنع *mumtaná'*. Things —ed, محرمات *muhramát*; مناهی *manáhí*; *pr. p.*, ناهی *náhí*; تحریم *tahrím* (*n.*).

Prohibition, منع *man'* (*k.*); مانع *máni'* (*k.*); نهی *nahí* (*k.*); ممانعت *mumána'at*.

Projecting, میفاء *mífá'*; اختراع *ikhtirá'* (*k.*).

Prolix, مفصل *mufassal*.

Prolixity, اطناب *itnáb*.

Prolongation, امتداد *imtidád* (*k. y.*).

Prolonging, متمادی *mutamádí*.

Promenade, سیر *sair* (*k.*).

Promise, *v.*, دست دادن *dast d.*; زبان دادن *zabán-d.*; *pa. p.*, موعود *mau'úd*; *pr. pa.*, واعد *vá'id*; *n.*, عهد *'ahd* (*k.*); وعده *va'dah* (*k.*); پیمان *paimán*; موء *mau'id*.

Promontory, شناخ *shinákh*; راس *rás*.

Promotion, ارتقاء *irtiká* (*d.*); ترقی *tarakkí* (*d.*).

Promptitude, شتاب *shitáb*; زودی *zúdí*.

Promptly, زود *zúd*.

Promulgated, شایع *sháyi'* (*k.*).

Prong, چنك *chang*.

Pronoun, ضمیر *zamír*.

Pronunciation, تلفظ *talaffuz* (*k.*).

Proof, برهان *burhán*; دلیل *dalíl*; حجة *hujjat*; ثبوت *subút*; نخشه *nakhshah*. A decisive —, دلیل قاطع *dalíl i kátí'*.

Prop, پشتیبان *pushtíbán*; عمود *'amúd*.

Propagation, انتشار *intishár* (*d.*).

Propensity, میل *mail*; مراغبت *murághabat*.

Proper, مناسب *munásib*; واجب *vájib*; سزاور *sezávar*. Not —, نباید *na-báyad*.

Property, مال *mal*; املاك *imlák*; مملوکة *mamlúkat*; ملك *milk*. A man of —, مایه دار *máyah-dár*. — and effects, مال و متاع *mál u mitá'*; (quality), خاصیت *khássiyet*, *pl.* خصائص *khasáis*.

Prophecy, نبوت *nubuvvat* (*n.*); کهانت *kahánat*.

Prophet, نبی *nabíy*, *pl.*, انبیآء *ambiyá*; رسول *rasúl*; پیغمبر *paighamber*.

Propinquity, قرب *ḳurb*.

Propitiation, تکفیر *takfír* (*k*.).

Propitious, خجسته *khujisteh*.

—ness, مساعدت *musá'adat*.

Proportion, مقدار *miḳdár*; نسبت *nisbat*.

Propose, پیش کرفتن *písh-gr*.

Proposition, مسئله *mas-aleh*.

Proprietaryship, مالکیت *málikíyet*.

Proprietor, مالك *málik*.

Proprietry, شایستکی *sháyistagí*; درستي *durustí*; صلاحیت *saláhiyet*.

Prose, نثر *nasr*.

Prosecution, *n*., پیروی *pairaví*; مرافعت *muráfa'at* (*k*.).

Proselyte, جدید *jadíd*.

Prosody, عروض *'arúz*.

Prospect, منظر *manzar*.

Prosper (him, may God), روزی کناد *rúzí kunád*.

Prospering, موفق *muvaffiḳ* (*n*.).

Prosperity, اقبال *iḳbál* (*n*.). May his — be lasting, دام اقباله *dáma iḳbáluhu*; برکت *barakat*; فرخي *farrukhí*; میمنت *maimanat*; یسارت *yasárat*; افلاح *ifláh*.

Prosperous, اقبالمند *iḳbálmand*; مفلیح *muflíh*; دوست کام *dúst i kám*; کامیاب *kám-yáb*.

Prostitute, قحبه *ḳahbah*; روسپی *rúspí*; لوند *lavand*; سلیطه *salíteh*; کسبی *kasbí*; زنچه *zanicheh*; جنده *jindeh*.

Prostitution, جندکی *jindegí*.

Prostrate, ساجد *sájid*; برجا *barjá*; *v*., افتادن *uftádan*.

Prostration, استلام *istilám*, *in pl*., سجدات *sijdát*.

Protected, محروس *mahrús* (*k*.).

Protection, حمایت *himáyet* (*d*.); زنهار *zinhár* (*k*.).; سایه *sáyah* (*n*.); پناه *panáh* (*d*.); امانی *amání* (*d*.); پرورش *parvarish*.

Protector, پرورنده *parvarendah*.

Protégé, پرورده *parvardeh*.

Protest, اشتهاد *iṣhtihád* (*k*.).

Protestation, ایضاح *ízáh*.

Protracting, ابطآء *ibtá* (*k*.)

Protracted, دراز *diráz*.

Protraction, تمادی *tamádí* (*n*.).

Proud, مغرور *maghrúr* ; متکبر *mutakabbir* ; مستکبر *mustakbír* ; گردن فراز *gardan-faráz*.

Prove, *v.*, ثابت کردن or شدن *sábit k.* or *sh.* ; تصدیق نمودن *tasdíḳ n.*

Provender, علوفه *'ulúfah*.

Proverb, مثل *masal*, *pl.*, امثال *amsál*.

Proverbial, ضرب المثل *zarb ul masal*.

Provide, درست ساختن *durust s.*

Providence, رزاق *Razzáḳ* ; پروردگار *Parvardagár* ; رازق *Rázik*.

Provident, آخربین *ákhir-bín* ; دور اندیش *dúr-andísh*.

Province (small), کوره *kúreh* ; (large), مملکت *mamlakat*.

Provision (for a journey), توشه *túshah* ; زاد (راه) *zád (i ráh)* ; رسد *rasad*, *pl.* خوردنی *khur-daní* ; ارزاق *arzáḳ* ; ذخر *zukhr*.

Provocation, تحریك *tahrík* (*k.*).

Provoke, خیزانیدن *khízánídan*.

Prow, راس *rás*.

Prowess, دلاوری *dilávarí*.

Proximity, نزدیکی *nazdíkí*.

Proxy, وکیل *vakíl*.

Prudence, هشیاری *hushyárí* ; هوشیاری *húshyári* ; هوشمندی *húsh-mandí* ; خرد منشی *khirad-manishí*.

Prudent, هوشمند *húsh-mand* ; لبیب *labíb* ; آخربین *ákhir-bín*. —ly, اختیاطاً *ikhtiyátan*.

Prune (plum), الو بخارا *álú bu-khárá* ; *v.*, خشودن *kha-shúdan* ; حطاب کردن *hitáb k.*

Prurience, هوس *havas*.

Prurient, هوسمند *havasmand*.

Prying, تفتیش *taftísh* (*k.*).

Psalms (of David), زبور *zabúr*.

Puberty, بلوغ *bulúgh*.

Public, the, ملاء *malá'* ; مردم *mardum*. — audience, بار عام *bár i 'ám* ; (notorious), عرفی *'urfí* ; جهراً *jahran*. — life, علانیة *'aláníyet*. To be made —, بر ملاء افتادن *bar malá' uftádan*. —ly, صحاراً *siháran* ; آشکارا *ásh-kárá*.

Publication, ابراز *ibráz* ; اشتهار *ishtihár* ; افشاء *ifshá* ; اعلام *i'lám* ; اعلان *i'lán*.

Publishing, ابانت *ibánat* (*k.*); اباحت *ibáhat* (*k.*); شیوع *shuyú'* (*dsh.*).

Pudendum virile کیر *kir*; آلت *álat*; ذکر *zakar*. — muliebre, کس *kus*; فرج *farj*; چوز *chúz*.

Puerility, طفلی *tiflí*.

Puff, پوف کردن *púf k.*

Pugnacious, لجوج *lajúj*.

Pull, کشیدن *kashídan*. — out hairs, etc., نتف کردن *natf k.*; نتش کردن *natsh k.*

Pullet, جوجه *júj eh*.

Pulley, غرغره *ghargharch*.

Pulp, مغز *maghz*.

Pulpit, منبر *minbar*.

Pulsation, نبض *nabz* (*gr.*). One —, نبضت *nabzat*.

Pulse (pea), کرسنه *karsaneh*.

Pump, طلمبه *tulumbah*.

Pumpkin, کدو *kaddú*.

Pun, تجنیس *tajnís*; لطیفه *latífah*.

Punctual, بالوقت *bilvakt*.

Puncture, خلیدکی *khalídagí*; ابر *abr*.

Pungent, تیز *tíz*.

Pungency, تیزی *tízí*.

Punish, *v.*, سیاست کردن *siyásat k.* — by mutilating the criminal, نسق کردن *nasak k.*

Punisher, معاقب *mu'ákib*.

Punishment, عقوبت *'ukúbat* (*n.*).; معاقبت *mu'ákabat*; نکال *nakál*; نقمت *nakmat*.

Puny, یکوجبی *yek vajabí*.

Pupil, یتمان *yatmán*; شاکرد *shágird*. — of the eye, مردمك چشم *mardumak i chashm*.

Puppet, لعبة *la'bat*. — show, لعبت بازی *la'bat bází*.

Puppy, توله *tuleh*; بچه *bacheh*.

Purblind, روز کور *rúz-kúr*; شب کور *shab-kúr*.

Purchase, *v.*, خریدن *kharídan*; اشتراء کردن *ishtirá k.*

Purchaser, مشتری *mushtarí*; خریدار *kharídár*.

Pure, پاك *pák*; خالص *khális*; ناب *náb*; طاهر *táhir*; نظیف *nazíf*; نقی *nakíy*; صفی *safíy*; سارا *sárá*; صمیم *samím*; (holy), منزه *munazzah*; (in colour), ناصع *nási'*.

Purgation, تنقیه *tankíh* (*n.*).

Purgative, مسهل *mus-hil* (*gr.*); جلاب *julláb*.

Purgatory, اعراف *i'ráf.*

Purged, مسهل *mus-hal* (*sh.*).

Purging, اسهال *is-hál* (*gr.*).

Purification, تصفيه *tasfíyeh* (*n.*); (before prayer), وضو *vuzú* (*k.*); (with sand or dust, when water cannot be had), تيمم *tayammum* (*k.*). Ceremonial —, طهارت *tahárat* (*k.*); تطهير *tathír* (*k.*).

Purified, مبرور *mabrúr*; مجهور *majhúr.*

Purifier, مطهر *mutahhir.*

Purity, صافى *sáfí*; پاكى *pákí*; صفاء *safá'*; صفوت *safvat*; خلوص *khulús*; نقاوت *naḳávat*; تزكية *tazkíyat*; تنقى *tanaḳḳí.*

Purple, ارغوان *arghaván*; قرمز *ḳirmiz.*

Purport, مطلب *matlab.*

Purpose, عمد *'amd* (*k.*); قصد *ḳasd* (*k.*); مقصود *maḳsud*; عزيمت *'azímat.* On —, عمداً *'amdan*; قصداً *ḳasdan.*

Purring, خرخر *khar-khar* (*k.*).

Purse, كيسه *kísah*; صرة *surrat*; هميان *himyán.* Cut —, طرار *tarrár.*

Purslain, خرفه *khurfah.*

Pursue, عقب رفتن *'aḳab r.*; در پى رفتن *dar pai r.*

Pursuit, تعقب *ta'aḳḳub* (*k.*).

Pus, ريم *rím*; هپر *hapar.*

Push, هول *húl* (*d.*); تكان *takán* (*d.*).

Pusillanimous, بيدل *bí-dil.*

Pustule, كرك *kurk.*

Put, *v.*, گذاشتن *guzáshtan*; نهادن *nihádan*; نهستن *nihistan.* — anything on the back of a beast of burden, ترك بستن *tark bastan.* — out the light, چراغ كشتن *chirágh-kushtan.* — in motion, جنبانيدن *jumbánídan.* — on garments, ملبوس كردن *malbús k.*

Putrified, پوشيده *púshídeh*; گنديده *gandídeh.*

Putrify, گنديدن *gandídan.*

Putrid, رميم *ramím.* Becoming —, تعفن *ta'affun* (*n.*).

Puzzle, *n.*, رمز *ramz*; لغز *lughz*; *v.*, سر بسر گذاشتن *sar-ba-sar guzáshtan.*

Pyramid, هرم *haram.*

Q

Quack, عیار *'ayyár.*

Quadrangular, مربع *murabba'.*

Quadruped, چهار پایه *chehár-páyah;* چار پایه *char-páyah;* چاروا *chárvá, pl.* ذوات الاربع *zavát ul arba';* دواب *davább.*

Quaff, نوشیدن *núshídan.*

Quail, *n.,* سمانه *sumánah;* بلدرچین *bildarchín.*

Quaking, هراسان *harásán (sh.).*

Qualified, متصف *muttasif.*

Qualifying, توصیف *tausíf (k.).*

Quality, صفت *sifat, pl.* صفات *sifát;* خصلت *khaslat, pl.* خصال *khisál;* حالة *hálat, pl.* حالات *hálát;* وصف *vasf, pl.* اوصاف *ausáf.* Innate —, شمایل *shamáil.* Best — (goods), فرد اعلی *fard i a'lá.*

Quantity, کمیت *kamíyet;* قدر *kadr;* انداز *andáz;* موازی *muvází.*

Quarrel, جنگ *jang (k.);* نزاع *nizá' (k.);* شتلم *shutulum.*

Quarrelsome, جنگجو *jang-jú;* فسادی *fasádí;* ستیزنده *sitízendah.*

Quarry (stone), کان *kán.*

Quarter (fourth), ربع *rub';* چهار یك *chehár yek;* (side), جانب *jánib;* (granted to an enemy), امان *amán.* Town —, محله *mahallah, pl.* محلات *mahallát.* Four —s of the world, چهار دانك *chehár-dáng.*

Quatrain, رباعی *rubá'íy.*

Quay, بندر گاه *bandar gáh.*

Queen, ملکه *malikah.* — at chess, فرزین *fárzín.*

Queer, غریب *gharíb.*

Quell, تسلی کردن *tasalli k.*

Quench (thirst), تسکین دادن *taskín d.;* (fire), خاموش کردن *khámúsh k.;* طفوء کردن *tufú' k.*

Question, *n.,* سوءال *su'ál (k.);* پرسش *pursish;* مسأله *masalah, pl.,* مسائل *masáil; v.,* پرسیدن *pursídan.*

Quibble, ایهام *íhám.*

Quick, زود *zúd;* جلد *jald;* سریع *sarí';* مسرع *musri';* (hasty), عاجل *'ájil.* —ly, بزودی *bizúdí.* — lime, کلس *kils;* آهك *áhak.*

Quickness, زودی *zúdí*. — of apprehension, باریك بینی *bárík-bíní*.

Quicksand, دزدریك *duzd-ríg*.

Quicksilver, سیم آب *sím-áb*; جیوه *jívah*; زیبق *zíbak*.

Quiescence (of a letter), سکون *sukún*.

Quiescent (ditto), ساکن *sákin*.

Quiet, *n*. *a*., مرفه *muraffah*; راحت *ráhat*; آسایش *ásáyish*; *v*., آرام دادن *áräm d*.; ترفیه کردن *tarfíyeh k*. —ly, یواش *yavásh*.

Quilt, توشك *túshak*; لحاف *laháf*.

Quilting, سوزنی *súzení*; بخیه *bakhyah*.

Quince, به *bih*; سفرجل *safarjal*.

Quinine, کنه کنه *kineh-kineh*.

Quinsy, خناق *khunák*.

Quintessence, ذات *zát*.

Quire, دسته *dastah*.

Quit, گذاشتن *guzáshtan*; فرو گذاشتن *farú-guzáshtan*.

Quite, بالکل *bilkull*.

Quittance, برات *barát*.

Quiver, تیر دان *tír dán*; جعبه *ja'bah*; ترکش *tarkash*; مقوس *mikvas*.

Quotation, ایراد *írád* (*k*.).

Quoted (from the Korán), مقتبس *muktabas*.

Quoting (from the Korán), اقتباس *iktibás* (*k*.).

Quotient, حاصل *hásil*.

R.

Rabbit, خرکوش *khar-gúsh*.

Race, اصل *asl*; نسل *nasl*; نسب *nasab*.

Race-course, میدان *maidán*; شرط *shart*.

Racing, مسابقت *musábakat*.

Rack, شکنجه *shikanjah* (*k*.).

Radiance, سطع *sat'*.

Radiant, منور *munavvar*.

Radical, اصلی *aslí*. —ly, اصلاً *aslan*.

Radish, ترب *turb*; فجل *fujul*.

Radius, نیم قطر *nim kutr*.

Raft, کلك *kalak*.

Rafter, تیر *tir*.

Rag, پاره *páreh*.

Rage, قهر *kahr*; غیظ *ghaiz*; خشم *khishm*.

Ragged, پاره پاره *páreh páreh*.

Rai (the ancient Rhagis), ری *Rai.*

Railer, عذال *'azzál.*

Railroad, راه آهن *ráh-i-áhan.*

Raiment, لباس *libás.*

Rain, *n.*, باران *bárán*; بارش *bárish*; *v.*, باریدن *báridan.*

Rainbow, قوس قزح *kaus i kuzah.*

Rainy, مطیر *mutír.*

Raise, بر آوردن *bar ávardan*; بالا کردن *bálá k*; *pr. p.*, تشیید *tashyíd* (*n.*); رافع *ráfi'* (*k.*).

Raiser, فرازنده *farázendah.*

Raisins, کشمش *kishmish*; مویز *maviz.*

Rake, خاک کش *khák kesh.*

Ram, غوچ *ghúch*; قوچ *kúch*; (sign of the Zodiac), حمل *hamal*; *v.*, آکندن *ákandan.*

Rambling (in speech), درهم برهم *dar ham bar ham.*

Rampart, بارو *bárú.*

Ramrod, میل *míl.*

Rancid, ترش *tursh.*

Rancour, کین *kín.*

Random (at), بیمقصود *bí maksúd.*

Rank (degree), مرتبه *martabah*; قدر *kadr*; پایگاه *páigáh*; رتبة *rutbat.* Of elevated —, والا جاه *válá-jáh*; (file), صف *saff*, *pl.* صفوف *sufúf*; *in pl.* (soldiers), مصاف *masáff.* Breaking the —, صف در *saff-dar.*

Ransom, *n.*, فدیه *fidyah* سر بها *sar-bahá* (*d.*).

Rapacious, درنده *darandeh.*

Rapacity, طمع *tama'.*

Rape, زنا *ziná* (*k.*).

Rapid, تند *tund.* —ity, تندی *tundí.*

Rapine, غارت *ghárat* (*k.*); نهب *nahb* (*k.*).

Rapture, بیخودی *bí-khudí.*

Rare, نادر *nádir*; کمیاب *kamyáb.* — things, نوادر *navádir.*

Rarity, ندرت *nudrat*; طرفکی *turfagí*; نادره *nádirah*, *pl.* تحفجات *tuhfaját*; تحائف *tahá'if.*

Rascal, جوولاغی *jauvalághí*; اوباش *aubásh.*

Rash, بی تحاشا *bí-tahúshá.*

Rashness, دلبازی *dil-bází.*

Rasp, سوهان *súhán* (*k.*).

Rat, موش *músh.*

Rate, انــدازه *andázeh.* The market —, نرخ بازار *nirkh i bázár.* At any —, بهر حال *behar hál.*

Rather, بیشتر *bíshtar.*

Ratification, تصدیق *tasdíḳ* (*n.*).

Ratified, قرار دار *ḳerár dár.*

Ratio, مقدار *miḳdár.*

Rationally, عاقلانه *'áḳilánah.*

Rations, جیره *jíreh.*

Ratsbane, سم الـفـار *samm ul fár.*

Ravage, تاراج *táráj* (*k.*).

Ravelled, برهـم زده *bar ham zadeh.*

Raven, غراب *ghuráb.*

Ravenous, درنده *darandah.*

Ravine, تنك *tang.*

Raving, شوریده *shúrídeh.*

Ravished, مفتضح *muftazah* (*k.*).

Ravisher, ربانـنده *rubánindah.*

Ravishing, دلستان *dilsitán.*

Raw, خام *khám.*

Rawness, خامی *khámí.*

Ray, پرتو *partav*; شعاع *shu'á'*, *pl.*, اشعه *ashi'ah.*

Raze, منـهـدم كـردن *munhadim k.*

Razor, موسی *músá.*

Reach, *n.*, اندازه *andázah*; *v.*, دست بردن *dast burdan.*

Read, خواندن *khándan.*

Readiness, آمـادكی *ámádagí*; تهیة *tahíyeh*; تیاری *taiyárí.*

Reading, خوانـد كی *khándagí*; (the Ḳorán), قراءت *ḳirá'at*; تلاوت *tilávat* (*k.*).

Ready, حاضر *házir*; آماده *ámádah*; تـیـار *taiyár*; مهیا *muhaiyá*; در حضور *dar huzúr*; كمر بسته *kamar-bastah.*

Real, عینی *'ainí.*

Reality, حقیة *haḳḳíyet.* In —, وقیعاً *vaḳí'an*; در حقیقت *dar haḳíḳat.*

Realm, مملكت *mamlakat.*

Reap, خسوردن *khasúrdan*; درو كردن *diro k*; درویدن *diravídan*; درودن *durúdan*; *pr. p.*, حصاد *hisád*, or *hasád* (*k.*).

Reaper, درونـــده *diravendah*; حصاد *hassád.*

Reaping-hook, داز *dáz.*

Rear (of an army), چـنـداول *chandávul*; *v. t.*, (a child), پروردن *parvardan*; *v. i.*, (a horse), سـكـزیـدن *sikízídan*; *pr. p.* (a horse), چـراغ پـا *chirágh-pá* (*sh.*).

Reason (wit), عقل *'aḳl*; (cause), سبب *sabab*. By — that, برای آنکه *berâyi ánkeh*.

Reasonable, معقول *ma'ḳúl*.

Rebeck, رباب *rabáb*.

Rebel, طاغی *tághí* (*sh.*); باغی *bághi*; عاصی *'ásí* (*sh.*), *pl.* عصاة *'usát*; *v.*, سرکشیدن *sar-ksh.*; سر بر داشتن *sar bar dsh.*; کردن کشیدن *gardan ksh.*

Rebellion, عصیان *'isyán* (*k.*); بغی *baghy*; معاصات *mu'ását* (*n.*); بغاوت *bagháνat*; اغتشاش *ightishásh*; طغیان *tughyán*.

Rebellious, مستعصی *musta'sí*.

Rebuke, زجر *zajr* (*n.*).

Receipt (discharge), قبض الوصول *ḳabz ul vusúl*; (medical, etc.), نسخه *nuskheh*; (getting), بازیافت *bázyáft*; رسید *rasíd*; (entry in an account), داخله *dákhilah*. — and disbursement, دخل و خرج *dakhl u kharch*.

Receipts, مداخل *mudákhil*.

Receive, گرفتن *giriftan*.

Receiver, کاسب *kásib*. — of good news, مبتشر *mubtashir*.

Receiving a bribe, راشی *ráshí*.

Recent, تازه *tázeh*.

Recess, گوشه *gúsheh*.

Recitals, تقاریر *taḳárír*.

Recite, بر خواندن *bar khándan*.

Reciter of stories, دستان سرای *dastán saráí*.

Reckon, شمردن *shumurdan*; شماریدن *shumárídan*.

Reckoning, شمار *shumár* (*k.*); احتساب *ihtisáb*.

Reclining, تکیه *takiyeh* (*z*).

Recluse, زاهد *záhíd*, *pl.* زهاد *zuhád*; تجرد گزین *tajarrud-guzín*; خلوت نشین *khalvat-nishín*; — وتی *khalvatí*. Like a —, زاهدانه *záhidanah*. The life of a —, زاهدی *záhidí*.

Recognition, تشخیص *tashkhís* (*d.*).

Recollect, یاد آوردن *yád a.*

Recollection, یاد *yád*.

Recommend, سپاریدن *sipárídan*.

Recommendation, سفارش *sifárish* (*k.*); توصیه *tausíyeh* (*k.*).

Recompence, پاداش *pádásh* ; عوض *'ivaz* (*d.*) ; مکافات *mukáfát* (*k.*) ; مزد *muzd.*

Recompensed, ماجور *ma'júr* ; مثاب *musáb.*

Recompensing, مثوب *musvib* (*n.*).

Reconciliation, صلح *sulh* (*k.*) ; تصفیه *tasfíyeh* (*n.*).

Reconnaissance, جاسوسی *jásúsí* (*k.*).

Record, *v.*, ثبط کردن *sabt k.*; *n.*, دفتر *daftar* ; سجل *sijil.*

Recourse to, متوسل *mutavassil*; رجوع *rujú'* (*k.*).

Recover (find), باز یافتن *báz y.*

Recovery (of health), افاقت *ifáḳat* (*y.*); شفا *shifá* (*y.*).

Recreation, تفرج *tafarruj.*

Recrimination, ملامت *malámat* (*k.*).

Recruit, جدید *jadíd.*

Rectifier, مصلح *muslih* ; مقوم *muḳavvim.*

Rectifying, مصداق *misdáḳ* (*n.*).

Rectitude, راستی *rástí* ; سداد *sadád* ; صواب *saváb* ; صلاح *saláh* ; رشد *rushd* ; قدوی *ḳadvá* ; استقامت *istiḳámat.*

Rector (of a University), رئیس مدرسه دار العلوم *raís i madrasah i dar ul 'ulúm.*

Recurrence, مراجعت *murája'at* (*k.*).

Red, سرخ *surkh* (*k.*) ; احمر *ahmar* ; قرمز *ḳirmiz.*

Redeem, وا خریدن *vá-kharídan.*

Redeemer, نجات دهنده *niját dihandeh.*

Redemption, رهائی *rihái.*

Red-lead, شنکرف *shingarf.*

Redness, سرخی *surkhí* ; حمرت *humrat.*

Redolent, معطر *mu'attar.*

Redoubt, قلعه *ḳal'ah.*

Redoubtable, مهیب *muhíb.*

Redress, چاره *cháreh.* Seeking —, استغاثه *istighásah.* — of grievances, فریاد رسی *faryád-rasí.*

Redresser (of grievances), فریاد رس *faryád-ras.*

Reduce, کم کردن *kam k.*

Reduced (to poverty), مفتقر *muftaḳar.* To be — to beggary, در بدر شدن *dar ba dar shudan.*

Redundancy, فضله *fazlah, pl.* فضلات *fazalát.*

Redundant, زاید *záid.*

Reed, نی *nai;* قصب *ḳasab.* A place where —s grow, نیستان *naiyistán.*

Reedy, نئین *na'ín.*

Reel, *n.*, پیلی *pílí; v.* (totter), یله شدن *yaleh sh.*

Refer, نسبت کردن *nisbat k.;* رجوع کردن *rujú' k.*

Reference, مرافعت *muráfa'at* (*n.*); نسبة *nisbat.*

Refine (butter, etc.), صاف کردن *sáf k.;* (metals), قال کردن *ḳál k.*

Refinement, تربیت *tarbiyat.*

Refiner, قالگر *ḳálgar.*

Reflection (thought), فکر *fikr* (*k.*); امعان *im'án* (*n.*); (shadow), عکس *'aks.*

Reform, *v.*, اصلاح کردن *isláh k.*

Reformer, مصلحت جو *maslihat-jú.*

Refraction, انحراف *inhiráf* (*n.*).

Refractory, عنید *'anid;* بد مست *bad-mast;* سر کش *sar-kash.* Being — تمرد *tamar-rud.* —ness, سرکشی *sar-kashí.*

Refrain, *v.*, وا ایستادن *vá ís-tádan.*

Refreshing, روان اسا *raván-ásá.*

Refreshment, غذا *ghizá.*

Refrigerator, یخچال *yakh-chál.*

Refuge, پناه *panáh;* بست *bast* (*gr.*); معاذ *ma'áz;* مأمن *ma'man.* Taking —, ملتجی *multají* (*n.*); التجاء *iltijá* (*k.*). A place of —, مفر *mafarr.* We seek — in God, نعوذ بالله *na'úzu billáhi.* God is my —, معاذ الله *ma'áz Alláh.*

Refund, باز دادن *báz d.*

Refusal, انکار *inkár* (*gf.*); نفی *nafí* (*k.*).

Refuse, *n.*, فضله *fazleh.*

Refusing, رافض *ráfiz.*

Refutation, رد کلام *radd i kalám* (*k.*).

Regal, شهوار *shahvár.*

Regard (affection), احترام *ihtirám* (*k.*); التفات *iltifát* (*k.*); (look), نظر *nazar* (*k.*). With — to, در باب *dar báb.* —less, غافل *gháfil.*

Regency, حکومت *hukúmat.*

Regent, نايب السلطنت *náib us Sultanat.*

Regiment, فوج *fauj.*

Region, اقليم *iḳlím ;* مرز *marz.*

Register, *n.*, دفتر *daftar;* سجل *sijil, pl.* سجول *sujúl ;* جريده *jarídah, v.;* to — a letter, سفارش كردن *sefáresh k.*

Regret, غم *gham (kh.);* افسوس *afsús (kh.) ;* حسرت *hasrat ;* تحسر *tahassur ;* فكنت *fuknat.*

Regretting, متأسف *muta'assif (h.).*

Regular, مستمرى *mustamirrí.*

Regularity, نظام *nizám (d.).*

Regulating, مدبر *madabbir (k.) ;* انتظام *intizám (n.).*

Regulation, آئين *á-ín ;* قاعده *ḳá'ideh ;* دستور العمل *dastúr ul 'amal.*

Rehearsal, تكرار *takrár (k.).*

Reign, *n.*, پادشاهى *pád-sháhí (k.);* حكمرانى *hukmrání (k.).* (time), جاوس *julús.*

Reinforcements, امداد *imdád (d.).*

Reins, عنان *'inán ;* جلو *jilau (ksh.).*

Reiteration, تاكيد *taakíd (n.).*

Rejection, رد *radd (k.).*

Rejoice, شاد شدن *shád sh ;* تهليل كردن *tahlíl k ; pr. p.,* مبهج *mubhij (n.) ;* منبسط *mumbasit.* — at another's misfortunes, شماتت *shamátat (k.).* — at good news, ابشار *ibshár (n.).*

Rejoiced (with good news), مبشر *mubashshar (h.).*

Rejoin, باز آمدن *báz ámadan.*

Rejoinder, رد جواب *radd i javáb.*

Relapse, نكس *nuks (k.).*

Relate (a story), آوردن *ávardan.*

Related, منسوب *mansúb ;* نسبتى *nisbatí.*

Relation (story), حكايت *hikáyat ;* (reference), نسبة *nisbat ;* (relative), رشته دار *rishtah-dár ;* قريب *ḳaríb.*

Relations (kindred), خويشان *khíshán ;* اقارب *aḳárib ;* قرباء *ḳurabá.*

Relationship, قربى *ḳurbá ;* قرابت *ḳarábat ;* خويشى *khíshí ;* مقربت *muḳrabat.*

Relator, محدث *muhaddis.*

Release, *n.*, خلاص *khilás* (*d.*); *v.*, رهانـدن *rahándan*; رهـا کردن *rahá k*; *pa. p.*, مستخلص *mustakhlas.*

Relenting, رحم *rahm* (*k.*).

Reliable, معتمد *mu'tamad.*

Reliance, وثوق *vasúk*; اعـتـمـاد *i'timád*; اتکا *ittiká.*

Relied (upon), معول *mu'avval.*

Relief, عون *'aun.*

Relieve, فارغ کردن *fárigh k.*

Religion, ديـن *dín*, *pl.* اديـان *adyán*; مذهب *muzhab*; ملت *millat*, *pl.*, مـلل *milal*; کيش *kish.* Of the same —, همکيش *ham-kish.* Promoter of —, دين پرور *dín-parvar.* Belonging to —, دينی *díní.*

Religious, خـدا مشرب *khudá mashrab*; دين دار *din-dár.* A — life, زهادت *zahádat.*

Relinquishing, ترك *tark* (*k.*).

Relinquishment, فـرو گـذاشت *farú-guzásht.*

Relish, مـزه *mazah*; *pr. p.*, مـتـلـذذ *mutalazziz*; مـزه دار *mazah-dár.*

Reluctance, ابا *ibá.*

Reluctant, ابی *abí.*

Relying upon, متکی *muttakí.*

Remain, ماندن *mándan.* To — fixed in the memory, ياد بودن *yád búdan.*

Remainder, مـاباقی *mábákí*; ما بقی *má baki*; باقی *báki*; بقيه *bakiyeh.*

Remains (of victuals), نيم خورد *ním-khurd*; الــش *alush*; الوش *alúsh.*

Remand, موقف *muvakkaf* (*n.*).

Remark, نظر کردن *nazar k.*

Remarkable, غريب *gharíb.*

Remedy, چاره *chárah*; عـلاج *'iláj*; درمان *darmán.* Applying to a —, مـداوات *mudávát* (*n.*); معالج *mu'álij* (*n.*).

Remember, يـاد داشـتـن *yád-dáshtan.*

Remembrance, يـاد آوری *yád ávárí*; يـاد کاری *yád-gárí*; ذکر *zikr.*

Remind, ياد دادن *yád-d.*

Remission, معافی *mu'áfí.*

Remissness, مواهنت *muváhanat*; تراخی *tarákhí.*

Remit (sin, etc.), آمـرزيـدن *ámurzídan.*

Remittance, ارسال *irsál* (*n.*).

Remnants, بقيتی *bakiyatí.*

Remonstrance, مواخذة *muvákhazat n.*; معارضه *mu'árezeh* (*k.*).

Remorse, ارمان *armán*; تاسف *taassuf.*

Remote, دور *dúr*; مقصى *muḳsá.* —ness, دوری *dúrí.*

Removal (from office), عزل *'azl* (*k.*); خلع *khal'* (*k.*).

Removing (to a distance), تبعيد *tab'íd*; ابعاد *ib'áb.*

Remuneration, اجرت *ujrat.*

Remunerative, مفيد *mufíd.*

Rend, دريدن *darídan.*

Render, پس دادن *pas d.*

Rendezvous, ميعاد *mí'ád.* — for troops, عرض گاه *'arzgáh.*

Renegade, مرتد *murtadd.*

Renewal, تجديد *tajdíd* (*k.*).

Renewing, مجدد *mujaddid* (*n.*).

Rennet, مايهٔ شير *máyah i shír*; شير مايه *shír-máyah*; پنير مايه *panír-máyah.*

Renounce, انكار كردن *inkár k.*

Renown, نيك نامی *ník námí.*

Renowned (person), مشهور *mash-húr*, *pl.*, مشاهير *mashá-hír.*

Rent (fissure), چاك *chák.* — (hire), كرايه *kiráyah*; جيره *jíreh*; اجاره *ijáreh* (*d.*). — free, لا خراج *lá kharáj.* — roll, هست و بود *hast u búd.*

Renunciation of one's kindred, قطع (رحيم) *kat' (i rahím).*

Repairing, مرمت *marammat* (*k.*); تعمير *ta'mír* (*k.*); رتق *ratḳ* (*n.*).

Reparation, تدارك *tadáruk.*

Repairs, اصلاح *isláh.*

Repartee, لطيفه *latífeh.*

Repeal, نسخ *naskh* (*k.*).

Repeat, باز گفتن *báz gf.*; *pa. p.*, مكرر *mukarrar* (*k.*).

Repeatedly, مكرراً *mukarraran.*

Repelling, نافي *náfí* (*k.*); رادع *rádi'*; استرداد *istirdád* (*n.*).

Repentance, توبه *taubeh* (*k.*); انابت *inábat*; پشيمانی *pashímání* (*k.*); ندامت *nadámat* (*ksh.*).

Repenting, تائب *ta'ib.*

Repetition, اعادة *i'ádat.*

Replete, مملو *mamlú.*

Repletion, امتلآء *imtilá.*

Reply, جواب *javáb* (*d.*); *v.*, باز گفتن *báz gf.*

Report, آوازه *ávázah ;* شهرة *shuhrat*, or *shuhrah (d.).*

Reporter, ناقل *nákil.* Government —, روز نامه نویس *rúznámah navís ;* وقایع نویس *vakáʻi navís;* وقایع نگار *vakáʻi nigár.*

Repose, *n.*, راحت *ráhat ;* آرام *árám.* Enjoying —, مطمئن *mutmain ; v.*, آرامیدن *árámidan ;* آسودن *ásúdan.*

Reprehended, ملوم *malúm (s.)* ; معاتب *muʻáteb (k.).*

Reprehensible, مقصر *mukassar.*

Represent, *v.*, اظهار کردن *izhár k. ; pa. p.*, معروض *maʻrúz.* Necessary to be —, واجب العرض *vájib ul ʻarz.*

Representation, گذارش *guzárish.* To make a —, غرض کردن *ʻarz k.*

Reprieve, مهلت *muhlat (d.).*

Reprimand, تعذیر *taʻzír (d.).*

Reprisal, قصاص *kisás.*

Reproach, *n.*, دشنام *dushnám ;* عتاب *ʻitáb (d.)* ; طعن *taʻn ;* ملام *malám ;* ملامت *malámat (k.)* ; *v.*, نکوهیدن *nikúhídan ; pr. p.*, تعتب *taʻattub ;* تشنیع *tashníʻ;* نکوهش *nikúhish.*

Reprobate, مردود *mardúd.*

Reproof, سر زنش *sar-zanish.*

Reprover, لایم *láim.*

Reptile, حشرة *hashrat, pl.* حشرات *hasharát ;* هوام *havámm.* Noxious —, هوام ضرر رسان *havámm i zararrasán.*

Republic, جمهور *jamhúr.*

Repudiation, تطلیق *tatlík (k.).*

Repugnance, نفرت *nifrat.*

Repugnant, مخالف *mukhálif.*

Repulsed, منفی *manfí ;* مردود *mardúd ;* مندفع *mundafíʻ.*

Repulsion, رد *radd (k.)* ; دفع *dafʻ (k.)* ; مدافعت *mudáfaʻat.*

Repulsive, زشت *zisht.*

Reputable, محترم *muhtaram.*

Reputation, آبرو *ábrú ;* نیک نامی *ník-namí ;* ناموس *námús ;* حرمة *hurmat.*

Repute (of good), نکو نام *nikúnám.*

Request, در خواست *dar-khást ; n.*, خواهش *kháhish ; v.*, در خواستن *dar-khástan.*

Require, لازم داشتن *lázim dsh*; خـواسـتـن *khástan*; *pa. p.*, مطلوب *matlúb*; مقتضی *muḳtazá*. Not —, نا خواست *ná khást*; *pr. p.*, مستلزم *mustalzim*; مقتضی *muḳtazí*.

Requisite, درکار *dar-kár*; طلبی *talabí*, *in pl.*, لوازم *lavázim*.

Requisitions, مبتـغـیات *mubtaghayát*.

Requital, مجازات *mujázát* (*k.*).

Rescue, رها *rihá* (*d.*).

Research (deep), توغل *tavaghghul*; غور رسی *ghaur-rasí*.

Resemblance, مشاکلت *mushákalat*; تمـثـال *timsál*; تشبیه *teshbíh*, *pl.* تشابه *tashábih*.

Resemble, مانستن *mánistan*; *pr. p.*, همانند *ham-mánand*; مـشـاکل *mushákil*; مـتـشـابـه *mutashábih*.

Resentment, خشم *khishm* (*n.*).

Reserve, برودت *barúdat*.

Reserved, برود *barúd* (*h.*).

Reservoir, حوض *hauz*.

Reside, ساکن بودن *sákin b.*

Residence, تمکن *tamakkun*; بود باش *búd-básh*; سکونت *sukúnat*. A place of —, مرز بوم *marz-búm*.

Resident (political), بـالـیـوس *báliyús*.

Residue, بقیه *baḳiyyeh*.

Resignation (official), رخصت *rukhsat* (*qr.*); (of mind), تسلیم *taslím*.

Resistance, مقاومت *muḳávamat* (*k.*); مخـالـفـت *mukhálafat* (*n.*).

Resolute, مستمر *mustamirr*.

Resolutions, تقالیب *taḳálíb*.

Resolve, *n.*, عـزم *'azm*; *pr. p.*, جـازم *jázim*; تـصـمـیـم *tasmím* (*k.*).

Resort, مأب *ma'áb*.

Resource, چاره *ch※reh*.

Respect, احـتـرام *ihtirám* (*k.*); تکریم *takrím* (*n.*); توقر *tuvaḳḳur*; *pr. p.*, اعـــزاز *i'záz*; *pa. p.*, معتبر *mu'tabar*. Not —, بی اعتبار *bí-i'tebár*.

Respectful, متواضع *mutavází'*.

Respecting, در باره *dar báreh*.

Respiration, تنفس *tanaffus*.

Respite, اهمال *ihmál* (*k.*).

Resplendent, رخشان *rakhshán*.

Respond, اجابت کردن *ijábat k.*

Responsible for, ضامن *zámin* (*h.*).

Responsibility, التزام *iltizám*.

Rest, *v.*, آسائیدن *ásá'ídan*; آرامیدن *árámídan*; *n.*, (repose), آسایش *ásáyish*; راحت *ráhat*; (remainder), باقی *báḳí*.

Resting-place, آرامگاه *árám-gáh*; تکیه گاه *takyeh-gáh*.

Restitution, وا پس *vá-pas*; استرداد *istirdád* (*k.*).

Restive, سرکش *sar kesh*.

Restless, بیکل *bi-kal*; بیقرار *bí-ḳarár*.

Restoration, اصلاح *isláh* (*k.*); (building), تعمیر *tá'mír* (*k.*).

Restore, وا دادن *vá d.*

Restrain, *v.*, باز داشتن *báz dsh*; *pa. p.*, محتبس *muhtabis*; *pr. p.*, احتباس *ihtibás*. — one's passion, اعتکاف *i'tikáf* (*n.*).

Restraint, امتناع *imtiná'*; قید *ḳaid*.

Restriction, حصر *hasr* (*k.*).

Restricted (to a certain time), موقت *muvaḳḳat*.

Result, نتیجه *natíjah*, *pl* نتائج *natáij*; انجام *anjám*.

Resume, باز یافتن *báz yáftan*.

Resurrection, رستخیز *rasta-khíz*; نشور *nushúr*; (the day of), قیامت (روز *rúz-i-*) *ḳiyámat*.

Resuscitation, احیا *ihyá* (*k.*).

Retail, خرده *khurdah*; (فروختن *farúkhtan*).

Retain, نگاه داشتن *nigáh dsh.*

Retaliation, قصاص *ḳisás* (*k.*); پاداش *pádásh* (*d.*).

Retention, حبس *habs*.

Retentive, حافظ *háfiz*.

Retinue, کوکبه *kaukabeh*; اتباع *atbá'*; خدم و حشم *khadam o hasham*.

Retire, *v.*, باز گشتن *báz gashtan*. Permission to —, رخصت *rukhsat*; *pa. p.*, محتجب *muhtajib*; *pr. p.*, مدبر *mudbir*.

Retirement, عزلت *'uzlat*; خلوت *khalvat*; (religious), گوشه نشین *gúshah-nishín*.

Retraction (of words), رد سخون *radd-i-sukhún* (*k.*).

Retreat, قهقری *ḳahḳará* (*k.*); *v.*, پشت دادن *pusht d.*

Retribution, سزا *sazá*; مکافات *mukáfát*.

Retrospection, باز پس *báz-pas*.

Return, *n.*, بازگشت *bázgasht*; مراجعت *murája'at* (*k.*); رجاع

rija' (*n.*); رجوع *rujú'* (*k*). The place of —, مرجع *marji'*; *v.*, باز کشتن *báz gashtan*; برکشتن *bar-gashtan*; *pr. p.*, معاودت *mu'ávadat*; اعادة *i'ádat*; *pa. p.*, مسترد *mustaradd*.

Reveal (a secret), فاش کردن *fásh k.*; (a religion), الهام کردن *ilhám k.*; *pa. p.*, مکشوف *makshúf*; *pr. p.*, (a secret), پرده بر انداز *pardah-bar andáz*.

Revealer, معلن *mu'lin*; کشاف *kashsháf*.

Revel, ولیمه *valímah*.

Revelation, تنزیل *tanzil*; وحی *vahí*.

Revelry, عیش و عشرت *'ísh o 'ishrat*.

Revenge, انتقام *intiḳám* (*k.*); قصاص *ḳisás* (*gr.*).

Revenue, مالیات *máliyát*; مالگذاری *málguzárí*.

Reverence, تعظیم *ta'zím* (*k.*); پا بوسی *pá búsí*.

Reverie, خیال *khayál*.

Reverse, عکس *'aks*.

Review (troops), سان دادن *sán-d.*

Reviling, سب *sabb* (*k.*).

Revision, تصحیح *tas-híh* (*k.*).

Revive, زنده کشتن *zindah gashtan*; *pr. p.*, احیا *ihyá* (*k.*); منشیر *munshír*.

Revocation, رد *radd*.

Revolt, بغی *baghí* (*k.*); یاغیگری *yághí garí* (*k.*).

Revolution, گردش *gardish*; دور *daur*; دوره *daurah*. — of the heavens, دور چرخ *daur i chirkh*; (change), انقلاب *inḳiláb*; اختلال *ikhtilál*.

Revolving, دایر *dáir*; دوار *davvár* (*n.*).

Reward, اجر *ajr*; مزد *muzd*; اجرت *ujrat*.

Rhetoric, نطق *nutḳ*. —al, —ian, منطقی *mantiḳí*.

Rheum, زکام *zukkám*.

Rheumatism, باد *bád*.

Rhinoceros, کرکدن *karkaddan*.

Rhubarb, ریوند *rívand*. China —, ریوند چینی *rívand i chíní*.

Rhyme, قافیه *ḳáfiyeh*.

Rhythm, سجع *saj'*.

Rhythmical, مسجع *musajja'*.

Rib, دنده *dandah*.

Riband, قور *ḳaur*.

Rice, برنج birínj. — seller, رزاز razzáz.

Rich, دولتمند daulat-mand; غنی ghaníy; توانگر taván-gar; با نوا bá-navá. — men, اغنیآء aghniyá.

Riches, مال و اموال mál u am-vál; غناء ghaná'; توانگری tavángarí; دول daval. Be-longing to —, مالی málíy.

Rickety, لك lak.

Riddle, چیستان chístán; رمز ramz.

Ride, v., سوار شدن suvár sh., سواره رفتن suváreh r.

Rider, سوار suvár; راکب rákib.

Ridge, ثغر sughr, pl. ثغور sughúr.

Ridicule, خه khah; ریشخند rísh-khand (k.); تسخر tas-khar (n.).

Ridiculing, مستهزی mustahzí (n.).

Ridiculous, مضحك muzhik; مسخره maskhareh (s.).

Riding side by side, همعنان ham-'inán. — coat, بارانی báráni.

Rifle, تفنك tufang. Long —, شمخال shamkhál.

Right (true), درست durust; صائب sáib; سدید sadíd; حق hakk, pl. حقوق hukúk. — or wrong, nolens volens, خواه مخواه kháh makháh; حق نا حق hakk ná hakk; (side), راست rást; میمنه maimanah; یمین yamín. To the — hand, یمیناً yamí-nan.

Righteous, صالح sálih. — men, صلحاء sulahá. — ness, صواب saváb.

Rigid, جامد jámid. —ity, سختی sakhtí.

Rigour, شدت shiddat.

Rim, لب lab.

Rind, پوست púst. — of a poppy, یلغز yalghaz.

Ring, حلقه halkah. Finger —, انگشتری angushtarí. — dove, قمری kumríy; فاخته fákhtah.

Ringlet, زلف zulf; طره tur-rah; گیسو gísú; کلاله kulálah.

Ringworm, بهق bahak.

Riot, غوغا ghaughá.

Rioter, اوباش *aubásh.*

Rip up, بر دریدن *bar darídan.*

Ripe, رسیده *rasídah.*

Ripen, پختن *pukhtan.*

Ripeness, رسیدگی *rasídagí.*

Rise, بر شدن *bar shudan;* بر خاستن *bar khástan;* خاستن *khástan;* خیزیدن *khízídan.*

Rising (of the sun, &c.), طلوع *tulú'.*

Risk, *n.*, خطر *khatar; v.*, (one's life), سر باختن *sar-bákhtan; pr. p.*, (one's life), جانباز *ján-báz.*

Rissole, کوفته *kúftah.*

Rite, طریقت *taríkat.*

Rival, حریف *haríf, in pl.* اغیار *aghyár.*

Rivalry, رقابت *rakábat.*

River, رود *rúd;* نهر *nahr.* Large —, دریا *daryá.* Small —, جوی اب *júy áb;* جوی *júy.* Bed of a —, رود بار *rúd-bár;* رود خانه *rúd kháneh.*

Rivet, پرچین *parchín (k.).*

Rivulet, دریاچه *daryácheh.*

Road, راه *ráh;* ره *rah;* سمت *samt;* طریق *taríḳ, pl.* طرق *turuḳ;* سبیل *sabíl;* مسلك *maslik.* High —, ره کذر *rah guzar;* شاهراه *sháh-ráh;* سر راه *sar i ráh.* Rugged —, شرفنج *sharfanj.* — guide, راه بر *ráh-bar;* بلد *balad.* — watch, کذر بان *guzar-bán.*

Roan (horse), قزل *ḳizil.*

Roar, غریدن *ghurídan.*

Roaring, غرنده *gharendah.*

Roast, کباب *kabáb (k.).*

Rob, دزدیدن *duzdídan.*

Robber, دزد *duzd.* Highway —, ره زن *rah-zan;* سالوك *sálúk;* صعلوك *sa'lúk;* حرامی *harámíy;* قزاق *ḳazzáḳ;* قاطع الطریق *ḳáti' ut taríḳ.* —s' den, یتیم خانه *yatím khánah.*

Robbery, دزدی *duzdí;* رهزنی *rahzaní.*

Robe, کسوت *kisvat.*

Robust, تنومند *tanúmand;* یلوك *yalúk.* — ness, تنومندی *tanúmandí.*

Rock, صخره *sakhrah.*

Rocket, تیر هوا *tír-i-havá.*

Rocky, سنکی *sangí.*

Rod, چوب *chúb.*

Roe (deer), آهو *áhú;* (of fish), تخم ماهی *tukhm-i-máhí.*

Rogue, گربه مسکین *gurbah-i-miskín*; جو ولاغي *jo valághí*.

Roll, طومار *túmár*; لوله *lúlah*. Rent —, طومار جمع *tumár i jama'*.

Rolling, غلطان *ghaltán* (*k.*). — pin, وردانه *vardánah*.

Romance, افسانه *afsánah*.

Romp, بازی *bází* (*k.*).

Roof, بام *bám*; (ceiling), سقف *saḳf*. High pitched —, خر پشته *khar-pushtah*. Arched —, طارم *táram*.

Rook, کلاغ *kallágh*.

Room, اطاق *otáḳ*. — on roof, بالا خانه *bálá kháneh*; Pillared —, طالار *tálár*.

Root, بیخ *bíkh*; اصل *asl*; *pl.* اصول *usúl*; بن *bun*. — and branch, سر و شاخ *sar u shákh*; سر و بن *sar u bun*.

Rope, رسن *rasan*; ریسمان *rísmán*; طناب *tanáb*, or تنف *tenef*; حبل *habl*. — for strangling, خناق *khináḳ*. — for binding the load upon a beast of burden, شریط *sharít*. — with which the fore feet of a horse are tied, پا بند *pá-band*. — dancer, دار بار *dár-bár*. — maker, رسن گر *rasan-gar*; حبال *habbál*.

Rosary, سبحه *subhah*; تسبیح *tasbíh*.

Rose, گل *gul*; ورد *vard*. Wild white —, نسرین *nisrín*. — bud, همسود *hamsúd*. — garden, گلستان *gulistán*; گلشن *gulshan*. — tree, گلبن *gulbun*. — water, گلاب *guláb*. Conserve of —, گل قند *gul-ḳand*; گل شکر *gul-shakar*.

Rosin, سقز *saḳíz*.

Rosy, وردی *vardí*. — cheeked, گل رخ *gul-rukh*.

Rot, پوسیدن *púsídan*.

Rotten, پوسیده *púsídáh*.

Rouge, غازه *gházah*.

Rough, درشت *durusht*; خشن *khushn*; وعر *va'r*; نا تراشیده *ná-taráshídah*.

Round, گرد *gird*; مدور *mudavver*; مستدیر *mustadír*. — about, گرداگرد *gird á gird*.

Rouse, *v. t.*, بیدار کردن *bídár k.*; *pr. p.*, بعث *ba's* (*n.*).

Rout, انهزام *inhizám* (*k.*); هزیمت *hazímat* (*n.*).

Row (rank), *n.*, قطار *ḳitár*; صف *saff*; سطر *satr*; *v.*, (a boat), پارو کشیدن *párú ksh.*

Royal, شاهانه *sháhánah*; سلطانی *sultání*; شاهوار *sháh-vár*; ملکی *malikí*; ملوکانه *mulúkánah*; خسروی *khusraví*. — edict, طمغا or طمغه *tamghá*. — entertainment, شیلان *shílán*. — mandate, یاسا *yásá*; یرلیغ *yarlígh*.

Royalty, شهی *shahí*; شاهی *sháhí*.

Rub, مالیدن *málídan*; فرسودن *farsúdan*.

Rubbed out, سوده *súdah*.

Rubbing, مالش *málish* (*k.*).

Rubbish, خاشاك *kháshák*; خلاشه *khaláshah*; خس و خاشاك *khas u kháshák*; خار و خس *khár u khas*; حطام *hutám*.

Ruby, لعل *la'l*; یاقوت *yaḳút*.

Rudder, دنبال *dumbál*.

Rude, گستاخ *gustákh*; بیعنایت *bi'ináyat*; گاو زور *gáu-zúr*; نا ملایم *ná-muláyim*; بی ادب *bí-adab*. —ness, نا مردمی *ná-mardumí*; گستاخی *gustákhí*.

Rue (herb), سداب *sudáb*.

Rueful, غمگین *ghamgín*.

Ruffian, اوباش *aubásh*.

Rug, فرش *farsh*.

Rugged, درشت *durusht*.

Ruin, خرابی *kharábí*; پایمال *pái-mál*; پامال *pámál*; دمار *damár*.

Ruined, خراب *kharáb* (*k.*); تباه *tabáh*; مخروب *makhrúb*. برباد *bar bád*.

Ruining, اضاعت *izá'at* (*k.*).

Rule (dominion), حکم رانی *hukm-rání* (*k.*); (custom), قاعده *ḳá'idah*, *pl.* قواعد *ḳavá'id*; رسم *rasm*; طریقه *taríḳah*; ضابطه *zábitah*. By one —, یکزده *yak-zadah*.

Ruler (for lines), مسطر *mastar* (*k.*); خط کش *khatt-kash*; (sovereign), فرمان ده *farmán-dih*; فرمان روا *farmán-ravá*.

Rules (usages), رسمیات *rasmíyát*; سنن *sunan*.

Rumination, نشخوار *nish-khár* (*k.*).

Rumours, اراجیف *arájíf*; گفتگو *guftogú*.

Rump, سرین *surín*.

Run, دویدن *davídan ;* تاختن *tákhtan.* — away (said of horses), رم کردن *ram k.*

Runaway, *n.*, فراری *farárí.*

Runner, دونده *davendah.*

Running, دو *dav.* — away (as a slave), اباق *ibáḳ.* — over, لبریز *labríz.* — fast, دوان *daván.*

Rupee, روپیه *rúpíyah.*

Rupture, ruptured, دبه *dabah ;* (hernia), فتق *fatḳ.*

Rural, روستائی *rustá-í.*

Ruse, حیلة *hílat ;* مکیده *makídah.*

Rush (reed), پیزر *pízar ;* (spring), هجوم *hujúm* (*ḳ.*). — mat, بوریا *búriyá.*

Rust, زنك *zang.*

Rustic, روستا زاده *rústá zádah.*

Rusty, زنك گرفته *zang girifteh.*

Rye, گندم سیه *gandum i siyah.*

S.

Sabbath, سبت *sabt.*

Sable, سمور *sammúr.*

Sabre, شمشیر *shamshír.*

Sack, *n.*, چوال *chuval ;* جوال *juvál.* —cloth, پلاس *palás.* — making, جوال دوزی *juvál-dúzí ; v.*, (a city), غارت کردن *ghárat k.*

Sacred, حرم *haram ;* مقدس *muḳaddas.* —ness, قدس *ḳuds.* — sites, معابد *ma'ábid.*

Sacrifice, *n.*, قربان *ḳurbán* (*ḳ.*); فدا *fidá* (*ḳ.*) ; ذبح *zabh* (*n.*) ; *v.*, بسمل کردن *bismil kerdan ; pa. p.*, ذبیح *zabíh ; pr. p.*, نحر *nahr.*

Sacrificer, ذابح *zábih.*

Sacrilegious, پلیدانه *palídánah.*

Sad, دلتنك *dil-tang* (*s.*) ; دل گیر *dil-gír* (*s.*) ; غمگین *ghamgín.*

Saddle, زین *zín* (*ḳ.*) ; سرج *sarj.* —bags, خرجین *khurjín.* —cloth, غاشیه *gháshiyeh ;* زین پوش *zín-púsh ;* برزغه *barazghah.* — straps, فتراك *fitrák.*

Saddled, مسرج *musarraj.*

Saddler, زین ساز *zín-sáz ;* زین گر *zín-gár.*

Sadness, ملال *malál ;* ملالت *malálat ;* غم *gham.*

Safe, امین *amín ;* ایمن *aíman ;* سالم *sálim.*

Safer, safest, اسلم *aslam.*

Safety, سلامت *salámat*; امان *amán.*

Saffron, زعفران *za'farán*; نجوان *najván.* Wild —, لاژه *lázhah.* — coloured, مزعفر *muza'far.*

Sagacious, نكته دان *nuktah-dán*; دانا *dáná*

Sagacity, فراست *firásat*; كيس *kais*; فطنت *fitnat*; زيركى *zírakí.*

Sagapenna (medicinal herb), سكبينج *sakbínaj.*

Sage (herb), سالبيه *sálbiyah*; (man), حكيم *hakim.*

Sago, سابو دانه *sábú-dánah.*

Sail, بادبان *bád-bán*; شراع *shirá'* (*ksh. z.*); جل *jall*, or *jull.*

Sailor, ملاح *malláh.*

Saint, ولى *valí*; پير *pír.*

Sake of, از براى *az berái.* For the —, بواسطه *beváseteh*; من اجل *min ajl*; پاسخاطر *pás-khátir.*

Salamander, سمندر *samandar.*

Sal-ammoniac, نشادر *mushádir*; نوشادر *núshádir.*

Salary, مواجب *mavájib*; ساليانه *sáliyánah*; ادرار *idrár*; جامقيه *jámikíyeh*; جامكى *jámagí.*

Sale, فروخت *farúkht*; فروش *farúsh*; بيع *bai'.* — by auction, مزاد *muzád.*

Salep (medicinal root), ثعلب مصرى *sa'leb i misrí.*

Saline, نمكزار *namakzár.*

Saliva, خيو *khíyú*; آب دهن *áb i dahan.*

Sallying forth, خروج *khurúj* (*k.*).

Salmon, آزاد ماهى *ázád máhí.*

Salt, نمك *namak*; (brackish), شور *shúr.* —cellar, نمكدان *namak-dán.* —marsh, شورستان *shúristán.* —pan, نمكزار *namak-zár.* —works, خالرى *khálari.*

Salted, مالح *málih*; نمكين *namakín.*

Saltpetre, شوره *shúrah.*

Salubrious, صحت بخش *sihhat bakhsh.*

Salubrity, عافيت *'áfiyat.*

Salutary, سازكار *sáz-kár.*

Salutation, سلام *salám* (*k.*); تحية *tahíyat* (*k.*), *pl.* تحيات *tahíyát* (*k.*).

Salvage (seam), درز *darz.*

Salvation, سلامت *salámat.*

Salve, ضماد *zamád.*

Salver, سینی *síní.*

Same, همین *hamín ;* همان *hamán ;* مثل *misl.*

Sample, نمونه *namúnah.*

Sanctified, مقدس *muḳaddas* (*k.*).

Sanctifying, تقدیس *taḳdís* (*n.*).

Sanction, اذن *izn* (*d.*).

Sanctity, قدس *ḳuds.*

Sanctuary (holy place), حریم *harím.* Place of —, بست *bust.*

Sand, ریك *ríg ;* رمل *raml.* — grouse, قطا *ḳatá.*

Sandal, نعلین *na'lín.* —wood, سندل *sandal ;* صندل *sandal ;* چندن *chandan.*

Sanguinary, خونخوار *khún-khár.*

Sanguine, متوقع *mutavaḳḳi'.*

Sap, شیره *shírah.*

Saphena vein, صافن *sáfin.*

Sapper, بیلدار *bíldár.*

Sapphire, یاقوت کبود *yáḳút i kabúd.*

Sarcasm, طنز *tanz ;* هجو *hajv.*

Sarcastic, مستهزی *mustahzí.*

Sarcophagus, تابوت *tábút.*

Satan, شیطان *shaitán.*

Satiated, سیر *sír* (*sh*).

Satiety, شبع *shab'* ; سیری *sírí.*

Satin, اطلس *atlas.*

Satire, هجو *hajv* (*k.*).

Satirist, هاجی *hájí.*

Satisfaction, رضا مندی *rizá mandí.* Mutual —, تراضی *tarází.*

Satisfied, راضی *rází* (*k.*) ; موفی *muvaffá* (*n.*). Soon —, سبك سیر *sabuk-sír.*

Satisfying the heart, دل نشین *dil-nishín.*

Saturation, شبع *shab'.*

Saturday, شنبه *shambeh.*

Saturn, کیوان *kaiván ;* زحل *zuhal.*

Sauce, چاشنه *cháshnah.*

Saucepan, دیك *dig.*

Saucer, نالبکی *nálbegí.*

Saucy, گستاخ *gustákh.*

Savage, جنگلی *jangalí.*

Save, *v.*, نجات دادن *naját d.* ; خلاص کردن *khilás k.*

Saviour, نجات دهنده *niját dihandeh.*

Savour, خوش ذائقه *khush-záiḳah.*

Saw, ارّه *arrah* (*ksh.*); منشار *minshár*; یوسه *yúsah.* — dust, رندش *randish.*

Saxifrage, قلت *ḳalt.*

Say, گفتن *guftan.*

Saying, قال *ḳál*; قول *ḳaul.*

Scab, گر *gar.*

Scabbard, غلاف *ghiláf.*

Scabby, گرگین *gargín.*

Scaffold, دار *dár.*

Scalding, سوزان *súzán.*

Scale, درجه *darajeh.* Fish-—, پولك *púlak.* In ascending —, متصاعد *mutasá'id.*

Scales (weighing), ترازو *tarázú*; (dross), نخجد *nakhjad*; خراشه *khuráshah.*

Scalp, شوات *shavát.*

Scalpel, مشرط *mishrat.*

Scandalize, بهتان *buhtán.*

Scandalous, زبون *zabún.*

Scanning (verse), تقطیع *taḳtí'* (*k.*).

Scar, داغ *dágh.*

Scarce, کم *kam.*

Scarcely, با دقت *bá diḳḳat.*

Scarcity, گرانی *garání*; قلة *ḳillat.*

Scare-crow, نطار *nuttár.*

Scared, نفار *naffár.* To be —, شمیدن *shamídan*; رمیدن *ramídan.*

Scarlet, قرمز *ḳirmiz.*

Scarred, داغ دار *dágh-dár.*

Scatter, فشاندن *fishándan*; افشاندن *afshándan*; پراکندن *parágandan*; *pa. p.*, ریخته *ríkhtah.*

Scavenger, کناس *kannás.*

Scene, مجلس *majlis.*

Scent, بو *bú.*

Scented, بودار *bú-dár.*

Sceptic, شکاك *shakák.* —ism, شبهه *shubheh.*

Scheme, اختراع *ikhtirá'.*

Schism, بدعت *bid'at.*

Schismatics, خوارج *khavárij.*

Scholar, تلمیذ *talmíz*, *pl.* تلامیذ *talámíz*; تلامذه *talámizah.*

School, مکتب *maktab*; کتاب *kuttáb.* —fellow, همسبق *ham-sabaḳ*; —master, استاد *ustád.*

Sciatica, عرق النسا *'irḳ un nísá.*

Science, علم *'ilm*, *pl.* علوم *'ulúm*; فن *fann*, *pl.* فنون *funún*; دانش *dánish.*

Scientific, علمی *'ilmíy.*

Scimitar, شمشیر *shamshír*.

Scissors, قیچی *ḳaichí*; مقراض *miḳráz*.

Scoff, استهزا *istihzá* (*k.*).

Scold, طعن زدن *ta'an z.*

Score (mark). بت *bat.*

Scorn, نکوهش *nikúhish.* —ful مهین *muhín* (*k.*).

Scorpion, عقرب *'aḳrab.*

Scoundrel, پاجی *pájí.*

Scourge, تازیانه *táziyánah* (*z.*).

Scout, جاسوس *jásús.*

Scrap, پرزه *purzah*; خورده *khurdah.*

Scrape, ستردن *suturdan.*

Scratch, خراشیدن *kharáshídan*; خاریدن *khárídan.*

Scream, داد و فریاد کردن *dád o faryád k.*

Screen, پرده *pardah.* — of split bamboos, چق *chiḳ.*

Screw, پیچ *pích* (*k.*). —bolt, نرماده *narmádah.*

Scribe, کاتب *kátib*; قلمزن *ḳalam-zan.*

Scriptures, کتب مقدس *kutub i muḳaddas.*

Scrofula, خنازیر *khanázír.*

Scrotum, فوطه *fútah.*

Scruple, شك *shakk* (*dsh.*). —ous وسواسی *vasvásí.*

Scrutinizing, اکتناه *iktináh* (*k.*); تدقیق *tadḳíḳ.*

Scrutiny, لحاظ *laház.*

Scuffle, کشمکش *keshmakesh.*

Scull, کله *kallah.*

Sculptor, کالبد کر *kálbad-gar*; نقاش *naḳḳásh.*

Scum, کف *kaf.*

Scurf, سبوسه *sabúsah.*

Scurrility, فحش *fuhsh.*

Scurrilous, بد زبان *bad zabán.*

Scurvy, جرب *jarab.*

Scythe, دهره *dahrah.*

Scythia, خطای *Khatáy.*

Sea, دریا *daryá*; بحر *bahr.* R d —, بحر قلزم *Bahr i Ḳulzum*; Circumambient —, (ocean), بحر محط *Bahr i Muhít.* Ægean —, بحر یونان *Bahr i Yúnán.* Caspian —, بحر خزر *Bahr i Kh :zr.* Mediterranean —, بحر سفید *Bahr i Sufíd.* The salt —, دریای شور *daryái shúr.* — shore, یالود *yálúd*; کنار دریا *kinár i daryá.*

Seal, مهر *muhr* (*k.*); خاتم *khátam.*

Sealed, مختوم *makhtúm* (*k.*); ممهور *mamhúr* (*s.*).

Seal-engraver, مهرکن *muhr-kan.*

Sealing-wax, لاك *lák.*

Seam, دوخت *dúkht.*

Seaman, جاشو *jáshú.*

Search, *n.*, تلاش *talásh* (*k.*); تکوپو *tagupú* (*k.*); تکاپو *takápú*; تجسس *tajassus*; جویا *júyá*; *v.*, پوئیدن *pú-ídan*; جستن *justan.*

Searching, جویاءی *júyái*; جویان *júyán.*

Season, موسم *mausam*; فصل *fasl.* — of scarcity, تنك سال *tang-sál.*

Seat, کرسی *kursí*; مقعد *maḳ'ad*; نشیمن *nashíman.* — of empire, دار السلطنت *dár us saltanat.*

Seceder, معتزل *mu'tazil.*

Secession, اعتزال *i'tizál* (*k.*).

Second, ثانی *sání*; دویم *dúyum*; دوم *duvum*; (of time), دقیقه *daḳiḳah.* The — person, مخاطب *mukhátib.*

Secondly, دیکرانه *dígaránah.*

Secrecy, سریرت *sarírat.*

Secret, سر *sirr*; راز *ráz*; رمز *ramz*; خفیه *khufyah.* In —, در خفیه *dar khufyah.* Keeping a —, پرده پوش *pardah-púsh.*

Secretary, منشی *munshí*; میرزا *mirzá*,

Sect, مذهب *mazhab*, *pl.* مذاهب *mazáhib*; فرقه *firḳah*; امت *ummat*; طائفه *táifah.*

Section, فصل *fasl*, *pl.* فصول *fusúl.*

Secular, دنیوی *dunyaví.*

Secure, مسلم *musallam*; مامون *mámún* (*s.*).

Security (bail), کفیل *kafíl.* Taking —, تکفل *takafful* (*k.*); (safety), امان *amán.*

Sedateness, وقار *vaḳár.*

Sedative, مسکن *musakkin.*

Sediment, ته نشین *tah-nishín*; کسافت *kasáfat*; راسب *rásib.*

Sedition, فتنه *fitnah*; فساد *fasád.*

Seditious, شور انکیز *shúr-angíz*; فتنه انکیز *fitnah-angíz.*

Seduce, فریفتن *faríftan*; *pr. p.*, مضل *muzill* (*n.*).

Seducer (of women), هتاك عرض *hiták i 'irz.*

Seduction, اضلال *izlál.*

Seductive, دلفریب *dilfiríb.*

Sedulous, مقید *muḳayyid.*

See, دیدن *dídan*; نگاه کردن *nigáh k*; *pr. p.*, مشاهد *musháhid.*

Seed, تخم *tukhm* (*k.*); بزر *bizr*; بذر *bazr.* Carraway —, زیرهٔ رومی *zírah i Rúmí.* Cummin —, or aniseed, زیره *zírah.* Mallow —, تودری *túdari.*

Seek, جوئیدن *júídan*; *pr. p.*, پویا *púyá*; پویان *púyán.*

Seeking enjoyment, کام جو *kám-jú.*

Seem, نمودن *namúdan.*

Seeming, ظاهر *záhir.* —ly, ظاهراً *záhiran.*

Segment, حصه *hissah.*

Seize, گرفتن *giriftan*: ستاندن *sitándan*; ربودن *rabúdan*; ربائیدن *rubáidan*; ربانیدن *rubánídan*; در ربودن *dar rabúdan.*

Seized, گرفتار *giriftár* (*k.*).

Seizer, قابض *ḳábiz.*

Seizing, گیر *gír*; منتزع *muntazi'*; اتخاذ *ittikház* (*n.*); اخذ *akhz* (*k.*).

Seldom, کمتر *kamtar.*

Select, بر گزیدن *bar guzídan*; *pa. p.*, چیده *chídah*; مصطفی *mustafá*; *pr. p.*, منتقی *muntaḳí.*

Selection, انتخاب *intikháb* (*k.*).

Self, خود *khud.* — complacency, ابراح *ibráh.* — complacent, خود پسند *khud-pasand.* —conceit, پنداری *pindárí*; خودی *khudí.* —, conceited, خود پرست *khud-parast.* — interested, خود غرض *khud-gharz.* — praise, خود آرا *khud-árá.* — restraint, احتباس *ihtibás.*

Selfish, خود خواه *khud-kháh.*

Sell, فروختن *farúkhtan.*

Seller, فروش *farúsh*; بائع *bá'i.* — of horse-provender, علاف *'alláf.* — of wood, خشاب *khashsháb.*

Semblance, مثال *misál.*

Semen, نطفه *nutfah.*

Semi, نیم *ním.*

Send, فرستادن *firistádan.* — away, روان کردن *raván k.*;

روانه کردن *raváneh k.* — back, واپس فرستادن *vá-pas firistádan.* — into confinement, بند فرمودن *band farmúdan.*

Senior, اکبر *akbar.*

Senna, سنا *saná.*

Sense (feeling), حس *hiss;* حواس *haváss.* The five —s, حواس خمسه *havássi khamsah.* Common —, حس مشترك *hiss i mushtarek.* The external —s, مشاعر *mashá'ir.* — of smell, مشام *mashámm;* شم *shamm.* Belonging to the —s, حسی *hissí.* — (meaning), معنی *ma'ná.*

Senseless, بیخود *bí-khud;* مخدر *mukhaddar.*

Sensible, با هوش *bá húsh;* معقول *ma'kúl.*

Sensitive, محس *muhiss.*

Sensual, نفس پرور *nafas-parvar;* نفسانی *nafsání.*

Sensualist, شهوت پرست *shahvat-parast.*

Sensuality, نفسانیت *nafsániyat;* بوالهوسی *bú'lhavasí.*

Sentence (judicial), فتوی *fatvá;* حکم *hukm (d.).*

Sentiment, پندار *pindár.*

Sentinel, پاسبان *pás-bán;* قراول *ḳeráúl.*

Separate, علیحده *'alá-hiddah;* جدا *jidá (s.).*

Separated, متفرق *mutafarraḳ;* منفصل *munfasil;* مفروق *mafrúḳ.* Being —, انفراق *infiráḳ (k.).*

Separately, جدا جدا *judá-judá;* جداگانه *judáganah;* واحداً *váhidan;* فراداً *furádan.*

Separating, مفارق *mufáriḳ (n.).*

Separation, تفریق *tafríḳ (k.);* فرقت *furḳat;* فراق *firáḳ;* مهاجرت *muhájarat;* مباینت *mubáyanat;* مفارقت *mufáraḳat;* جدائی *judái;* افتراق *iftiráḳ;* انفصال *infisál;* تفرقه *tafriḳah;* تفرد *tafarrud (n.);* تجرید *tajríd.*

Separator, فاصل *fásil.*

Sepulchre, گور *gúr;* مرقد *markad;* مقبره *maḳbarah.*

Sequel, نتیجه *natíjah.*

Sequestration, ضبط *zabt (k.).*

Seraglio, حرم سرا *haram-sará.*

Sergeant, وکیل *vakíl.*

Seriatim, موالیا *muváliyá.*

Series, سلك *silk*; صف *saff*; ترادف *taráduf*; تسلسل *tasalsul*.

Serious, موقر *muvakkar*.

Sermon, خطبه *khutbah*; وعظ *va'z*.

Serpent, مار *már*.

Servant, بنده *bandah*; نوکر *naukar*. Body —, خدمتکار *khidmat-gár*; خدمتگذار *khidmat-guzár*; خادم *khádim*, *pl.* خدام *khuddám*; ملازم *mulázim*. Fellow —, همخدمت *ham-khidmat*. Maid —, داه *dáh*; کنیز *kaníz*. Menial —, شاگرد پیشه *shágird píshah*.

Service, خدمت *khidmat* (*k.*); چاکری *chákarí*; نوکری *naukarí*; ملازمت *mulázamat* (*k.*). Pressed —, سخره *sukhrah*.

Servile, پست *past*.

Servility, دونی *dúní*.

Servitude, بندگی *bandagí*; عبودیت *'ubúdíyet*.

Sesame, سمسم *simsim*.

Sessions, مقامات *mukámát*.

Set, *v.*, گذاشتن *guzáshtan*; گذاردن *guzárdan*. — off on the march, نهضت فرمودن *nahzat f.*

Setting forth clearly, تصریح *tasríh* (*k.*). — at liberty, اعتاق *i'ták* (*d.*).

Settled, معین *mu'ayyin*.

Settlement, بندوبست *band u bast*; انتظام *intizám*. A — by instalment, قسطبندی *kast-bandí*.

Seven, هفت *haft*; سبع *sab'*. — hundred, هفتصد *haftsad*.

Seventh, هفتم *haftum*; سابع *sábi'*.

Seventeen, هفده *hafdah*.

Seventeenth, هفدهم *hafdahum*.

Seventieth, هفتادم *haftádum*.

Seventy, هفتاد *haftád*; سبعین *sab'ín*.

Sever, بریدن *burídan*.

Several times, باری چند *bárí chand*.

Severe, درشت *durusht*; مبرح *mubarrih*; عنیف *'aníf*.

Severity, عنف *'unf*; درشتی *durushtí*.

Sew, دوختن *dúkhtan*; آزدن *ázadan*.

Sewer, آبریز ábríz.

Sewing, خیاطت khiyátat; رفو rafú (k.). — thread, خیطه khaitah.

Sex, جنس jins. The fair —, خوبان khúbán.

Sexual intercourse, مجامعه mujámaʻah.

Shackle, بند band (k.)

Shaddock, بتاوی batávi.

Shade (glass), لاله lálah.

Shadow, سایه sáyah; ظل zill (as ظل الله zill Ullah, the — of God; title given to the Shah).

Shady, سایه دار sáyah dár.

Shagreen, سغری saghrí.

Shake off, تکانیدن takánídan.

Shaken, منفوض manfúz (sh.).

Shaking, جنبان jumbán. — hands, مصافحه musáfahah (k.).

Shallow, پایاب páyáb.

Sham, بهانه baháneh (k.)

Shame, شرم sharm; هنومند hanú-mand; حجلت hijlat; نا داشت ná dásht. —ful things, فواحش fawáhish.

Shameless, بی شرم bí-sharm.

Shape, شکل shakl; پیکر paikar.

Share, نصیبه nasíbah; حصه hissah, pl. حصص hissas; قسمت kismat (k.). The proprietor's share of the produce of the soil, مالکانه málikánah.

Shark, بنبك bambak.

Sharp, تیز tíz (k.); برنده burendah; حاد hádd. —ness, تیزی tízí; حدت hiddat.

Shatter, پاره پاره کردن páreh páreh k.

Shave, v., استردن usturdan; ستردن saturdan.

Shavings, نشارت nushárat.

Shawl, شال shál. Cashmir —, شال ترمه shál i termah. Imitation Cashmir —, شال ترمه نما shál i termah numá. — merchant, سمسار simsár.

She, او ú.

Sheaf, دسته dastah.

Shears, کاز káz; مقراض mikráz (k.).

Sheath, نیام niyám; نیاب niyáb; غلاف ghiláf (k.).

Shed, v., ریختن ríkhtan.

Shedding blood, هدر hadr (k.). — tears, اشکبار ashkbár.

Sheep, گوسفند *gúsfand.* — fold, آغل *ágil.* — skin, (dressed), نری *narí.* —'s trotters, کله پاچه *kallah-páchah.*

Sheet, چادر *chádar ;* ملافه *malá-feh ;* (of paper), ورق *varaḳ.*

Shelf, رفرف *rafraf ;* طاقچه *taḳ-cheh.*

Shell, صدف *sadaf ;* (kowrie), خرمهره *khar-muhrah.*

Shelter, پناه *panáh* (*d.*) ; پوشش *púshish.*

Shepherd, چوبان *chúbán ;* چوپان *chúpán ;* شبان *shabán,* or *shubán.*

Sherbet, شربت *sharbat.*

Shield, سپر *sipar ;* یلب *yalab.*

Shin, ساق *sáḳ.*

Shine, رخشیدن *rakhshídan ;* درخشیدن *dirakhshídan ;* تابیدن *tábídan ;* درفشیدن *dirafshídan.*

Shining, رخشان *rakhshán ;* درفشان *dirafshán ;* تابان *tábán ;* درخشان *dirakhshán ;* درخشنده *dirakhshendah ;* منیر *munír ;* لمعان *lama'án ;* شارق *shárik ;* ساطع *sáti'.*

Ship, جهاز *jaház ;* کشتی *keshtí ;* (small), سفینه *safínah.* — wrecked, کشتی شکسته *kishtí-shikastah* (*sh.*).

Shirt, پیراهن *piráhan ;* قمیص *ḳamís.*

Shiver, لرزیدن *larzídan ; pr. p.,* لرزه *larzah.*

Shoal, پایاب *páyáb.*

Shock, جنبش *jumbish.*

Shocked, مضطرب *muztarib.*

Shoe, کفش *kafsh ;* پاپوش *pá-púsh ;* پای پوش *pái-púsh.* Horse —, نعل *na'l.* To — (a horse), نعل بستن *na'l bastan,* — maker, کفش دوز *kafsh-dúz.*

Shoot (of plant), نهال *nihál.* New —, نو دمیده *nau-damí-dah ; v.,* زدن *zadan.*

Shooting (archery), رمایت *rimáyet* (*k.*). — stars, رجم *rujum.*

Shop, دوکان *dúkán ;* دکان *du-kán.* Small —, دکانچه *du-káncheh.* — keeper, دوکان دار *dúkán-dár.* — keeping, دوکانی *dúkání.*

Shore, کنار *kinár ;* ساحل *sáhil.*

Short, کوتاه *kútáh* (*k.*) ; قصیر *ḳasír.* In —, بالجمله *bi'l-*

jumlah ; فی الجمله *fi'l jumlah* ; الغرض *algharz* ; القصه *al-kissah.* —ened, مقصور *maksúr* (*k.*). — ness, کوتاهی *kútáhí.*

Shot (ball), گلوله *galúlah.* Small —, ساچمه *sáchmeh.*

Shoulder, دوش *dúsh.* — blade, شانه *sháneh* ; کتف *katif.*

Shout, آواز *áváz* ; بانك *báng* (*z.*) ; *v.*, نعره زدن *na'rah z.*

Shovel, پارو *párú* ; مسحاة *mas-hát.*

Show, *n.*, تماشا *tamáshá* ; *v.*, نمودن *namúdan* ; وا نمودن *wá-n.* ; فرا نمودن *fará n.*

Showing, نما *namá* ; نماینده *namá-yendah.* — respect, or attention, ملتفت *multafit* (*sh.*) ; احترام *ihtirám* (*k.*).

Shower (rain), باران *bárán.*

Shred, پاره *páreh.*

Shrewd, چست *chust.* —ness, ذهن *zihn.*

Shriek, فریاد *faryád* (*k.*).

Shrill, تیز *tíz.*

Shrimp, میگو *maigú* ; جراد البحر *jarádu 'l bahr.*

Shrine, مزار *mazár* ; قدمگاه *kadam gáh.*

Shrink, or Shrivel, تنك شدن *tang sh.*

Shroud, کفن *kafan.*

Shrub, بوته *bútah.*

Shudder, هراسان *hirásán* (*k.*).

Shunning, احتراز *ihtiráz* (*k.*). ; اجتناب *ijtináb* (*k.*).

Shut, بستن *bastan* ; مسدود کردن *masdúd k.*

Shutting and opening, رتق و فتق *ratk u fatk.*

Shutter, دریچه *daricheh.*

Shuttle, ماکو *mákú.*

Shy, *v.*, رمیدن *ramídan.*

Sick, بیمار *bímár* (*sh.*) ; ناخوش *ná khúsh* (*sh.*) ; مریض *maríz* ; علیل *'alíl.* Attendant on the —, رنجور دار *ranjúr-dár.*

Sickle, داس *dás* ; منجل *minjal.*

Sickness, سقم *sukm*, or *sakam* ; سقام *sakám.*

Side, طرف *taraf*, *pl.* اطراف *atráf* ; جانب *jánib* ; پهلو *pahlú* ; صوب *saub* ; سو *sú* ; سوی *súy* ; کنار *kinár* ; پره *parrah.* Both —s, طرفین *tarafain.* — of a mountain

كاچه *káchah*. One —, يكسو *yaksú*. Every —, هرسو *harsú*. Back —, دبر *dubr*.

Siege, محاصره *muhásarah*.

Sieve, كربال *girbál*; غربال *ghirbál*; پرويزن *parvízan*; منخل *minkhal*. Large — for sifting gravel, &c., خاك بيز *khák-bíz*.

Sift, بيختن *bíkhtan*.

Sigh, دريغ *darígh*; دود دل *dúd i dil*.

Sight, باصره *básirah*; نظر *nazar*; بصارت *basárat*; بصيرت *basírat*; رويت *rúyat*. Clear —ed, صاحب نظر *sáhib-nazar*.

Sign, *n.*, نشان *nishán*; كنايه *kináyah*; علامة *'alámat*, *pl.* علامات *'alámát*; *v.*, (a name), امضاء داشتن *imzá dáshtan*; *pa. p.*, رقم زده *raḳam zadah*.

Signal, غمز *ghamz*; اشارة *isháráh* (*k.*).

Signature, دستخط *dast-khatt*; دسخط *das-khatt*; امضآء *imzá* (*k.*). Royal —, دسخط خاص *daskhatt i kháss*; طغرا *tughrá*.

Signet, خاتم *khátim*.

Signification, فحوى *fahvá*; معنى *ma'ni* (*dsh.*); مضمون *mazmún*.

Signified, مشار *mushár*.

Signifying, مشعر *mush'ir*.

Silence, سكوت *sukút*; صمت *samt*.

Silent, خاموش *khámúsh* (*k.*); ساكت *sákit* (*k.*); صامت *sámit*. To be —, دم داركشيدن *dam dár ksh.*; خاموشيدن *khámúshídan*. Very —, سكيت *sikkít*. — man, ساكوت *sákút*.

Silk, ابريشم *abrísham*; آبريشم *ábríshum*; حرير *harír*. Raw —, خز *khaz*. — stuff, اورمك *úrmek*. Painted Chinese —, پرنيان *parniyán*. —worm, دود الحرير *dúd ul harír*; ديوه *dívah*.

Silliness, ابلهى *ablahí*.

Silly, بيمعنى *bí ma'ní*.

Silver, نقره *nuḳrah*. Bad —, سيم سيه *sím i siyah*. Made of —, نقرئى *nuḳraí*.

Silvery, سيمين *símín*.

Similar, مثل *misl*; مطابق *mutábik*.

Similitude, مشابهت *mushábahat*; مثال *misál*.

Simmering, نیم جوش *ním júsh* (*k.*).

Simple, بسیط *basít.*

Simpleton, ساده دل *sádah-dil.*

Simplicity, سادگی *sádagí.*

Simulation, تجاهل *tajáhul.*

Simultaneity, مقارنت *muḳáranat.*

Simultaneous, مقارن *muḳárin.*

Sin, گناه *gunáh* (*k.*); تقصیر *taḳsír* (*k.*); اثم *ism*, *pl.* آثام *ásám*; خطاء *khatá'*, *pl.* خطایا *khatáyá.*

Since, زانکه *zánkih.*

Sincere, مخلص *mukhlis*; اخلاصمند *ikhlásmand*; نصیح *nasíh.* — friend, خلص *khils.* — friendship, خلالت *khilálat.* —ly, مخلصانه *mukhlisánah.*

Sincerity, صداقت *sadáḳat*; اخلاص *ikhlás*; خلوص *khulús*; مباحت *mabáhat.*

Sine, جیب *jib.*

Sinew, پی *pay*; عصب *'asab.*

Sinful, نا صواب *ná-saváb.* —ness, گناه کاری *gunáh kárí.*

Sing, *v.*, سریدن *sarídan*; سرودن *surúdan*; سرائیدن *sará'ídan.*

Singe, *v.*, سوختن *súkhtan.*

Singer, مغنی *mughanní* (fem. مغنیه *mughanniyah*); قوال *ḳavvál.*

Singing, خنیا *khunyá*; سراینده *saráyandah*; مترنم *mutarannim.* — in time with one another, هم آواز *ham-áváz.*

Single, فرد *fard*; فرید *faríd*; وحده *vahdahu*; یکتا *yaktá*; یکلو *yaklú.*

Singular, مفرد *mufrad.*

Singularity, یکانگی *yagánagí.*

Sink, *v.*, غرق کردن *gharḳ k.*

Sinless, بیگناه *bígunáh*; معصوم *ma'súm.*

Sinner, گنهکار *gunahgár*; گناهکار *gunáh-gár*; بزه کار *bazah-kár*; روسیاه *rú-siyáh*; تر دامن *tar-dáman*; سیه کار *siyah-kár*; عاصی *'ási.*

Sip, نوشیدن *núshídan.*

Sir! اغا *ághá*; صاحب *sáhib.*

Sirius, شعری *shi'rá.*

Sirup, شیره *shírah.*

Sister, خواهر *kháher*; همشیره *ham-shírah*; باجي *bájí.*

Sit, نشستن *nishastan.* To cause to — on, بر نشاندن *bar nishándan.*

Sitting, قاعد *ḳá'id* ; جالس *jális*. — at the same table, همسفره *ham-sufrah*.

Site, جا *já*.

Situated, واقع *váki'* (*sh.*).

Situation, وضع *vaz'*.

Six شش *shash* ; ست *sitt* ; ستة *sittah*. — hundred, ششصد *shash-sad*.

Sixteen, شانزده *shánzdah*.

Sixteenth, شانزدهم *shánzdahum*.

Sixth, ششم *shashum* ; سادس *sádis*. — part of a dram, &c., دانق *dánaḳ* ; دانك *dának*.

Sixtieth, شصتم *shastum*.

Sixty, شصت *shast* ; ستين *sittín*.

Size, مقدار *miḳdár* ; اندازه *andázeh*.

Skein, پيچك *píchak*.

Skeleton, تشريح *tashríh*.

Sketch, مسوده *musavvadah* ; خاكه *khákah*.

Skewer, سيخچه *síkhchah*.

Skiff, قايق *ḳáiḳ*.

Skilful, حاذق *háziḳ* ; پر كار *pur-kár* ; اهل *ahl* ; كار اكاه *kár-ágáh* ; قابل *ḳábil* ; كار شناس *kár-shinás*.

Skill, استعداد *isti'dád* ; قابليت *ḳábiliyat*.

Skilled in the law, متشرع *mutasharri'*. — in genealogy, نسابت *nassábat*. — in war, جنك آزموده *jang ázmúdah*.

Skim, كف كرفتن *kaf gr.*

Skimmer, كفكير *kaf-gír*.

Skin, پوست *púst* ; جلد *jild*, *pl.* جلود *julúd*. — for water or milk, مشك *mashk* ; خيك *khík* ; خي *khí*.

Skirt, دامن *dáman* ; دامان *dámán* ; ذيل *zail*.

Skull, كاسهء سر *kásah i sar* ; قحف *ḳihf* ; جمجمه *jumjumah*. —cap, عرقچين *'araḳ chín*.

Sky, آسمان *ásmán* ; فلك *falak* ; سماء *samá*. — light, تابدان *tábdán* ; روشندان *raushandán*.

Slab, تخته *takhtah*.

Slain, مقتول *maḳtúl*.

Slaking (thirst), تسكين *taskín* (*d.*).

Slander, غمازى *ghammází* ; بهتان *buhtán* (*bs.*) ; نميمه *namímah*.

Slanderer, نميم *namím* ; مفترى *muftarí*.

Slap, سیلی *sílí* (*z.*); لتم *latm.*

Slaughter, قتل *ḳatl* (*k.*); قتال *ḳitál.* Place of —, مقتل *maḳtal.*

Slaughtered, مذبوح *mazbúh.* Half —, نیم بسمل *ním-bis-mil.*

Slave, بنده *bandah, pl.* بندگان *bandagán*; عبد *'abd, pl.* عبید *'abíd*; غلام *ghulám.* Purchased —, مملوك *mam-lúk.* Female —, جارية *jári-yet.* — born in the house, خانه زاد *khánah-zád.*

Slavery, رقیه *riḳḳíyat.*

Slay, کشتن *kushtan.*

Sledge-hammer, چاکوچ *chá-kúch*; جاکوج *jákúj.*

Sleep, *n.*, خواب *kháb*; نوم *naum*; منام *munám*; هجوع *hujú'.* First —, سر خواب *sar-kháb*; *v.*, خوبیدن *khá-bídan*; خواب کردن *kháb k.* To go to sleep, خواب رفتن *kháb r.*

Sleepy, خوابناك *kháb-nák*; خواب آلوده *kháb álúdah.*

Sleeper (great), بسیار خسپ *bis-yár-khasp.*

Sleeplessness, بی خوابی *bí-khábí*; سهر *sahar.*

Sleeve, آستین *ástín.*

Sleight of hand, شعبده *shu'b-dah.*

Slender, نازك *názuk.*

Slice, تراشه *tirásheh.*

Slime, لجن *lajan.*

Sliminess, لعاب *lu'áb.*

Sling, فلاخن *falákhan.*

Slinger, کلوخ انداز *kulúkh-andáz*; سنك انداز *sang-andáz.*

Slip, *n.*, زل *zall, pl.* زلات *zal-lát*; *v.*, لیزیدن *lízídan*; لغزیدن *laghzídan.*

Slipping, لغزان *laghzán.*

Slipper, پاپوش *pá-púsh.* —s worn over the boots, خارکش *khár-kesh.*

Slippery place, مزلقه *mazlaḳah*; مزلات *mazallát.*

Slit, چاك *chák* (*k.*).

Sloe, الوچه *álúcheh.*

Slope, شیب *shíb.*

Sloth, کاهلی *káhilí.* —ful, کاهل *káhil.*

Slow, دیر *dír*; درنك *dirang.* —ly, یواش *yavásh.* —ness, کسالت *kasálat*; آهستکی *áhistagí.*

Sluice gate, آبکیره *ábgírah.*

Slumber, *v.*, غنودن *ghunúdan.*

Slut, پلشت *pilisht.*

Sly, حیلة باز *híleh báz.*

Smack (of the fingers), زنجیر *zinjír* (*k.*).

Small, کوچك *kúchik*; خورد *khurd*; صغیر *saghír*; یسیر *yasír*

Smaller, or Smallest, اصغر *asghar.*

Smallness, خردی *khurdí*; خوردي *khúrdí*; صغارت *saghárat.*

Small-pox, جدری *jadaríy*; چچك *chichak*; چیچك *chíchak.*

Small, or ape-nosed, ذلف *zulf.*

Smash, خورد کردن *khúrd k.*

Smear, اندودن *andúdan.*

Smell, *n.*, بو *bú*; بوی *búy*; شامه *shámmah*; *v.*, بوئیدن *bú-ídan.* — ing, استشام *istishám* (*k.*); مستنشی *mustanshí* (*h.*).

Smile, تبسم *tabassum* (*k.*); ابتسام *ibtisám* (*n.*).

Smith, آهنگر *áhangar.*

Smoke, دود *dúd* (*ksh.*); دخان *dukhán.*

Smooth, مسطح *musattah*; هون *haun.* —ing, نحت *naht* (*k.*).

Smother, خفه *khuffah* (*k. sh.*).

Snail, خانه بدوش *khánah badúsh.*

Snake, مار *már*; افعی *af'á.* — bitten, مار گزیده *márgazídah.* — catcher, مار گیر *már-gír.*

Snap asunder, گسلیدن *guslídan*; گسلانیدن *guslánídan.* — off, بر گسلیدن *bar guslídan.* — the fingers, بر فشاندن *bar fishándan.*

Snare, دام *dám* (*an.*).

Snatch, بر گسلانیدن *bar guslánídan.*

Sneeze, عطسه زدن *'atsah z.*; خفیدن *khafídan.* — ing, عطس *'ats*; (of animals), کداس *kudás.*

Snore, خراخر زدن *kharákhar z.* — ing, خرخرا *kharkhará.*

Snout, پوز *púz.*

Snow, برف *barf*; *v.*, برف باریدن *barf báridan.*

Snuff, انفیه *anfíyeh.* Medicinal —, سعوط *sa'út.* — the candle, چراغ گرفتن *chirágh-giriftan.*

Snuffers, گلگیر *gul-gír.*

So, چنین *chanín*; چنان *chanán.*

And so on and so forth, هلم جراً *hallumma jarran.* So and so, ذيت كيت *zait-kait.*

Soak, آغشتن *ághushtan.*

Soap, صابون *sábún.*

Sob, *n.*, گريه *geryeh* (*k.*); *v.*, سكليدن *saglídan.*

Sober, نا مست *ná mast.* Becoming —, صحو *sahv* (*k.*).

Society, صحبت *suhbat*; صحابت *sahábat*; مصاحبت *musáhabat*; رفاقت *rifákat*; همراهی *ham-ráhí.*

Sock, جرابه *jurábah*; پاتابه *pátábah.*

Socket (of the eye), چشمخانه *chashm-khánah.*

Soda, نطرون *natrún.*

Sodomite, لوطی *lutíy*,

Sodomy, بچه بازی *bacheh bází.*

Soft, *s.*, نرم *narm*; ناعم *ná'im*; نسود *nasúd.*

Softening, ملين *mulaiyin* (*k.*).

Softly, نرم نرم *narm narm*; آهسته *áhistah.*

Softness, ملايمة *muláyamat*; نرمی *narmí.*

Soil, *n.*, خاك *khák*; *v.*, آلودن *álúdan.* —ed, تنجس *tanajjus.*

Sojourn, اقامت *ikámat* (*k.*).

Solace, سلوت *salvat.*

Sold, فروخته *farúkhtah*; مبيع *mabí'.*

Solder, قلع *kal'*; *v.*, جوش خوردن *júsh khurdan.*

Soldier, سارباز *sárbáz*; سپاهی *sipáhí*; لشكری *lashkarí.* Fellow —, همجنك *ham-jang.* —ship, سپاهكری *sipáhgarí.*

Sole (of the feet), كف پا *kaff i pá*; (alone), تنها *tanhá*; (fish), كوشك *kaushak.*

Solemn, محترم *muhtaram.*

Solemnity, هيبت *haibat.*

Solicitation, الحاح *ilháh* (*k.*); التماس *iltimás* (*k.*).

Solicitude, پروا *parvá.*

Solid, يكپاره *yak-párah*; صلد *suld*; محشو *mahshúv.* —ity, رصانت *rasánat.*

Solitary, مفرد *mufarrad*; مجرد *mujarrad.*

Solitariness, يكانيت *yagáníyet.*

Solitude, تنهای *tanhái*; وحدت *vahdat*; تجرد *tajarrud.*

Solstice (Summer), راس السرطان *rás us saratán.* (Winter), راس الجدی *rás ul jidy.*

Solution (of question), حل *hall* (*k.*); (in water, etc.), گداخته *gudákhtah*.

Solvent, گدازنده *gudázendah*.

Some, بعضی *ba'zí*; قدری *ḳadrí*; چند *chand*.

Somebody, شخصی *shakhsí*; هیچکس *hích-kas*; یکی *yakí*.

Something, چیزی *chízí*.

Sometime, چند گاه *chandgáh*.

Sometimes, گاه گاه *gáh-gáh*; احیاناً *ahyánan*.

Somewhat, برخ *barkh*; برخی *barkhí*; قدری *ḳadrí*; یك چند *yak-chand*.

Somersault, پشتك *pushtak* (*z.*).

Somnolent, نعاس *na'ás*.

Son, پسر *pise'*; فرزند *farzand*; ولد *valad*; ابن *ibn*, *pl.* بنی *bení*; in comp., زاده *zádeh*; (as, — of a Bey, بکزاده *beg-zádah*). — in-law, داماد *dámád*. —'s son, نبیره *nabírah*; نبیر *nabír*. Daughter's —, سبط *sabt*.

Song, نوا *navá*; نغمة *naghmah*; غناء *ghiná'*.

Sonnet, غزل *ghazal*.

Soon, زود *zúd*. As — as, هماندگاه *hamán-gáh*; همانکه *hamángah*.

Soot, دوده *dúdah*.

Soothing, تعلیل *ta'líl*.

Soothsayer, فال کو *fál-gú*; کاهن *káhin*; رمال *rammál*.

Soothsaying, کهانت *kahánat*.

Sorcerer, ساحر *sáher*.

Sorcery, جادو *jádú*.

Sordid (men), لیام *liyám*; طمعکار *tama'kár*.

Sore, قرحة *ḳarhat*; زخم *zakhm*; ریش *rísh*.

Sorrel, حماض *humáz*; ترشك *turshek*. Wild —, ترشه *turshah*.

Sorrow, افسوس *afsús* (*kh.*); غم *ghamm* (*kh.*), *pl.* غموم *ghumúm*; دل نکرانی *dil-nigarání*.

Sorrowful, or Sorry, غمکین *gham-gín*; ناخن بدندان *ná-khun ba-dandán*; اندوهکین *andúhgín*; سوکوار *súg-vár*.

Sort, صنف *sinf*, *pl.* صنوف *sunúf*; جنس *jins*, *pl.* اجناس *ajnás*; قسم *ḳism*, *pl.* اقسام *aḳsám*; نوع *nau'*, *pl.* انواع *anvá'*. Of various —s, رنكارنك *rang-á-rang*.

Soul, روح *rúh* ; جان *ján* ; نفس *nafas*, *pl.* نفوس *nufús* ; روان *raván*. Captivating the —, جانربا *ján-rubá*.

Sound, صدا *sadá* (*k.*) ; صوت *saut* ; آواز *áváz* ; نشدت *nishdat*.

Soup, شوربا *shurbá*; آبگوشت *ábgúsht*.

Sour, ترش *tursh* ; حمض *hamz*. — cherry, آلو بالو *álú bálú*.

Source, مصدر *masdar* ; اصل *asl*.

South, جنوب *janúb*.

Southern, جنوبی *janúbí*.

Souvenir, یادکار *yádgár*.

Sovereign, پادشاه *pádsháh* ; شاه *sháh*. — sway, ملك رانی *mulk-ráni*.

Sovereignty, داوری *dávarí* ; دارائی *dárái* ; جهانداری *jahán-dárí*.

Sow (pig), ماده خوك *mádeh khúg*.

Sow, *v.*, کاشتن *káshtan* ; کاریدن *kárídan* ; کشتن *kishtan*.

Sower, زارع *zári'*

Sown (field or seed), مزروع *mazru'*.

Space, حوز *hauz* ; فسحت *fushat* ; عرصه *'arsah* ; (of time), برهة *burhat*.

Spacious, باسط *básit* ; وسیع *vasi'*.

Spade, بیل *bíl* ; کلند *kaland*, or *kuland*.

Spain, اندلوس *Andalús*.

Span, شبر *shibr* ; بلست *bilist*.

Spare, *a.*, لاغر *lághir*.

Spark, پرکاله *parkálah* ; شراره *sharáreh*, *pl.* شرار *sharár* ; شرر *sharar*.

Sparkling, تابان *tábán*.

Sparrow, کنجشك *kunjishk*. — hawk, قراغوش *ḳarághúsh* ; باشه *báshah*.

Spasm, تشنج *tashannuj*.

Spavin, قرقوش *ḳarḳúsh*.

Spawn, اشپل *ishpul*.

Speak, کفتن *guftan* ; حرف زدن *harf z.* زبان کشادن *zabán-kushádan*. — obscenely, افساریدن *afsárídan*. — elegantly, تحبیر کردن *tahbír k.*

Speaker, کوینده *gúyandah* ; قایل *ḳáil* ; متکلم *muta-ḳallim*.

Spear, نیزه *nízah* ; حربه *harbah* ; رمح *rumh*. — head, سنان *sinán* ; پیکان *paikán*.

Special, مخصوص makhsús. More or most —, اخص akhass.
Specially, مخصوصاً makhsúsan.
Specialty, اختصاص ikhtisás.
Species, اجناس ajnás; نوع nau'.
Specific, نوعی nau'í.
Specifying, تعیین ta'yín k.
Specimen, نمونه namúnah.
Specious, وجیه vajíh. — ness, تصنع tasannu'.
Speck, ذره zarreh.
Speckled, لکه دار lakkeh dár.
Spectacle, تماشا tamáshá; نظاره nazárah. Looking at a —, نظارگی nazzáragí.
Spectacles, عینك 'ainak.
Spectator, بینا bíná; تماشاءی tamáshái, pl. حضار huzzár; نظارکان nazzáragán.
Spectre, خیال khiyál.
Speculation, معامله mu'ámaleh (k.).
Speech, تکلم takallum (k.); تقریر takrír (k.). ; کویاءی gúyái; نطق nutk; نطوق nutúk; کلام kalám; کفتار guftár. Inconsiderate —, لغو laghv. Idle —, ژاژ zházh. Incoherent —, طامات támát. —less, بیزبان bízabán.
Speed, زودی zúdí; جلدی jaldí. Full —, جلو ریز jalav-ríz.
Spell, n., افسون afsún.
Spelling, املا imlá (k.).
Spend, خرج کردن kharj k.
Spent, مصروف masrúf.
Spew, قی کردن kai k.
Sphere, چرخ charkh; مرکز markaz; کردون gardún.
Spice, ادویه adviyeh.
Spider, عنکبوت 'ankabút. —s web, پرده عنکبوت pardah-i-'ankabút.
Spike, میخ míkh.
Spikenard (Indian), سادج sádij; سنبل الطیب sumbul ut tíb.
Spill, ریختن ríkhtan.
Spilt, منشق munshakk.
Spin, رشتن rishtan.
Spinage, اسفاناج isfánáj; شومین shúmín.
Spindle, دوك dúk. — case, دوکدان dúk-dán.
Spine, عصعص 'us'us.
Spinner, ریسنده rísandeh.
Spinning-wheel, چرخه charkheh.

Spirit, روح rúh ; بال bál. —of God (Jesus Christ), روح الله rúh Ulláh. Faithful— (Gabriel), روح الامين rúh ul amín. Vegetable —, روح نباتی rúh i nabátí. Animal—, روح حیوانی rúh i haiwání. —less, بیحمیت bí-hamíyet ; بیغیرت bí-ghairat. — of wine, عرق 'arak. Extra strong —, عرق سه آتشی 'arak i sih átishí.

Spiritual, نفسی nafasí ; روحانی rúhání. — guide, پیر طریقت pír i taríkat.

Spit, n., سیخ síkh ; v., سلف انداختن suluf andákhtan.

Spite, کینه kínah. —ful, شریر sharír.

Spittle, ریق rík ; آب دهن áb-i-daham ; تف tuff (z.) ; بزاق buzák.

Spleen, طحال tihál ; سپرز supurz.

Splendid, جلوه گر jilvah-gar ; لامع lámi'.

Splendour, فروغ furúgh ; لمع lam' ; اشراق ishrák ; آب áb ; درخش durukhsh ; جلوه jilvah ; رونق raunak.

Splice, وصل vasl (k.).

Splint (bandaging), جبیره jabíreh ; (of horse), قرقوش karkúsh.

Split, v., شکافتن shikáftan ; pa. p., منفتق munfatik ; منخرق munkharik ; منفطر munfatir ; pr. p., فالق fálik ; خارق khárik.

Spoil, تاراج táráj ; چپو chapau (k.) ; غنیمة ghanímat (k.), pl. غنائم ghanáim.

Spoiling, افساد ifsád (k.) ; مخل mukhill ; مفسد mufsid (n.).

Spoilt, معیوب ma'yúb.

Spoke (of wheel), دیره dírah.

Sponge, ابر abr ; (parasite), طفیل tufeil.

Sponsor, ضمین zamín ; کافل káfil.

Spoon, قاشق káshuk ; (large), چمچه chamchah ; چمچم cham-cham.

Sport, بازی bází ; بازیچه bázícheh ; لهو و لعب lahv o la'b.

Sportsman, شکارچی shikár-chí.

Spot, لکه lakkah.

Spotted, داغی dághí.

Spousal, عروسی 'arúsí.

Spout, ناو دان *náv-dán* ; میزاب *mízáb*.

Sprain, *n.*, پیچش *píchesh* (*kh.*).

Spread, گستردن *gustardan* ; *pa. p.*, مبسوط *mabsút* ; مفروش *mafrúsh* (*k.*) ; سرکشاده *sar-kushádah*.

Spring (season), بهار *bahár* ; ربیع *rabí'* ; (of steel), کمان *kamán* ; فنر *fanar* ; (water), چشمه *cheshmeh*. Early — rain, وسمي *vasmíy* ; *v.*, جهیدن *jihídan*.

Springing upon, بر جستگی *bar jastagí*.

Sprinkle, پاشیدن *páshídan*.

Sprinkling, پاش *pásh* (*k.*) ; رش *rash*.

Sprout, غصن *ghusn*.

Sprung up (newly), رستخیز *rus-takhíz*.

Spur, مهمیز *mihmíz* (*z.*).

Spurious, قلب *ḳalb*.

Spurt, فش *fish* (*k.*).

Spy, خبر گیر *khabar-gír* ; جاسوس *jásús* ; زبان گیر *zabán-gír*. — glass, دور بین *dúr bín*. —ing, خبر گیری *khabar-girí* (*k.*) ; تجسس *tajassus* (*n.*) ; جاسوسی *jásúsí*.

Squabble, شلوك *shulúk* (*k.*).

Squadron, دسته *dastah*.

Squalid, پلشت *pilisht*.

Squalor, قشف *ḳashf*.

Squander, اسراف کردن *isráf k.*

Square, چار گوشه *chár-gúshah* ; مربع *murabba'*. — root, جذر *jazr*.

Squeeze, افشاردن *afshárdan* ; افشردن *afshurdan* ; فشردن *fashurdan* ; بر فشاندن *bar fishándan*.

Squib, مهتاب *mahtáb*.

Squills, اسقیل *asḳail*.

Squinting, احوال *ahvál* (*k.*) ; لوچ *lúch* (*k.*).

Squirrel, موش پران *músh parrán* ; موش پرنده *músh parandah*. Grey —, سنجاب *sinjáb*.

Stability, ثبات *sabát* ; قرار *ḳarár* (*gr.*).

Stable, طویله *tavílah* ; آخور *ákhur* ; اصطبل or اسطبل *istabl*.

Stack, توده *túdah*.

Staff, عصا *'asá* ; چوب *chúb*.

Stage, منزل *manzil*, *pl.* منازل *manázil*.

Stagnant, نا روان *ná-raván*.

Stain, آلودن álúdan; pr. p., لطخ latkh; pa. p., خضیب khazíb.

Stairs, پله pillah; درجه darajeh.

Stake, چوب chúb. Impaling —, سولی súlí; خازوق kházúk.

Stale, مانده mándah; شبانه shabánah.

Stalk, شاخه shákhah.

Stall (cattle), آخر ákhur. Thumb —, شست shast.

Stallion, نریان naryán.

Stammer, زبان کوفتن zabán-kúftan. —er, الکن alkan. —ing, تعثر ta'assur (k.); لکن lakan; لکنت làknat.

Stamp, v., (a document), سجل کردن sijil k. Official —, n., تمغا tamghá; مهر muhr. —ed (a document), مسجل musajjal.

Staunch, v., موقوف کردن maukúf k.

Stand, v., استادن istádan; ایستادن ístádan; ستادن sitádan. —, n., (for a lamp), چراغدان chirágh-dán.

Standard, رایت ráyat, pl. رایات ráyát; لیواء liwá', pl. الویه alviyeh; علم دار 'alam dár; نشان nishán. — bearer, علم بردار 'alam bardár.

Standing, قایم káim; قیام kayám.

Stanza, بیت bait.

Staple, ریزه rízah.

Star ستاره sitárah; نجم najm, pl., نجوم nujúm; کوکب kaukab, pl., کواکب kavákib; اختر akhtar, in pl. فندق سیم funduk i sím. Fixed —, ثابته sábitah. Morning —, شب آهنك shab-áhang. Two stars near the pole, فرقدان farkadán.

Starch, نشاشته nasháshtah.

Stare, وانکرستن vá-nigristan.

Starling, سارك sárak.

Starting (on a journey), ارتحال irtihál (k.); نقل مکان nakl í makán (k.).

Startle, ترسانیدن tarsánídan.

Starvation, فاقه fákah; کرسنکی gurisnagí (ksh.).

State (condition), حال hál; کیفیت kaifiyet; ماهیت máhíyet; چهره، حال chihrah i hál. Proper —, بحال ba-hál. — of facts, رویداد

rúydád; (empire), دولت *daulat*; (degree), شان *shán*.

Stated time, میقات *míkát*.

Statement, توجیه *taujíh*; توضیح *tauzíh*.

Statesman, مدبر *mudabbir*.

Station, موقف *maukif*, *pl.* مواقف *mavákif*; جایگاه *jáygáh*; مکان *makán*; موضع *mauza'*.

Stationary, ساکن *sákin*.

Statuary, بت تراش *but tarásh*.

Statue, صورت *súrat*.

Stature, قد *kadd*; قامت *kámat*.

Statute, قاعده *ká'idah*.

Stay, ماندن *mándan*. — behind, واماندن *wá-mándan*.

Steady, ثابت قدم *sábit-kadam*; استوار *ustuvár*.

Steal, دزدیدن *duzdídan*; دزدی کردن *duzdí k*.

Steam, بخار *bukhár*. — ship, واپور *vápúr*.

Steed, مرکب *markab*.

Steel, فولاد *fúlád*; پولاد *púlád*.

Steep, ژرف *zharf*; سرا بالا *sará-bálá*. — acclivity, گریوه *girívah*.

Steer, *v.*, راندن *rándan*.

Stem (of a hookah), نایچه *náichah*.

Stench, بد بو *bad bú*.

Step, گام *gám*; قدم *kadam* (*z.*); پایه *páyah*; درجه *darajah*, *pl.* درجات *daraját*; مدارج *madárij*; خطوة *khatvat*. — daughter, ربیبه *rabíbah*. — father, راب *ráb*. — mother, رابه *rábeh*. — son, ربیب *rabíb*.

Stercorare, ریدن *rídan*.

Sterile, عقیم *'akím*; شوره *shúrah*.

Sterling, صادق *sádik*.

Stern, متعبس *muta'abbis*. —ness, درشتی *durushtí*.

Stew, قورمه *kavurmah*.

Steward, ناظر *názir*. — ship, نظارت *nazárat*.

Stick, چوبدستی *chúb-dastí*. Drum —, چوبك *chúbak*; *v.*, چسپیدن *chaspídan*.

Sticky, چسپناك *chaspnák*.

Stiff, سخت *sakht* (*k.*). — necked, یاغی *yághí*. —ness, سختی *sakhtí*.

Stifle, خفه شدن *khuffah shudan* (or *k.*).

Stigma, عيب *'aib.*

Still, *a.*, ساكت *sákit* (*k.*); خاموش *khámúsh* (*k.*); (already), تا هنوز *tá hanúz*; (for spirits), انبيق *ambík.* —ness, خاموشى *khámúshí.*

Stimulation, تحريك *tahrík* (*k.*).

Sting, نيش *nísh* (*z.*); (of a scorpion, &c.), لسع *las'*; ابر *abr.*

Stingy, بخيل *bakhíl.* —ness, طمع *tama'.*

Stink, *n.*, كند *gand*; *v.*, كنديدن *gandídan*; *pr. p.*, كنده *gandah.*

Stipend, جامقيه *jámikíyeh*; جامكى *jámagí*; وظيفه *vazífah.*

Stipulated, مشروط *mashrút.*

Stipulation, قيود *kuyúd* (*k.*); شرط *shart* (*bs.*).

Stir up, برهم زدن *bar ham z.*

Stirring up strife, محرب *muhrib* (*n.*).

Stirrup (a), ركاب *rikáb.*

Stitch, دوختن *dúkhtan.*

Stitching together, لفق *lafk* (*n.*); تلفيق *talfík* (*k.*).

Stock (capital), مايه *máyah*; سرمايه *sar-máyah*; دست مايه *dast-máyah.* — of gun, قنداغ *kundágh.*

Stocking, جراب *juráb.*

Stocks, كنده *kundah.*

Stolen (goods), بلكه *balgah.*

Stomach, شكم *shikam*; معده *mi'dah.*

Stone, سنك *sang*; حجر *hajar*, *pl.* حجار *hijár.* A large —, خرسنك *kharsang.* Ring —, فص *fuss*; نكين *nigín.* — for a sling, ملچخ *malchakh.* Date —, وخچى *vakhchí.* Bezoar —, پادزهر *pád-zahr.* Fruit —, خستو *khastú.* Blood —, شادنه *shádnah.* Hard —, سنك خارا *sang i khárá.* Mill —, سنك آسيا *sang-ásyá.* A small piece of —, سنك خرده *sang-khurdah.* — in the bladder, حصاة *hesát*; سنك مثانه *sang i masánah.*

Stoning to death, سنك سار *sang-sár* (*k.*); رجم *rajm* (*k.*).

Stony (heavy), سنكى *sangí* — country, سنكستان *sangistán.* — place, سنكلاخ *sang-lákh.*

Stool, کرسی *kursí.*

Stoop, خم شدن *kham sh.*

Stop! وا ایست *vá íst; v.,* ایستادن *ístádan.*

Store, ذخیره *zakhírah, pl.* ذخایر *zakháir;* مایه *máyah.* — house, خزانه *khizánah.*

Stork, لقلق *laḳlaḳ;* حاجی لك لك *háji lak-lak.*

Storm, طوفان *túfán.*

Storming, هجوم *hujúm* (*a*).

Story, قصة *ḳissah;* حکایت *hikáyat.* — teller, قصه کو *ḳissah-gú;* قصه خوان *ḳissah-khán.* Idle —, خرافة *khuráfeh, pl.* خرافات *khuráfát.* Relating a —, محاکات *muhákát* (*n.*). — (of a house), طبق *tabaḳ.* Lower —, طبقهٔ پائین *tabaḳah i páin.* Upper —, طبقهٔ بالا *tabaḳah i bálá.*

Stout, جسیم *jasím.*

Stove, کلخن *gulkhan;* دیکدان *díg-dán.*

Straight, راست *rást* (*k.*); مستقیم *mustaḳím;* سهی *sahí.*

Straightened, مقوم *muḳavvam.* — in means, تنك روزی *tang-rúzi.*

Strain, پالودن *pálúdan.*

Strainer, صافی *sáfí.*

Strait, تنك *tang.*

Strange, عجب *'ajab* عجیب *'ajíb.*

Strangeness, نا محرمیت *ná-mahramíyet.*

Stranger, بیکانه *bígánah;* نزیل *nazíl;* نا محرم *ná-mahram.*

Strangle, طناب انداختن *tanáf* (*tenef*) *andákhtan;* خفه کردن *khuffeh k.*

Strangler, خناق *khannáḳ.*

Strangling, دغر *daghr.*

Strangulation, خبه *khabah;* خفکی *khaffagí.*

Strangury, برمیو *barmíyú.*

Strap, دوال *duvál.*

Stratagem, حیله *hílah;* کول *gúl.*

Straw, کاه *káh;* صمان *samán, in pl.* کاهریز *káh-ríz.*

Strawberry, توت فرنکی *tút-i-farangí.*

Straying, ضال *záll* (*n.*).

Strayed away, دور افتاده *dúr uftádah;* کم راه *gum ráh* (*sh.*).

Stream, جو *jú* ; آب *áb*. Dried-up —, خشك رودی *khushk-rúdí*. A pure limpid —, سلسال *salsál*.

Street, کوی *kúy* ; کوچه *kúchah* ; مشرع *mashra'*.

Strength, قوت *ḳúvat* ; زور *zúr* ; زور مندی *zúr-mandí* ; استواری *ustuvárí* ; نیرو *nírú* ; سر پنجکی *sar-panjagí* ; تقویة *taḳvíyet*.

Strengthened, مشید *mushaiyad* ; مقوی *muḳavvá* ; مؤید *mu'aiyad*.

Strengthening, موثق *músiḳ*.

Strenuous, جداً *jiddan*. —ly, بشدت *beshiddat*.

Stretch, کشیدن *keshídan*.

Strew, ریختن *ríkhtan*.

Stricken (in years), پیر سال *pír-sál*.

Strict search, جست و جو *just u jú*.

Stricture, ملامت *malámat*.

Stride, قدم *ḳadam* (*z.*).

Strife, ستیز *sitíz* ; ستیزه *sitízah* ; یارغو *yárghú*.

Strike, زدن *zadan* ; یاختن *yákhtan* ; ضرب کردن *zarb k.* To — together, برهم زدن *barham z.*

Striker, زننده *zanendah* ; ضارب *zárib*.

String, ریسمان *rísmán*. — of the drawers, ازاربند *izárband*. Bow —, زه *zih* ; وتر *vatar*.

Strip, پارچه *párchah*.

Stripe, خط *khatt*.

Striped (garment), مخطط *mukhattat*.

Stripped, سلیب *salíb* ; لخت *lukht*.

Strive, کوشیدن *kúshídan*.

Striving, مجهد *mujhid* (*n.*) ; مجتهد *mujtahid*. — to please, دل جو *dil-jú*.

Stroke, *n.*, شلق *shalḳ* ; داو *dáv*.

Stroll, گردش *gardesh* (*k.*).

Strong, سخت *sakht* ; قوی *ḳavvíy* ; مضبوط *mazbút* ; استوار *ustuvár* ; سخت پی *sakht-pai* ; زورمند *zúr-mand*. A — fort, رزین *razín* ; رصین *rasín* ; حصین *hasín*.

Strongly prohibiting, مناع *manná'*.

Structure, بنیه *bunyah*.

Struggle, چالش *chálish* (*n.*).

Strumpet, قحبه *kahbeh* ; لوند *lavand* ; جنده *jindeh.*

Stubble, کاهبان *káh-bán.*

Stubborn, متمرد *mutamarrid.*

Stucco, گچ *gach.*

Stud (metal), گل *gul.*

Studded with jewels, مرصع *murassa'.*

Student, طالب العلم *tálib ul'ilm*, *pl.* طلباء *tulabá* ; متعلم *muta-'allim* ; شاگرد *shágird.*

Study, دراست *dirásat* ; *v.*, درس خواندن *dars khándan.*

Stuff (cloth), قماش *kumásh.* — and non-sense ! این پشم است *ín pashm íst* ; *v.*, طپاندن *tapándan* ; آغندن *ághandan* ; آگندن *ágandan.*

Stuffed (with feathers), آگنده پر *ágandah-par.*

Stuffing (of a pillow, &c.), حشو *hashv* ; انبارش *ambárish.*

Stumbling, افتان *uftán* (*k.*).

Stump, تنه *tanah.*

Stunned, بیهوش *bí-húsh* (*k.*).

Stupefied, مدهوش *madhúsh* (*g.*).

Stupid, نا فهم *ná-fahm* ; بیوقوف *bí-vukúf* ; احمق *ahmak* ; سفیه *safíh.*

Stupidity, بلاهت *baláhat* ; احمقی *ahmakí* ; سفاهت *safáhat* ; حمق *humk.*

Stupor, غش *ghash.*

Sturgeon, مرسین *marsín.*

Stutter, لکنت کردن *luknat k.*

Stutterer, هاکره *hákrah* ; هاکله *háklah.*

Sty (eye), سنده سلامی *sindah salámí.*

Style, عبارت *'ibárat.* Attentive to —, عبارت سنج *'ibárat-sanj.*

Styptic, عفص *'afis* ; زمخک *zumukhk.*

Suavity, لطف *lutf.*

Subaltern, زیر دست *zír-dast.*

Subdue, غلبه کردن *ghalabeh k.* ; *pa. p.*, مقهور *mak-húr* ; منفتح *munfatih* ; مسخر *musakh-khar* ; *pr. p.* تسخیر *taskhír* (*n.*) ; قاهر *káhir.*

Subject, رعیت *ra'íyat*, *pl.* رعایا *ru'áyá.* — (matter), ضمن *zamn* ; باره *bárah.* — of disputation, مبحث *mabhas.*

— to palpitation, خفقانی *khafakání.*

Subjected, محکوم *mahkúm.*

Subjection, انقیاد *inkiyád.*

Sublime, سامی *sámí ;* عالی *'álí.*

Sublimity, علو *'ulúv ;* رفعت *rif'at.*

Submission, اطاعت *itá'at ;* خضوع *khuzú' ;* منقاد *minkád.*

Submissive, مخفوض *makhfúz.*

Submit, مطیع شدن *mutí' sh. ;* سپر انداختن *sipar andákhtan ;* سر فرو آوردن *sar farau-áverdan.*

Subordinate, زیر دست *zír dast.*

Subscribe, زیر نوشتن *zír navish-tan.*

Subsequently, من بعد *min ba'ad.*

Subserviency, ابتهال *ibtihál.*

Subservient, متعلق *muta'al-lak.*

Subsist, زیستن *zístan.*

Subsistence, رزق *rízk ;* برك و نوا *barg u navá.* Means of —, سر و برك *sar u barg.*

Substance, کنه *kunh ;* جوهر *jauhar.*

Substantial, جسیم *jasím.*

Substantialness, مادیت *máddí-yat.*

Substantially, الحق *al-hakk.*

Substantive, اسم *ism.*

Substitute, *n.*, بدل *badal (k.) ;* بدلا *badlá.*

Substitution, تعویض *ta'víz (n.) ;* تبدیل *tabdíl (k.).*

Subterfuge, فریب *faríb.*

Subtile, چست *chust.*

Subtilty, باریکی *báríkí ;* نکته *nuktah, in pl.* رقائق *rakáik ;* دقائق *dakáik.* — of genius, خرده بینی *khurdah-bíní.*

Subtraction, منها *minhá (k.).*

Suburbs, گرد شهر *gird i shahr ;* حوالیٔ شهر *haválí e shehr.*

Success, انجاح *injáh (y.) ;* نجاح *najáh ;* نجح *nujh (y.).*

Successful, نجیح *najíh ;* کامیاب *kámyáb (sh.).*

Succession, میراث *mírás (y.) ;* مرادفت *murádafat (n.) ;* تناسل *tanásul ;* تواتر *ta-vátur.*

Successive, متعاقب *muta'ákib ;* مترادف *mutarádif ;* متوالی *mutaválí.*

Successively, متواتر *mutavátir ;* پی در پی *pai dar pai ;*

پی پیا پی *pai á pai;* پی هم *pai-ham.*

Successor, خالف *khálif;* خلف *khalf.*

Succour, غیاث *ghiyás;* امداد *imdád* (*k.*).

Succulent, آبدار *ábdár.*

Such, همچو *hamchú;* چنان *chunán.* — as, چنانچه *chunánchih.* — as that, آنچنان *ánchunán.* — a one, فلان *fulán.*

Suck, مکیدن *makídan.*

Suckle, *v.*, سیر دادن *shír d.*

Suckling a child, مراضعت *muráza'at* (*n.*); مرضع *murzi'.* A —, *n.*, شیر خوارگی *shír-kháragí;* رضاع *rezá'.*

Sudden death, مرك مفاجات *marg i mufáját.*

Suddenly, یکایك *yakáyak;* ناگاه *ná-gáh;* بیکبار *ba-yek-bár;* نا گهان *ná-gahán;* نا گرفت *ná-girift.*

Suddenness, مفاجات *mufáját.*

Suet, پیه *píh.*

Suffer, *v.*, زحمت کشیدن *zahmat ksh.*

Suffering, زحمت *zahmat;* درد *dard.*

Sufficiency, کفایة *kifáyat;* اکتفاء *iktifá.*

Sufficient, بس *bas;* بسنده *ba sendah.;* کافی *káfí;* مقنع *makna'.*

Suffocation, خفه *khafah* (*k. sh.*); غصه *ghussah;* خفگی *khafagí.*

Suffocating, خنق *khanik.*

Sugar (candied), قند *kand;* (moist), سکر *sukkar;* شکر *shakar.* — cane, نبات سکر *nabát i sukkar;* نی شکر *nai shakkar.* — plantation, شکرستان *shakaristán.*

Suggestion, اشاره *isháreh* (*k.*). Evil —, وسوسه *vasvasah*, *pl.* وساوس *vasávis.*

Suit, *v.*, شایستن *sháyistan;* *n.*, (for judgment), دعوا *da'vá.* Bringing a — before a judge, محاکمت *muhákamat.*

Suitability, مناسبت *munásabat.*

Suitable, بواجبی *bavájibí;* شایسته *sháyistah;* در خور *dar-khur.*

Suite, خدم و حشم *khadam o hasham.*

Suitor, شاکی *shákí.*

Sullen, عبوس *'abús.*

Sully, آلودن *álúdan.*

Sulphur, کبریت *kibrít;* کوگرد *gaugird.*

Sultan, سلطان *sultán, pl.* سلاطین *salátín.*

Sum (of money), مبلغ *mablagh.* — total, خبیره *khabírah;* جمله *jamlah.* Principal —, زر اصل *zar i asal.*

Summarily, سخن کوتاه *sukhan-kotáh;* مجملاً *majmalan.*

Summary, مجمل *majmal.*

Summer, تابستان *tábistán;* صیف *saif.*

Summit, سر *sar;* ذروه *zurvah.*

Summon, طلبیدن *talabídan;* احضار نمودن *ihzár n.*

Summons, طلب نامه *talab-námah.*

Sumptuous, فاخر *fákhir.*

Sun, آفتاب *áftáb;* (poetic or obsolete), شمس *shems;* خورشید *khurshíd;* هور *húr;* چشمهٔ هور *chashmah i húr;* نیر *naiyar;* یوسف روز *yúsuf i rúz;* هورخش *húrakhsh;* قبهٔ زرین *kubbah i zarrín;* قباس *kubás;* نان زرین *nán i zarín.* The Order of the Lion and the —, نشان شیر خرشید, *nishán i shír khurshíd.*

Sunday, یکشنبه *yak-shambah;* یوم الاحد *yaum ul ahad.*

Sundry, بعضی *ba'zí.*

Sunflower, شترپا *shutur-pá.* آفتاب گردان *áftáb-gardán.*

Sunk, مستغرق *mustaghrak.*

Sunnite, سنی *sunní.*

Sunrise, طلوع آفتاب *tulú' i áftáb.*

Sunset, غروب *ghurúb;* غروب آفتاب *ghurúb i áftáb.*

Sun-worshipper, آفتاب پرست *áftáb-parast.*

Superabundance, استفاضه *isti-fázah.*

Superabundant, افزون *afzún.*

Superb, معظم *mu'azzam.*

Supercilious, مغرور *maghrúr.* —ness, تکبر *takabbur.*

Supererogatory (prayers), نافله *náfilah.*

Superficial, ظاهر *záhir.*

Superficies, بساط *basát.*

Superfluity, افراط *ifrát.*

Superfluous, فاضل *fázil.*

Superintendence, نضارت *na-zárat (k.).*

Superintendent, داروغه *dárú-ghah;* ناظر *názir.* — of the police, شحنه *shahnah.*

Superior, اعظم *a'zam*; زبرین *zabarín*; فایق *fáiḳ*; مسلط *musallat*; مرجح *murajjah*; فوقانی *fauḳání*.

Superiority, غلبة *ghalabat*; پیشی *píshí*; دست برد *dast burd*.

Superlative, افضل *afzal*.

Superseded, منسوخ *mansúkh* (*k. sh.*).

Superstition, وسواس *vasvás*.

Superstitious, وسواسی *vasvásí*.

Supper, شام *shám*.

Supping, تعشی *ta'ashshí* (*n.*).

Supple, نرم *narm*.

Supplement, تتمه *tatimmah*, ضمیمة *zamímah*, *pl.* ضمائم *zamáim*.

Suppliant, عارض *'áriz*.

Supplicate, یشتن *yashtan*; التماس کردن *iltimás k.*

Supplication, نیاز *niyáz k.*; عرض *'arz* (*k.*); استدعاء *istid'á* (*n.*); ابتهال *ibtihál*; تضرع *tazarru'*; ملتمس *multamis n.*; لاوه *lávah*.

Support, *n.*, پشتی *pushtí*; *v.*, تحمل کردن *tahammul k.*

Supported, مستظهر *mustazhar*.

Supporter, ظهیر *zahír*; مدد کار *madad-gár*.

Supporting, متحمل *mutahammil*; اعتضاد *i'tizád* (*n.*).

Suppose, پنداشتن *pindáshtan*; (for example), مثلاً *masalan*.

Supposition, قیاس *ḳiyás* (*k.*). On —, بر تقدیر *bar taḳdír*.

Suppression, تسکین *taskín* (*k.*).

Suppuration, چرك *chirk* (*k.*).

Supreme, اعلی *a'lá*.

Surcingle, زبر تنك *zabar-tang*.

Sure, یقین *yaḳín*.

Surety (bail), ضامن *zámin*. Becoming —, متکفل *mutakaffil*.

Suretiship, ضامنی *záminí*.

Surface, صفحه *safhah*: سطح *sath*, *pl.* سطوح *sutúh*. — of the earth, عرصه زمین *'arsah i zamín*.

Surfeit, سیری *sírí*.

Surge, *v.*, موج زدن *mauj-z.*

Surgeon, جراح *jarráh*.

Surgery, or Surgical, جراحی *jarráhí*.

Surmise, قیاس *ḳiyás* (*k.*).

Surname, لقب *laḳab.*

Surnamed, ملقب *mulaḳḳab.*

Surpass, سبق بردن *sabḳ burdan.*

Surplus, صرفه *sarfah*; افزونی *afzúní.*

Surprise, تعجب *ta'ajjub* (*n.*); حیرت *hairat* (*k.*).

Surprised, متعجب *muta'ajjib* (*sh. h.*).

Surrender, تسلیم *taslím k.*

Surround, گرد کردن *gird-k.*; *pa. p.*, محاط *muhát*; *pr. p.*, احاطه *ihátah* (*k.*); محیط *muhít*; طائف *táif.*

Surveillance (under), نظر بند *nazar-band.*

Survey, مساحت *masáhat* (*k.*).

Suspect, شبهه کردن *shubheh k.*

Suspected, متهم *muttaham.*

Suspecting, متوهم *mutavahhim.*

Suspend, (بر) آویختن (*bar*) *ávíkhtan*; در آویختن *dar ávíkhtan.*

Suspended, بردار *bardár*; معلق *mu'allaḳ.*

Suspense, تعویق *ta'víḳ.*

Suspension, آویزش *ávízish*; تعلیق *ta'líḳ.*

Suspicion, گمان *gumán*; ظنه *zinnah*; شائبه *sháibah*; توهم *tavahhum*; اتهام *ithám.*

Suspicious, ظنی *zanní*; ظان *zánn*; وهام *vahhám.*

Sustain, بر داشتن *bar dáshtan.*

Sustenance, طعام *ta'ám.*

Swaddling clothes, قماط *kamát.*

Swallow, *n.*, پرستك *piristuk*, vulg., پرستو *piristú.* Mountain —, وطواط *vatvát*; *v.*, بلعیدن *bal'ídan.*

Swallowing, بلع *bal'* (*k.*); سرط *sarat.*

Swamp, خلاب *khaláb.*

Swan, قو *ḳú.*

Swarm, انبوه *ambúh.*

Swarthy, گندم گون *gandum-gún.*

Sway, حکمرانی *hukmráni.*

Swear, یمین کردن *yamin k.*; قسم خوردن *ḳasam kh.*; سوگند خوردن *saugand kh.*

Sweat, خوی *khúy*; عرق *'araḳ* (*k.*)

Sweating, متعرق *muta'arriḳ.*

Sweep (to), رفتن *ruftan*; روبیدن *rúbídan.*

Sweeper, خاکروب khák-rúb; کناس kannás.

Sweet, شیرین shírín (k.); حلو hulúv; نوشین núshín; با مزه bá-mazah; عذب 'azb; طاب táb. — smile, شکر خنده shakar-khandah.

Sweetheart, دل آزار dil-ázár; جانان jánán.

Sweetmeat, شیرینی shíríní; بتاشه batáshah; حلواء halvá'.

Sweetness, شیرینی shíríní; عذوبت 'uzúbat; حلاوت halávat.

Swell, آماسیدن ámásídan.

Swelling, آماس ámas.

Swerved, معدول ma'dúl (k.).

Swerving, عدول 'adúl (k.).

Swift, تیز رو tíz-rav; تند tund. — as the wind (a horse), بادپا bád-pá. — footed, سبك پا sabuk-pá. — paced, چابکخرام chábuk-khirám. — winged, سبك پر sabuk-par.

Swifter, or Swiftest, اسرع asra'.

Swiftness, تندی tundí.

Swim, شنا کردن shiná k.; شنو کردن shinau k.

Swimmer, سناور shinávar.

Swimming, n., شناوری shináverí.

Swindle, فریب دادن fíríb d.

Swindler, غدار ghaddár; فریبنده fíribandeh.

Swine, خوك khúg.

Swing, n., سرند sirind; هلاجین halájín; هلوجین halújín; v., آویختن ávíkhtan.

Switch, قمچی kamchí.

Swoon, غش ghash; بیهوش bíhúsh (sh.).

Sword, شمشیر shamshír; سیف saif; تیغ tígh. Small —, نیمچه ním-chah; (poetical), حسام hisám; صمصام samsám; نصل nasl.

Sword-belt, حمایل himáyil.

Swordsman, سیاف saiyáf.

Sycamore, چنار chinár.

Sycophancy, چاپلوسی cháplúsí.

Sycophant, طفیل tofail.

Syllable, هجا hijá.

Syllogism, قیاس kiyás.

Symbol, علامت 'alámat (b.).

Symmetry, تناسب tanásub.

Sympathizing, همدرد ham-dard (b.).

Sympathy, دردمندی *dard-mandí.*

Synonymous, هم معنی *ham-ma'ní.*

Syntax, نحو *nahv.*

Syphilis, کوفت *ḳúft.*

Syphon, انبوب *ambúb.*

Syrian, شامی *shámí ;* سریانی *suriyání.*

Syringe, حقنه *huḳnah.*

Syrup, شیره *shíruh.*

System, ضابطه *zábiteh.*

Systematic, مترتب *mutarattib.*

T.

Table, میز *míz.*

Tablecloth, سفره *sufrah.*

Table-decker, سفره چی *sufrah-chí.*

Tablet, تختی *takhtí.*

Taciturn, خاموش *khámúsh.* —ity, صمت *samt.*

Tail, دم *dum ;* ذنب *zanab ;* دنبال *dumbál.* The fat of a sheep's —, دنبه *dumbah.* Having a —, دمدار *dum-dár.*

Tailor, درزی *darzí ;* خیاط *khay-yát.*

Tainted, پوسیده *púsídeh.*

Take, گرفتن *giriftan ;* ستیدن *sitídan ;* ستدن *sitadan.* — up, بر گرفتن *bar giriftan.* — away, بر داشتن *bar dásh-tan.* — a siesta, چارت زدن *chárt z.* — care ! خبر دار *khabar dár.*

Taking, اخذ *akhz (k.).* — legal possession of, تصاحب *tasáhub (n.).*

Talc, طلق *talḳ.*

Tale, قصة *ḳissah, pl.* قصص *ḳisas ;* حکایت *hikáyat ;* نقل *naḳl ;* دستان *dastán ;* داستان *dástán.*

Talent, ذهن *zihn.*

Talisman, طلسم *tilsam, pl.* طلاسم *talásim.*

Talk, *v.,* حرف زدن *harf z. ;* گفتن *guftan ; n.,* گفتگو *guftogú (k.);* مقال *maḳál.*

Talker, سخن گو *sukhan gú.* Idle —, بطال *battál ;* بوالفضول *bu'lfuzúl.*

Tall, بلند *buland ;* دراز *diráz.* — of nature, درز قد *daráz-ḳadd.*

Tallow, پیه *píh.*

Talons, چنگال *changál.*

Tamarind, تمر هندی *tamar i hindí.*

Tamarisk-tree, طرفاء *tarfá'*; گز *gaz*; بان *bán.*

Tambourine, طنبور *tambúr*; خنجری *khanjarí*; دف *daf.*

Tamo, رام *rám* (*k.*); داجن *dájin.*

Tank, حوز *hauz*; دریاچه *daryácheh.*

Tanned, مدبول *madbúl* (*k.*).

Tanning, دباغت *dibághat.*

Tape, بافته *báfteh.*

Taper, شمع *sham'.*

Tapestry, فرش *farsh.*

Tar, قیر *ḳír.*

Tarantula, رتیل *rutail.*

Tardy, وقاف *vakḳáf.*

Tares, کاکلك *kákulak.*

Target, هدف *hadaf.*

Tarnish, تیره کردن *tírah k.*

Tarragon, ترخون *tarkhún.*

Tatar, تاتار *Tátár*; یوزبك *Yúz-beg*; تتر *Tatar.*

Tartarian, تتری *tatari.*

Task, شغل *shughl.*

Tassel, منگله *mangulah.*

Taste, *v.*, چشیدن *chashídan*;—*n.*, مزه *mazah* (*gr.*); ذوق *zauḳ*; چاشنی *cháshní.*

Tasting, ذائق *záiḳ*; طعم *ta'm* (*k.*); مذاق *muzáḳ.* The sense of —, ذایقه *záiḳah.*

Tasteless, بی نمك *bí-namak*; بیمزه *bí-mazah.*

Taster, بکاول *bakával.*

Tattered (garments), خلقان *khulḳán.*

Tattooing, وشم *vashm* (*k.*); خال *khál* (*k.*).

Taunt, طعنه زدن *ta'neh z.* One who —s, طاعن *tá'in*; *pa. p.*, مطعون *mat'ún.* —ing, نزغ *nazgh* (*k*).

Tavern, میکده *mai-kedah*; ماخور *mákhur*; خمخانه *khum-khánah*; خماره *khammárah*; خرابات *kharábát.*

Tax, باج *báj*; خراج *kharáj*; وضیعت *vazí'at.*

Taxation, تسعیر *tas'ír.*

Taxgather, باجدار *báj-dár.*

Tea, چای *chái.* — pot, قوری *ḳúrí.*

Teach, آموختن *ámúkhtan*; در آموختن *dar ámúkhtan*;

درس دادن ـ كفتن ـ خواندن *dars d.*, *gf.*, or *khándan.*

Teacher, اوستاد *ústád ;* استاد *ustád ;* آموز كار *ámúzgár ;* معلم *mu'allim.*

Teak-tree, ساج *sáj.*

Tear, *n.*, اشك *ashk ;* سرشك *sirishk ;* دمع *dam'*, *pl.* دموع *dumú'.* —ful, آبديده *áb-dídah ;* دامع *dámi'.*

Tear, *v.*, دريدن *darídan;* كسستن *gusistan ;* كسيختن *gusíkhtan.* — up, بر كندن *bar kandan ;* *pr. p.*, اختراق *ikhtirák (k.) ;* انتزاع *intizá' (n.).*

Tease, *v.*, آزار كردن *ázár k.*

Teat, ضرع *zir';* سر پستان *sar-i-pistán.*

Technical, مصطلح *mustalih.* —terms, اصطلاحات *istiláhát.*

Tedious, مفصل *mufassal.* —ness, تفصيل *tafsíl.*

Teeth, اسنان *asnán;* ضرس *zars*, *pl.* اضراس *azrás.* — of a saw, دندانه *dandánah.*

Telegram, تلكرافنامه *talgeráf-námeh.*

Telegraph, تلكراف *talgeráf.* —ist, تلكرافچی *talgeráfchí.*

Telescope, دوربين *dúr bín.*

Tell, كفتن *guftan ;* خبر كردن, دادن *khabar d.*, or *k.*

Tell-tale, نمام *nammám.*

Temerity, جسارت *jasárat.*

Temper, خوى *khúy ;* طبع *tab'.*

Temperament, سيرت *sírat ;* مزاج *mizáj.*

Temperate, معتدل *mu'tadil.*

Temperature, كرمى *garmí.*

Tempest, تندباد *tund-bád ;* طوفان *túfán.*

Temple, هيكل *haikal.* — of Jerusalem, هوخ *húkh.* — of Mecca, كعبه *ka'bah ;* (brow), جبين *jabín ;* شقيقه *shakíkah.*

Temporal, زمانى *zamání;* هنكامى *hangámí.*

Tempt, اغوا كردن *ighvá k.*

Temptation, ابتيلاء *ibtílá (n.).*

Tempter, فاتن *fátin ;* مغوى *mughví.*

Ten, ده *dah ;* عشر *'ashar.* — or twenty, ده بست *dah-bist,*

Tenacity, چسپيدكى *chaspí-dagí.*

Tenant, اجارہ دار *ijáreh dár.*

Tendency, میل *mail.*

Tender, ملایم *muláyim* ; مناعم *muná'im.* —ness, ملایمت *muláyimat.*

Tending (the sick), تیمار *tímár* (*k.*).

Tendon, عصب *'asab.*

Tenet, عقیدہ *'akídah.*

Tense, حالت *hálat.*

Tent, خیمہ *khaimah* ; چادر *chádir.* Small —, سراچہ *sarácheh* ; سرایچہ *saráycheh.* A — pitched without a pole, بیچوبا *bí-chúbá.* Royal —, خرگاہ *khargáh.* To pitch a —, خیمہ زدن *khaimah z.* — maker, خیام *khayyám.* — peg, میخ *míkh.*

Tenth, دہم *dahum.* A — part, عاشر *'áshir* ; عشیر *'ashír.*

Tepid, ملول *malúl.*

Term, *n.*, مدت *muddat* ; *v.*, مسمی نمودن *musammá n.*

Terminate, تمام کردن *tamám k.*

Terminated, متناہی *mutanáhí.*

Termination, اتمام *atmám* (*rs.*).

Terrace (roof), بام *bám.*

Terrestrial, ارضی *arzí.*

Terrible, ہولناک *haul-nák* ; مرہوب *marhúb* ; ہایل *háil.*

Terrify, ترسانیدن *tarsánídan* ; رمانیدن *ramánídan* ; *pa. p.*, مرعوب *mar'úb* ; مخوف *mukhavvaf* ; متوحش *mutavahhish* ; *pr. p.*, موحش *múhish* ; منفر *munfir.*

Territory, بلاد *belád.*

Terror, ترس *tars* ; رعب *ra'b* ; بیم *bím* ; ہراسہ *hirásah* ; ہراس *hirás.*

Test, عیار *'iyár* (*k.*) ; امتحان *imtihán* (*n.*).

Testament, وصیت *vasíyat.* Old —, تورات *taurát.* New —, انجیل *anjíl.*

Testator, موصی *muvassí.*

Testicle, خصیۃ *khusyat* ; in *dual.*, خصیتان *khusyatáni* ; خایہ *kháyah.*

Testimony, شہادت *shahádat* (*d.*) ; گواہی *gaváhí* (*d.*).

Testing, تجریب *tajríb* (*n.*).

Text, متن *matn* ; آیت *áyat.*

Texture, نسیج nasíj.

Than, از az.

Thank God, شکر ایزد shukr i ízad ; شکر خدا shukr i khudá. — you, لطف شما زیاد lutf-i-shumá ziyád.

Thanked, مشکور mashkúr.

Thanking, شاکر shákir (h.).

Thanks, شکر shukr.

Thanksgiving, سپاس sipás.

That, آن án (gen. pron. ún). From —, زان zán. — very, همون hamún.

Thatch, پوش púsh.

Thaw, یخاب yakháb (sh.).

Theatre, تماشگاه tamásha-gáh.

Theft, دزدی duzdí ; سرقة sarḳat ; مسارقت musáraḳat.

Them, their, ایشان íshán ; شان -shán.

Then, آنگه ángah ; پس pas.

Thence, از آنجا az ánjá.

Theology, حکمت الاهی hikmat i iláhí.

Theory, علم 'ilm قیاس ḳiyás.

There, آنجا ánjá ; هناك hunák.

Therefore, لهذا liházá ; از آن سبب az án sabab ; فلهذا faliházá.

Thermometer, درجه darajeh.

These, اینان ínán ; اینها ínhá.

They, ایشان íshán ; آنها ánhá.

Thick, کلفت kuluft ; غلیظ ghalíz ; بلما balmá ; هنگفت hunguft ; ستبر sitabr.

Thickness, کلفتی kuluftí ; ضخامت zakhámat ; ستبری sitabri ; غلظت, ghalzat, or ghulzat ; حجم hajm.

Thief, دزد duzd ; سارق sáriḳ.

Thigh, ران rán.

Thimble, انکشتانه angushtánah ; — rig, حقه بازی huḳḳah bází ; — rigger, حقه باز huḳḳah-báz.

Thin, باریك bárík ; نازك názuk ; رقیق raḳíḳ ; رکیك rakík ; رق raḳḳ.

Thing, چیز chíz ; شی shai, pl. اشیاء ashyá', in pl. اسباب asbab. — given in charge, حوالات haválát.

Think, اندیشیدن andíshídan ; پنداشتن pindáshtan ; سکالیدن sikálídan, or sigálídan ; انکاشتن angáshtan.

Thinking, حدس hads (k.) ; فکر fikr (k.).

Thinness, باریکی báríkí.

Third, سوم *sivum*; سیوم *síyum*. The — (an arbitrator), ثالث *sális*. A — part, ثلث *suls*.

Thirdly, سیومین *síyumín*.

Thirst, تشنگی *tishnagí*; عطش *'atsh*.

Thirsty, تشنه *tishnah*; عطشان *'atshán*; ظامی *zámí*.

Thirteen, سیزده *sízdah*.

Thirteenth, سیزدهم *sízdahum*.

Thirtieth, سیم *síyum*.

Thirty, سی *sí*.

This, این *ín*. In —, درین *darín*.

Thistle, شوك *shauk*.

Thong, تسمه *tasmah*.

Thorn, خار *khár*; شوك *shauk*. Hedge of —, خاربست *khár-bast*.

Thorny, خار دار *khár-dár*.

Thorough, تام *támm*.

Thoroughbred, اصیل *asíl*.

Thoroughfare, راه *ráh*.

Those, آنها *ánhá*; آنان *ánán*.

Thou, تو *tú*.

Though, اگرچه *agarcheh*.

Thought, تفکر *tafakkur* (*k.*); هواجس *havájis*; فکر *fikr*; سگال *sikál*, or *sigál*, *in pl.* ظنون *zunún*.

Thoughtful, متفکر *mutafakkir*; اندیشناك *andíshanák*.

Thousand, هزار *hazár*. Ten —, تمن *tuman*, or تومان *túmán*.

Thrash, مالش کردن *málish k.*

Thrashing-floor, خرمن گاه *khirman gáh*.

Thread, رشته *rishtah*; تار *tár*; نخ *nakh*; کلاوه *kalávah*. Raw —, کلابه *kalábah*. Brahminical or Guebre's —, زنار *zunnár*. A — upon which pearls, &c., are strung, سمط *simt*.

Threat, تهدید *tahdíd* (*k.*); وعید *va'íd*.

Threaten, ترسانیدن *tarsánídan*; *pr. p.*, تحذیر *tahzír*.

Three, سه *sih*; ثلاث *salás*. — hundred, سهصد *sihsad*. — sixes (a throw at dice), سه شش *sih-shash*.

Threshold, آستان *ástán*; عتبه *'atabah*.

Throat, گلو *gulú*; حلق *halk*. To have a sore —, گلو گرفتن *gulú gr.*

Throb, حرکت *harakat* (*k.*).

Throne, سریر *sarír*; تخت

takht ; مسند masnad ; اریکه arikah ; اورنك aurang.

Throng, جماعت jamá'at.

Throttled, خفه khaffah (k.).

Through, ازمیان az miyán.

Throw, انداختن andákhtan ; افگندن afgandan ; فکندن fikandan. — down, زپای در آوردن zi pái dar a.

Thrush, سار sár.

Thrust, زدن zadan.

Thumb, شست shast ; ابهام ibham.

Thunder, رعد ra'd ; تندر tundar. It —s, رعد صدا میکند ra'd sadá mí kunad ; v., غریدن ghurídan.

Thursday, پنج شنبه panj-shambah.

Thus, همچنین hamchunín ; کذا kazá.

Thyme, اپار ipár.

Tick (cattle), کنه kanah.

Tickling, نشکنج nishkunj ; قلقلی ḳilḳilí (k.).

Tide (ebb), جزر jazr ; فرو آمدن دریا farau ámadan i daryá ; (flow), مد madd ; بالا آمدن دریا bálá ámadan i daryá.

Tidings, اخبار akhbár. Glad —, خوش خبر khush-khabar ; مژده muzhdah.

Tie, ربط rabt ; عقد 'aḳd (k.). Marriage —, عقد نکاح 'aḳd i nikah. To — down, فرو بستن farú bastan.

Tied, منعقد muna'ḳíd (sh.) ; tongue —, زبان بریده zabán-burídah.

Tiger, پلنك palang ; ببر babr.

Tight, تنك tang (ksh.).

Tightness, تنك جای tang-jái ; ضیق zaiḳ.

Tigris, دجله Dijlah, or Dajlah.

Tile کاشی káshí.

Till, تا tá ;—v., (ground), زرع کردن zar' k.

Tillage, زراعت zirá'at.

Timber, چوب chúb ; هیزم heizum.

Time, که gah ; گاه gáh ; وقت vaḳt, pl. اوقات auḳát ; هنگام hangám ; زمان zamán ; زمانه zamánah ; روز گار rúz-gár ; حین hín ; (turn), نوبت naubat. Space of —, مدت muddat. Every —, هر بار har bár. — stated for payment, عهده بندی 'uhdah *bandí.* At the same —, هموقت *ham-vaḳt.* This —, انبار *imbár.* Appointed — (death), اجل *ajal;* موءجل *mu'ajjal.* One —, دفعه *daf'ah;* يك دفع *yek daf'ah.* Convenient —, سر وقت *sar i vaḳt.* Life—, عمر *'umr;* حين حيات *hín i haiyát, in pl.* ايام *aiyám;* ازمان *azmán;* آوان *áván;* ازمنه *azminah;* دوران *daurán;* دفعات *dafa'át* Hundred —s as much, صد چندان *sad chandán.* To beat —, خنبيدن *khumbídan.*

Time-server, زمانه‌ساز *zamánah-sáz.*

Tinid, ترسنده *tarsendah;* خايف *kháif;* هيدان *haidán;* رمنده *ramendah;* رمان *ramán;* خشى *khashí;* خاشى *kháshí.*

Timidity, وحشة *vahshat.*

Tin, ارزين *arzín.* A — حلبى *halabí.* Made of —, قلعى *ḳal'iy.*

Tincture, رز *raz.*

Tinder, قو *ḳú.*

Tinge, رنك *rang* (*k. z.*).

Tinged, مصبغ *musabbagh.*

Tip, سر *sar.* — of the ear, نرمه كوش *narmah i gúsh.* — of a pen, ناخن خامه *nákhun i khámah.* — of the finger, سرانكشت *sar-angusht;* سر دست *sar-dast.* — of the tongue, سر زبان *sar i zabán.*

Tipsy, مست *mast.*

Tired, خسته *khasteh* (*k. sh.*); ستوه *sutúh;* ملول *malúl* (*sh.*); مبتلى *mubtalá* (*sh.*); فرو مانده *farú-mándah.*

Tithe, عشر *'ushr;* ده يك *dah yek.*

Title, لقب *laḳab, pl.* القاب *alḳáb;* خطاب *khitáb.* — page, عنوان *'anván.*

To ب *ba;* الى *ilá;* (until), تا *tá.* — him, بوى *ba vai;* بدو *badú.*

Toad, قرباغه *ḳurpághah.*

Toadstool, قارچ *ḳarch.*

Tobacco, توتن *tútun,* for *ḳaliyán;* تنباكو *tam-bákú.*

To-day, امروز *imrúz.*

Toe, انكشت *angusht.*

Together, باهم *báham;* بهم

baham; باهم دیکر *báham digar*; (all at once), یکقلم *yak-ḳalam.*

Toil, زحمت *zaḣmat.*

Toilet, زینت *zínat.*

Token, علامت *'alámat.*

Tolerant, صبور *sabúr.*

Toleration, اجازت *ijázat* (*d.*).

Toll, *v.*, زدن *zadan.*

Tomb, قبر *ḳabr*, *pl.* قبور *ḳubúr*; مزار *mizár*; تربت *turbat.*

To-morrow, فردا *fardá.* The day after —, پس فردا *pas fardá.*

Tongs, گاز *gáz*; کلبتان *kal-batán.*

Tongue, زبان *zabán*; لسان *lisán.* — tied, خفاجل *khu-fájil.*

Too, (also) ایضاً *aizan.* — much زیاد *ziyád.*

Tool, آلت *álat*, *pl.* آلات *álát*; دست افراز *dast-afráz.* —

Tooth, دندان *dandán.* Canine —, سگ دندان *sag-dandán.* — pick, خلال *khilál.*

Top, سر *sar*; قله *ḳullah*; بالا *bálá*; اوج *auj*, — of the head, تارك *tárak.*

Topaz, زبرجد *zabarjad.*

Topsy-turvy, زیر و بالا *zír u bálá*; زیر و زبر *zír u zabar*; سرنگون *sar-nigún*; تار و مار *tár u már*; ته و بالا *tah u bálá.*

Torch, مشعل *mash'al.* Small —, مشعله *mash'alah.* — bearer, مشعلچی *mash'alchí.*

Torment, عذاب *'azáb* (*k.*). —ing, اعذاب *i'záb* (*k.*); تعذیب *ta'zíb* (*n.*).

Tormentor, ظالم *zálim*; خلق آزار *khalḳ ázár.*

Torn, دریده *darídah*; پاره *páreh*; فرسوده *farsúdah.* — out, منقلع *munḳala'.*

Torpid, سست *sust.*

Torpor, خدر *khadar.*

Torrent, سیل *sail*; سیلاب *sailáb.*

Torrid, حار *hárr.*

Tortoise, سنگ پشت *sang-pusht.*

Torture, شکنجه *shikanjeh* (*k.d.*).

Total, جمله *jumleh.*

Totality, جملگی *jumlagí.*

Totally, سر بسر *sar-ba-sar*; سرتا پا *sar tá pá*; سرتا سر *sar tá sar.*

Totter, طپیدن *tapídan.*

Tottering (pace), فراخیز *ferá-khíz.*

Touch, لمس *lams;* مس *mass* (*k.*); *pr. p.*, لامس *lámis;* مساس *misás.* — hole, کداره *gudárah.* — stone, محك *mahakk.* — wood, وریت *varíyat;* پیفه *pífah.*

Tough, سخت *sakht* (*s.*).

Tour, سیر *sair* (*k.*).

Tow, *n.*, کنف *kanaf;* *v.*, (drag), کشیدن *kashídan.*

Towards, سوی *súy;* سمت *samt;* طرف *taraf.*

Turned, معطوف *ma'túf.*

Towel, دستمال *dastmál;* بشکیر *bashgír.*

Tower, برج *burj, pl.* بروج *burúj;* قبة *ḳubbeh, pl.* قباب *ḳibáb.*

Town, شهر *shahr;* قصبه *ḳasbah.*

Toy, *n.*, بازیچه *bázícheh;* *v.*, غنجیدن *ghanjídan.*

Traces (vestiges), آثار *ásár.*

Track, نشان *nishán;* (path), جاده *jádeh.*

Tracts, صفاح *sifáh;* اقطار *aḳtár.*

Trade, *n.*, تجارت *tijárat;* بازر کانی *bázar-gání;* سودا *sauda;* کسب *kasb;* حرفة *hurfat;* *v.*, معامله کردن *mu'ámalah k.*

Trader, کار و باری *kár u bárí.*

Tradition, روایت *riváyat;* (oral), سماعی *samá'íy;* (of the Prophet), حدیث *hadís.*

Traditional, نقلی *naḳlí.*

Traducement, بهتان *buhtán* (*bs.*).

Traffic, عبور و مرور *'ubúr o murúr;* معامله *mu'ámeleh* (*k.*).

Tragedy, مرثیه *marsiyah.*

Tragic, مغموم *maghmúm.*

Trail, سراغ *surágh.*

Train, حشم *hashm.* — of artillery, توپخانه *topkhánah.*

Trained (by the hand), دست آموز *dast-ámúz.*

Trained (horse), سوغانی *sava-ghání* (*gr.*).

Training, to go into (a horse), روغن کرفتن *raughan gr.*

Traitor, غادر *ghádir;* بد عهد *bad-'ahd.*

Trample on, پایمال کردن *páí mál k.*

Trance, غش *ghash.*

Tranquil, آسوده *ásúdah* (*k.*); آرام *aram* (*d.*).

Tranquility, استراحت *istiráhat;* فراغبال *farágh i bál;* امن *amn;* سکینه *sakínah.*

Transaction (business), کار و بار kár o bár; (doing), اجرا ijrá (k.).

Transcript, or Transfer, نقل naḳl (k.).

Transfix, سفتن saftan.

Transformation, مسخ maskh.

Transformed, متغیر muta-ghayyir.

Transgression, تجاوز tajávuz (k.).

Transgressing, مجاوز mujáviz (k.).

Transgressor, متجاوز mutajáviz.

Transitory, فنا پذیر faná-pazír; زایل záil; فانی fání.

Translation, ترجمه tarjumah (k.).

Translator, مترجم mutarjim; ترجمان tarjumán.

Transmigration, تناسخ tanásukh.

Transmitting, بلاغ balágh (n.); انفاذ infáz (dsh.).

Transmutation, تبدیل tabdíl (k.).

Transparent, شفاف shaffáf.

Transoxania, ما وراء النهر Má vará an nahr.

Transport, نقل naḳl (k.).

Transportation, تبعید tab'íd.

Transposition, Transubstantiation, تبدیل tabdíl (k.).

Trap, دام dám (an.).

Travail, درد زی dard-i-zí.

Travel, راه بریدن ráh burídan; سفر کردن safar k.; در نوردن dar navardan. Foreign —, n., سیاحت siyáhat (k.); غربت ghurbat.

Traveller, مسافر musáfir; راه رو ráh-ro; راهبان ráhbán; سیاح saiyáh; رونده ravendah; سالك sálik; رهور rah-var; ره رو rah-ro; سافر sáfir; راهی ráhí; (poetical), جهان نورد jahán-navard; جهان کرد jahán-gard; ابن السبیل ibn us sabíl. — by sea, دریا نورد daryá-navard. Fellow —, همتك ham-tag; همرو ham-ro; همره ham-rah; همراه ham-ráh.

Travelling, مسیر masír (k.); سیاحت siyáhat (k.); سایر sáir.

Tray, سینی síní; خوان khán; طبله tablah. Small —, خوانچه khánchah. Cover of a —,

خوان پوش *khán-púsh.* — of a pair of scales, كفه *kaffah.*

Treacherous, دغلی *daghalí;* خاین *kháin.*

Treachery, غدر *ghadr.*

Treacle, نوشدارو *núshdárú.*

Treason, خیانت *khiyánat.*

Treasure, کنج *ganj;* کنجور *ganjvar;* کنز *kanz, pl.* کنوز *kunúz.* Buried —, دفینه *dafínah, pl.* دفائن *dafáin.*

Treasurer, خزینه دار *khazínah dár;* خازن *kházin;* خزانچی *khezánchí.*

Treasury, خزینه *khazínah;* خزانه *khizánah;* گنجینه *ganjínah.* Imperial or public —, خزانهٔ عامره *khizánah i 'ámirah.*

Treatise, رساله *risálah.*

Treatment (medical), مداوات *mudávát (n.).*

Treaty, صلح نامه *sulh-námah;* عهد نامه *'ahd-námah;* پیمان *paimán;* قولنامه *kaul-námah.*

Tree, درخت *dirakht;* شجر *shajar.* Young —, نو نهال *nau-nihál.* Box —, شمشاد *shamshád.*

Trefoil, هلندور *halandúr.*

Tremble, لرزیدن *larzídan.*

Trembling, زلازل *zalázil.*

Tremour, زلزال *zalzál;* لرزه *larzah;* رعشه *ra'shah.*

Trench, خندق *khandak.*

Trencher, خوانچه *kháncheh.*

Trepidation, بیم *bím;* باك *bák.*

Trespass, تعدی *ta'addí.*

Tresses, کیس *gís.*

Trial, امتحان *imtihán (k.);* ابتلاء *ibtilá (n.);* ابلاء *iblá (k.);* تجویز *tajvíz.*

Triangle, سه کوشه *sih-gúshah.*

Triangular, مثلث *musallas.*

Tribe, قبیله *kabílah, pl.* قبایل *kabáil.* Nomade —, ایل *íl, pl.* ایلات *ílát;* قوم *kaum;* طایفه *táifeh.*

Tribunal, دیوان *díván;* محکمه *mahkamah.* — of justice, دار القضاء *dar ul kazá.*

Tributary, خراج کذار *kharáj-guzár;* باجکذار *báj-guzár.*

Tribute, باج *báj;* خراج *kharáj;* اخراجات *ikhráját;* سا *sá.*

Trick, بازی *bází;* مکر *makr;* کول *gúl (z.);* توطیه *tautíyeh;* شید *shaid.*

Trickery, تسویل *tasvíl.*

Trickle, چکیدن *chakídan.*

Trifle, ژاژ خای *zházh-kháy*; مزجات *mazaját*; پوچ *púch*, *in pl.* خردوات *khurdavát*; *v.*, در باختن *dar-bákhtan.*

Trigger, ماشه *másheh.*

Triliteral, ثلاثی *sulásí.*

Trimming, سجاف *sajáf.*

Trinity, ثالوث *sálús.*

Trip up, پا لغزیدن *pá laghzídan.*

Tripe, شکنبه *shikambah.*

Triple, مثلث *musallas.*

Tripod, سه پا *seh pá.*

Triumph, ظفر *zafar* (*y.*).

Triumphant, غالبانه *ghálibánah*; مظفر *muzaffar.*

Trivet, سپا *sipá.*

Troop, فوج *fauj*, *pl.* افواج *afváj*; فریق *faríḳ*; جوق *jauḳ.*

Troops, جنود *junúd*; جیش *jaish.*

Trooper, سوار *sovvár*; دواسپه *dú-aspah.*

Tropics, گرمسیر *garmsír.*

Trot, لکه *lukkah* (*z.*).

Trouble, رنجه *ranjah*; ازی *azá*; تکلیف *taklíf*; کلفت *kulfat*; ازار *ázár* (*k.*); اختلال *ikhtilál*; *v.*, آزاردن *ázárdan.* To give —, زحمت دادن *zahmat d.* To take —, زحمت کشیدن *zahmat ksh.*

Troubler, مصدع *musaddiʿ*; متکلف *mutakallif.*

Trough, ناوه *náveh.*

Trousseau, جهاز *jaház.*

Trout, قزل آلا *ḳizil álá.*

Trowel, ماله *málah*; برز *burz.*

Trowsers, شلوار *shalvár*; پاجامه *pá-jámah.* Ladies' — for out-door wear, چاهچور *cháhchúr.*

Truce, متارکه *mutárakeh.*

Truculent, جبار *jabbár.*

True, راست *rást*; صحیح *sahíh*; صدیق *siddíḳ*; حقانی *haḳḳání.* More or most —, اصح *asahh.*

Truly, بدرستی *ba-durustí*; محققانه *muhaḳḳiḳánah.*

Trumpet, کرنا *karná* (*z.*); بوق *búḳ* (*z.*); سورنا *súrná*; سورنای *súrnáy* (*z.*); شیپور *shaipúr*; بوری *búrí*; ناقور *náḳúr*; گاو دم *gáu-dam.*

Trunk (elephant's), خرطوم *khartúm*; (of a tree), تنه *tunah.*

Trust (in), اعتماد *i'timád* (*k.*); اعتقاد *i'tiḳád* (*k.*); (to), سپرد *sipurd* (*k.*).; ذمه *zimmah.* — in God, توكل *tavakkul* (*k.*). In —, وديعة *vadi'at.*

Trusted (fit to be), سپردنی *sipurdaní.*

Trusting (in God), متوکل *mutavakkil.*

Trustworthy, معتمد *mu'tamad.*

Trusty, موءتمن *mu'taman.* — friends, ثقات *siḳát.*

Truth, حق *haḳḳ;* صدق *sidḳ;* هستو *hastú;* حقانیت *haḳḳáníyet.* In —, برحق *bar haḳḳ;* حقاً *haḳḳan;* فی الحقیقة *fi'l haḳíḳat.* Addicted to the —, حق پرست *haḳḳ parast.* Addiction to —, حق پرستی *haḳḳ-parastí.* Seeking —, حق جو *haḳḳ-jú.*

Truthful, صادق *sádiḳ;* راست سخن *rást-sukhan;* راست کو *rást-gú.* — ness, تحقیق *tahḳiḳ.*

Try, سعی کردن *sa'í k;* آزمودن *ázmúdan;* عیار گرفتن *'iyár gr.;* *pa. p.*, مجرب *mujarrab.*

Tub, سطل *satl.*

Tube, نیچه *naichah;* ناو *náv.*

Tubercle, آماس *ámás.*

Tuberose, گل مریام *gul i maryám.*

Tuesday, سه شنبه *sih shambah.*

Tuition, تعلیم *ta'lím* (*d.*).

Tulip, لاله *lálah.*

Tumble, غلطیدن *ghaltídan.*

Tumbler (glass), معلق زن *mu'allaḳ-zan;* استقان *istaḳán.*

Tumour, ورم *varam.*

Tumult, هرج *harj;* غلغل *ghulghul;* دغدغه *daghdaghah;* دار و کیر *dár u gír;* شولوق *shúlúḳ;* شلتاق *shiltáḳ;* خرخشه *kharkhishah.*

Tumultuous, هنکامه کیر *hangámah-gír.*

Tune, آواز *áváz.*

Tunic, قباچه *ḳabácheh;* چوخا *chúkhá.*

Turban, دستار *dastár;* عمامه *'amámah.*

Turbid, مکدر *mukaddar.* —ness, کدورت *kudúrat;* کدر *kadar;* تکدر *takaddur.*

Turbulence, فساد *fisád.*

Turbulent, لجوج *lajúj.*

Turk, ترك *Turk*; (Ottoman), عثمانلو *'Osmanlú* or *'Osmanlí.*

Turkey (bird), فيل مرغ *fíl-murgh*; (country), روم *Rúm.*

Turkish, تركى *Turkí.*

Turmeric, زرد چوب *zard-chúb*; هرد *hurd.*

Turn, *v. i.*, گرديدن *gardídan*; *v. t.*, گردانيدن *gardánídan.* — away, تافتن *táftan*; (spin), چرخ زدن *charkh-z.*

Turned (on a lathe), منخرط *munkharit* (*sh.*); مخروط *makh-rút.* — back, منصرف *mun-sarif.* — towards, منعطف *mun'atif.*

Turning, گردان *gardán* (*k.*). Art of —, خراطت *kharátat*; خرط *khart.* — lathe, خراد *kharád.*

Turner, خراط *kharrát*; خرادى *kharádí.*

Turnip, شلغم *shalgham*; سلجم *saljam.*

Turnscrew, آچار *áchár*; پيچ *pích.*

Turpitude, شنيعت *shaní'at.*

Turquoise, فيروزه *fírúzah.*

Turret, مناره *minárah*; كنگره *kangurah.*

Turtle, كاسه پشت *kásah pusht.* — dove, يمام *yamám*; قمرى *kumrí.*

Tuck, دندان *dandán.*

Tutor, آخون *ákhún*; آخوند *ákhund*; اديب *adíb*; اتاليق *atálík.*

Tutty, توتيا *tútiyá.*

Tweezers, موچينه *mú-chínah*; خار چينه *khár-chínah.*

Twelfth, دوازدهم *duvázdahum.*

Twelve, دوازده *duvázdah.*

Twentieth, بستم *bistum.*

Twenty, بيست *bíst*; عشرين *'ishrín.*

Twice, دو تا *dú-tá.*; دو چند *dú-chand.*

Twig, شاخچه *shákhchah.*

Twilight, هوا گرك و ميش *havá i gurg o mísh*; (morning), صبح كاذب *subh i kázib.*

Twin, توءام *tav'ám*, *in dual*, توءامان *tav'ámán*; همزاد *ham-zád.*

Twine, *v.*, تافتن *táftan.*

Twinge, درد *dard.*

Twinkling (of an eye), طرفة العين *tarfat ul 'ain.*

Twist, *n.*, پيچ *pích*; *v.*, پيچيدن *píchídan*; تافتن *táftan*;

بر تافتن *bar táftan*; تنیدن *tanídan*; ریستن *rístan*; ریسیدن *risídan*; پیختن *píkhtan*; نوردن *navardan*.

Twisted, تافته *táftah*; مفتل *muftall*; مفتول *maftúl*.

Two, دو *do*; اثنانی *isnáni*. — or three, دوسه *do-seh*. —s, دو گان *dú-gán*. — faced, دو روی *do-rúí*.

Tyrannical, ظلوم *zalúm*; جائر *jáir*.

Tyranny, ظلم *zulm*; دراز دستی *diráz-dastí*; دست درازی *dast-dirází*; ظلمیت *zulmíyet*; تطاول *tatávul*; جور *jaur*; حیف *haif*.

Tyrant, ظالم *zálim*; ظلم پیشه *zulm-píshah*; ستم کار *sitam-kár*; جور پیشه *jaur-píshah*.

U.

Udder, پستان *pistán*.

Ugliness, زشتی *zishtí*.

Ugly, زشت *zisht*; نغام *nagham*; ستیزه رو *sitízah-rú*. — fellow, نا فرهخته *ná-farhikhtah*.

Ulcer, چبان *chabán*; قرح *kurh*, *pl.* قروح *kurúh*.

Ultimately, عاقبت الامر *'ákibat ul amr*.

Umbrage, خفت *kiffat*.

Umbrella, چتر *chatr*.

Umpire, حکم *hakam*.

Un- (in comp.), نا *ná*, بی *bí*.

Unable, ناتوان *nátaván*.

Unacceptable, نا مقبول *ná-makbúl*.

Unacquainted (with the roads), نا بلد *ná-balad*.

Unaided, نا مساعد *ná-musá'id*;

Unanimity, یك جهتی *yak jihatí*.

Unanimous, یکدل *yak-dil*; یکروی *yak-rúí*; همدل *ham-dil*; همساز *ham-sáz*. —ly, یکزبان *yak-zabán*.

Unappropriate, نا مخصوص *ná-makhsús*.

Unattainable, نا میسر *ná-muyassar*; نا یاب *ná-yáb*.

Unbecoming, نا شایسته *ná-sháyistah*; نشاید *nasháyad*.

Unbeliever, کافر *káfir*.

Unblemished, بیداغ *bí dágh*.

Uncalled, نا طلب *ná-talab*.

Uncertainty, شك و شبهه *shakk o shubheh.*

Uncivil, بی ادب *bí-adab.*

Uncle (paternal), عم *'amm ;* عمو *'ammú ;* (maternal), خال *khál ;* خالو *khálú.*

Unclean, نجس *najis.*

Uncleanness, رجس *rijs.*

Uncommon, شاذ *sházz.*

Unconcerned, بی غم *bí-ghamm.*

Unconnected, نا مربوط *ná-marbút*

Unconscious, بیخود *bíkhud.*

Uncovered, منکشف *munkashif.*

Uncultivated, بایر *báir.*

Undeniable, بیدریغ *bí-dirígh.*

Under, زیر *zír ;* فرود *farúd ;* تحت *taht.* —mined, منقوب *mankúb (sh.).*

Understand, فهمیدن *fahmídan.*

Understanding, فهم *fahm ;* هوش *húsh ;* هنك *hang ;* تفهم *tafahhum ;* تعقل *ta'akkul ;* مدرکه *madrikah.* Good —, مصافات *musáfát.*

Understood, مفهوم *mafhúm ;* ذهن نشین *zahan-nishín.*

Undertaking, عزم *'azm (k.) ;* کار *kar (k.) ;* متعهد *muta-'ahhid (k.).*

Undeserving, نا مستحق *ná-mustahikk.*

Undesirable, نا مرغوب *ná-marghúb.*

Undetermined, نکره *nukrah.*

Undiminished, نا کاسته *ná-kástah.*

Undo, وا کردن *vá k.*

Undress, جامه بیرون کردن *jámeh bírún k.*

Undulation, اهتزاز *ihtizáz (k.).*

Uneasiness, آزردگی *ázardagí ;* دقت *dikkat.*

Uneasy, بیقرار *bí-karár.* To be —, آشفتن *áshuftan.*

Unemployed, بیکار *bí-kár.* Being —, تعطل *ta'attul (sh.).*

Unencumbered, سبکبار *sabuk-bár.*

Unfeigned (friendship), خلا ملا *khalá-malá.*

Unfit, نا شایسته *ná-sháyistah ;* نا اهل *ná-ahl ;* نا قابل *ná-kábil.* — for business, هیچکاره *hích-kárah.*

Unfortunate, کم بخت *kam-bakht ;* شوریده بخت *shúrídah-bakht ;* حوادث زده *havádis-zadah ;* بخت بر کشته *bakht-*

bar-gashtah ; شور بخت *shúr-bakht*; نا مبارك *ná-mubárak*; مصيبت زده *masíbat zadah* ; نحوس *nahús* ; منحوس *man-hús* ; سيه روز *siyah-rúz* ; ميشوم *maishúm* ; تيره بخت *tírah-bakht* ; تيره روز كار *tírah rúzgár* ; بد روز كار *bad-rúzgár*.

Ungathered, نا چيده *ná-chídah*.

Ungrateful, نا سپاس *ná-sipás* ; بيوفا *bí-vafá* ; نمك حرام *namak-harám* ; كافر نعمت *káfir i ni'mat* ; نان كور *nán-kúr* ; حق نا شناس *hakk ná shinás*.

Unguent, ادهان *adhán*.

Unhappy, غمگين *ghamgín*.

Unhealthy, نا گواره *ná guváreh*.

Uniform (soldier's) رخت نظام *rakht-i-nizám* ; — with مطابقت *mutábakat*.

Uninformed, بي خبر *bí-khabar*.

Unintentionally, عارضا *'árizan*.

Union, اتفاق *ittifák* ; اتحاد *ittihád* ; امتزاج *imtizáj*.

Unique, يكتاى *yaktái* ; يتيم *yatím*.

Units, وحدان *vuhdán* ; آحاد *áhád*.

Unitarianism, توحيد *tauhíd*.

Unite, پيوستن *paivastan*.

United, متفق *muttafik* (*k*.) ; متحد *muttahid* (*sh*.) ; مجتمع *mujtama'* ; شامل *shámil*.

Unity, وحدانيت *vahdáníyet* ; احديت *ahadíyat*.

Universal, عميم *'amím* ; اجمعين *ajma'ín*.

Universality, جامعيت *jámi-'íyet*.

Universally, كلى *kulliy* ; على الاطلاق *'ala 'l itlák* ; قاطباً *kátiban*.

Unjust, ناحق *ná-hakk* ; بي انصاف *bí-insáf* ; بيداد *bí-dád*.

Unkind, بيمروت *bí-muruvvat* ; بيعنايت *bí-'ináyet* ; بد مهر *bad-mihr*.

Unknown, نا معلوم *ná-ma'lúm* ; مجهول *majhúl*.

Unlawful, حرام *harám*.

Unlearned, امى *ummí*.

Unleavened, فطيرى *fatírí*.

Unless, گرنه *gar-nah* ; مگر *magar* ; الا *illa*.

Unlevel, نا هموار *ná-hamvár*.

Unlimited, غير منتهاى *ghair-muntahái*.

Unlucky, بدبخت *bad-bakkt*; شوم *shúm*. Being —, نحوست *nuhúsat*.

Unmarried, عذب *'azab*.

Unmask, *v.*, حجاب بر داشتن *hijáb bar dsh.*

Unmeaning, بیمعنی *bí-ma'ní*.

Unnecessary, غیر لازم *ghair lázem*.

Unpaid, مفت *muft*.

Unpierced, نا سفته *ná-suftah*.

Unpleasant, نا پسند *ná pasand*.

Unprincipled, بیراه *bí-ráh*.

Unprofitable, بی حاصل *bí-hásil*.

Unpunctuality, بیوقت *bí-vakt*.

Unripe, نا رس *ná-ras*; نا رسیده *ná-rasídah*. — corn, خوید *khavíd*.

Unseen, نا دیده *ná-dídah*.

Unsheathe, آهیختن *áhíkhtan*.

Unsheathed (a sword), مسلول *maslúl*.

Unskilful, خام کار *khám-kár*.

Unsound, نا چاق *ná-chák*.

Unsuccessful, خایب *kháib*; بد فرجام *bad-farjám*.

Unsuitable, نا مناسب *ná munásib*.

Until, حتی *hattá*; تا *tá*.

Untimely, بیگاه *bí-gáh*; بیوقت *bí-vakt*; بی هنگام *bí-hangám*.

Untravelled, راه نبرده *ráh naburdah*.

Untried, نا آزموده *ná-ázmúdah*.

Untrue, or Untruth, دروغ *durúgh* (*gf.*).

Unwary, غافل *gháfil*.

Unwashed, نا شسته *ná-shustah*.

Unwelcome, نا مطلوب *ná matlúb*.

Unwholesome, نا گوار *ná-gavár*; وخیم *vakhím*.

Unwilling, نا خواه *ná-kháh*.

Unwise, بی دانش *bí-dánish*; نا بخرد *ná-bakhirad*.

Unworthy, نا سزا *ná-sazá*.

Up, بالا *bálá*.

Upon, بر *bar*; روی *rúy*. — the whole, الغرض *al-gharz*; الحاصل *al-hásil*.

Upper, زبرین *zabarín*. To get the — hand, بالا گرفتن *bálá-gr.* — chamber, بالا خانه *bálá-khánah*.

Upright (steady), قایم *káim*; (in character), حق گذار *hakk-*

guzár ; راست نما *rást-numá.*
—ness, راستی *rástí.*
Uproar, غوغا *ghaughá.*
Upset, وارونه *várúnah* (*k.*).
Upside-down, سر زیر *sar-zír* (*k.*).
Urbanity, ادب *adab.*
Urgency, تقاضی *taḳází* ; ضرورت *zarúrat* (*k.*) ; تحریك *tahrik* (*k.*).
Urine, بول *baul* (*k.*) ; پیشاب *písháb* (*k.*) ; شاشه *sháshah* (*k.*). —bladder, کمیز دان *kumíz-dán* ; مثانه *masánah.*
Urinometer, قاروره *ḳárúrah.*
Urn (tea), سماوار *samávár.*
Us, مارا *márá.*
Usage, دستور *dastúr* ; رایج *ráij, in pl.* مراسم *marásim.*
Use, *n.*, فایده *fáideh* ; مصرف *musraf.* To be of —, بکار آمدن *bakár ámadan.* To —, تصرف کردن *tasarruf k.*
Useful, کار آمدنی *kár-ámadaní* ; مفید *mufíd* ; ورنان *varnán.*
Useless, نا کاره *ná-kárah* ; بی فائده *bí-fáidah* ; نا بکار *ná-bakár* ; نا بنوا *ná-binavá.* Rendering —, تعطیل *ta'tíl* (*k.*).
Usual, معمول *ma'múl.*
Usually, عموماً *'umúman.*
Usurer, ربا خور *ribá-khur* ; سود خور *súd-khur.*
Usurpation, غصب *ghasb.*
Usurper, غاصب *ghásib.*
Usury, ربا *ribá.*
Utensil, ظرف *zarf.*
Uterine, شکمی *shikmí.*
Utility, انتفاع *intifá'* ; فایده *fáideh.*
Utmost, غایت *gháyat.* To the —, حتی الوسع *hattá 'l vas'.*
Utter, فرو خواندن *farú-khándan.*
Utterance, تلفظ *talaffuz.*
Utterly, بالکل *bilkull.*
Uvula, کنج *kanj.*

V.

Vacancy, خلاء *khalá'.*
Vacant, خالی *khálí* (*k.*).
Vacation, تعطیل *ta'tíl.*
Vaccination, آبله کوبی *ábilah kúbí* (*k.*).
Vacuity, خلو *khalú.*
Vagrancy, هرزه گردی *harzah-gardí.*
Vagrant, هنجام *hanjám.*

Vain, بیهوده *baihúdah*; عبث *'abs*; یاوه *yávah*; هوا پرست *havá-parast*; in —, بـاطل *bátil*; بطال *battál* (*sh.*). — promise, برات برشاخ آهو *barát bar shákh i áhú.*

Valiant, دلاور *dilávar*; بهادر *bahádur*; قویم *ḳavím.*

Valid, درست *durust.*

Valley, دره *darreh*; جلغه *jul-ghah, in pl.* بقاع *biḳá'.*

Valour, شجـاعـت *shajá'at*; غیرت *ghairat.*

Valuable, قـیـمتی *ḳaimatíy*; ثمین *samín.*

Valuation, ارزش *arzish.*

Value, قـیـمـت *ḳaimat* (*k.*); ماهیت *máhíyet*; قدر *ḳadar*; ارج *arj*; ارز *arz.*

Valve, غطا *ghitá.*

Vanguard, قراول *ḳarául*; طلیعه *talí'at.*

Vanish, غایب شدن *gháib sh.*

Vanity, زیـاده سـری *ziyádah-sarí*; بطالت *batálat.*

Vanquish, فتح کردن *fath k.*; ظفر یافتن *zafar y.*

Vanquisher, منصور *mansúr.*

Vapour, تف *taf*; بخار *bukhár.*

Variation, تـفـاوت *tafávut* (*dsh.*).

Variegated, بو قـلـمـون *bu-ḳalamún.*

Variety, اختلاف *ikhtiláf.*

Various, گونا گون *gún á gún*; متلون *mutalavvin.*

Varnish, روغن *raughan* (*z.*).

Vast, وسیع *vasí'.*

Vault, قـبـه *ḳubbah*; گـنبذ *gumbaz.*

Vaunting, مفاخرت *mufákharat* (*k.*).

Veal, گوشت گوساله *gúsht-i-gausáleh.*

Vegetable, رستنی *rustaní*; نباتی *nabáti.*

Vegetation, نما *namá.*

Vehemence, تـنـدی *tundí*; هیجان *haiyaján*; شدة *shid-dat.*

Vehement, شدید *shadíd.*

Veil, رو بـنـد *rú band*; پـرده *pardah*; حجاب *hijáb*; نقاب *niḳáb*; ستر *sitr*; سجف *sajf*; برقع *burḳa'* (*z.*).

Veiled, محجوب *mahjúb.*

Vein, رگ *rag*; عـرق *'irḳ, pl.* عروق *'urúḳ.* Cephalic —,

قيفال *kifál*. Jugular —, حبل الوريد *habl ul varíd*.

Vellum, رق *rikk*.

Velvet, مخمل *makhmal*.

Venerable, or Venerated, مكرم *mukarram* (*dsh.*).

Veneration, احترام *ihtirám* (*k.*).

Venereal (disease), آتشك *átishak*; سوزنك *súzanok*.

Vengeance, انتقام *intikám*; كينه *kínah*.

Venom, زهر *zahr*; سم *samm*; ذئفان *zi'fán*. Bezoar antidote against —, زهر دارو *zahr-dárú*.

Venomous, زهر دار *zahr-dár*; زهرناك *zahr-nák*.

Ventilator (of a house), باد كير *bád gír*.

Venus (planet), ناهيد *náhíd*; زهره *zuhrah*.

Veracity, صدق *sidk*; صداقت *sedákat*.

Verb, فعل *fe'el*.

Verbal, قولى *kaulí*; زبانى *zabání*.

Verbatim, لفظ بلفظ *lafz be lafz*.

Verbose, مفصل *mufassal*.

Verdant, سرسبز *sar-sabz*; مخضر *mukhazzar*.

Verdict, حكم *hukm* (*k.*).

Verdigris, زنجار *zinjár*.

Verdure, سبزه *sabzah*.

Verified, متحقق *mutahakkak* (*sh.*). Anything —, ما صدق *má sudik*.

Verifying, متحقق *mutahakkik* (*k.*); تصديق *tasdík* (*k.*); محقق *muhakkik* (*n.*); مصدق *musaddik*.

Vermilion, زنجرف *zinjarf*.

Vermin, جانورك *jánvarak*.

Vernal, بهارى *bahári*; ربعى *rib'íy*.

Versatile, سبك پا *sabuk pá*.

Verse, بيت *bait*, *pl.* ابيات *abyát*; آيت *áyat*. — of the Korán, *pl.* آيات *áyát*. In —, نظم *nazm*.

Versified, منظومه *manzúmah*.

Vertebrate, ذوالفقار *zú'l fakár*.

Vertical, قايم *káim*.

Vertigo, كيج *gíj*.

Very, خيلى *khailí*; بسيار *bisyár*.

Vessel (ship), مركب *markab*; (vase), ظرف *zarf*; آناء *iná*. Glazed —, مرطبان *martabán*. Earthenware —, لولين *lúlín*; خزف *khazf*. — for holding water, آبدان *ábdán*. — for measuring, مکیال *mikyál*.

Vest, ارخلق *arkhaluḳ*; خفتان *khuftán*.

Vestibule, دالان *dálán*.

Vestige, اثر *asar*, *pl.* آثار *ásár*; قطف *ḳataf*.

Vex, هنجیدن *hanjídan*. —ing, متصدع *mutasaddi'* (*k.*). To be —ed, رنجیدن *ranjídan*.

Vexation, اذی *azá* (*d.*); دق *diḳḳ*; تصدیع *tasdí'* (*n.*); هنجار *hanjár*; سر دردی *sar-dardí*.

Vexatious, متاعب *matá'ib*.

Viands, اطعمه *at'imah*; خوراکی *khúrákí*.

Vibration, تکان *takán* (*k.*).

Vices, خبائث *khabáis*; معایب *ma'áib*; شنایع *shanáï*; عیوب *'uyúb*; in the sing. عیب *'aib*; نقیصت *naḳisat*. Carpenters —, گیره *gírah*.

Viceroy, فرمانفرما *farmán farmá*; نائب مناب *náib munáb*. — of Egypt, خدیوی *Khidívi*.

Viceroyalty, وکالت *vikálat*.

Vicinity, جوار *javár*; تجاور *tajávur*.

Vicious, بی پیر *bí-pír*; معیوب *ma'yúb*; فاسد *fásid*.

Vicissitudes, صوارف *savárif*; انقلابات *inḳilábát*.

Victorious, مظافر *muzáfir*; منصور *mansúr*; فیروز *fírúz*; مظفر *muzfir*. Being —, تغالب *taghálub* (*sh.*).

Victim, فدیه *fidyah*.

Victor, غالب *ghálib*.

Victory, فتح *fath* (*y. k.*), *pl.* فتوح *futúh*; فتوحات *futúhát*; ظفر *zafar* (*y.*); فوز *fauz*.

Victuals, خورش *khurish*; خوردنی *khúrdaní*.

Videlicet, یعنی *ya'ní*.

View, چشم انداز *cheshm andáz*. In —, پیشدید *písh-díd*.

Vigilance, انتباه *intibáh*; بیداری *bídárí*; حزم *hazm*.

Vigilant, آگاه *ágáh*; سبك خیز *sabuk-khíz*.

Vigorous, چاق *cháḳ*; توانا *taváná*.

Vigour, قوت *ḳuvvat*.

Vile, زبون *zabún*; لیم *liyam*.

Vileness, ابتذال *ibtizál*; خساست *khasásat*.

Village, ده *dih*; روستا *rústá*; قریه *ḳaryah*, *pl.* قری *ḳurá*.

Of the same —, همقریه *ham-ḳiryah*. The chief of a —, دیهبان *dihbán*.

Villager, دهاتی *diháti*; دهقان *dihḳán*.

Villain, شفك *shafak*; بد ذات *bad zát*.

Vindication, حمایت *himáyat* (*k*.).

Vindicative, کینه کش *kínah kesh*.

Vine, تاك *ták*; درخت انکور *dirakht-i-angúr*.

Vinegar, سرکه *sirkah*; خل *khall*.

Vineyard, باغ مو *bágh i mau*; آبسال *ábsál*; رز *raz*.

Vintage, قطاف *ḳatáf*, or *ḳitáf*.

Vintner, می فروش *mai-farúsh*.

Violating, مفترع *muftari'* (*k*.); نقض *naḳz* (*k*.).

Violence, زور آوری *zúr-ávarí*; اشتداد *ishtidád*; جفا *jafá*; جور *jaur*.

Violent, شدید *shadíd*; شداد *shidád*. —ly, بزور *bizúr*.

Violet, بنفشه *benafshah*; خیاری *khayárí*.

Violin, کمانچه *kamáncheh*.

Viper, افعی *af'í*.

Virgin, بکر *bikr*; دختر *dukhtar*; باکره *bákirah*; دوشیزه *dúshízah*.

Virginity, بکارت *bakárat*; دوشیزکی *dúshízagí*.

Virgo, سنبلة *sumbulat*.

Virile, مردانه *mardáneh*. Semen —, منی *miná*.

Virility, رجولیت *rujúliyet*; باه *báh*.

Virtue, فضل *fazl*, *pl*. افضال *afzál*; منقبت *manḳabat*; فضیلت *fazílat*, *pl*. فضایل *fazáil*; هنر *hunar*, *in pl*. محاسن *mahásin*.

Virtuous, هنر پیشه *hunar-píshah*.

Virulence, شدت *shiddat*.

Virulent, شدید *shadíd*.

Virus, ریم *rím*.

Visage, رو *rú*.

Visible, نمودار *namúdár*; پدید *padíd*; پیدا *paidá*.

Visibly, ظاهراً *záhiran*.

Vision, خیال *khiyál*.

Visionary, محال اندیش *mahál-andísh*; خیال پرست *khayál-parast*.

Visit, زیارت *ziyárat* (*k*.); لقاء *liḳá'*. To come on a —,

تشریف آوردن *tashríf a.* To go on a —, تشریف بردن *tashríf burdan.*

Visiting, متلقی *mutalakkí (n.).*

Visitor, زایر *záir.*

Visual, بصیره *basírah.*

Vitality, زندگی *zindagí.*

Vitiated, معیوب *ma'yúb (s.).*

Vitriol, زاج *záj ;* زاك *zág.* Blue —, زاج کبود *záj i kabúd.* Green —, زاج سبز *záj i sabz.* Water of —, زاکاب *zág-áb.*

Vituperation, فحش *fuhsh (d.).*

Vivid, منیر *munír.*

Vizier, وزیر *vazír, pl.* وزراء *vuzará'.*

Vocabulary, لغت *loghat.*

Vocal, صوتی *sautí.*

Vocation, حرفت *hirfat.*

Voice, آواز *áváz.* Having a sweet —, خوش آواز *khush-áváz ;* خوش خوان *khush-khán.*

Void, خالی *khálí (s.).*

Volley, شلیك *shalík (k.).*

Volume, جلد *jild, in pl.* مصاحف *masáhif ;* دفاتر *dafátir.*

Voluntarily, خود بخود *khud ba khud.*

Voluptuary, عیاش *'ayyásh.*

Voluptuous, تن پرور *tan-parvar.*

Vomit, *v.,* هراشیدن *haráshídan ; n.,* هراش *harásh.*

Vomiting, قی *kai (k.).*

Voracious, اکول *akúl.*

Voucher, ضامن *zámin.*

Vow, نذر *nazr (k.) ;* شرط *shart (n.) ;* یمین *yamín.*

Vowel (short), حرکت *harakat ;* (long), حرف علت *harf-i-'illat.* — points, اعراب *i'ráb.*

Voyage, سفر *safar (k.).*

Voyager, سافر *sáfir.*

Vulgar, عامه *'ámmah.* The —, عوام الناس *'avvám un nás.*

Vulture, نسر *nasr ;* کرکس *kar-gas.*

W.

Wadding (for gun), کهنه *kuhnah.*

Wading, غور *ghaur (k.).*

Wafer, گرده *girdah.*

Wager, شرط *shart (k. bs.).*

Wages, اجرت *ujrat* ; مواجب *mavájib* ; دست مزد *dast-muzd.*

Waggon, عرابه *'arábeh.*

Wailing, ناله *náleh* (*k.*) ; شیون *shaivan* (*k.*).

Waist, کمر *kamar* ; میان *miyán.*

Wait, ماندن *mándan* ; منتظر هستن *muntazir h.*

Waiter (at baths), دلاك *dallák.*

Waiting, انتظار *intizár* (*ksh.*); رقابت *raḳábat.*

Wakefulness, بیداری *bídárí.*

Waking, بیدار *bídár* (*k. sh.*).

Walk, *v.*, راه رفتن *ráh-raftan* ; (gracefully), چمیدن *chamídan* ; خرامیدن *khará-mídan.*

Walking, سیر *sair* (*k.*) ; گردش *gardesh* (*k.*) ; رفتار *raftár* ; (jauntily), تبختر *tabakhtur.*

Wall, دیوار *dívár* ; حائط *háit* ; جدار *jidár* ; (rampart), سور *súr.* City —, شهر بند *shahr-band.* High outer —, شهدیوار *shah-dívár.* — of a tent, قنات *ḳanát.*

Wallet, بقچه *buḳchah* ; انبان *ambán* ; خورچین *khurchín.*

Dervish's —, کشکول *kashkúl.*

Walnut, گردو *girdú* ; گردگان *gurdagán* ; چار مغز *chár-maghz* ; جوز رومی *jauz i rúmí.*

Wand, عصا *'asá.*

Wander, وا رفتن *vá-raftan* ; گشت کردن *gasht k.*

Wandering, سیار *saiyár.*

Wanderer, آواره *avárah* (*g.*). State of —, آوارگی *ává-ragí.*

Want (wish), *v.*, خواستن *khástan* ; *n.* (necessity), حاجت *hájat* (*dsh*), *pl.* حاجات *háját* ; احتیاج *ihtiyáj* (*n.*) ; قلت *ḳillat.*

Wanting, معیل *mu'íl* ; ونکول *vankúl* ; کم *kam* ; (petitioner), خواستکار *khástgár.*

Wanton, شوخ *shúkh.*

War, جنك *jang* (*a. k.*) ; حرب *harb*, *pl.* حروب *hurúb* ; پرخاش *purkhásh* ; رزم *razm* ; محاربة *muhárabat* ; وغا *vighá* ; هیجاء *haijá.'* Holy —, جهاد *jihád* ; (raid), غزا *ghazá.* Making —, غزو *ghazv* (*k.*).

Warder, سرایدار *saráy-dár.*

Wardrobe, صندوقخانه *sandúḳ-khánah*; توشك خانه *túshak-khánah*; جامه خانه *jámah-khánah*.

Wards (of a key), نژ *nazh*.

Warehouse, انبار *ambár*.

Warlike, جنكي *jangí*; نبرده *naburdah*.

Warm, كرم *garm* (*s.*); تفته *taftah*. Being —, ابت *abt*. To —, تفيدن *tafídan*. To grow —, تفسيدن *tafsídan*.

Warmth, تفت *taft*; حرارت *harárat*.

Warn, *v.*, خبر دادن *khabar d.* One who warns, نذير *nazír*.

Warning, نذارت *nazárat* (*k.*).

Warp, پود *púd*. — and woof, تاروپود *tár u púd*.

Warrant, *v.*, ضمانت كردن *zamánat k.*

Warrior, مبارز *mubáriz*; محارب *muhárib*; (for religion), مجاهد *mujáhid*; غازي *ghází*.

Wart, ثوءلول *sú'lúl*, *pl.* ثاليل *sa'álíl*; زكيل *zigíl*.

Wash, *v.*, شستن *shustan*; شويدن *shúidan*; *pa. p.*, مغسول *maghsúl*; *pr. p.*, غسل *ghusl* (*k.*); شستكي *shustagí*. — and cleansing, شست و شو *shust u shú* (*k.*). A place for — (especially of dead bodies), مغسل *maghsal*.

Wasp, زنبور *zambúr*. — nest, زنبورخانه *zambúr-khánah*.

Waste, تلف *talaf* (*k.*); اتلاف *itláf* (*n.*).

Wasting, تضييع *tazyí'* (*k.*).

Watch (time piece), ساعت *sá'at*. The — is fast, ساعت تند كار مي كند *sá'at tund-kár mí kunad*. The — is too slow, ساعت كند كار مي كند *sá'at kund-kár mí kunad*. To wind up a —, ساعت را كوك كردن *sá'at-rá kúk k.* — maker, ساعت ساز *sá'at-sáz*. The first — of the night, عشا *'ashá*. Keeping —, پاسباني *pás-bání*.

Watching, مترصد *mutarassid*; رصيد *rasíd*; حراست *hirásat*; كرد آوري *gird-ávarí*.

Watchman پاس *pás*; (in a vineyard), ناطور *nátúr*; هركش *harkush*. Head —, سر پاس *sar-pás*; ديد بان *díd-bán*. Night —, عسس *'asas*; رقيب *raḳíb*, *pl.* رقباء *ruḳabá'*.

Watchword, اسم شب *ism-i-shab.*

Water, آب *áb;* ماء *má.* The — of immortality, آب حیات *ábi haiyát;* ماء الحیاة *má ul haiyát.* Shallow —, تنك آب *tang-áb.* Deep —, غرقاب *gharḳ-áb.* Limpid —, زلال *zulál.* Polluted —, منجلاب *manjaláb.* To make —, شاشیدن *sháshídan.* — carrier, آبکش *áb-kesh;* سقا *saḳḳá.* — course, آبراه *áb-ráh.* — fall, آبشار *ábshár.* — fowl, مرغابی *murgh-ábí.* — lily, نیلوفر *nílúfar.* — melon, هندوانه *hinduvánah.* — skin, قربه *ḳirbah;* مشك *mashk.* — supply, سقایت *saḳáyet.* — wagtail, سریچه *saricheh.* — wheel, دولاب *dúláb;* دوالیب *daválíb.*

Watering-place, منهل *minhall, pl.* مناهل *manáhil;* موارد *mavárid.*

Watery, آبی *ábí;* مائی *má'í.*

Wave, موج *mauj;* خیزاب *khiz-áb.*

Waving, نواس *navvás (k.);* تکان *takán (d.).*

Wax, موم *múm;* شمع *sham'.* Sealing —, لاك *lák.* — chandler, شماع *shammá'.* — cloth, موم جامه *múm-jámah.*

Waxen, مومی *múmí.*

Way, راه *ráh;* سلوك *sulúk;* وتیره *vatírah;* سبیل *sabíl, pl.* سبل *subul;* سمت *samt, pl.* سموت *sumút, in pl.* مسالك *masálik.* High —, شهراه *shah-ráh;* صراط *sirát;* شارع *shári';* منهج *minhaj.* A long —, خیلی راه *kheilí ráh.* By one —, یکره *yak-rah.* By — of, از روی *az rú i.* To find the —, رهبردن *rah-burdan.*

We, ما *má.*

Weak, ضعیف *za'íf* Most —, اضعف *az'af;* فاتر *fátir;* واهی *váhí.* — in understanding, سخیف *sakhíf.* — in the loins (a horse), کمری *kamaríy.* — with age or infirmity, هار *hár.*

Weakening the animal spirits, جان کاه *ján-káh.*

Weakness, ضعف *zu'f;* خذلان *khizlán;* وهن *vahn;* کلال

kalál; رکاکت *rekákat*; عجز *'ajz*.

Wealth, دولت *daulat*; مال *mál*, *pl.* اموال *amvál*; مالیت *máliyet*; ثروت *sarvat*.

Wealthy, مالدار *máldár*; تونکر *tavangar*; دولتمند *daulat-mand*.

Weaned, فطیم *fatím*.

Weaning, فطام *fitám* (*k.*).

Weapon, سلاح *saláh*, *pl.* اسلحه *aslihah*.

Wear (clothes), پوشیدن *púshídan*; (out), سودن *súdan*.

Wearing, مویار *múyár*. — out the life, جان فرسا *ján-farsá*.

Wearied out, *v.*, بجان آمدن *baján ámadan*.

Weary, خسته *khasteh*.

Weasel, راسو *rású*.

Weather, اب و هوا *áb o havá*. — cock, باد نما *bád-numá*.

Weave, بافتن *báftan*; *pr. p.*, نسج *nasj* (*k.*).

Weaver, بافندد *báfendah*; جولاه *júláh*; نساج *nussáj*. — of mats, بوریاباف *búriyábáf*. —'s shop, هف *haf*.

Web, طاقه *tákeh*; ثوب *saub*.

Wedding, عروسی *'arúsí*.

Wedge, فانه *fánah*; چوب شکاف *chúb-shigáf*; میخ شکاف *míkh i shikáf*.

Wednesday, چهار شنبه *chehár-shambah*.

Weed, خس *khas*.

Week, هفته *haftah*.

Weep, کرستن *giristan*; کریستن *giristan*; نار افشاندن *nár-afshándan*.

Weeping, کریان *giryán*; کریه *giryah*; نیاح *niyáh*.

Weevil, سوفته *súftah*.

Weigh, سنجیدن *sanjidan*; سختن *sakhtan*; *pa. p.*, موزون *mauzún*.

Weight, وزن *vazn* (*k.*), *pl.* اوزان *auzán*; سنجه *sanjah*. Make —, پاسنك *pásang*. Of the same —, همسنك *ham-sang*.

Weighty, وزین *vazín*; کران *girán*; سنکین *sangín*.

Welcome, اهلاً وسهلاً *ahlan va sahlan*. To be —, خوش آمدن *khush ámadan*.

Weld, کوفتن *kúftan*.

Welfare, خیریت *khairiyat*; بهبود *bih-búd*.

Well (good), خوب *khúb*; فبها *fabihá*; خوشا *khushá*. Very

—, خیلی خوب khailí khúb.
— born, اصیل asíl. — disposed, خوش طبع khush-tab'.
— wisher, هوا خواه havá-kháh ; نکو خواه nikú-kháh.
— (pit), چاه chah ; بئر bi'r.
— at Mecca, زمزم zemzem.
— digger, چاه کن cháh-kan.

Wen, غده ghuddah.

West, مغرب maghrib.

Westerly, غربی gharbíy.

Western, مغربی maghribí.

Wet, تر tar (s. sh.) ; نم nam (s. sh.).

Wetness, رطوبت rutúbat.

Whale, وال vál.

What, چه chih. — is it? چیست chíst. — will you take, چه چیزمیل می دارید chih chíz meyl mí daríd.

Whatever, انچه ánchih ; هر چه har-chih. — is at hand, ما حضر má hazar.

Whatsoever, هرانچه haránchih.

Wheat, گندم gandum ; حنطه hintah.

Wheel, چرخه charkhah. Water —, دولاب dúl-áb.

Whelp, بچه bacheh.

When, کی kai — and wherefore, چون و چرا chún u cherá. — (relative), چو chu ; چون chun ; وقتیکه vaktíkeh.

Whenever, هرگاه har gáh.

Whence! ازکجا az kujá.

Where? کجا kujá. — (relat.), جایکه jáikeh.

Wherefore, چرا cherá.

Whether - or, یا - یا yá - yá.

Whetstone, فسان fasán.

Whey, پنیر آب panír ab ; ماء الجبن má ul jibn.

Which? کدام kudám. — (relat.), چه cheh ; که keh.

While, وقتیکه vaktíkeh ; ما دام má dám.

Whip, تازیانه táziyanah ; قمچی kamchí.

Whirlpool, گرداب girdáb ; شار shár ; ورطه vartah.

Whirl-wind, گرد باد gird-bád.

Whiskers, بروت burút ; سبلت sabalat.

Whisper, نجوی گفتن najvá guftan.

Whisperer, واشی váshí.

Whistle, v., هشتیدن hashtídan.

Whistling, صفیر safír (z.).

White, سفید *safíd*; ابیض *abyaz*; بیضاء *baizá*; یلق *yalak*. Anything —, یلاغ *yalágh*. — or gray horse, خنك *khing*. — wine, آب زر *áb i zar*.

Whiteness, بیاض *baiyáz*.

Whitlow, ناخن پال *nákhun-pál*.

Who, که *kih*. — is it? کیست *kíst*=که است

Whoever, هرکه *harkeh*.

Whosoever, هرانکه *haránkih*.

Whole, تمام *tamám*; کل *kull*; همه *hammah*; مجموع *majmú'*. On the —, فی الجملة *fil-jumlah*.

Wholesome, خوش کوار *khush-guvár*; نجیع *nají'*; نقیع *nakí'*; نمیر *namír*.

Wholly, بالکل *bil-kull*.

Whore, قحبه *kahbeh*; لوند *lavand*; جنده *jindah*.

Whoremonger, زنا کار *zená kár*.

Whose? مال که *mál-i-kih*.

Why, چرا *cherá*; برای چه *birâyi chih*; بچه *ba chih*.

Wick, فتیله *fatílah*; پلیته *palítah*.

Wicked, بد *bad*; شریر *sharír*; منکار *munkár*; خبیث *khabís*; ردی *radíy*; تباه *tabáh*.

Wickedness, بدی *badí*; خباثت *khabásat*; شر *sharr*.

Wide, پهنا *pahná*; فراخ *farákh*; عریض *'aríz*; کشاد *gushád*.

Widow, بیوه *bívah*.

Widower, ارمل *armal*.

Width, پهن *pahn*; عرض *'arz*.

Wife, زن *zan*; زوجه *zaujah*; اهلیه *ahlíyeh*. Temporary —, متعه *mut'ah*; صیغه *sígheh*. Lawful —, منکوحه *mankúhah*. —'s brother, خسر پوره *khusar-púrah*. Disreputable —, زنقحبه *zan-i-kahbah*.

Wild, بیابانی *biyábání*; بری *barrí*; دشتی *dashtí*; صحرائی *sahráí*; متابد *muta'abbid*; خود رو *khud-rau*.

Wilderness, بیابان *biyábán*.

Wile, کول *gúl* (z.); حیله *híleh*.

Wilful, خود سر *khud sar*. —ly, عمداً *'amdan*.

Will, خواهش *kháhesh*; مراد *murád*; (testament), وصیت *vasíyat* (k.).

Willing, خواهان *kháhán.* —or unwilling, کام نا کام *kám-ná-kám.* —ly, طوعاً *tau'an.*

Willow, بید *bíd.* Musk —, بید مشك *bíd-i-mushk.* Weeping —, بید مجنون *bíd i majnún.*

Wily, غدار *ghaddár.*

Win (at play), بردن *burdan.*

Wince, رمیدن *ramídan.*

Wind, *n.*, باد *bád.* To break —, گوزیدن *gúzídan.* Whirl —, دیو باد *dív-bád.* Fair —, شرطه *shurtah.* Cold boisterous —, صرصر *sarsar.* Hot pestilential —, سموم *samúm.* Blustering —, ناشره *náshirah.* South —, نعامی *nu'ámí.* ...ng —ed, دراز نفسی *daráz-nafasí.*

Wind, *v.*, تافتن *táftan.*

Winding-sheet, كفن *kafan.*

Windlass, منجنق *manjaniḳ.*

Windmill, آسیا باد *ásyá-bád.*

Window, پنجره *panjareh;* دریچه *darícheh;* روزن *rauzan.* Sash —, ارسی *urusí.*

Windpipe, حنجره *hanjarah;* مریء *marí'.*

Windy, بادی *bádí.*

Wine, شراب *sharáb;* (poetical), می *mai;* باده *bádah;* خمر *khamr;* نبیذ *nabíz;* راح *ráh.* Red —, صهباء *sahbá';* یاقوت روان *yáḳút i raván.* — boiled down to a third, سیکی *síkí.* —coloured, میگون *mai-gún.* — bottle, چارپر *chárpar.*

Wing, پر *par;* بال *bál;* کنف *kanaf;* بازو *bázú;* (of army), جناح *janáh, pl.* اجنحه *ajnihah.* —ed, فروند *farvend.*

Wink, کرشمه *kirishmah;* چسمق *cheshmaḳ* (z.).

Winnow, هید *haid; v.*, افشندن *afshandan.*

Winter, زمستان *zamistán;* سرما *sarmá.*

Wintry, سرمائی *sarmáí.*

Wipe, روبیدن *rúbídan;* پاك کردن *pák k.; pa. p.*, ممسوح *mamsúh; pr. p.*, مسح *mas-h;* تمییز *tamyíz* (k.).

Wire, تار *tár;* سیم *sím* (s.). — drawer, تارکش *tárkesh.*

Wisdom, حکمت *hikmat;* خردمندی *khiradmandí;* خرد *khirad;* دانشوری *dánishvarí;* دانائی *dánáí;* فرزان

farzán ; فرزانـكـى farzánagí; بخردى ba khirdí. Practising —, خرد مشرب khirad-mashrab ; خـرد پـيـشـه khirad-píshah.

Wise, هوشيار húshyár ; دانشور dánishvar ; عـلـيـم 'alím ; دانشمند dánishmand ; خردمند khiradmand ; حـازم házim. —ly, خردمندانه khiradmandánah.

Wish, خواهش kháhesh (k.) ; خواست khást ; تمنا tamanná ; مـنـيـت munyat ; آرزو arzú (n.) ; v., خواستن khástan ; pr. p., مـتـمنى mutamanní ; خواه kháh ; راغب rághib.

Wisher, خواهـنـده kháhendah. Well —, خـيـر خـواه khair-kháh ; دولـت خـواه daulat-kháh ; نيك خواه ník-kháh.

Wit (joke), ظرافت zaráfat ; (person), بذله كو or بـزلـه كو bazlah-gú.

Wits, عقل 'akl.

Witch, ساحره sáhirah.

Witchcraft, سحر sihr.

With, به ب ba ; ب bi ; با bá ; از az (lit. from) ; مع ma'. — him, بـاوى bá-vai. — whom? باكـه bákih. To do —, to agree —, در ساختن dar sákhtan.

Withdraw, كنار رفتن kenár r.

Wither, پژمردن pazhmurdan ; پـوسـيـدن púsídan. —ed, پژمان pazhmán ; پژمرده pazhmurdah ; افـسرده afsurdah ; يـبـس yabis.

Withers, حارك hárik.

Withhold, باز داشتن báz dsh.

Within, انـدرون andarún ; درون darún ; داخل dákhil ; توى tuí.

Without (exterior), بـيـرون bírún ; (less), بدون bidún ; بـلا bilá ; غـيـر ghair ; بى bí. — ceremony, بى تـكـلف bí-takalluf. — delay, بـيدرنك bí-dirang. — deceit, بيغل وغش bí-ghill u ghashsh. — deliberation, بى تـدبـيـر bí-tadbír. — discernment, بى تـمـيـز bí-tamíz. — doubt, بى كمان bí-gumán. — limit, بى حد bí-hadd. — measure, بى انـدازه bí-andázah. — provisions, بى توشه bí-túshah. — remedy, بـيدرمان bí-darmán. — trouble, بى آزار bí-ázár.

Witness, شاهد *sháhid*; شهيد *shahíd*, *pl.* اشهاد *ash-hád*; شواهد *shaváhid*; شهود *shuhúd*. To bear —, شهادت بردن *shahádat burdan*.

Witticisms, لطيفه *latífeh*; نكات *nukát*.

Witty, ظريف *zuríf*.

Woe, غم *gham*. —ful, غمناك *ghamnák*.

Wolf, گرگ *gurg*; ذئب *zi'b*.

Woman, زن *zan*; ضعيفه *za'ífeh*, *in pl.* نسوت *nisvat*; نسوان *nisván*. — in childbed, زجه *zajah*; زچه *zachah*. Pregnant —, حبلى *hablá*; زن بار دار *zan i bár-dár*. Free —, حرة *hurrah*. Old —, عجوز *'ajúz*. Wanton —, يار باز *yár-báz*. Tire —, مشاطه *mashshátah*. Married —, ناكح *nákih*; نكاحى *nikáhí*. Modest —, مستوره *mastúrah*. Women's attire, رخت زنانه *rakht i zanánah*. Addicted to women, زندوست *zan-dúst*.

Womanly, زنانه *zanánah*.

Womb, رحم *rahim*; زهدان *zihdán*.

Wonder, تعجب *ta'ajjub* (*k.*). Causing —, تعجيب *ta'jíb*(*n.*); عجب *'ajab* (*m.*), *pl.* عجائب *'ajáib*; غريبه *gharíbah*, *pl.* غرائب *gharáib*; شگرف *shigarf*; طرفه *turfah*.

Wonderful, عجب *'ajab*; عجيب *'ajíb*; رايق *ráik*; بديع *badí'*. — thing, بو العجب *bu'l'ajab*.

Wood, چوب *chúb*. Fire —, هيزم *haizum*; هيمه *haimeh*; (forest), جنگل *jangal*. Fragrant aloes —, عود *'úd*. —ed country, مشجر *mushajjar*.

Woodcock, زيرك *zírak*.

Wooden, چوبين *chúbín*.

Woodman, هيزم كش *haizum-kesh*.

Wool, پشم *pashm*; صوف *súf*.

Woollen, پشمينه *pashmínah*.

Word, سخن *sukhan* (*gf.*); كلمه *kalimah*; لفظ *lafz*. — and deed, قول و فعل *kaul u fi'l*; (gossip), قال *kál*; قيل و قال *kíl u kál*.

Work, كار *kár* (*k.*); كار وبار *kár o bár*; عمل *'amal* (*k.*), *pl.* اعمال *a'mál*. Collected works of an author, كليات

kullíyát. Good —s, مثوبات *masúbát;* مبرات *mabarrát.*

Workman, کاریکر *kárígar.*

Workshop, کارخانه *kár-khánah.*

World, جهان *jahán;* دنیا *dunyá;* عالم *'álam;* روز کار *rúz-gár;* کیهان *kíhán;* کیتی *gítí.* This — (house of transience), دار الفنا *dár ul faná;* سپنجی سرای *sipanjí saráy;* (land of delusion), سرابستان *sarábistán;* (mansion of darkness), ظلمت کده *zulmat-kedah.* Belonging to this —, دنیوی *dunyaví.* The inhabited quarter of the —, ربع مسکون *rab' i maskún.*

Worldly, عالمی *'álamíy;* دهری *dahríy.*

Worm, کرم *kirm.* Glow —, شب چراغ *shab-chirágh;* کرم شب تاب *kirm i shabtáb.* Ship —, زیو *zív.* Silk —, کرم پیله *kirm i pílah* — wood, درمنه *dirmanah.*

Worn out, مندرس *mundaris;* مسحوق *mas-húk;* نیم کار *ním-kár;* (hollowed —), ناخر *nákhir.*

Worse, بدتر *bad-tar;* بتر *bat-tar;* اشر *asharr.*

Worship, عبادت *'ibádat (k.);* پرشتش *parastish (k.);* پا بوس *pá-bús.* A place for —, معبد *ma'bad; v.,* پرستیدن *parastídan.*

Worshipper, پرستنده *parastendah;* عابد *'ábid;* معبد *mu'abbid.* — of fire, کبر *gabr;* in comp., پرست *parast,* as, — of wealth, مالپرست *mál-parast.*

Worst, بدترین *badtarín.*

Worth, قیمت *ḳaimat (dsh.).* To be —, ارزیدن *arzídan.*

Worthless, ناقز *náḳiz;* نا کس *ná-kas;* نا مستحسن *ná-mustahsin;* نکاره *nakárah.*

Worthy, لایق *láiḳ;* سزاوار *sazá-vár;* شایکان *sháigan;* شایان *sháyán;* فرزام *farzám;* فراخ خور *ferákh-khur.* To be —, سزاییدن *sazáídan;* سزیدن *sazídan;* شاییدن *sháyídan.*

Would that! کاش *kásh.*

Wound, زخم *zakhm (z. kh.);* جرح *jarh;* ریش *rísh:*

جراحت *jiráhat.* To —, خستن *khastan.*

Wounded, مجروح *majrúh;* زخمخورده *zakhm-khurdah;* زخم دار *zakhm-dár;* زخم زده *zakhm-zadah;* زخمی *zakhmí.*

Woven, بفت *baft;* بافته *báftah;* منسوج *mansúj.*

Wrangler, جادل *jádil.*

Wrangling, جدال *jidál.*

Wrath, غیظ *ghaiz.*

Wreck, تباهی *tabáhí* (*k.*).

Wrench off, بر کسلانیدن *bar guslánídan.*

Wrestler, کشتی گیر *kushtí-gír;* پهلوان *pahlaván.*

Wrestling, کشتی *kushtí* (*gr.*); مصرعة *musara'at* (*k.*).

Wretched, غمگین *ghamgín.* — ness, دلتنگی *dil-tangí.*

Wrinkle, چین *chín.*

Wrinkled, پرچین *pur chín* (*sh.*).

Wrist, رسغ *rusgh;* معصم *mi'sam.*

Write, نوشتن *navishtan;* رقم زدن *rakam z.* — with a nice appreciation of the beauties of the language, داد سخن دادن *dád i sukhan dádan.*

Writer, نویسنده *navísandah;* محرر *muharrir;* کاتب *kátib;* راقم *rákim;* دبیر *dabír.*

Writhing, تقلب *takallub* (*k.*).

Writing, تحریر *tahrír* (*n.*); نوشته *navishtah, pl.* نوشتجات *navishtaját;* کتابت *kitábat;* رقم *rakam* (*z.*); نگارش *nigárish;* ترقیم *tarkím* (*n.*); رقیم *rakím.* Fine —, خوش خط *khush-khatt.* Error in —, تصحیف *tas-híf.* Prescribed form of —, رسم الخط *rasm ul khatt.* Committed to —, رقم پذیر *rakam pazír.*

Written, مکتوب *maktúb;* مرقوم *markúm.*

Wrong, نا راست *ná rást;* ناحق *ná hakk;* نادرست *ná-durust.*

Wrought, بفت *baft.*

Wry, کج *kej.*

Y

Yard (of house), حیاط *hayát*; (measure), ذرع *zár'*.

Yarn, کلابه *kalábah*.

Yawn, یازیدن *yázídan*; فازیدن *fázhídan*. —ing, یازش *yázish* (*k.*); غمیار *gham-yár*.

Year, سال *sál*. Solar —, سال شمسی *sál i shamsíy*. Lunar —, سال قمری *sál i ḳamaríy*; سنه *sannah*, *pl.* سنین *sanín*; سنوات *sanavát*; سنون *sunún*. A few —s, سالی چند *sálí chand*; سالیان *sáliyán*. The — before last, پراسال *parásál*. Last —, پارسال *pár-sál*. This —, امسال *imsál*. One — old, یکساله *yak-sálah*.

Yearly, سالانه *sálánah*.

Yearning, رقت *riḳḳat* (*dsh.*).

Yeast, مایه *máyeh*.

Yell, بانك *báng* (*z.*).

Yellow, زرد *zard*; اصفر *asfar*.

Yellowish, زرد فام *zard-fám*.

Yellowness, زردی *zardí*; صفرت *sufrat*.

Yew, کاج *káj*.

Yes, بلی *bali*; آری *ári*; نعم *na'am*. — and no, لا و نعم *lá wa na'am*.

Yesterday, دیروز *dí-rúz*.. The day before —, پری روز *parí-rúz*.

Yesternight, دیشب *díshab*.

Yet, هنوز *hanúz*; اما *ammá*.

Yezd, یزد *Yezd*; (surnamed, دار العبادة *dár ul 'ibádat*).

Yoke (oxen), جغ *jugh*; یوغ *yúgh*.

Yolk, زرده *zardah*.

You, شما *shumá*, *pl. of pl.* شمایان *shumáyán*.

Young, جوان *javán*. Quite —, نوجوان *nau-javán*. The — of man or any animal, بچه *bachah*.

Your, مال شما *mál i shumá*.

Youth, جوان *javán*; شاب *shább*; برنا *barná*, or *burná*. Beardless —, امرد *amrad*. Promising —, جوان بخت *javán bakht*.

Youthful, نو خاسته *nau-khástah*. —ness, جوانی *javání*; شباب *shebáb*.

Z

Zeal, غيرت *ghairat;* شوق *shauḳ.*

Zealot, زاهد *záhid.*

Zealous, سرگرم *sar-garm.*

Zedoary, جدوار *jadvár.*

Zenith, اوج *auj.*

Zendavesta, follower of the, زند خوان *Zend-khán.*

Zephyr, بادصبا *bád i sebá;* صبا *sabá;* نسيم *nasím, pl.* نسائم *nasáim.*

Zero, صفر *sifr.*

Zest, ذوق *zauḳ.*

Zinc, روح *rúh.*

Zodiac, منطقة البروج *mantiḳa ul burúj.*

Zone, منطق *mintaḳ.* The seven zones, i.e. the whole world, هفت اقلم *haft iḳlím;* هفت كشور *haft kishvar.*

Zoological Gardens, باغ وحوش *bágh-i-vuhúsh.*

Zoology, حيوانات *haivánát.*

Zoroaster, زردشت *Zardusht.*

FINIS.